Mark Hildebrand

3

THE MODERN HISTORY OF JAPAN

THE MODERN HISTORY

OF

JAPAN

W. G. BEASLEY

PRAEGER PUBLISHERS
New York · Washington

BOOKS THAT MATTER

Published in the United States of America in 1963
by Praeger Publishers, Inc.
111 Fourth Avenue, New York, N.Y. 10003

Seventh printing, 1970

© 1963 by W. G. Beasley

Library of Congress Catalog Card Number: 63-20665

Printed in the United States of America

CONTENTS

CONTENTS

CONTENTS

ILLUSTRATIONS

ACKNOWLEDGMENTS

I am grateful to the following publishers for permission to reprint short passages from the works stated: Columbia University Press for *Sources of the Japanese Tradition* by W. T. de Bary, Allen and Unwin for *Anthology of Japanese Literature from the Earliest Era to the Nineteenth Century* edited by Donald Keene, for *Japan under Taisho Tenno 1912–1926* by A. M. Young, for *Imperial Japan 1926–1938* also by A. M. Young; also Oxford University Press for *Select Documents on Japanese Foreign Policy 1853–1868* edited by W. G. Beasley, the Japan Society, New York, for the *Complete Journal of Townsend Harris* edited by M. E. Cosenza, the Asiatic Society of Japan, Tokyo, for *Japanese Government Documents*, edited by W. W. McLaren, John Murray for *A Handbook for Travellers in Japan* edited by B. H. Chamberlain and W. B. Mason, Princeton University Press for *The Economic Development of Japan. Growth and Structural Change 1868–1938* by W. W. Lockwood, Chatto and Windus for *The Double Patriots: a Study of Japanese Nationalism*, and Harvard University Press for *Kokutai no Hongi. Cardinal Principles of the National Entity of Japan*, edited by R. K. Hall.

I should also like to express my thanks to Mr Jiro Numata of the Shiryo-hensanjo, Tokyo University, for his help in obtaining photographs for use as illustrations; and to my wife, without whose assistance in such matters as typing and the preparation of maps this book would still be far from being finished.

W. G. Beasley

London, 1962

JAPANESE NAMES

Japanese personal names are given in this book in the order in which they are used by the Japanese themselves: family name first, followed by given name.

CHAPTER I

JAPAN IN THE EARLY
NINETEENTH CENTURY

*Decay of feudalism—changing role of the samurai—growth of
merchant guilds—rural society*

WHEN EUROPEAN explorers of the sixteenth century rounded
the Malay peninsula and moved into Far Eastern waters they
confronted a civilization quite different from those which they
had found in India and western Asia. Over an area extending
from Tongking in the south to Korea in the north they met with
a culture which was in origin Chinese, its members looking to
China as the heart of their international structure and the
source of their dominant beliefs. It was not an entirely uniform
culture, for the degree and nature of Chinese influence had
varied with both time and place. Nevertheless the differences
between one part of the region and another were no greater
than those to be found within the boundaries of Europe, certainly not great enough to make invalid the application of a
common label to the whole.

Japan was part of this civilization. From earliest times she
had been affected by Chinese ideas, deriving from China many
important elements of her culture: her written language, most
of the literary forms which it employed, her concepts of king-
ship and family, the Buddhist religion, the tenets of Confucian
philosophy. Even Japanese art, however original in detail or
in treatment, remained recognizably Chinese in derivation. On
the other hand, political relationships between the two countries had rarely been as close as this might seem to imply.
Sometimes Japan had shown herself willing to accept an inferior status because of the economic benefits it could bring.
Sometimes she had rejected it with scorn, even at the risk of

war. Nor had China ever been able to assert control by force. Morever, political institutions in the two countries had developed on very different lines. Where China had evolved an imperial bureaucracy, dependent largely on the services of a class of scholar gentry, Japan in the twelfth century had turned away from Chinese models towards something much more akin to European feudalism. The phase persisted, despite important changes in both leadership and structure, into the nineteenth century.

Meanwhile, during the decade 1630-40, Japan's rulers had decided to shut out the outside world. Seeking to control all factors that might threaten political stability, they prohibited Japanese from leaving the country and banned foreign priests and traders from coming in, making exceptions only of a handful of Dutch and Chinese merchants who were allowed to visit Nagasaki. The latter, and the books they were sometimes allowed to bring, were thereafter Japan's only source of knowledge about conditions overseas. Nor were Japanese encouraged to extend that knowledge. Until 1800, or even later, their view of international relations was determined largely by what they had learnt in the seventeenth century. In addition, the technology they had then begun to acquire, such as that which had enabled them to start the manufacture of firearms and cannon of a Western type, was checked in its development, so that their country's defences at the beginning of the nineteenth century were still those of a seventeenth-century European state; while the network of trade and settlements they had established since about 1590 in the countries bordering China were allowed entirely to disappear.

For two hundred years this system of *sakoku*, 'the closed country', was maintained. In the nineteenth century, however, it began to weaken in the face of increasing encroachment from an industrialized and expanding West, until treaties were signed and trade resumed. This was in the period 1853-8. Ten years later, under a combination of domestic and foreign pressures, Tokugawa rule was overthrown and the way was cleared for new leaders to seize power, men by whose decision Japan was exposed fully to Western influence. As a result, by the end of the century the derivatives of Western civilization had come to determine, if not the fact of change, at least its direction in Japan, so that in politics, economic organization, literature, philosophy, law, social custom and personal behaviour, in almost every aspect of life, in fact, Europe replaced China as the country's source of models and ideas. It is with this process, and with the events that followed from it, that much of this book will be concerned.

In 1800 Japan was still in many respects a feudal state. Feudalism, it is true, was in decay. A money economy, dominant in the towns and already penetrating the villages, had begun to weaken the bonds of feudal loyalty. Financial chaos threatened the stability of feudal government. Yet the samurai—the knights and men-at-arms of Japanese chivalry—still dominated political society. As a military caste they comprised the country's only army, holding rank, office and land by virtue of this function. One of them, indeed, exercised supreme administrative authority: as Shogun, an office which had been hereditary in the Tokugawa family since 1603, each succeeding head of the Tokugawa house became the emperor's military deputy and therefore *de facto* ruler of Japan. He exercised a power which extended to all men and all places, even to the Imperial Court itself. In Kyoto, the emperor's capital, he was represented by a governor, chosen from among his own relatives or vassals. Court nobles appointed to act in his interests had to swear a special oath of allegiance to him and through them he controlled the appointment of all senior officials at the Court. These, though their titles recalled the days when emperors had both reigned and ruled, were now required to perform duties which were no more than a time-consuming and complex ceremonial. For recompense they depended on the Shogun's favour, which was rarely generous. The wealthiest Court nobles had a rice income smaller than that of many of the Shogun's household officers, while most, though outranking the majority of feudal lords, were forced by poverty to live at a standard much like that of a minor lord's retainers. Their life was regulated in its every detail by the Shogun's laws: their dress, marriages and behaviour, even their literary pursuits and pastimes. The emperor himself was a Tokugawa pensioner and virtually a prisoner in the palace.

In sharp contrast to the Court nobility were the men at

3

the Shogun's capital of Edo (later to become modern Tokyo). These were the real rulers of Japan, the Shogun being the greatest of them, not only by virtue of his office but also because as a feudal lord he held lands whose estimated yield was some 15 per cent of that of Japan at large.[1] His retainers, excluding those who counted as vassals-in-chief, held as much again. The administration of these vast estates involved thousands of officials, great and small, whose labours brought together the revenue from which were paid the Shogun's household expenses, official salaries, stipends for those of his followers who had no land, and grants in aid to the loyal but impoverished. From the same source came the funds for governing Japan. In Tokugawa Japan, as in medieval Europe, the monarch was expected to live off his own.

The central administration served the Shogun in both his capacities, as imperial deputy and as feudal lord. In theory he was an autocrat, but after 1650 the Tokugawa line rarely produced a man capable of exercising personal authority. Some fell under the influence of favourites from their palace entourage, though in the nineteenth century this was exceptional; for the most past, decisions were taken by officials appointed from the ranks of the Shogun's vassals. Most powerful were the Councillors of State (*Roju*), usually four or five in number, who were responsible for general policy and for supervision of the great lords. Next came the members of the Junior Council, controlling the samurai of lesser rank, and other officials who supervised shrines and temples. All these, as well as the governors of Kyoto and Osaka, were *daimyo*, vassals-in-chief whose lands were valued at or above 10,000 *koku* (50,000 bushels) of rice a year. They were assisted by a number of officials of lower rank. The most important were the Edo magistrates (*machi-bugyo*), who administered the capital with its huge samurai population; the finance commissioners (*kanjo-bugyo*), whose duties included the handling of revenue and the government of the Shogun's own domains; and the censors (*metsuke*), whose task it was to watch for disaffection or maladministration among officials and feudal lords. Of about the same rank, or near it, were the governors of a handful of key cities like Nagasaki, which were under direct Tokugawa rule, and the stewards of the larger Tokugawa estates.

The administrative machine was slow and cumbersome, involving a system of checks and balances which seemed more designed to protect the regime from the ambitions of its own officials than to make any positive contribution to governing the country. Offices were often held by more than one man at a time, the incumbents taking it in turns to carry out the duties appropriate to them. Rarely was it possible to say precisely where the functions of one official ended and those of another began. Nor was it always clear who had the power to take decisions, though the detailed regulation of rank and seniority at least ensured that there would be no doubt about questions of formal precedence. One result of all this was to make it very difficult for an individual or clique to acquire lasting power by monopolizing a few great offices. Another, achieved by restricting all office to direct retainers of the Shogun or those lords bound traditionally to support him, was to give certain groups a vested interest in maintaining Tokugawa power.

Feudal lords were classified in terms of their relationship to the Tokugawa. First came those who were of Tokugawa blood: the *Sanke* (Three Houses) of Kii, Owari and Mito, descended from the founder of the line, Tokugawa Ieyasu; the *Sankyo* (Three Lords) of Tayasu, Hitotsubashi and Shimizu, descended from two eighteenth-century rulers, Yoshimune and Ieshige; and the *Kamon* (Related Houses), more numerous, who usually bore the family's original name of Matsudaira. The first two might provide an heir if the direct line failed. The *Kamon* might fill important office in times of emergency. It was the next group, however, who usually furnished the Shogun's senior advisers: the *fudai* ('dependent') lords, about 120 in all, the descendants of men who had become vassals of Ieyasu during his rise to power. They alone had the right to be appointed to the two councils of state and similar offices. Their leading families were always consulted on decisions of major importance and were qualified to provide a regent should need arise. In all this they differed sharply from the hundred or so *tozama* ('outside') lords, whose families had only submitted to Tokugawa control after the battle of Sekigahara in 1600, for the *tozama* were permanently excluded from office in the central government on the grounds that they were potentially subversive.

All feudal lords were in some degree free from government interference. Within the boundaries of a domain—and for the most powerful this might encompass a whole province, sometimes more—the lord was absolute master. His administration was usually patterned on that of the Tokugawa, senior councillors being chosen from collateral branches of his house or from a few families of leading retainers, while other posts were filled by samurai of middle or lower rank, who served in the specialist bureaucracy of the castle-town or as intendants governing rural districts. In none of this were they directly accountable to the Shogun and his officers. Nor did the domain owe taxes to the central government. On the other hand, the lord as a person had no such freedom: the Shogun had the power to transfer him from one fief to another, reduce the size of his holding, or even confiscate it altogether if he failed in his loyalty or duties. Although military service had become largely nominal in the long years of peace after 1650, once in a generation or so a *daimyo* was likely to find himself called upon to carry out expensive public works, like flood control, road building, or structural repairs to buildings, such as were often made necessary by fire or earthquake. Marriage alliances were subject to the Shogun's approval. So was the building or repair of castles. Most important of all, each lord was required to spend six months of the year in Edo, leaving members of his family there as hostages when he returned to his own province. This system, known as *sankin-kotai* ('alternate attendance'), was fundamental to the whole mechanism of control.

In the last resort, it was the distribution of land which enabled the Tokugawa to enforce these measures, for in a feudal society land was the basis of military strength and force was the ultimate sanction. The early Tokugawa rulers—Ieyasu, his son and grandson—had carried out a major redistribution of fiefs, by which they and their supporters had acquired not only the lion's share of the whole, but also control of all strategic areas. The Shogun and his retainers held between them land estimated as yielding some 30 per cent of Japan's annual agricultural production. In addition, Tokugawa branch families contributed another 10 per cent and the *fudai* lords twice as much again. Most of these holdings were concentrated in central Japan, thus ensuring that the regime could dominate the two capitals, Edo and Kyoto, and the whole length of the great road which connected them, the Tokaido. By contrast, the *tozama* lords, aggregating only 40 per cent of the whole by land value, were situated largely in the south and west or in the north-east, the most powerful of them being subject to the watchful attentions of a *fudai* established on their borders.

It must not be thought, however, that the *fudai* lords were individually the stronger, for it had always been the policy of the Tokugawa to avoid giving their followers domains large enough to make them a threat to the house they served. Indeed, while the *fudai* together controlled some six million *koku* out of a national total of just under thirty million, only one had a personal holding of over 200,000 *koku*. This was Ii of Hikone, whose lands straddled the eastern approaches to Kyoto. Of the Tokugawa branch houses, Aizu, Fukui and Mito were about the same size as Hikone, whereas Wakayama (Kii) and Nagoya (Owari) both exceeded half a million *koku*.[2] Yet some of the *tozama* were wealthier still. Kanazawa, north of Kyoto on the Japan Sea coast, was rated at over a million *koku*. Four others were more than half that size: Sendai in the north-east and the three Kyushu domains of Kagoshima (Satsuma), Kumamoto and Fukuoka. This still left eleven *tozama* domains of 200,000 *koku* and over. Several of them played an important part in the history of the period and are worth mentioning by name: Saga (Hizen) in Kyushu; Yamaguchi (Choshu), on the straits between Kyushu and Honshu; Hiroshima and Okayama, farther east on the shores of the Inland Sea; and Kochi (Tosa) in the southern part of the island of Shikoku.

The domain values cited above are those which were officially recorded by the Shogun's government. In the seventeenth century they had been fairly realistic estimates of the crop. In the two hundred years that followed, however, peace and technical improvements had brought great increases in agricultural production in some areas, without any corresponding adjustment in rated values, so that by 1800 some domains were notoriously 'rich', yielding far more than the official figure, while others were just as notoriously 'poor'. What is particularly significant about this is that the change had been to the relative disadvantage of the Shogun and his vassals. This was chiefly because increases had been greater at the periphery than in the centre. In the provinces round Edo and Kyoto, where most Tokugawa and *fudai* domains were found, the land had been longer settled and harder worked. It therefore offered less margin for development. By contrast, in the north-east and south-west it was easier to find new land to bring under cultivation, a fact which was soon reflected in the tax yields of the local lords, most of whom were *tozama*. Moreover, some of these lords benefited from a growing diversity in crops and economic activity in general, which eventually made it possible for villages to bear a higher rate of tax, especially along the shores of the Inland Sea and in parts of Kyushu and Shikoku. In such areas, tax yields of the nineteenth century were sometimes more than double those of the seventeenth. One result was that the domains in question were better able to cope with the financial problems brought by economic change than were the majority of those on which the stability of the regime depended—a by-product of the Tokugawa pattern of land distribution which was both unforeseen and most unwelcome to officials.

One might also argue that Tokugawa policies were responsible for a good deal of the social change which took place in the period, though this was directly contrary to their purpose. Official doctrine propounded a view of society which was one of fixed stratification: a hierarchy of samurai, farmer, artisan, and merchant, each segment subdivided and the distinctions between them rigidly maintained. The samurai was soldier and ruler. The farmer produced rice—and taxes—and was therefore honoured as the foundation of the state. The artisan's role was useful but subordinate. Merchants came last, because they engaged chiefly in the pursuit of profit, and opinions differed about whether they were merely a necessary evil, or more positively something parasitic and corrupting. Yet the debates on this subject, which were many, proved little to the purpose. Long before the nineteenth century the merchant had assumed a place in Japanese society bearing little relation to that which the traditionally-minded thought it proper to accord him, while the processes of change had done much to destroy the satisfying simplicity that was supposed to characterize the life of samurai and farmer.

8

In earlier periods the samurai had been a farmer-warrior, tilling the land in times of peace and following his lord into battle in times of war; but with the increasing scale and complexity of warfare in the fifteenth and sixteenth centuries fighting had tended to become a specialist activity, so that the functions of the samurai and the farmer became distinct. In the end the farmer was forbidden to carry arms, the samurai was incorporated into something very like the garrison of an occupied territory, living in a strongly-defended castle from which the surrounding countryside was governed. It was in this way that the typical domain of the Tokugawa period took shape. It was large and geographically compact. Within its frontiers the lord brooked no rival to his authority over men and land, whether from the once-powerful shrines and temples or from his followers, only a few of whom were allowed to retain fiefs of their own. These were subject to a system of control which was a replica in miniature of that which the Shogun imposed on Japan at large. Ordinary samurai for the most part lost their land entirely. Required to be in attendance on their lord and live in or around his castle, they were no longer able to supervise in person either cultivation or the collection of dues, these rights being assumed by the feudal lord acting through officials. In return, the samurai was granted a stipend from the domain treasury, its value determined by the estimated annual yield of the piece of land from which it was nominally derived. Many lost even this final link with the village: their stipends were fixed arbitrarily, in extreme cases at a sum payable in cash.

The transformation of the samurai was carried a stage further by the Tokugawa success in restoring and then maintaining law and order after centuries of civil war. Peace made the samurai less needed as a soldier. On the other hand, the nature of the new domains made him all the more important as an administrator. In every castle-town there was a multitude of posts to be filled, their duties ranging from the formulation of policy to the government of a rural district, from control of finance or archives to service as attendants, guards and messengers. All were filled by samurai, usually samurai of a specified rank. So great was the preoccupation with civil office that a famous scholar, Yamaga Soko, writing towards the end of the

9

seventeenth century, was able to describe the life of a samurai as follows:

'In minor matters, such as dress, food, dwelling, and all implements and their uses, he must live up to the best samurai traditions of good form . . . Among major matters there are the maintenance of peace and order in the world; rites and festivals; the control of feudal states and districts; mountains and forests, seas and rivers, farms and rice fields, temples and shrines; and the disposition of suits and appeals among the four classes of people.'[3]

Yamaga, as his writings showed elsewhere, did not by any means despise the samurai's place in warfare. None the less, his outlook takes us a long way from the concept of the samurai as a rough and uncouth soldier.

Once it had been deprived of battle as a lubricant of social mobility, Japanese society quickly became preoccupied with questions of personal and family status. The samurai found himself the possessor by virtue of birth or adoption of a position which it was a great deal easier to lose by failure to fulfil ceremonial duties than it was to improve by meritorious service. Ranks tended to proliferate, as did the regulations concerning them. For all this it is possible to identify three broad divisions of the feudal class. First came those who were linked with the lord's own house by blood or long service: the upper samurai, few in number, much wealthier than the rest and often holding land of their own. Second were the middle samurai, full members of their class by rank and privilege, but usually excluded from the very highest posts. Last were those who are often called the lesser samurai, a group rather more numerous in most domains than the other two together. They were men whose military duty as foot-soldiers and the like gave them some claim to samurai status and access to the minor offices of government, but whose economic and social position was vastly inferior to that of the samurai proper. Indeed, it is not easy to recognize some of them as members of a ruling class at all.

It was extremely difficult to move upward from one of these divisions to another. An able man might sometimes achieve promotion for himself, while two or three generations of able men might do so for a whole family, but for the majority rank was hereditary and fixed. All manner of things were determined

by it: access to office, type of education, even habits of speech.
If they belonged to the same domain, men of the same rank
were likely to know each other well, since the regulations
about place of residence made it almost certain that their families were neighbours. Their houses and dress would be similar,
though they might differ considerably in wealth. They had
almost certainly gone to the same school. This made the
groups within the castle-town community exceedingly close-
knit—even in the largest domain there was not likely to be
more than 5,000 families of middle and upper samurai, in the
smaller ones only a few hundred—but this very fact helped to
accentuate the barriers which cut groups off from one another.
In a society where every man knew his place, it is not surprising that the ruling philosophy was of a kind calculated to
keep him in it. The Confucian ideas associated with the name
of the Sung philosopher, Chu Hsi, were admirably suited to
this purpose, for they emphasized the subordination of wife to
husband, of son to father, of subject to ruler, in a manner
which in Tokugawa Japan brought about a natural alliance
between feudal authority and Confucian scholarship. The duties
of loyalty and service were expounded in official schools maintained by the Shogun's government and feudal lords. To them
went almost all samurai of middle and upper rank to learn the
duties of their station, to learn above all that a man's own
welfare counted for less than that of the group, whether family
or domain, to which he belonged. The attitude was reinforced
by the pervading social and religious concept of obligation
(*ho-on*). This brought together strands from Buddhist as well
as Confucian thought, emphasizing that man's primary task
was to live in such a way as would constitute a return for
favours received: to the deity for his blessings, to the universe
which supported life, to parents for their love, to political
superiors for their protection. Thus loyalty and filial piety
came together and were given religious sanction.
    These ideas, in association with elements from an older
tradition, became part of *bushido*, the code of the warrior class.
In its Tokugawa form this was as much a code of the bureaucrat as of the soldier. Death in the service of one's lord remained the ultimate expression of loyalty, bringing something
not far short of salvation in a religious sense; but if this could

not be, then dutiful service and honest advice were not to be despised. Learning and scholarship were also to be valued for the training they gave, though it was a training more appropriate to administration than the battlefield. Even the time-honoured military virtues of austerity and frugality were given a new gloss. Diligence and economy were the form in which they were now enjoined, the one to ensure the maximum contribution in service, the other the minimum consumption by way of recompense. This, too, was a kind of loyalty.

Ideals of behaviour which the ruling class prescribed for itself were readily adopted by the rest of society. In this sense, *bushido* influenced all groups, at least all those which sought social recognition. On the other hand, this did not make its rules any easier to observe, especially where they ran counter to economic change. Frugality was one of them. Peace and the growth in agricultural production had contributed to a rapid development of commerce in the seventeenth century, making possible a rise in standards of living which was enjoyed in most parts of the country. Even in remote castle-towns one could now obtain products from as far afield as Kyushu and Hokkaido. In the great cities of Edo, Kyoto and Osaka luxuries abounded. Edo, especially, played a major part in samurai life, since feudal lords, accompanied always by a large retinue of followers, were required to live there for half the year. Here were many temptations by way of goods and entertainment, temptations which most found it impossible to resist. Unfortunately, they had to be paid for, usually in cash. For samurai—of whatever rank—who received their incomes in rice, the provision of money to be spent in Edo became a serious problem, one which could be solved only with the help of the merchant and financier. The improvident soon found that their new habits had left no margin to meet the sort of unexpected expenditure or loss of income which might be occasioned by fire or flood. For them the merchant became moneylender, making advances against future income. Others, who were more careful, were eventually caught in the same web despite themselves, for city prices rose faster than crops increased and it was easier to acquire expensive tastes than to lose them. By 1700 the whole samurai class was in a state of chronic debt.

In the eighteenth century samurai indebtedness continued

to grow, despite efforts which feudal rulers made to check it. Moreover, since the Tokugawa and domain governments faced the same difficulties as did individuals, they were rendered unable to help their retainers to any great extent and were often forced to levy new imposts on them. These levies, euphemistically described as loans, might amount to half a samurai's stipend. They caused great discontent, the tenets of *bushido* notwithstanding. In many domains this led the middle samurai, blaming their troubles on the incapacity of their superiors, to agitate for, and sometimes obtain, a larger share in administration. Lesser samurai, whose case was far worse, also tended to become supporters of reform movements of various kinds, while many sought personal solutions outside the existing feudal framework altogether, relinquishing their samurai status to become farmers or merchants, or using the devices of marriage and adoption to bring wealth into the family in return for social standing. This process, familiar enough among impoverished aristocracies at any time or place, helped to induce a greater degree of social mobility at the lower levels of the ruling class, to which officialdom contributed by engaging in what was virtually a sale of rank. It was the merchants and a new class of rural landlords who largely benefited.

Indeed, the corollary of samurai debt was merchant wealth. As domestic commerce grew in scale so it had become more complex, with townsmen (*chonin*) emerging as specialists in a wide range of different occupations: wholesaling, warehousing, transport, rice-broking, money exchange, credit transactions, speculative dealing of every kind. Typical is this description of a Kyoto merchant, taken from one of the stories of the novelist, Ihara Saikaku, written in 1688:

'As the clerks from the money exchanges passed by he noted down the market ratio of copper and gold; he inquired about the current quotations of the rice brokers; he sought information from druggists' and haberdashers' assistants on the state of the market in Nagasaki; for the latest news on the prices of ginned cotton, salt, and saké, he noted the various days on which the Kyoto dealers received dispatches from the Edo branch shops. Every day a thousand things were entered in his book. . . .'[4]

With specialized knowledge so important, it is not surprising that the samurai left the handling of his finances to the merchant, or that in the process he became indebted to him. All the same, merchants did not easily gain the upper hand. The feudal lord and his retainers still possessed authority, as well as prestige, and did not hesitate to use it. Repayment of loans was difficult to enforce against members of a ruling class, particularly when their refusal to honour debts was likely to be upheld by a central government which officially despised trade and was not above confiscating a merchant's goods in their entirety if its own interests were at stake. Faced with this situation, merchants began to organize themselves into monopoly guilds, seeking security through collective action. In part they were successful. The guilds, membership of which was a valuable commodity, capable of being bought and sold, became characteristic of the eighteenth century. They helped to keep prices and profits high. Moreover, they came frequently into alliance with the Tokugawa and domain governments, acting as bankers, official purveyors or agents in the marketing of rice and other products, their members receiving in return social privileges and protection. The effects of this on the feudal structure we must consider in the next chapter. Here it is enough to emphasize that one result was to give the privileged merchants of the towns a status more in keeping with their wealth than hitherto. Many of them became city elders, firmly subordinated to feudal control but exercising a good deal of authority in local matters.

Not all town-dwellers were rich, of course. There was a host of small traders, struggling to make ends meet, as well as apprentices, journeymen, pedlars and day labourers, their ranks constantly swollen by new recruits. Most of the latter came from the countryside, where harsh taxes and bad harvests combined to drive a succession of impoverished farmers to seek their fortune in the town; and although the majority found only a different kind of poverty, their total numbers helped to change the nature of society by making the urban element of significant size for the first time in Japanese history. Kyoto, a political and commercial centre, famous also for its craftsmen, had long been a great city. In size and importance, however, it now had to take second place to Edo, which grew from being a mere fishing village in 1590 to a huge conglomeration with

a population, excluding samurai, of over 500,000 in 1721.[5]
Samurai accounted for at least half as much again and made
this by far the country's largest consumer market. Osaka, by
contrast, was a city of merchants. It was rather smaller than
Kyoto—under 300,000 to Kyoto's 400,000 in the seventeenth
century—but it was the focus of large-scale commerce and
finance for all except the north-east provinces. Apart from
these, and perhaps Nagasaki, Japan had no true cities. Yet
there were many country towns, their size varying with that of
the domains for which they served as markets and administrative centres.

Town life in the Tokugawa period, especially that of Edo
and Osaka, contributed a new element to Japanese culture. It
was an element of noise and turbulence and colour, quite unlike
the restraint proper to a long-established aristocracy, and it
derived from that part of the population which might be
described as *nouveaux riches*, the great merchants and their
households. To cater to their whims and those of their feudal
overlords, there developed what contemporaries called *ukiyo*,
the floating world: a world, in the words of a modern historian,
'of fugitive pleasures, of theatres and restaurants, wrestling-
booths and houses of assignation, with their permanent population of actors, dancers, singers, story-tellers, jesters, courtesans, bath-girls and itinerant purveyors, among whom mingled
the profligate sons of rich merchants, dissolute samurai and
naughty apprentices'.[6] It was with this world that much of
the period's art and literature were concerned. Colour prints
depicted actors and famous courtesans, as well as street scenes
in busy commercial quarters. The theatre, especially the puppet
drama, found its themes in subjects which the townsmen
loved: the clash between feudal loyalty and personal inclination
—typical of Tokugawa Japan and popular because it took its
audience into high society—or the fortunes, good and bad, of
rich merchants and poor journeymen, of their mistresses and
wives. Novels and short stories followed the same course. It
was not a literature for the prudish, but it was bursting with
life. By comparison, the verse and landscapes of the Chinese
tradition seemed anaemic and artificial.

For those who could afford it life in the city was one of
extravagant costume, exotic foods and elaborate pastimes.

Samurai, without doubt, were attracted by it. However, the more serious-minded were distrustful, thinking it something calculated to rob a man of his substance and to weaken his moral fibre, something that would make him a worse soldier and retainer. Hence reformers fulminated against the city's luxury and corruption. So, too, did spokesmen of the merchant class, for the greater respectability which the privileged townsmen had achieved led them to affirm, not to reject, the dominant values of society. They, as much as the samurai, aspired to a code of loyalty, filial piety and frugality in service. They were as much to be blamed if they abandoned themselves to a life of pleasure.

Still more shocking by the canons of the age was the spectacle of farmers enjoying some of the same luxuries. It was bad enough that many should be forced by poverty to abandon their land and flock to the city, to the obvious detriment of agricultural production. It became worse when a few, though remaining in the village, acquired wealth enough to ape their betters. That they had the facilities to do so was a reflection of commercial growth, making available in rural areas what had at first been limited to the towns. That they had the money was a reflection of economic development in a wider sense. This, by the nineteenth century, had brought about far-reaching changes in landholding and the structure of village wealth.

The classic pattern of the Tokugawa village was that of the early seventeenth century: a community consisting of peasant farmers bound to the soil, each cultivating a plot large enough to support his family and paying the whole of any surplus to his lord as feudal dues. This was the ideal—a sort of equality in misery—which feudal officials sought to maintain. Yet inequalities had in fact existed from the beginning. Farmers of substance usually had dependants of one kind or another to help them on their land, men who were bound to them either by ties of blood and marriage or by traditional bonds not far short of slavery. Some villagers were distinguished also by hereditary rights to local office, often backed by claims that they were the 'old' families, descended from original settlers of the area. It was from such groups that the village headmen and councillors were drawn. They played an influential part in village life, it being their duty to apportion individual shares of taxation, which the domain imposed simply on the village as a unit, as well as to settle local disputes, arrange details of irrigation, organize festivals and so on. Above them were a number of district officials, who were also local residents, though they often ranked as minor members of the feudal class. To most Japanese these were the most familiar representatives of authority. The samurai official proper, from the Shogun's capital or the lord's castle, was an exalted and rather terrifying figure, appeal to whom was very much a last resort.

The increase in the area of land under cultivation and in yield per acre, which went on throughout the seventeenth century and well into the eighteenth century in many places, tended to enlarge the existing disparities of wealth within the village since it was mostly those who already held plots larger than the average who had the resources to open up new land or pay for improvements in technique. However, it was the development of a commercial economy, especially in central, south and west Japan, that finally proved disruptive of the traditional village structure. It not only brought to the farmer new implements, fertilizers and strains of seed, but also made possible a decrease in local self-sufficiency. Once trade became widespread, it was no longer necessary for every man to grow his own grain. Instead, where conditions favoured it, he could turn to one of the cash crops for which the growth of city culture and the rise in standards of living had created a demand: silk, cotton, paper, wax, rape seed, indigo and others. These became ancillary crops for many, main crops for some. The result, in areas where this occurred, was to involve the village deeply in the commercial sector of the economy, making the farmer's prosperity subject to market fluctuations which were completely outside his own control.

The change did not make life any easier for the majority. Speculation, natural disasters and occasional ill-advised interference by feudal governments helped to make selling prices vary widely. Costs for such things as fertilizers were kept high by the monopoly rings of city merchants. Moreover, there was always the danger that domain governments might take a proprietary interest in any really profitable commodity, declaring it an official monopoly and buying in the crop at forced prices. With all this, as well as high taxation, the farmer's life and income were precarious. More and more had recourse to the moneylender, often losing their land because of it, at least in part, so that many independent cultivators of the earlier period became tenants or even landless labourers. Some made their way to the towns. Others remained to form a pool of workers for the local industries which began to spring up in rural areas, such as cotton spinning and weaving, dyeing, the brewing of saké (rice wine), or the manufacture of paper.

These developments were at their height during the last quarter of the eighteenth century and the first quarter of the nineteenth, a period which saw also the emergence of a class of rural entrepreneurs whose wealth was not based exclusively on land. For the most part they, too, originated in the ranks of peasant cultivators. Unlike their fellows, however, they were the sort of men who seized the opportunities which the new economy presented and were able by thrift, hard work and good judgment to extend their operations into retailing, moneylending, manufacture and similar non-agricultural pursuits, retaining an interest in the soil as landlords but devoting relatively little of their time to its management. Among them were some who handled the marketing of commercial crops, others who organized a putting-out system which harnessed the surplus labour capacity of farming households to the manufacture of textiles, even a few who established small-scale factories. Such men were to be found in almost every village in the provinces round Kyoto and along the Inland Sea.

In food, dress, education and entertainment they lived like samurai of middle rank or better. Yet no matter how great their wealth it was not easy for them to win formal recognition. In some areas they engaged in a bitter and eventually successful struggle to secure appointment to village office, important to them not only for the prestige it conferred, but also because it provided a means of manipulating tax assessments and other matters vital to their interests. Elsewhere they acquired status by marrying into the families of minor domain officials. In many domains they were even able to gain it in their own right, for, as financial pressure on governments increased, so did the temptation to raise money by the sale of rank. The newly rich of the countryside were invited to subscribe to so-called loans, their reward for doing so being a grant of rank which was in strict proportion to the size of contribution. In this way many a farmer, turned moneylender, acquired the right to bear a family name and wear the two swords of the samurai.

Tokugawa Ieyasu, it is said, expected most of his descendants to be mediocrities, or worse, and set out to create an administrative machine which would protect them from their own folly. Certainly the regime he founded gave every sign of being dedicated to the task of self-preservation. The country's rulers, both Shogun and feudal lords, tried to freeze society in the pattern it had assumed at the end of the sixteenth-century civil wars, a pattern in which they shared between them a more effective authority than had ever before been achieved in Japanese history. The result was an age of political conservatism and rigid class structure, of rule and precedent, place and privilege.

The attempt to outlaw change was remarkably successful. Nevertheless, as we have seen, by the beginning of the nineteenth century it had failed in a number of important ways. This was partly because new forms of wealth fell into the hands of groups which did not already have prestige and power, making them potentially subversive of the existing order: the merchants of the towns and the entrepreneurs of rural areas. The former proved less of a threat to samurai dominance than one might have supposed, for during the eighteenth century they entered into a kind of symbiotic relationship with feudal government, putting their commercial and financial skills to the service of the ruling class in return for rank, security and profit. On the other hand, rich villagers were likely to be more dangerous. They invested their profits heavily in land and thereby touched the regime at a sensitive point. The castle-town system, while leaving the samurai dependent on the land for his income, had removed him from direct participation in its use and management, thus making it possible for the new landlords to interpose themselves, as it were, between feudalism and the farm. It was a situation that had occurred several times in Japanese history and had always been the prelude to the replacement of one regime by another.

This is not to imply that there was any immediate danger of a concerted attempt by the landlords to overthrow feudalism or the Tokugawa. Indeed, most of them seemed satisfied with the semi-samurai status which their wealth had gained them, while in many parts of the country the village economy—and hence its social structure—had as yet been hardly touched by change at all. More immediate difficulties arose from the financial chaos which had overtaken both central and domain governments and from the disorder to which it led in the countryside. Attempts by the domain to improve its finances by increasing taxation, their effects accentuated in some areas by the stresses in village life which accompanied the enrichment of the few and the impoverishment of the many, brought a rising level of peasant revolt. After 1800, outbreaks averaged five or six a year, the most frequent objects of violence being the residences of moneylenders, landlords or unpopular village and domain officials.

The middle and upper samurai were quick to recognize that these developments might eventually break their own hold on Japanese society. Many of them called for reform, though they could not agree upon its nature. Some urged in effect a return to the past, a policy which was to be carried out by means of sumptuary laws, limitations on the growth of towns, even a redistribution of the land, all aimed at reducing trade and forcing the population back to its old habits. Others planned to ride the tiger, that is, to come to terms with the new trends and use them to bolster traditional authority. Both groups, not only by what they did, but also by the struggles into which they entered to secure the power to do it, played an important part in shaping Japan's political future. It is therefore desirable that we should consider their problems and their policies in greater detail.

CHAPTER II

ECONOMIC PROBLEMS
AND REFORMS

Mizuno Tadakuni—Zusho Hiromichi—Murata Seifu

IN THE eighteenth century money became of prime concern to Japan's feudal rulers. From the Shogun to the humblest samurai, from the central government to that of the smallest domain, failure to adjust to the needs of a changing economy brought growing financial stress. It was a stress, moreover, due in large measure to factors outside their own control. The concentration of the ruling class in castle-towns, especially the huge agglomeration that was Edo, had acted as a stimulus to trade. Commercial efficiency, in turn, had put temptations in the way of buyers. Since most samurai had been reduced to idleness by the years of peace, encouraged to engage in scholarship and martial exercises or to perform administrative tasks which rarely took up all their time, it is not surprising that their tastes and habits grew expensive. Income, despite the rise in agricultural production, failed to keep pace with costs. This was often as much a result of laxity among tax-collectors, the almost inevitable concomitant of hereditary office-holding, as it was of higher standards of living; but it meant, whatever the cause, that a misfortune like fire or flood, bringing an increase in expenses or a drop in revenue, put a domain almost invariably in debt to the city rice-brokers who handled its finances. Individual samurai suffered by a similar process, though on a smaller scale. At the opposite extreme, the Tokugawa government succumbed slowly but inexorably to the same pressures. And once in debt, neither the samurai nor his lord found it easy to recover.

Intermittent attempts at reform in the eighteenth century proved to have only a local and temporary effect, so that by the time Tokugawa Ieyoshi succeeded his father as Shogun on October 1, 1837, the situation had reached a stage of crisis. Ieyoshi was not the man to take much interest in questions of government finance. Nor were his ministers concerned with the economic problems of Japan at large. Nevertheless, it was during the period of his rule, which lasted till 1853, that officials in Edo and several of the great domains initiated economic policies that were to have a considerable bearing on the fate of the regime. It is therefore at this point that a discussion of late Tokugawa history can conveniently begin.

The finances of the Tokugawa government—the Bakufu, or 'tent government', as it was called, because of its origins as the Shogun's military headquarters—depended in the first place on rice. Most dues from rural areas were paid in it. Most normal expenditure was calculated in it: household expenses, official salaries, samurai stipends. The actual amounts involved were capable of considerable variation, depending both on the harvest and on the efficiency to be expected from officials—in 1742-51, for example, after a period of administrative reform, the annual average rice revenue rose to 800,000 *koku* (1 *koku* = 5 bushels approximately), whereas in 1782-91, which were years of atrocious weather, it was only just over 600,000 *koku*—but in general it was a great deal more likely that revenue would drop, because of bad luck or bad management, and that expenditure would rise, because of luxurious living, than the reverse. A minister of character and determination, having the Shogun's confidence, could do much to improve administration and cut expenses. Such a circumstance, however, was fortuitous and rare. More often appeals for economy fell on deaf ears and officials were left with no other recourse than to seek ways of increasing government income.

An essential difficulty was that there was a limit to the amount which farmers could be made to pay. Where dues were comparatively low, or farm output was increasing, it was possible to tap the surplus by a variety of devices. They ranged from the imposition of supplementary taxes to the use of false instruments in conducting surveys. It was even possible in some respects to reduce the annual variations. Thus in the eighteenth century tax-collectors began to levy dues on the basis of periodic averages, instead of fixing the amount after inspection of the crop, a change that transferred to the farmer the responsibility for providing against future fluctuations in the harvest. All the same, there was a point beyond which tax could be made neither heavier nor more predictable, namely, that at which demands provoked the cultivator to revolt or to abandon his land. Samurai officials frequently misjudged it, but it put an effective ceiling on the revenue they raised.

Faced with this problem the Bakufu turned to sources of revenue in cash. Some of these it had possessed from the beginning: profits from gold and silver mines, most of which were under Tokugawa control; certain small amounts paid by the villages as taxation on minor crops; a tax on house property in the towns; and several miscellaneous dues, such as transit charges on the movement of goods. Profits from mining, the only item on this list which was of any consequence, declined sharply towards the end of the seventeenth century because the most easily worked deposits of the precious metals had been exhausted, but a substitute was soon found in debasement of the coinage. Beginning in 1695, this rapidly became one of the most regular and profitable ways of raising funds. To it after 1721 was added a levy on merchant associations, usually taking the form of annual cash payments made in return for a grant of monopoly rights.

These innovations enabled the Bakufu in the first half of the eighteenth century to supplement its rice revenue by cash receipts which varied between about 1·5 and 2 million gold *ryo* a year.[7] To set against this were expenditures of something like 1·2 million *ryo* in a good year, 1·6 million in a bad one, so that it was possible, given sound administration, to make ends meet. On the other hand, administration was not always sound and these resources were not invariably sufficient to maintain a balance. Officials, therefore, continued their search for something new to tax. Opening up fresh land was one possibility, but most of what was suitable had already been exploited earlier in the Tokugawa period and further efforts at reclamation were handicapped by technical difficulties beyond the power of the age to solve. Another possibility, direct taxation of the feudal lords, was politically dangerous, as the Shogun Yoshimune had discovered when he attempted it in 1722-31. This left only commerce. Most of the country's wealth, or so it seemed to contemporary observers, was now finding its way into the hands of city merchants. It appeared reasonable that they should contribute part of it to ease the burdens of the state. Means of effecting this were eventually found by levying forced loans, known as *goyo-kin*; and although these were hardly taxation in the strict sense, since they were irregular in timing and arbitrary in amount, they were usefully high in yield. The first to be recorded, that of 1761-2, raised 700,000 *ryo* from Osaka merchants, out of a total of 1·7 million *ryo* which had been demanded. Later ones were smaller, but after 1800 they became frequent enough to rival recoinage as a source of government funds. Thus in the years 1853-60 about 1·4 million *ryo* was received from loans of this kind, some 900,000 *ryo* coming from Edo and Osaka, the rest from rich residents of the countryside.

One trouble with these policies, especially debasement of the coinage, was that they pushed up prices. By so doing they introduced an element of contradiction into feudal rule. It was obviously necessary, if political stability were to be preserved, that ministers should retain the loyalty of the feudal class. This involved among other things ensuring its members a degree of economic privilege. Yet the very actions of government in its search for solvency were of a kind to increase the upward spiral of commodity prices, making it more and more difficult for retainers to live on a fixed stipend payable in rice. Officials sought constantly for a way out of this dilemma, or rather, one might say, tried solutions first for one part of it, then the other, without always recognizing the connection between the two. A common response was to blame human behaviour: merchants for taking excessive profit, samurai for abandoning their traditional frugality. Hence exhortation became a conspicuous feature of reform. It was reinforced by a number of more practical measures, designed to encourage samurai virtue by a system of rewards and punishments or to discourage luxury by sumptuary laws. In addition, Bakufu statesmen tried to control the interest payable on samurai debts, though in this they were more often than not defeated by the men they meant to aid, since the latter, finding themselves unable to live without credit and equally unable to get it at the official rates, simply evaded the regulations. None the less, the authorities usually found ways in a crisis of robbing the moneylender of part of his profits and protecting the samurai from the worst results of his improvidence. Certainly a merchant who wished to recover money from a defaulting samurai could expect scant help or sympathy from those in power.

There were, then, two main elements in economic reform as the later Tokugawa rulers saw it, on the one hand, an attempt to restore government finances, on the other, an attack on the problem of samurai impoverishment. Both emerged clearly in the work of Tokugawa Yoshimune, Shogun from 1716 to 1745, though he was more successful in bequeathing to his son a full treasury, the fruits of long and careful administration, than in overcoming the difficulties that faced his vassals. Even what he did achieve depended so greatly on his personal supervision and example that it barely survived his death. In fact, forty years later all was to be done again. This time the reformer was Matsudaira Sadanobu, Yoshimune's grandson and Bakufu chief minister from 1786 to 1793. His measures included a cancellation of samurai debts, encouragement of military training and an insistence on Confucian orthodoxy in the official schools, together with a whole quiverful of rules about dress, food, hairstyles, gifts and similar matters. Once again, however, the effects were short-lived, Sadanobu's edicts being ignored and his reserves dissipated well before his own life ended.

The first three decades of the nineteenth century saw a considerable increase in the level of commercial activity in Japan and as a consequence a worsening economic situation for the Bakufu and its retainers. In the period 1834–41 expenditure exceeded normal cash revenue by over half a million *ryo* a year, with the result that only a series of desperate expedients prevented total financial chaos. In the same years, moreover, there was increasing evidence of unrest in the form of peasant revolts. Rioting, accompanying demands for tax relief, had begun in the previous century, but the number of outbreaks had increased sharply since 1800 and their scale had grown. In January 1823, for example, a mob said to be 70,000 strong stormed the town of Miyazu, a little north-west of Kyoto, in protest against a special tax designed to repay money which the feudal lord had borrowed. Six months later a still more serious rising occurred in the Tokugawa domain of Kii. In 1836 the whole of Kai, a province under Bakufu control, broke into revolt, this being the largest of some twenty-six incidents recorded for that year, while in 1837 a minor Bakufu official, Oshio Heihachiro, planned a rising in Osaka because of his indignation at local maladministration and maintenance of high, rice prices in a time of great distress. His plot was betrayed and Oshio committed suicide after achieving no more than a minor disturbance, but news of the affair provoked outbreaks as far afield as Hiroshima in one direction and Niigata in the other.

It is against this background that one must set the reforms undertaken by the *fudai* lord, Mizuno Tadakuni, in the first few years of Ieyoshi's rule. As an ambitious young man, Mizuno had accepted a transfer from the fief of Karatsu in Kyushu to the rather less valuable but more central one of Hamamatsu, not far from Nagoya, in order to improve his chances of a political career. This was in 1817, when he was twenty-three. He then served in turn as governor of Osaka and governor of Kyoto, until in 1828 he was made senior adviser to Ieyoshi, the Shogun's heir. Promotion to the Council of State followed in 1834. The accession of Ieyoshi increased his influence, but it was not until 1841, with the death of Ieyoshi's father, that he achieved complete control of policy and announced his intention of carrying out reforms on the lines laid down by Yoshimune and Matsudaira Sadanobu. For the next two years decrees flowed from his office in a steady stream.

Mizuno's methods of raising revenue were not strikingly original and cannot really be described as reforms. His main recourse was to recoinage and forced loans, the yields from which were considerable: 1·6 million *ryo* from recoinage in 1841–2, equal to a whole year's revenue, and an estimated one million *ryo* in loans collected from Edo and Osaka merchants in 1843. Attempts were also made to increase the returns from land tax. In 1842 these provoked a brief revolt in Omi province, just east of Kyoto, when local inhabitants discovered that a Bakufu survey party was accepting bribes as well as using false instruments; but financially they achieved little more than those of Mizuno's immediate predecessors. Of more interest was his long-term plan for reversing the drift of rural population to the towns. Orders were issued in the spring of 1843 which forbade new emigration into Edo, directed those residents of the city who had no family and no permanent job to return to their former homes, and put limits on the period for which farmers were allowed to engage in casual urban employment. All these were measures designed to increase the available sources of agricultural labour.

In his attitude towards samurai debt, Mizuno did not go as far as Matsudaira Sadanobu, who had cancelled old debts and tried to limit interest on new ones, but he nevertheless ordered a reduction of interest rates to 10 per cent in September 1842. He also instituted a system of debt redemption, though it was not generous enough to the samurai to win him much popularity. It was the attempt to reduce commodity prices, however, which was the outstanding feature of his reforms. An attack on luxury and immorality, which involved restrictions on theatres, brothels and other temptations to extravagance, in addition to the customary injunctions about simplicity in food and dress, was supplemented by a series of moves against the city merchants. One of the first was the dissolution of privileged merchant associations, on the grounds that their monopoly practices were keeping prices high. In 1842 the government also prohibited attempts to corner the market in particular commodities and issued a warning against holding back goods in the hope of greater profits. Meanwhile, attention was turned to the retail trade. After several months of investigation by Bakufu agents, Edo drapers were ordered to cut prices on some items by as much as half, a general price reduction of 20 per cent being decreed shortly after. Some tradesmen tried to evade the laws by giving short measure and poor quality, or chose to ignore them altogether; but this was dangerous, since the customer might prove to be a spy from the magistrate's office sent to test conformity with the regulations, as many merchants soon discovered to their cost.

For all this, the controls on commerce were self-defeating. Many businesses closed their doors to wait for better times and it was soon made clear that nothing could force goods on to the market when prices were artificially low. Even the abolition of merchant monopolies was not an unmixed blessing, since it destroyed the credit system on which the whole structure of trade depended. The resulting dislocation, far from reducing prices by enlivening competition, raised them higher still.

From this point of view, Mizuno's experiment was an unmistakable failure. And failure was something a man in his position could ill afford. Able himself, he made use of able subordinates; but he never created a personal following bound to him by special bonds of loyalty, partly because he never identified himself fully with any particular group, partly because of of an unsympathetic quality in his character which made him isolated, a Puritan in an age which was far from puritanical. By contrast, he made enemies freely: the city merchants; rivals for power; those who suffered by his policy of retrenchment (like the ladies of the Shogun's household). Previous reformers had been able to sustain themselves in such a situation by their own high rank—Yoshimune a Shogun, Sadanobu a Shogun's grandson—but Mizuno was a mere *fudai* lord of 60,000 *koku* and as such depended heavily on the support of members of the Tokugawa family. With one of them, Tokugawa Nariaki of Mito, he quarrelled over foreign policy in 1842, when the question arose of modifying the seclusion laws. Others were alienated by his plan, announced in the late summer of 1843, to take over in the Shogun's name all land in the immediate vicinity of Edo and Osaka, offering annual stipends to the existing holders by way of compensation. A storm of protest forced him to drop the scheme, but it was already too late to save his power. On November 4, 1843, he was dismissed from office; and though he was recalled briefly to handle a foreign crisis in the following year, this was the end of Mizuno's active career as a reformer. It was also the end for the time being of attempts at Bakufu reform.

The great domains were influenced indirectly by Bakufu economic policies, since these modified the general situation with which they had to deal, but they were not immediately subject to the Shogun's officers and did not have to enforce within their own boundaries any of the reform edicts issued in his name. They sometimes followed a similar course because

28

they faced similar problems. Sometimes, however, their leaders found different solutions and achieved more lasting success.

Many domains were in financial straits long before the end of the seventeenth century, especially those, like Satsuma and Choshu, which had been reduced in size after suffering defeat at the hands of the Tokugawa. Nor were the others far behind. By 1750 it was a commonplace among contemporary writers that all *daimyo* were indebted to the great Osaka merchants. Fundamentally the reasons for this were the same as those which impoverished the Bakufu—a cash expenditure rising faster than a rice revenue—but there were certain respects in which the domains had less responsibility for their own misfortunes and less means of avoiding them. For example, the *sankin-kotai* system required a lord to spend six months of every year in Edo. While there he was expected to live in state, for part of the object was to weaken him financially, with the result that anything up to half his revenue had to be spent on the upkeep of a permanent establishment in the capital and his own expenses while living in it. From time to time, moreover, he would face Bakufu demands for the carrying out of public works or for troops to take part in the manning of coast defences. These were costly items. Since they could rarely be anticipated and few domain governments held a reserve from which to pay them, each such demand, like the damage caused by earthquake or typhoon, threatened to push the level of expenditure above that of income. Once it did so, recourse was had to loans from city merchants and payment of interest was thereafter added to existing burdens.

For these reasons most domains ended by incurring debts which were proportionately far greater than those of the Bakufu. For example, Kanazawa, the largest of the *tozama* holdings, had gold and silver debts in 1785 of over 2 million *ryo*, equivalent to something like three or four years revenue. Satsuma was in much the same position, or worse, being in debt to the extent of 1·3 million *ryo* in 1807 and about 5 million in 1829, by which time officials were finding it difficult to raise funds even for day-to-day administration, while Choshu owed a little over 1·3 million *ryo* in 1840. In each case most of the creditors were the financiers of Osaka and Edo.

Very little of a feudal lord's rice revenue was available for interest payments on, or redemption of, these debts. The assessed value of his domain—a million *koku* for Kanazawa and almost 800,000 *koku* for Satsuma, to take these as examples— was a statement not of revenue but of estimated total crop, between thirty and fifty per cent of which was likely to be collected in dues. Some of this went to those members of his family, senior retainers, shrines and temples who still held land direct. Some was earmarked for the payment of samurai stipends. From the rest the fief treasury had to provide for all the lord's private and public expenditure within his own territories, before converting what was left into cash for use elsewhere. The balance available for this purpose was very small: about 100,000 *koku* in Kanazawa, only 20,000 *koku* in Satsuma, though there were some domains which specialized in rice production for the market, like Sendai, and were able to spare a great deal more. In addition there were the dues received in cash, which were of a similar kind to those levied by the Bakufu. Almost all these were spent outside the domain, but their yield was low, averaging perhaps 5 per cent of total revenue in the middle of the nineteenth century.

Raise Money

Like the Tokugawa, domain governments were forced by this situation to try new ways of raising money. The prospects of their taxing merchants were much less, of course, since the commercial wealth of a single castle-town was not at all comparable with that of the great cities under Tokugawa rule. Furthermore, they were not permitted to issue coinage and hence had no opportunity to debase it. Their efforts therefore took a different form. The forced loans to which they had recourse were often required of samurai, for example, as well as merchants, a departure from tradition that for the samurai marked a growing divergence between his own interests and those of his lord. Nor were the amounts negligible in themselves. In Kanazawa they were 10 to 15 per cent of samurai stipends in 1794, the higher rate operating for those with larger incomes. This was cut to between 5 and 10 per cent in 1810, but a higher level was restored in 1830, as financial difficulties grew, while in 1837 special Bakufu demands on the fief caused a levy of 50 per cent for the next three years. After this, samurai distress again led to a general reduction, until in 1852 the rate was down to as little as 5 per cent for the majority.

By comparison, the figures for the Shikoku domain of Tosa seem to have been much higher. Beginning in 1728 with a complex system of levies graded from nil to 50 per cent in accordance with rank and income, they fluctuated throughout the rest of the century, with the maximum occasionally forced down to 25 per cent by samurai opposition. Indeed, samurai poverty was so great by 1800 that the practice was abandoned altogether. It was re-established a few years later, however, when the maximum was again set at 50 per cent, this being the level at which Tosa officials seem always to have aimed, though they did not always achieve it.

Another device by which funds were raised was that of monopoly trading. For the most part this was undertaken in co-operation with the privileged merchants of the castle-town —who stood in much the same relationship to the domain as did those of Edo and Osaka to the Bakufu, though their activities were on a provincial rather than a national scale—and was directed not only at increasing revenue, but also at acquiring profit from markets outside the domain boundaries. For this reason the monopolies were in 'export' goods, that is, those for which there was a steady demand in other parts of the country. Organization usually took one of two forms. Under the first, a group of merchants would be granted exclusive rights to purchase a given local product, on condition that they subsequently turned it over to officials for shipment to Edo and Osaka, where it was sold on the wholesale market. In this way, the merchants took their profits from the producer, the domain from the buyer. Alternatively, the domain might control the whole process by establishing its own offices to buy the goods, as well as to ship and sell them. In this case the feudal lord was able to employ his political authority to fix prices and increase the profits, while appointing merchants to minor official posts to handle the detailed running of the system.

From the official viewpoint, one important advantage of the monopolies was that they produced an income in gold and silver. This not only represented 'real' wealth in the mercantilist terms common to Tokugawa Japan, but was also immediately available to meet the heavy expenses which were incurred in Edo. Moreover, the farmer-producer was often paid in the domain's own paper money, which he was required to accept at face value, or in some form of credit note which could be used only in certain permitted ways. In other words, he was forced to take a low price in a dubious form of payment. It is not surprising, therefore, that the introduction of monopolies brought more unrest in the countryside and that the merchant-officials who acted as the domain's agents were among the most frequent targets of peasant violence.

Monopoly arrangements of various kinds increased greatly in number between 1800 and 1830, affording evidence of the growing financial pressure on domains. They were not, however, universally successful as a solution to financial ills. In many cases there is no doubt that the lion's share of the profit found its way into the pockets of the merchants who administered the system, not into the treasury for whose benefit it was ostensibly run, and this, together with mounting signs of rural unrest, provoked many samurai to demand reform. In some fiefs, usually where the *daimyo* was himself a man of some ability, they were able to carry it out.

Economies in expenditure and improvements in administration were the most familiar features of a reformer's policy, just as they were in Edo; but, these apart, one can still identify two main differences of emphasis in what was done. The first constituted an attempt in the manner of Mizuno Tadakuni to strengthen the traditional sources of feudal revenue and protect these elements in society that did most to produce it, this involving an attack on the commercialization of agriculture, on luxury in the towns, on the decline in samurai standards of behaviour. The second aimed at achieving solvency by exploiting commercial wealth, subordinating the interests of the merchant to those of the domain, but co-operating with him to some extent in monopoly arrangements made at the expense of the farmer and the artisan. Both policies had their advocates, often within a single domain's officialdom. All the same one can readily cite examples of domains that chose to follow substantially one course or the other. Notable among them were Satsuma and Choshu.

Zusho Hiromichi's career as a reformer in Satsuma stands as one of the most successful of the period. Zusho was born in 1776 into a samurai family of low rank, but he entered his lord's household and rose steadily to high office in it by 1825. A few years later he was made responsible for financial reform, an event which marked his emergence into the domain government proper and was followed by new appointments and grants of rank. From 1833 until his death in 1848 he was senior minister with an annual stipend of a thousand *koku*, devoting こく his attention largely to the task of increasing Satsuma revenue いちま and redeeming the domain's enormous debts.

One of his early cares was to reduce waste in the collection of dues and in the shipment of rice to Osaka. He also took あか steps to improve the yield and quality of the fief's main crops. In more original vein, trade with the Ryukyu islands was encouraged, this being an indirect means of trade with China, with which country the islands still maintained a tributary relationship; and, most important of all, control over the sugar production of Oshima and neighbouring areas was greatly おしま tightened. The latter had been a source of income to Satsuma ever since sugar had first formed part of the Ryukyu tax payments in 1647, becoming more so in the eighteenth century, when the domain had begun to buy up the rest of the Oshima crop as well, making dealing in it an official monopoly. It was left to Zusho, however, to make the controls really effective. This he did by regulations issued in 1830, which provided that all sugar had to be sold to the domain for subsequent disposal in the Osaka market. The purchase price was fixed, crops were regularly inspected and the death penalty was imposed for any attempt at private trading, while profits were further increased by paying the producer in credit notes which he could only use to buy goods from official dealers at prices which were kept artificially high.

The result of these measures was a sharp improvement in domain finances. Annual proceeds from sugar sales rose from 136,000 *ryo* in 1830 to 235,000 *ryo* a decade later, this being entirely due to improvements in quality and handling, since quantities remained the same. The profit margin must also have risen, though no figures for it are available, in that the domain monopolized all operations, including shipping, up to the point where sugar was sold to wholesalers by competitive tender. One estimate has it that something like half the returns were profit, that is, about 100,000 *ryo* a year. Certainly there was enough, with the yields from Zusho's other measures, to make possible an expensive programme of military reform.

One factor that made such methods workable in Satsuma was the nature of the domain's political structure: the high proportion of samurai in the population, many of them living permanently in the countryside, whose numbers made peasant revolt wellnigh impossible and whose adherence to traditional virtues greatly eased the task of subjecting merchants to samurai control. In Choshu the position was different. There, too, samurai were numerous, at least by comparison with Tokugawa lands. Many of them were also resident in villages, though in this case it was to escape the higher cost of living in the castle-town. Economically, however, the domain lacked any single crop or product that could compare with Satsuma sugar as a source of profit, while in its wealthier areas, chiefly along the shores of the Inland Sea, development had been more complex, more closely linked with the commercial market and hence more difficult to regulate than in the backward regions. Monopolies had been created at various times in salt, wax, paper, indigo, saké and cotton, but none had brought in a substantial revenue for very long. On the other hand, all had proved unpopular, the reactions of the farmers ranging from evasion to outright revolt. Thus it was anti-monopoly demonstrations near the town of Mitajiri that touched off widespread —if abortive—riots throughout the province in the summer of 1831, these being followed by further outbreaks in 1832, 1833 and 1837.

In 1838 a new *daimyo*, Mori Yoshichika, decided to initiate reforms, entrusting their execution to Murata Seifu, a samurai now raised to high office for the first time, who began in the usual manner with exhortations to frugality. Three years later he evolved a more far-reaching plan, designed to base fief finances on the encouragement of agriculture and the limitation of expenditure. This his lord approved, together with its two corollaries: first, that official participation in monopolies should end—except for a profitable shipping and warehousing organization in Shimonoseki—on the grounds that they benefited townsmen, not the treasury, and aroused hostility in rural areas; second, that men of ability be promoted to office, regardless of inherited rank, to ensure effective management and supervision.

It is not entirely clear how far these policies succeeded in restoring order to the Choshu finances in the next few years, though Murata was certainly able to build up a special reserve for emergency use and to reduce the burdens on samurai income. The result, so contemporaries reported, was a marked improvement in Choshu morale. All the same, opposition was not slow in coming. The merchants of the castle-town were inevitably hostile, especially after Murata announced a plan for redeeming the debts of both domain and samurai at rates that were not far short of total cancellation. Equally opposed to him were many members of the feudal class, who found it impossible to live without their merchant loans. Together these groups succeeded in bringing about his fall in 1844. They substituted a government with less inflexible convictions, men who were unwilling to attack vested interests to attain their ends; and they thereby began a struggle for power that lasted for the rest of the Tokugawa period. Involved on the one side was the party of monopolies and the established order. It had the backing of most upper samurai, if not always of the feudal lord, and stood for a conservatism that varied from the moderate to the extreme. On the other side were the advocates of austere reform, deriving support from elements that grew increasingly more varied and more radical: samurai looking to a feudal past, farmers seeking freedom from monopolist restraints, ambitious village headmen, young idealists. Twenty years later, transformed by time into an anti-Tokugawa movement, it was the reformers who finally gained the upper hand.

The reform movements of Ieyoshi's era played a significant part in the events which led to the Bakufu's fall. In the first place, the fact that a number of domains had greater success than the Tokugawa in overcoming financial crisis weakened the latter as compared with feudal lords who were potentially their rivals. This was merely to confirm a shift in the balance of economic power which was already taking place, arising, on the one hand, from the uneven growth in agricultural yields during the seventeenth and eighteenth centuries, which tended to benefit those whose holdings, because they were in peripheral regions, included more marginal land that could be brought under cultivation; and, on the other, from the development of a commercial economy in the fertile and thickly populated areas of the south and west, which increased the resources available to domains without as yet posing problems of organization of the same order as those that Edo found insoluble. Several domains found means to tap these new resources, raising their tax returns to an appreciably higher level. Some, moreover, were able to exploit particular advantages of geography and climate. Satsuma, for example, had access to the trade and sugar of Ryukyu; Choshu dominated the western approaches to the Inland Sea, most important of commercial shipping routes; Tosa had rich fishing grounds and a valuable paper industry. All three attained a degree of financial stability that enabled them to provide active leadership in the history of the next few decades.

The change involved political as well as economic factors. Among them must be counted the accident of personality, that is, the emergence of reforming *daimyo*, like Mori Yoshichika of Choshu and Shimazu Nariakira of Satsuma, who raised young men of modest rank—though always samurai rank, for this was a condition of entrance to the *daimyo's* household—to form a new administrative élite. They included, too, the environment that gave these young men drive and purpose: a combination of poverty and opportunity that had almost explosive force. Together they created an age of political faction and debate. There were those, as we have seen, who looked to agriculture as the basis of both respectability and finance. Others looked to trade, or at least had no desire to lose the comforts it made possible. In addition, there were samurai interest groups of a different kind: men of high rank and little energy, clinging grimly to power; exponents of traditional skills—in gunnery or fencing, for example—whose status and privileges were soon to be challenged by the importation of new techniques; and 'men of ability', usually from the middle or lower strata of the samurai class, seeking outlets for ambition as well as opportunities for reform. All tended to organize, to seek allies, to vie with each other for positions of authority. In the process they gave experience of politics and office to a widening circle, from which was to be drawn the future rulers of Japan.

Yet it would be unwise to assume that there was anything

like identity in the political patterns that took shape in different areas, or that a coherent national movement was emerging. Still less can one describe reform as anti-feudal or anti-Bakufu at this stage. On the contrary, it was designed, it has been said, 'to shake off the dead hand of conservatism and lethargy so characteristic of later Tokugawa rule . . . without precipitating any cataclysmic changes'.[8] It was not until the 1850s that extremer views gained hold, another decade before they became politically effective. The shift of emphasis, moreover, when it came, was to be linked with something new, a consciousness of external threat arising from relations with the West. It is to a consideration of this that we must therefore turn.

CHAPTER III

JAPAN AND THE WEST

Western attempts to open trade—the Opium War—Japanese reactions—developments in shipping and armaments

WHEN THE third Tokugawa ruler, Iemitsu, took the final steps in establishing Japan's policy of national seclusion in the seventeenth century, he did so for reasons that seemed to him practical and cogent. Christianity he regarded as an instrument of foreign ambitions, to be stamped out by every means at his disposal. Trade, which might provide guns and gold to a disaffected vassal, ought to be limited and controlled. Hence priests were excluded; those who brought them were punished; and the few Dutch and Chinese merchants still permitted at Nagasaki were closely watched. With the passage of time, trade itself came into disfavour, on the grounds that what the foreigners brought were luxuries and what they took were goods that Japan could hardly spare, while the suspicions on which Iemitsu had acted became inflated by constant repetition until the whole structure of his belief became hallowed as ancestral law.

The difficulty about enforcing this law, however, was that it depended on the willingness of other countries to accept the ban, as well as on Japan's ability to resist any demands they might make for its removal. In both respects the position changed gradually to Japan's disadvantage. Advances in European science and technology, unmatched elsewhere, had by the nineteenth century made it impossible for Japan to defend herself successfully in the event of war. Similarly, a new wave of European expansion, linked with the growth of industry and a search for markets, ensured that she would not be left alone for ever. In the south, after about 1775, Britain, followed by the

United States, began to establish an important trade with China. In the north, Russian settlements appeared on the Sea of Okhotsk, from which explorers eventually made contact with Japan.

Russian attention was first drawn to that country by the discovery of a Japanese castaway on Kamchatka in 1697. There followed a number of exploratory voyages to the Kuriles and Hokkaido, but it was not until 1792 that Adam Laxman, with Catherine the Great's approval, left Okhotsk in a formal attempt to communicate with Japan under the pretext of returning a group of shipwrecked seamen. He wintered in Hokkaido and had amicable discussions with officials there, but in July 1793 was told he must not continue to Edo. Nor was he allowed to open questions of trade, since this, it was said, could only be done at Nagasaki. However, he was given a permit for one Russian ship to visit that port for the purpose of making the request.

The permit was not used until after the establishment of the Russian-American Company in 1799, when Nikolai Rezanov, a shareholder in the company and an advocate of Russian commercial expansion in China and Japan, secured imperial approval for a further voyage, together with a letter from Alexander I for delivery to the Japanese government. He sailed from Kronstadt in 1803 and reached Kamchatka, via Cape Horn, in the following year, eventually arriving at Nagasaki on October 20, 1804. There his reception was far from friendly. His ship was put under close guard while a copy of the Tsar's letter was sent to Edo. Moreover, the accommodation provided for him ashore was more a prison than an ambassador's residence and he was forced to wait six months for the Bakufu's decision. When, after all this, permission to go to Edo was refused and all the Russian proposals were rejected, Rezanov was furious; and before returning home he left orders with two Russian officers in Okhotsk which led to a series of raids on Japanese settlements in the north during 1806 and 1807. This in turn embittered the Japanese, who had their revenge a few years later when they seized the captain of a Russian survey vessel, Vasilii Golovnin, who landed on one of the Kurile islands in July 1811, holding him prisoner in Hokkaido for a little over two years until his ship returned with official disclaimers of the 1806–7 raids from the governor of Irkutsk. Thereafter Russo-Japanese relations for a generation or more were reduced to scattered contact in the islands.

British relations with Japan in this period were equally sporadic. In 1791 a private trader, James Colnett, cruised up the west coast of Kyushu, trying cautiously to open trade by approaches to ships offshore, but his total failure seems to have discouraged others from repeating the experiment. Then in 1808 a British frigate, the *Phaeton*, entered Nagasaki harbour under Dutch colours and took hostages to ensure the prompt supply of stores. Such high-handed action caused a great commotion ashore, but it was in fact incidental to the *Phaeton*'s purpose: she was concerned merely to seize Dutch ships, as a part of wartime operations against Napoleon's empire. However, the incident had repercussions a few years later, when a deliberate attack on Japan's seclusion was planned by Thomas Stamford Raffles. As lieutenant-governor of Java, newly captured from the Dutch, Raffles tried twice in 1813–14 to substitute a British trade with Deshima for that of Holland. Each time the men he sent to carry out his orders were foiled by the Dutch factor at Deshima, Hendrik Doeff, who threatened to reveal their identity to Japanese officials and so involve them in the hostility incurred by the *Phaeton*'s action. The effectiveness of this threat depended partly on the fact that Raffles' policy had been coldly received in London and was actively opposed by the governor-general in Calcutta, which made it necessary for him to proceed with caution, but in any case the opportunity to act at all was not of long duration, since Java was handed back to the Dutch soon after.

In the next twenty years British interest in Japan was rare and action based upon it even rarer. An unsuccessful private voyage was made to Edo Bay in 1818 and on several occasions whaling vessels, now operating off the Japanese coast, came into contact with Japanese villagers, but this was all. A further attempt to open Japan did not come until 1837, when it took the form of a joint Anglo-American venture. The story of it began when a Japanese junk, on a coasting voyage to Edo at the end of 1832, was dismasted and driven off its course by a typhoon. Drifting for months across the Pacific, with a few of its crew managing to exist on rain-water and the ship's cargo of rice, it was wrecked on the north-west coast of America, where three survivors were rescued from the Indians in 1834 by the Hudson's Bay Company's factor at Fort Vancouver. Thinking it possible that they might be welcome as an excuse for negotiating with Japan, he sent them to London in 1835, but the British government showed little enthusiasm for this as a pretext for an official mission. They were duly transferred to Canton later in the year. Here Captain Elliott, Second Superintendent of Trade, evolved the same plan as had already occurred to the Vancouver factor. He wrote to Palmerston suggesting that the opportunity be taken to send the castaways back by warship and so open a correspondence with Japan, only to find himself firmly snubbed in a Foreign Office dispatch of September 1836. This put an end to any possibility of government action, though it still left the problem of how to get the men back to their own country, since the Foreign Office recommendation that they be sent 'quietly home' in a Chinese junk was impracticable for a variety of reasons.

A solution was found in the arrangements being made by two Americans, a merchant, C. W. King, and a missionary, Dr S. Wells Williams. They, too, had Japanese castaways— in this case, four from Manila—and hopes of gaining access to Japan. In consultation with Elliott they agreed to add his three charges to their company, the whole expedition, privately financed, to proceed to Edo Bay in the ship *Morrison* after calling at the Ryukyu capital of Naha. The plan was carried out in the summer of 1837, only to fail in both its public and its private objects. On July 30 of that year, the *Morrison* dropped anchor off Uraga and was visited by crowds of Japanese, both impassive officials and curious sightseers. Yet at dawn next day, before any formal discussions could take place, shore batteries opened fire on the anchorage, forcing the unarmed ship to sea. An attempt a few days later to establish communication with the shore at Kagoshima in the south of Kyushu met the same response. On August 27, therefore, with castaways, bibles and trade goods still intact, the *Morrison* returned to the China coast.

The *Morrison* affair, it transpired, marked the end of an era. A little over two years later war broke out between Britain and China, the so-called Opium War, which revolutionized the international politics of the region. By the treaty settlement of 1842–3 Britain acquired Hong Kong and opened additional Chinese ports to foreign trade as far north as Shanghai at the mouth of the Yangtse. This increased the possibility of visits to Japan, planned or unplanned, since Shanghai was a mere 500 miles from Nagasaki. Moreover, the resulting growth in trade soon meant that many more European merchants and far greater financial interests were involved, so that Japan was no longer to be regarded as beyond the farthest point of Europe's longest trade route, but rather as being on the fringe of an area of increasing concern to European governments. The Far East in general began to loom larger in the calculations of Western statesmen. Accordingly, they provided it with the appurtenances of modern diplomacy—consuls and gunboats —and by so doing made it easier to plan official missions to Japan. These could now be carried out with the resources of men and ships which were locally available. In other words, certain practical advantages in pursuing relations with Japan which only Russia had previously possessed were now extended to the maritime powers.

The change was reflected in the character of Japan's visitors in the next decade or so, almost all of whom were official representatives of their respective countries. For example, Japan, because its geography was so little known, acquired a certain importance as a possible danger to navigation. In 1843 a British survey ship, HMS *Samarang*, was put to work on the islands running north-east from Formosa and this brought her to Nagasaki in August 1845 with a request for stores. She carried out a surreptitious survey of the harbour before leaving. Four years later another vessel, HMS *Mariner*, arrived from Shanghai to survey the approaches to Edo; and despite Japanese objections she was able to acquire much useful information about the two ports of Uraga and Shimoda, and about Sagami Bay, which lies between them. All this was naval routine, without ulterior diplomatic motives, but it undoubtedly looked ominous to many observers.

There was, indeed, good reason for supposing that European governments would be forced by mercantile opinion at home to put an end to Japanese seclusion. There were many merchants, officials and even missionaries in the West who thought that what had been done to force trade on China was not only right in itself, but also exemplified a principle which should be applied to Japan as well. The *Edinburgh Review* put the argument as follows:

'The compulsory seclusion of the Japanese is a wrong not only to themselves, but to the civilized world . . . The Japanese undoubtedly have an exclusive right to the possession of their territory; but they must not abuse that right to the extent of debarring all other nations from a participation in its riches and virtues. The only secure title to property, whether it be a hovel or an empire, is, that the exclusive possession of one is for the benefit of all.'[9]

Ministers had henceforth to take this sort of thinking into account when framing policy.

It was in 1844 that Japanese attention was first directed officially to the situation which the Opium War had brought about. In the summer of that year a Dutch ship arrived at Nagasaki bringing a letter to the Shogun from the Dutch king, William II, setting out the changes which industrialization was causing in Europe's relations with the rest of the world and underlining their dangerous implications for Japan. The letter took the form of friendly advice, urging the Japanese government to reconsider the seclusion policy while it was still able to do so free from outside pressure. It was clear enough, however, that Holland hoped for advantages for herself and that the letter was meant to be a preliminary to negotiation. Edo certainly so regarded it. Nevertheless, the Bakufu's reply to the Dutch was negative and uncompromising. Dated July 5, 1845, it reiterated the traditional view: foreign trade was limited by ancestral law to China and Holland; its extension to other countries could not be considered; correspondence on this subject must therefore cease and never be resumed.

Such an answer would almost certainly have been rejected by Britain or Russia, but it happened that action on their part was prevented, or at least delayed, by other considerations. It was in 1845, in fact, that Britain first made secret plans for a mission to Japan, proposed in May by Sir John Davis, Superintendent of Trade at Hong Kong, and approved some months later by Aberdeen at the Foreign Office, with the expectation that they would be carried out during the summer of 1846; but in the event Davis allowed them to lapse because the navy's China squadron could not put at his disposal the amount of force which he considered necessary. And since there was not enough interest in the matter at Whitehall to make the government take action on its own, Davis's decision was accepted and the matter was allowed to drop, though subsequent Superintendents were provided with authority to go to Japan should a suitable opportunity arise. All of them proved too preoccupied with the affairs of China to try to do so.

For Russia the reasons were different but the effect the same. After the Opium War, Nicholas I had established a committee to review Russia's position in the Amur region in the light of new conditions; and a member of it, Rear-Admiral Putiatin, had put forward plans for surveying the Amur estuary and sending an expedition to Japan. They were approved by the Tsar in 1843, but were then opposed by the Foreign Minister, Nesselrode, on the grounds that Russia had no Pacific trade which was worth such effort. This proved decisive, with the result that, although the Amur survey was carried out on a small scale, nothing at all was done about Japan. The fact was that Japanese trade was never likely to be of more than subsidiary interest to Russia, important chiefly for its local value to her settlements round the Sea of Okhotsk. On the other hand, there were other motives than trade that might bring about negotiation. Russia was a territorial power in north-east Asia, with political and strategic interests there which made her inevitably concerned at any possible growth in the influence of other Western countries, such as might easily be occasioned by the opening of Japanese ports. She therefore watched closely the moves, not only of Britain, but also of the United States.

American interests in the Pacific were both commercial, like those of Britain, and strategic, like those of Russia, a combination which sufficiently explains why it was the United States that in the end successfully forced a way into Japanese waters. Her first official attempt to do so began in 1845, when a merchant, Aaron Palmer, persuaded his government that trade with Japan held out good prospects. At Palmer's urging, orders were given to Commodore James Biddle, in command of the Pacific squadron, permitting him to go to Japan and investigate the possibilities of agreement, an opportunity of which he took advantage in July 1846. Unfortunately for his chances of success, he had been instructed to avoid provocation. He therefore let pass an incident at the anchorage in Edo Bay which was widely interpreted as a gratuitous insult to his rank. This brought down on him more criticism from his fellow-countrymen and other Western residents on the China coast even than his readiness to accept a Japanese reply which was a flat refusal to grant trade or privileges and which was undated, unsigned and unaddressed. On all sides it was said that Biddle had left the situation rather worse than he had found it. His experiences certainly helped to persuade Sir John Davis to abandon the projected British mission. What is more, no greater success awaited another American venture three years later, when the USS *Preble* was sent to Nagasaki. Her commander secured the ostensible object of his voyage, the release of some seamen shipwrecked from an American whaler, but made no headway in his efforts to establish a consul in Japan and acquire a coaling station there.

On these occasions, American policy had not been pressed any more forcefully than that of Russia or of Britain. America's position with respect to the Pacific, however, was changing quickly. British recognition of US rights in the Oregon territory in 1846 and the acquisition of California after the war with Mexico in 1846–8 gave her a long Pacific coastline. A transcontinental railway was already being discussed, in terms of trade with Asia as well as of development at home, while the newly formed Pacific Mail Steamship Company was planning a route to China. Thus Japan suddenly became a factor of real importance. Her harbours—and reported coal deposits—lay directly on the route from San Francisco to Shanghai. Consequently her notorious lack of hospitality for seamen in distress or in need of supplies, displeasing enough when it affected only whalers, could not be tolerated any longer. For her coastal waters were to become a major shipping lane, used by steamers which at this early state of their development had a very limited range; and whether or not Japanese trade was likely to be of value, Japanese seclusion had therefore become an offence. The next attack on it was likely to be more determined.

This was made very clear in 1852 when it was announced

that a new American expedition would go to Japan under the command of Commodore M. C. Perry. He was to be accompanied by a sizeable force and would not be able lightly to turn away, for the whole world, including Japan, was told of the plan and its preparations. The Western press debated ends and means, confidently predicting that guns would be used if arguments failed. European governments, officially notified of America's intention, sought to clarify their attitude to it. Britain, it appeared, was prepared to let things take their course. 'Her Majesty's Government', the Foreign Secretary wrote to Hong Kong in July 1852, 'would be glad to see the trade with Japan open; but they think it better to leave it to the Government of the United States to make the experiment; and if that experiment is successful, Her Majesty's Government can take advantage of its success.'[10] Russia, by contrast, hurriedly revived the plans of 1843 and appointed Putiatin to take a squadron to Japan, with orders to watch over Russian interests and ensure that his country had a voice in any settlement. Thus Japan had become the destination, not of single ships, but of powerful and rival squadrons, one sailing from America's east coast in November 1852, the other leaving Europe two months later. To almost everyone it was apparent that the closed door must open or it would be broken down.

The development of Russian, British and American interest in the Far East, although known to Tokugawa officials, affected Japanese policy only in causing more attention to be paid to coast defence. Domains on the coast were told to keep watch for foreign ships and to have troops ready to repel them. In 1825 they were even ordered to fire on them at sight. This rule was cancelled in 1842, when Mizuno Tadakuni, influenced by events in China, issued instructions that vessels in distress were to be provided with essential stores before being ordered to depart, but he coupled this with a warning that the relaxation was not to become an excuse for carelessness over military precautions. His successor, Abe Masahiro, who became senior councillor in March 1845, was equally cautious. He showed himself willing to overlook Satsuma evasion of the strict letter of the seclusion laws in the Ryukyu islands, but not, as we have seen, to enter into negotiations with the occasional Western representatives who reached Japan. Until 1853, basic policies in this respect remained unchanged.

Yet this is not to say that basic policies were never questioned. From the end of the eighteenth century, Japanese scholars—most of whom were samurai, many of them having considerable influence as officials, teachers, or advisers to their lords—had begun seriously to debate the political and economic implications of seclusion. Among the first to do so were the Rangakusha, or 'Dutch scholars', those who studied the Dutch language in order to make use of books imported through the Deshima factory. Early representatives of the group had concentrated largely on European medicine and similar topics, but after 1790, as foreign visits to Japan increased, some of them turned to geography, world affairs and even politics. This led inevitably to a consideration of their country's foreign relations. One, for example, wrote a pamphlet in 1838 about the *Morrison* venture, under the title 'Story of a Dream'. His facts were garbled, but the point of his remarks was clear enough: Britain was a powerful adversary, well able to resent insult, and Japan had best beware how she treated British missions. In other words, seclusion might prove dangerous. For this, which officials chose to regard as an attack on the regime, the author was later imprisoned.

One of the most famous of the Rangakusha was Sakuma Shozan, a samurai of Matsushiro in Shinano, whose lord, Sanada Yukitsura, was appointed to the Council of State in Mizuno Tadakuni's time and put in charge of coast defence. A knowledge of and interest in defence policy, acquired through this connection, led Sakuma to a study of the Dutch language and Western military science, for he became convinced that only weapons of the Western type would enable Japan to defend herself successfully. It was a case which he proceeded to argue in a number of memorials to his lord. In 1842, pointing to the dangers of Russian and British attack, he urged that Japan must prepare for the struggle by purchasing modern armaments and by learning to make them, too. Within six years he had himself learnt the technique of casting cannon. Nor were his studies confined to the mechanical, though they continued to have a practical and military bent. In 1849 we find him petitioning Sanada for financial help in the preparation of a Dutch-Japanese dictionary and the publication of Dutch books, a plan he justified on the grounds that it was necessary 'to know one's enemy'.[11] In the following year he sought Bakufu help as well, arguing still more generally the superiority of Western science over that of China and Japan. Western countries had been able to achieve overwhelming material strength, he said, 'because foreign learning is rational and Chinese learning is not'.[12] It was China's failure to recognize this which had been responsible for her defeat; and if Japan wished to avoid the same fate she must study what the West had to teach her in a variety of fields, not merely those which were of direct application to war.

Notwithstanding his growing, if reluctant, admiration for the West's achievements, Sakuma always remained wedded to Japanese tradition in non-technical matters, an attitude he expressed in the slogan, 'Eastern ethics, Western science', which was to be not far short of an official doctrine for a time after the Meiji Restoration. Sakuma, however, never lived to see this happen. He died in 1864 at the age of fifty-three, murdered by an anti-foreign extremist from Choshu—an ironic ending for a man who had spent over twenty years seeking means to preserve Japan from foreign aggression and had not long before been in prison for criticizing the Bakufu's weakness in diplomatic negotiations.

Men like Sakuma became involved in politics because foreign affairs was a political issue. Others did so because they identified themselves from the beginning with proposals for reform within Japan. Among the latter, for example, was Sato Shinen (1769–1850), advocate of radical economic and political change, of military reform and overseas expansion. Some of his lack of orthodoxy was undoubtedly due to family background, since he came of a non-samurai family in northern Japan which for several generations had produced experts in agriculture, forestry and mining. But much of it was in the man himself. He travelled extensively throughout Japan, making careful notes of all that interested him, and acquired a knowledge of Dutch which he used in the study of Western geography, history, navigation and military science. As a result he was far better equipped than most of his contemporaries to prescribe cures for the country's ills. He was initially much in favour of expanding foreign trade. However, when news of the Opium War reached Japan he began to wonder whether the economic advantages of trade were commensurate with its political risks. The same period saw him become hesitant about the possibilities of empire. He had argued in earlier days that Japan's geographical position, organizing ability and superior moral fibre made it inevitable, as well as desirable, that she should dominate China and the areas further west; but he now began to dwell anxiously on the subject of defence, as Chinese defeats began to sap his confidence.

This was a common response to the Opium War among writers of the time. More interesting in many ways was Sato's recognition that economic and military strength could not be achieved independently of political structure. In one of his books he described the sort of state—as purposeful and highly regulated a state as Sparta—which he would wish to see established in Japan. Government, he maintained, should be conducted through separate departments handling agriculture, forestry and mining, finance and commerce, manufacture, and the army and navy, with the whole population divided into hereditary classes defined by function, each under the control of one of these departments. Change of occupation would be forbidden and each group segregated from the others. This would ensure that children acquired a knowledge of their family trade in their earliest years, thus increasing specialization and efficiency. From the age of eight, moreover, children would be entitled to free education in one of the provincial schools run by a Department of Education, receiving a training designed to increase their value to the state. There would also be a national university for the privileged and able, providing, in addition to traditional subjects like philosophy and religion, instruction in law, foreign languages and Western science. Sato's proposals foreshadow many features of Japanese life in the later nineteenth century, even—perhaps especially—in their disconcerting blend of the grim and the enlightened. Sakuma, too, provided ideas which were used by statesmen after 1868. In this respect they both, like other men of similar outlook, contributed to the process we call 'modernization'. On the other hand, it does not follow that they played a direct part in bringing about the fall of the Tokugawa, which was to be the prelude to modernization and the key to its success. In fact, the work of the early nineteenth century Mito scholars was far more relevant to this stage of the political process.

The Mito domain, held by one of the three senior Tokugawa branch houses, had long been a centre of Confucian scholarship. For generations its official scholars had engaged in writing a chronicle of early Japanese history, an undertaking which gave them a reputation for patriotism and, apparently, a lively interest in contemporary affairs. Certainly the new crisis in Japan's foreign relations which came in the eighteenth century caused them great concern. In 1797 one of them, Fujita Yukoku, warned his lord of the danger of Russian attack, criticizing the Bakufu for its failure to make adequate preparations to meet it and urging that Mito, as a coastal fief, had a special duty to do so on its own account. As means to this end he specified two things which were to be central to Mito thinking for sixty years: armaments and reform. He added that the country's leaders must show such resolution as would unite the nation, raise morale and so make victory sure.

These ideas were further developed by Aizawa Seishisai in a book called *Shinron* (New Proposals) written in 1825 and by Yukoku's son, Fujita Toko, in his *Hitachi obi* (Sash of Hitachi) twenty years later. Both argued that the urgent task was to arouse Japan to a sense of danger and to unite the country in its own defence. This done, the rest of their plans would have some meaning: the provision of new weapons, including Western-style ships; financial reform, to pay for them; and the promotion of men of ability, to secure sound administration on which all else depended. Yet a revival of traditional spirit, overcoming luxury and lethargy, could not be achieved by exhortation. Only one thing would suffice to do it, they said, an announcement that the government was resolved once and for all to reject foreign demands and fight to defend seclusion. The slogan must be 'expel the barbarian' (*jo-i*). In other words, the ports must remain closed and trade must be refused, even if this meant war.

By 1853, then, the Mito scholars had reached some very definite conclusions about foreign affairs. Japan, they believed, could only attain national strength and international equality by achieving unity at home. This, in turn, depended on war or the threat of war. Hence the Bakufu must be uncompromising in negotiation. Unfortunately, however, there was a danger that Bakufu officials, fearing defeat, might be willing to temporise in the hope of avoiding conflict, a possibility which called in question the Bakufu's capacity for leadership and shifted the discussion of reform to a new—and ominous— level. Suggestions were made that the Shogun should consult the great lords—those whose views were reliable, of course— in addition to the usual officials. There were even some who urged that success could never be complete until the emperor became once again a focus of national government, creating unity by transcending other loyalties.

This doctrine of imperial sovereignty had always been latent in Japanese thought. In the eighteenth century, however, it had emerged more widely because of attempts to revive the Shinto religion, which owed much to the studies of ancient Japanese literature and society by the scholar Motoori Norinaga (1730–1801). His work served to resurrect one particular set of Shinto beliefs that were ultimately of great political importance: briefly, that the Japanese emperor was descended directly from the sun-goddess; that his claim to temporal power rested on divine descent; that the Japanese islands and people were also of divine origin; and that Japan was by these facts made superior to other lands. The chauvinist element in this was made explicit in the nineteenth century by the publicist, Hirata Atsutane (1776–1843). 'Japanese', he wrote, 'differ completely from and are superior to the peoples of China, India, Russia, Holland, Siam, Cambodia, and all other countries of the world.'[13] It was a comforting thought to men who knew that Western countries possessed much power and an apparent willingness to use it against Japan.

Neo-Shinto ideas of this kind gained considerable influence among those who wrote on foreign affairs. This was largely, no doubt, because their anti-foreign flavour accorded well with the fears and suspicions aroused by Western encroachment, but it helped also to turn men's minds towards the emperor as a means of healing political divisions. Some of these divisions, after all, were the result of Tokugawa supremacy. Others deeply involved the samurai class, of which the Shogun was the appointed head. The Shogun, therefore, was not an entirely satisfactory focus of loyalty, whereas the emperor, being above the discord, was. Thus a second slogan, 'honour the emperor' (*son-no*), eventually came into being to reinforce that which called for expelling the barbarian.

In this way, foreign policy became linked with issues of domestic politics: first, because political and economic reform was regarded as an essential part of defence preparations; second, because men began to look to the emperor as a source of unity in the face of foreign threat. All the same, it would be quite wrong to describe this as being from the start a deliberate attack on Tokugawa authority. Even allowing for the fact that such ideas would have been dangerous to express, it is still significant that contemporary literature reveals practically nothing in the way of threats to overthrow the existing order. When the Mito scholars spoke of 'reform', they meant policies that would make the best of society as it was. When they talked of 'honouring the emperor', they meant to strengthen the Shogun's power in a time of growing unrest by using the emperor's name in the Bakufu's service. The way to unity was through a loyalty that must be duly hierarchical. As Tokugawa Nariaki, lord of Mito, wrote in 1842:

'If the Shogun takes the lead in showing respect for the throne, the whole country will naturally be united, but it is vital that in this each should preserve his proper place. The samurai shows respect for his lord, the lord shows respect for the Shogun, the Shogun shows respect for the Emperor.'[14]

One can hardly call this subversive.

It took the events of 1853–60, with which we shall deal in the next chapter, to make the ideas of the Mito school the basis for an anti-Tokugawa movement. By that time they had been disseminated widely by the writings and personal teaching of the domain's outstanding scholars, Fujita Toko and Aizawa Seishisai, the first of whom lived till 1855 and the second till 1863. Their fame was such that many came to study under them. Others met them in Edo or learnt their views at second hand, until it is fair to say that most samurai of the period knew at least their slogans.

This was to be enormously important. Nevertheless, their

only sure way of influencing policy, as distinct from opinion, was through their lord, Tokugawa Nariaki, whose actions in this period speak eloquently of their success. In 1842 he opposed Mizuno Tadakuni's plan to relax the seclusion laws, on the grounds that it was pusillanimous. In 1846 he urged Abe Masahiro, the senior Bakufu councillor, to arrange for translations of Dutch works on military subjects to be made widely available as a step towards improving Japan's defences. In 1853 and after he was a consistent opponent of diplomatic concession and an advocate of Bakufu reform. Since he was not only a senior member of the Tokugawa house, but also, through the marriage of his daughters and the adoption of his sons, closely connected with two leading families of the Imperial Court and several of the most powerful *tozama* lords, his advice was not lightly to be rejected or ignored. Nor did Nariaki confine himself to the giving of advice. Within the boundaries of his own domain he was free to do many things without interference from the Shogun and he therefore did what he could to prepare for the coming struggle. His financial and administrative reforms became a model. In addition, by encouraging the study and use of Western techniques which had military importance, he put Mito in the forefront of modernization in the 1850s, with an iron industry and western-style shipbuilding already established on a small scale by 1858. Meanwhile, however, his plans had brought him into conflict with Bakufu authority. In 1844, because he had begun casting cannon without Edo's permission—in direct contravention of the regulations governing internal security—he was ordered to retire from headship of the fief in favour of his son. This he did, but his personal standing was such that he continued to dominate Mito policies until his death in 1860.

Tokugawa Nariaki and Mito were not alone in turning to Western technology for anti-Western ends, though others did not always justify their actions by the same loyalist and chauvinistic reasoning. A number of domains, as well as the Bakufu itself, encouraged Dutch studies and established translation offices. One or two, those which had the necessary economic resources, tried to put what they learnt to use. Conspicuous among them were Hizen and Satsuma, the former under Nabeshima Kanso (1814–71), *daimyo* from 1831 to 1861, the latter under Shimazu Nariakira (1809–58), *daimyo* from 1851 to 1858.

Nabeshima, as the man responsible for the Nagasaki defences, was able to tackle the problems of cannon-founding with Bakufu support and Dutch technical advice. In 1850 his domain built Japan's first successful reverberatory furnace, thus obtaining the higher quality iron which was needed to replace copper in making modern cannon. Production of these began in 1853. Thereafter the technique was applied regularly to supply the Bakufu with weapons, while a number of other lords, including those of Satsuma and Mito, sent men to learn it. From guns Hizen turned to shipping, experimenting first with models and then ordering a complete shipbuilding plant from Holland in 1856. It proved too expensive and was handed over to the Tokugawa in 1859, but even without it Hizen was able to turn out a ship's boiler in 1861 and a small steamer in 1865. Three years later an agreement was made for joint operation of the Takashima colliery with a British firm.

Much of this development took place after the ports were opened in 1858, but it is significant that much of it had started well before. The same was true in Satsuma. Attempts to improve artillery methods there had begun under Zusho Hiromichi in 1842 and had been followed by the introduction of some Western techniques in gun-making in 1846. When Shimazu Nariakira became *daimyo*, however, the speed and scope of change increased considerably. In 1852 artillery specialists were ordered to learn Western drill, while in 1853, reverberatory and blast furnaces were built, copied from Hizen, so that Satsuma, too, was able to turn out modern weapons. In the same years Dutch infantry methods were studied, the castle-town samurai were reorganized into companies for training, and a start was made on creating a cavalry force after French models. In 1856 Satsuma began to train a Western-style navy with samurai volunteers. Docks had already been built at Kagoshima the previous year and a steamer launched, though most of the domain's modern ships were acquired by purchase from abroad: seventeen of them between 1854 and 1868. In addition, a number of non-military industries were established or improved by the use of the new technology, including the manufacture of leather goods, paper, iron tools, glass and porcelain. So rapidly were the results apparent that a Dutch visitor to Kagoshima in 1858, some months before Japan's ports were fully opened to foreign trade, estimated that over 1,200 men were employed in the domain's industrial undertakings.

In Bakufu territories it seems to have been more difficult for military reformers to make headway. Takashima Shuhan, for example, a minor official in Nagasaki, tried to persuade Edo in 1841 to adopt Western drill and use modern guns, like those he had just imported from Holland on his own responsibility. He was ordered to start a training school to teach his methods, but incurred the suspicions of jealous and conservative seniors, at whose instigation he was imprisoned the following year. A similar fate overtook many of the 'Dutch scholars', though the Bakufu had been sufficiently aware of their usefulness to establish a translation office as early as 1808. In fact, little was done in the way of modernization by the Shogun's government until Perry arrived in 1853. Even then progress was slow and depended on foreign technicians. A naval training school with Dutch instructors was founded in 1855 and shipbuilding was begun at Uraga and Shimoda in 1855-6. Work was started on constructing a Nagasaki iron foundry in 1857, again with foreign help, and this was completed in 1861, though its facilities for ship repair soon proved inadequate. Subsequently the Bakufu obtained French assistance and began to work on a larger scale, but this phase belongs to the years of the regime's fall and discussion of it is best left to a later chapter.

In all this the Bakufu acted too slowly and with too little imagination, letting the initiative in modernization fall into the hands of a few of the great domains, whose financial reforms had made such development possible and whose leaders recognized the need. As a result, the gap which had set the Tokugawa so much above their rivals a century earlier, already reduced by economic change, was narrowed further. Indeed, the effectiveness of the Bakufu's military establishment was soon brought to a level only slightly above that of its potential enemies. Its authority was diminished in proportion. Nevertheless, this alone did not ensure its fall. It was the treaty negotiations of 1853-8 and the diplomatic disputes of the years that followed, revealing an inability either to satisfy Western demands or to silence domestic critics, that were to provide the crucial, because public, evidence of Tokugawa weakness.

What is more, the same events were to convert a recognition of external threat, which, as we have seen, was already widespread in Japan, into something much closer to nationalism in the modern Western sense. The conclusion of 'unequal treaties', together with military failure, as exemplified in bombardments by foreign warships in 1863 and 1864, aroused anti-foreign sentiment, which had as one of its facets an enhanced consciousness of what it meant to be Japanese. This, in turn, had important repercussions on both domestic politics and foreign affairs. It gave an impetus to the search for national strength, and hence for unity, constituting on the one hand a move towards a new kind of patriotism, in which the country, rather than the province or domain, was to be the focus of loyalty, and on the other an emotional basis for attacks on a regime which was said to have failed in its duty of protecting the nation's honour. The Bakufu, by its inability to exploit the change—or even, perhaps, to recognize its importance—helped largely to seal its own fate.

CHAPTER IV

TREATIES AND POLITICS
1853-1860

*Trading agreements—repercussions in Japan—agitation for
reform*

COMMODORE MATTHEW CALBRAITH PERRY, whose ships
were the first modern Western squadron to reach Japan, was
a senior and distinguished officer of the United States Navy.
He had only accepted the Pacific command with reluctance, in
the expectation that he would be provided with a force commensurate with his rank and reputation, and he had no intention of suffering the same kind of treatment in Japan as had
been meted out to previous Western envoys. On July 8, 1853,
therefore, when his two steamers and two sailing vessels
anchored off Uraga, his orders were that no insults or slights
in any form were to be tolerated. The ships were to be cleared
for action at all times. Only officials were to be allowed on
board. These, moreover, were to be told that only an envoy of
high rank, appointed by the Japanese government, would be
permitted to see the commodore, who would deliver to him in
proper manner a letter from President Fillmore, together with
a number of presents for the Japanese ruler. The letter was
intended subsequently to form the basis of negotiations. Meanwhile, no matter what arguments and entreaties the Japanese
employed, the commodore was not prepared to go to Nagasaki
for discussions. Indeed, the only move he was prepared to consider was one which would take him nearer Edo.

In the Shogun's capital, Perry's arrival and the obvious
strength of his squadron caused consternation, even though
advance warning of it had been given by the Dutch several

months before. As a stopgap, it was decided to accept the letters, since to do so would give time for proper consideration of the questions which they raised, and the officials at Uraga were ordered to make appropriate arrangements. This they did, the ceremony taking place with great solemnity at Kurihama on July 14. Five thousand Japanese troops surrounded the temporary building erected for the purpose and the two American steamers were less than a gunshot offshore, when Perry duly handed over the elaborate boxes in which the President's letter and the commodore's credentials were enclosed. He also added a letter of his own; and whereas the President's was a firm but friendly document, emphasizing America's desire for proper treatment of shipwrecked seamen, for ports of refuge where ships could obtain coal and stores, and for the opening of trade, Perry's came close to being a threat. If these 'very reasonable and pacific overtures' were not at once accepted, he wrote, he would have to return for a reply next spring, this time 'with a much larger force'.[15] The point was underlined in the following two days, when he took part of the squadron well into Edo Bay before leaving for the China coast.

It was Abe Masahiro, senior councillor since 1845, who had to work out a policy in response to this American demand; and recognizing that recent events had provoked widespread discussion of defence policy in Japan, causing considerable divergence of views among samurai concerning the course it was best to follow, he set out to establish a rather broader base for Bakufu decisions than had been customary hitherto. One of his first actions was to seek the support of Tokugawa Nariaki. This proved embarrassing, for Nariaki proceeded to expound the so-called 'expulsion policy' of the scholars from his own domain of Mito (see Chapter III), making few concessions to the practical difficulties raised by Perry's military superiority. The first need, he argued, was to unite the country by sounding a call to arms. Thereafter defence preparations could be pushed forward, including importation of Western arms and if necessary Western experts, until Japan was in a position to resist any foreign attack. Ideally this should be averted: 'war at home, peace abroad' was the slogan Nariaki favoured, meaning that the country was to be roused by an avowal of war's inevitability, while diplomacy sought to prevent hostilities breaking out. But if in the last resort foreigners would not accept delay, then it would be better to fight and suffer defeat than to submit and destroy Japan's morale. After all, America's strength was naval. He saw no chance of her successfully invading the interior of Japan.

While trying to bring Nariaki to a less rigid viewpoint, Abe also sent out a circular asking for the advice of officials and feudal lords. It was an unprecedented step, generally interpreted as a confession of Bakufu weakness and indecision. What is more, the replies, which reached him between August and October, did little to resolve his problem, since they simply documented differences which he already knew to exist. A majority repeated time-worn arguments, perhaps because they thought these were what the government wanted: seclusion was ancestral law; Christianity was subversive; and trade was merely the exchange of Japan's essential ores for useless foreign textiles. Others maintained that once the ports were opened, on whatever pretext, Japan could not long escape the fate of China. Only a few spoke in favour of accepting the American proposals, this chiefly on the grounds that Japan did not have the strength to resist them. Yet one fact did emerge, namely, that most wanted peace. Those who followed Tokugawa Nariaki in preferring war to compromise were a small minority, for nearly all the men who urged that seclusion must be maintained ended by admitting that such rigidity could easily be fatal, that some kind of 'temporary expedient' would have to be accepted. Also in a minority were the men who wanted positive action of a different kind. The most radical suggestion was that the Bakufu should attempt to build up Japan's strength by engaging in overseas trade and creating a Western-style navy, which could one day meet the West on equal terms. It emanated from Ii Naosuke, head of the senior *fudai* house, who argued that 'when opposing forces face each other across a river, victory is obtained by that which crosses the river and attacks'.[16] This was far too adventurous an outlook for late Tokugawa Japan, and Naosuke, like Nariaki, gained only a handful of supporters.

Both Ii Naosuke and Tokugawa Nariaki were men of influence, but in this matter each could gain greater backing in opposing the other's views than he could on behalf of his own. In any case the opinion of officialdom was more in accord with that of the majority. Many Edo officials of middling rank, to whose hands the execution of policy was likely to be entrusted, favoured a cautious approach which would avoid all risk of hostilities until the Bakufu had time to prepare its defences, a matter of several years. They therefore proposed devices for achieving this, some ingenious, some irrelevant, some quite ludicrous. What mattered more, however, was their ability to exert pressure on Abe, who became the target of a paper war in which the Bakufu divided for and against the Mito recommendations. Since disparities of status often made it impossible for the participants to argue their differences face to face, the upshot was not agreement, but verbal compromise, emerging in the form of a decree dated December 1, 1853. This admitted that Japan's defences were inadequate. Accordingly, the only practical policy to be followed on Perry's return, it said, was one of peace and procrastination. In other words, an attempt would be made to persuade Perry to depart without a clear answer to his requests one way or the other, though if this failed and he resorted to force Japan must fight, thus making it the duty of all meanwhile to join loyally in warlike preparations.

As a call to arms this left much to be desired. It was also a poor basis for negotiations. When Perry returned in February 1854, this time with eight ships, it soon became clear that he would accept no answer of the kind the Bakufu envisaged. Step by step the Japanese negotiators, in constant touch with their superiors in the capital, were forced to give way; and it was only on the question of trade that they were able to hold their own, chiefly because Perry was less inclined to press for trade than for other matters. By the end of March a treaty had taken shape and on the last day of the month it was signed at Kanagawa in Edo Bay. It opened Shimoda and Hakodate as ports of refuge, where stores could be obtained through Japanese officials; it assured castaways of good treatment and return to their own country; and it authorized the appointment of consuls at a later date. To the Bakufu, this was making the best of a bad job. To Perry, despite the absence of specific permission for trade, it was a foundation on which others could build.

Perry's attitude was also that of other Western representatives who were in a position to negotiate at this time, those of Britain and Russia. Both were admirals and neither was interested primarily in trade. Indeed, their immediate preoccupation was the fact that from the end of March 1854 their countries were at war over the Crimea. News of the terms Perry had accepted discouraged Sir John Bowring, Britain's diplomatic representative at Hong Kong, from going to Japan in search of a commercial treaty, but the outbreak of hostilities gave Rear-Admiral Stirling, commanding the China squadron, a reason for going of a different kind. In September 1854 he arrived at Nagasaki in an attempt to ensure that Japan would not give shelter to the Russian warships which it was his duty to destroy. He failed completely to make himself understood in this, partly because of inefficient interpreting, partly because the context of his statements was an international code of which Japanese officials were entirely ignorant; but when the latter in despair offered him the same terms as had been won by Perry, he accepted, in the expectation that the foothold so gained could later be extended. Soon afterwards Rear-Admiral Putiatin, who had originally been sent to the area by Russia to keep an eye on American activities and had for some months past been playing hide-and-seek with Stirling up and down the Pacific coast of Asia, arrived in Shimoda to continue negotiations which he had started earlier in Nagasaki. His reception was comparatively friendly, not even the destruction of his flagship by a tidal wave in January 1855 interrupting the talks for long. Thus early in the following month he secured a convention of what now seemed to be the standard pattern, with the addition of a frontier agreement dividing the Kurile islands between Japan and Russia at a point between Uruppu and Etorofu.

The treaties signed by Perry, Stirling and Putiatin were quite unacceptable to merchant opinion in Europe, in America and on the China coast. Western governments therefore came under pressure from commercial interests to secure trading rights in Japan on the lines of those already obtained in China, though this proved to be a policy to which all subscribed but few found opportunity to attempt in practice. Until 1856 Britain,

France and Russia were too occupied with the Crimean War to spare resources for much else. Then in October of that year came fresh disputes with China, leading to the so-called Arrow War, which engaged the whole energies of British and French representatives in the area for two years more, especially as the military forces at their disposal were weakened by the need to suppress revolt in India. Russia, meanwhile, was consolidating her position in the north along the Siberian frontier and the Amur River. Hence none of the three Powers was able to give full attention to Japan, with the result that except for occasional warships, whose actions were sometimes threatening but whose objects were never diplomatic, Japanese officials were little troubled by foreign visitors.

This does not mean that they were left entirely in peace. The Dutch minister at Deshima, Donker Curtius, kept Edo fully informed of international developments and did his best to exploit Japanese fears to his own advantage. In August 1856 he warned the Bakufu that Britain planned a mission to Japan and advised conclusion of a commercial treaty with Holland to forestall unpleasantness, remarking as an added inducement that customs duties would be a useful means of increasing government revenue. Early in 1857 he passed on news of the Arrow War, emphasizing that it sprang from Chinese attempts to evade treaty obligations. Japan's policy was just as dangerous, he pointed out, and might well bring a similar result. The logical way to prevent this was to negotiate with Holland.

Similar arguments were used by Townsend Harris, the newly arrived American consul at Shimoda. Brought there in August 1856 by an American warship—the last he was to see for over a year, as he later complained—he established himself ashore after some acrimonious debate with local officials, who at first denied his right to be in Shimoda at all. They then, when this argument was beaten down by reference to the English text of the Perry convention, installed him in a small Buddhist temple and hedged him about with all manner of petty restrictions. For some weeks he was employed largely in getting these removed. Thereafter he turned to discussion of matters arising from Perry's agreement, which led eventually in June 1857 to a further convention, settling such details as use of currency, rights of residence in the open ports and legal jurisdiction over

American citizens in Japan. Well before this, however, he had set in train the first moves towards obtaining a full commercial treaty. In October 1856 he informed the governor of Shimoda that he had a letter from the US President which he must deliver in person at an audience with the Shogun. The occasion, he said, would provide an opportunity for discussing 'an important matter of state'—the nature of which was fairly obvious, since Harris handed over at the same time a Dutch translation of America's treaty with Siam—and would enable him to reveal what he had learnt in Hong Kong about British plans. Harris, in fact, like Curtius, was prepared to threaten the Bakufu with Britain's wrath even before the Arrow War broke out. The news of hostilities came aptly to reinforce his warning.

The Japanese officials with whom decision rested were readier now to look at foreign affairs in realistic terms. Abe Masahiro, though he lacked the resolution needed to impose a consistent policy on Edo's divided councils, had brought a number of able men into the administration and thereby greatly raised the level of discussion. As his own power waned—he resigned as senior minister in November 1855, though he remained a member of the Council of State for two years longer—these new men rallied to his successor, Hotta Masayoshi, who in the early autumn of 1856, as a result of Dutch and American warnings, initiated fresh discussions of foreign policy in anticipation of the arrival of a British envoy.

It was soon obvious that a substantial and influential group favoured permitting trade in some form, either to avert danger or as a means of strengthening Japan. Accordingly, despite the continued opposition of Tokugawa Nariaki, it was decided to make a more thorough investigation of the steps that might be taken. A commission was appointed to do so in November, with Hotta at its head and a membership which included most of those who had had direct dealings with foreigners so far, its proceedings, which were at first desultory, being given new urgency at the beginning of 1857 by reports of the war in China.

On March 19, 1857, the Council ordered all senior officials to submit their advice as to the best course for Japan to follow in the light of renewed British aggression on the mainland. The document made it clear that haste and a new approach were both required. 'Any attempt on our part', it said, 'to cling to tradition, making difficulties over the merest trifles and so eventually provoking the foreigners to anger, would be impolitic in the extreme'.[17] This was reinforced by a memorandum from Hotta, who argued, first, that to have any chance of success a policy must be worked out in advance, not as a result of intimidation during negotiations, and second, that the real issue was no longer whether to permit trade, but how to regulate it. After such a lead it is not surprising that few voices were raised in favour of seclusion. Yet there were still great differences of opinion. One group of officials came down strongly on the side of opening the ports, urging that students and consuls be sent abroad and that Japan's participation in world affairs be generally increased. Another group, slightly more senior, only grudgingly accepted the changing times and regarded innovation as bringing more dangers than it did benefits. Trade was inevitable, they said, not desirable. The Bakufu should therefore go no farther than circumstances made necessary, for fear that the attack on established habits, once begun, might spread from foreign to domestic affairs and put the whole regime in jeopardy: 'to change the superficial structure of a house according to the tastes of the moment will do no great harm to the building, but to change the framework or replace the pillars and foundation-stones is to introduce weaknesses and cause complete collapse'.[18]

Hotta sought to reconcile these differences by sending a representative of each viewpoint, the progressive and the conservative, to discuss with Curtius at Nagasaki in the summer of 1857 the provisions that might be incorporated in a commercial treaty. The move was successful, for by late August a treaty had actually been drafted and formally recommended to the Edo government. It still promised many restrictions on Dutch freedom of action, but it was much more generous than anything previously considered, permitting trade to an unlimited amount at Nagasaki and Hakodate, to be carried on by private merchants under official supervision and on payment of a considerable duty. Curtius found it very satisfactory. For their part, the Japanese investigators, who had never been given power to negotiate, asked that it be concluded as a matter of urgency, pointing out that if a British envoy arrived, as was very likely, it would be essential to have the Dutch agreement ready signed, so that it could be offered him as a model.

For two months, however, the men in Nagasaki waited in vain for a Bakufu reply to their proposals. In the interval they were brought up against the very crisis they had feared, with the difference that it was not a British, but a Russian, squadron that put in an appearance. Towards the end of September Putiatin arrived and announced his intention of seeking a new treaty. Talks were delayed for a week or two while he visited China, but when he returned on October 11 there was still no word from Edo and the Japanese officials decided to put into effect the plan they had recommended, namely, to sign the Dutch agreement as a prototype on which all others could be based. This they did on October 16. A week later Putiatin accepted similar terms, with the addition of a promise that another port would be opened instead of Shimoda.

These two treaties, accepted by the Bakufu after they were signed, became at once the basis of its policy. Unhappily they did not please Townsend Harris. As a former merchant he had firm views about conditions of trade and the treaties did not meet them. They were, he said later, 'disgraceful to all parties engaged in making them . . . not worth the paper on which they were written'.[19] They therefore did nothing to divert him from his intention of negotiating on quite different lines. In August he had already been promised that he should go to Edo; and the arrival of an American warship in September, making it possible for him to proceed by sea if all else failed, finally brought the Bakufu to the point of fixing a date. He left Shimoda two months later, travelling in state, and after a week of rehearsal and preparations in Edo had his audience with the Shogun on December 7, an event which cleared the way for diplomatic talks.

On December 12 Harris visited Hotta's residence and lectured him for two hours on world conditions. He repeated much that Curtius had already said, arguing that trade neither could nor ought to be refused, since it was for Japan a means to national wealth and for the countries of the West a right which they would not be denied. Britain, in particular, was ready to use force to secure it as soon as she was free of military commitments in China. It was therefore in Japan's own interest, he urged, to negotiate at once with America, peacefully and on equal terms. A fleet would certainly exact more than an ambassador—especially an ambassador deprived, like himself, of naval backing—and its manner of doing so would humble the Japanese government in the eyes of its people. (This was an argument well calculated to appeal to the susceptibilities of Bakufu officials.) For his own part, Harris concluded, he would be content with three changes in the terms embodied in the Dutch and Russian treaties: appointment of a resident American minister in Edo; trade without official interference; and an increase in the number of open ports.

Hotta decided to consult feudal opinion before taking a final decision on Harris's proposals. On December 16 he accordingly circulated to feudal lords and others a summary of what Harris had said, the replies he received during the following month revealing that most lords were now reconciled to the need for ending seclusion, though they had little idea of a policy to put in its place. Many, it is true, still dwelt hopefully on ways of postponing the inevitable. All the same, the number of those who were prepared to take positive action was slowly growing. The lord of Yanagawa urged the importance of promoting trade, increasing production and carrying out reform at home. So did the able Tokugawa relative, Matsudaira Keiei of Fukui, who wanted Japan to seize the initiative and 'shatter the selfish designs of the brutish foreigners' by building a fleet and annexing nearby territories, as well as encouraging commerce. At home, he wrote, 'the services of capable men must be enlisted from the entire country; peacetime extravagance must be cut down and the military system revised; the evil practices by which the *daimyo* and lesser lords have been impoverished must be discontinued; . . . the daily livelihood of the whole people must be fostered; and schools for the various arts and crafts must be established'.[20] This was innovation with a vengeance, and it is no wonder conservative officials were alarmed. Yet even that arch-conservative, Tokugawa Nariaki, had changed his ground under the pressure of events. He still objected strongly to any plan which would admit foreigners to Edo, but now proposed instead that he should himself be sent abroad as Japan's intermediary for trade—accompanied by lordless samurai, younger sons and others equally expendable!

The views expressed at this time are more important as evidence of a changing climate of opinion than they were for their impact on government decisions. Hotta had already made up his mind before hearing them that neither truculence nor a sulky acceptance of *force majeure* would any longer serve. Japan, he insisted, had to enrich herself by trade. She must rearm, conclude alliances, and generally adopt such foreign ways as would contribute to her national strength. This was much like the argument of Matsudaira Keiei, shorn of the latter's emphasis on reform at home. Moreover, it was supported by an important section of Bakufu officialdom, while those who still hesitated found that Hotta's position as senior minister was enough to tip the scales against them. On January 16, 1858, he summoned Harris to another interview, agreeing in substance to his previous stipulations, except that of opening more ports. It was on this basis that formal negotiations began.

The plenipotentiaries appointed by the Bakufu, knowing that Japanese opinion was divided, were in a difficult position. It was only with reluctance that they accepted Harris's draft, rather than the Dutch treaty, as a starting-point for the discussions, and in the weeks that followed they fought a stubborn rearguard action on its every detail. The number and choice of open ports, rights of travel in the interior, the place of residence for an American minister, all these matters were the subject of long debate. The delay exasperated Harris, who had thought after Hotta's statement that all would be plain sailing. Indeed, he prefaced his account of the proceedings with a sweeping indictment of Japanese diplomacy:

'In this *Journal* I shall confine myself to the main leading facts of actual transactions, omitting the interminable discourses of the Japanese where the same proposition may be repeated a dozen times; nor shall I note their positive refusal of points they subsequently grant, and meant to grant all the while; nor many absurd proposals made by them without the hope, and scarcely the wish, of having them accepted. . . .'[21]

The method, if irritating, was understandable: Japanese diplomats were having to feel their way in territory which was politically dangerous and quite unknown. Nor was the time taken so very great. By February 23 the last doubts were settled and the text of the treaty made ready for signature. What is more, Harris had got his way on all important questions. The American minister was to reside in Edo; trade was to be free of official intervention; and Japan was to open the ports of Nagasaki and Kanagawa in 1859, Niigata in 1860, Hyogo in 1863. This was in addition to Shimoda and Hakodate, already open, while traders were also to be admitted to the cities of Edo in 1862 and Osaka in 1863.

Before this agreement could be signed, however, there came a setback. In the middle of February, when it was clear what its terms would be, Hotta announced them to all feudal lords who were in Edo at the time, only to find that his critics far outnumbered his supporters. Many who had accepted the necessity for something like the Dutch treaty of October 1857 were horrified at the concessions made in this latest document. To others it was confirmation of their worst suspicions. So loud was the chorus of disapproval, in fact, that Hotta decided it would be unwise to take the matter further without doing something to reduce it. Accordingly he arranged with Harris to postpone signature of the treaty, proposing meanwhile to secure imperial sanction for his policy. To do this, his representatives explained, would be a matter of routine—a combination of threats and bribery—but once the emperor's approval was made public it would silence all those who dared to question the senior minister's decision.

In the event this optimism proved ill-founded. Notwithstanding Hotta's readiness to go in person to Kyoto to bring pressure on the Court, the Emperor and the majority of his courtiers continued to favour seclusion. Surprisingly, they were even prepared to insist on it against the Bakufu's advice. The emperor Komei himself objected to the provisions concerning Hyogo and Osaka on the grounds that these places were too near the imperial capital to be opened. He also enjoined the Bakufu to achieve unity in the face of crisis by giving more heed to the opinions of the great lords, a pronouncement which some of the latter had been intriguing busily to obtain for several weeks. It was with these two demands, therefore, that Hotta was faced when he arrived in Kyoto on March 19. After much discussion, during which it transpired that he could count on the support of the Kampaku and one or two other senior officials at the Court, an imperial decree was drafted which did not specifically approve the treaty, but recognized that decisions on foreign policy were the Bakufu's responsibility, a compromise which met Hotta's immediate needs. Even so the decree had to be forced through the imperial council against opposition and did not receive the emperor's sanction until April 27. At this point, Komei let it be known privately that he had been coerced into approving it against his will. The result was uproar, an uproar carefully organized by a small group of anti-foreign and anti-Bakufu nobles, which made it necessary for the draft to be revised and for Hotta to accept what was in effect a command to reconsider his policy. He had still been unable to get it modified when he left Kyoto on May 17.

The Court's treatment of Hotta reflected both a doubt about the Bakufu's capacity for leadership and a suspicion that its power was declining. It was certainly an affront which Edo took very seriously. Almost at once it was decided to appoint a Regent (*Tairo*), as could always be done when danger threatened, and on June 4, 1858, the Shogun announced the appointment of Ii Naosuke, head of the senior *fudai* house, who thereby superseded Hotta as the regime's most powerful official. One result was to give the Bakufu more decisive guidance than it had had for many years. Another, a few weeks later, was to settle the question of the treaty.

It was again events in China which raised this issue, just as Townsend Harris was beginning to despair of further progress. At the end of July he learnt that Britain and France had made a peace settlement with China and were planning to send an expedition to Japan, news which brought him at once to Kanagawa to urge the Japanese representatives to sign his treaty. They referred to Edo for instructions, where a council was hurriedly summoned. Most of its members advised the Regent to authorize signature without further reference to the Court, their argument being, as in the past, that Japan's first need was a model agreement which Britain would be likely to accept. Admitting the force of this, Ii gave the necessary orders and on July 29 the document was signed at last. It was only just in time. Curtius and Putiatin were already on their way and arrived soon after, concluding similar treaties on August 18 and 19 respectively. By then the British squadron, bearing Lord Elgin as plenipotentiary, had also put in an appearance, marking its independence by sweeping past Kanagawa to an anchorage off Edo, where in a mere two days of negotiation Harris's arrangements became the basis of a British treaty, too. It was signed on August 23, leaving only Baron Gros for France, who arrived in September and concluded a satisfactory agreement at the beginning of October.

It remained to regularize the position with the Imperial Court, a task which was eventually entrusted to Manabe Akikatsu, a loyal but not particularly able adherent of the Regent, who left for Kyoto in October. Like Hotta, he soon ran into difficulties. Despite long explanations of the reasons for Bakufu action, he failed for some weeks to change Komei's views and was told in December that the emperor firmly opposed any more extended foreign intercourse than Dutch and Chinese had been traditionally allowed. This brought a stiffer Bakufu response, implying that Edo would not reverse its decisions, whether the emperor approved of them or not. What the emperor could do, by giving his approval, was to make it easier to unite the country in the pursuit of national strength. A memorandum to this effect, accompanied by vague threats directed at the imperial advisers, proved sufficient to bring a compromise, this being embodied in a decree of February 2, 1859, by which the Court promised its 'forbearance' and the Bakufu undertook to prevent somehow the opening of Hyogo and Osaka. More important, both committed themselves publicly to revoking the treaties at some unspecified date: 'we must assuredly keep aloof from foreigners and revert to the sound rule of seclusion as formerly laid down in our national laws'.[22] In this were the seeds of future problems.

Some of these problems, as we shall see, were to arise from incidents concerning foreigners and the implementation of the treaties after 1859. Others had already begun to emerge from the political manoeuvrings within Japan in 1858. For the latter, if superficially a matter of treaty negotiation, had come to involve an implicit challenge to the Bakufu's authority as well.

This came in the first instance from a number of the more powerful feudal lords, motivated partly by rivalry with the

Tokugawa house, partly by a conviction that the quality of Bakufu leadership was inadequate to the tasks it had to perform. Thus the group included Tokugawa Nariaki, suspected by many in Edo of seeking to advance the interests of Mito to the detriment of those of the Shogun's hereditary retainers; Matsudaira Keiei of Fukui, whom we have already quoted as an advocate of new men and new measures in the administration; and two of the *tozama*, Shimazu Nariakira of Satsuma and Yamanouchi Yodo of Tosa, whose families were closely linked with the Tokugawa by marriage and tradition. None of these were revolutionaries, in the sense of men wishing to destroy the regime. None were openly anti-Tokugawa. On the other hand, all were reformers in their own domains, who believed that the Bakufu, too, must do some serious re-thinking if it were to overcome the difficulties it faced in finance and foreign affairs; and all were territorial magnates in their own right, anxious to secure some relaxation of Edo controls on their freedom of action. They accordingly coupled their advocacy of reform with proposals that the Shogun should consult the great lords on questions of policy and reduce the economic burdens he imposed on the domains, a means—ostensibly—of enabling the lords to devote their energies and resources to Japan's defence.

The issue which brought these men actively into politics was not diplomacy, on which they did not agree among themselves, but the succession. By the time Hotta set out for Kyoto in the spring of 1858 the childless Shogun, Iesada, was ailing and expected soon to die, a circumstance that made it urgent to choose his heir. Two candidates were favoured. One was Tokugawa Yoshitomi of Kii, nearest by descent but still only a boy. The other was Hitotsubashi Keiki, one of Tokugawa Nariaki's sons, adopted into the Hitotsubashi house and regarded as a young man of promise. It was urged on his behalf that in times of danger the Shogun must be both adult and able. For this reason he had the backing of his father, the reforming lords, and a number of Bakufu officials, especially among those of middle rank. Yoshitomi's claim was that of blood, which gave him the support of most senior officials and *fudai*, who chose to invoke the principle of heredity, to which they owed their power, and saw in Keiki the instrument of an

71

attack on privilege. This alignment made the succession dispute a conflict of interests as well as a struggle of factions.

Because of its composition the Kii party was better placed to influence Bakufu policy from within. Its opponents sought to do so from without. Many of them had close family or personal connections with nobles at the Imperial Court and they realized, like Hotta, that an imperial pronouncement, though unenforceable without Bakufu consent, would carry immense prestige. They therefore began to intrigue to obtain one in their favour, working meanwhile to prevent Hotta from securing the emperor's consent for the American treaty, in the hope of using this as an additional lever. In May, we have seen, the second part of this programme was accomplished. The effect, however, was to cause a crisis in Edo, which brought the appointment of Ii Naosuke as Regent and through it the failure of the Hitotsubashi faction's plans. Ii decided for Yoshitomi. He forced the Court after prolonged negotiation to give its consent and finally made the decision public at the beginning of August. Ten days later Iesada died and Yoshitomi succeeded him under the name of Iemochi.

For some weeks before this Ii had been taking steps to ensure that his authority would not be challenged. In the middle of June he had begun to remove or demote those officials who had supported Hitotsubashi. On August 2 he dismissed Hotta and another member of the Council, putting on them the blame for the Harris treaty. All were replaced by his own nominees. Then on August 13 he ordered into retirement or house arrest the feudal lords who had opposed his policies in Kyoto and Edo, including Tokugawa Nariaki of Mito and Tokugawa Yoshikatsu of the Owari branch, in addition to Shimazu and Yamanouchi. Many of their retainers were also punished.

One result was to disorganize the Hitotsubashi party while confirming its distrust of Bakufu power. A few years later, when its members again became active, they looked more than ever to the Court, urging what they called *kobu-gattai*, 'Court-Bakufu unity': in essence, a plan to use the emperor's prestige as a weapon to threaten Edo, and the imperial institution as cover for a new relationship between lords and Shogun. In the interval, however, some of the *dramatis personae* changed.

Shimazu Nariakira died in 1858, his place being taken by his brother, Hisamitsu, whose son succeeded to the Satsuma domain. Tokugawa Nariaki died two years later, causing a decline in the influence of Mito, though his son, Hitotsubashi Keiki, emerged as a major participant in events soon after. Matsudaira Keiei and Yamanouchi Yodo continued to play a leading role throughout the 'sixties. They were joined as a rule by Date Muneki of Uwajima, sometimes by Tokugawa Yoshikatsu of Owari and Matsudaira Katamori of Aizu.

A further result of Ii Naosuke's 'purge' was to make him virtually a dictator and—through the feeling of security that this engendered—to restore to Bakufu policy-makers the negative outlook of earlier years. Their prime task became that of preserving the regime. All attempts to take a fresh look at current problems, especially those of foreign affairs, vanished with the men who had negotiated the treaties. Most of them came under Ii's ban. For his own part, it is clear, Ii would have accepted plans for Japan to trade abroad as a means of securing military and financial benefit. Yet he was far from regarding the foreigners' coming as an opportunity for reform at home. Indeed, his whole attitude to admitting foreign trade and traders to Japan was one of suspicion and reserve, a fact which became apparent as soon as the ports were opened in 1859.

Despite this, Ii Naosuke was blamed at the time—and has been praised since—for opening the country. Such a reputation was important, for it brought into being certain political alliances which were to be vital in the next ten years. Because he stood so obviously for the preservation of the Shogun's power, he was opposed by all those who wished to weaken it, whether on behalf of the emperor, the great lords, or other sections of the population. Because he checked reform, he was hated by those who sought it. Finally, because he accepted responsibility for the signing of the treaties, he incurred the hostility both of patriots who objected to the manner of their negotiation and xenophobes who resented their terms. Thus 'honour the emperor', 'expel the barbarian' and 'reform' all became slogans which could be used against him. By association they were therefore anti-Tokugawa.

Increasingly these slogans were being used by samurai of middle, or even lower, rank, many of them brought into politics as agents in the intrigues of their seniors, many more infected by the atmosphere of danger and excitement occasioned by the coming of foreign warships to Japan. In Edo, the schools of gunnery and swordsmanship were agog, their students— young, ambitious, careless both of life and authority—vying with each other to achieve a name as monarchist or anti-foreign zealots. In Kyoto, now made a centre of politics by the disputes over the succession and the treaties, more active radicals found both a refuge and an opportunity. The patronage of Court nobles gave them some kind of protection. It also held out the prospect of influencing the decisions, first of the Court, then of the Bakufu, something they could hardly have dared to hope a few years earlier. Samurai, especially from the *tozama* domains, began to flock there in considerable numbers.

These men, who abandoned fiefs and families at the risk of loss of rank and even severer punishments, were all critical of the Tokugawa government: of its 'weakness' abroad, of its 'autocracy' at home. They were therefore the material from which a revolutionary movement might be formed. Nevertheless, such a movement cannot be said to have existed in 1858. Few in Kyoto had the qualities to organize it or to carry out a successful *coup d'état*, most of the samurai there being fanatics, sincere but impractical, or mere youths, attracted by the prospects of adventure. Most of them, one is tempted to say, thought of themselves as leaders. Then there were the impoverished and the discontented, who had fled their villages to seek fortune and hoped to find it through their swords. In such a milieu, assassination and threats of it were common. Yet they were rarely the prelude to an attempted seizure of power. It was to be several years before a new kind of organizer emerged to give the anti-Tokugawa movement coherence and effective strength.

Characteristic of this early period—of its dreams and even its ineffectiveness—was Yoshida Shoin, teacher and samurai of Choshu, to whom many of the hotheads turned for inspiration. Born in 1830 and adopted into a family of minor feudal rank, Yoshida travelled widely as a youth and studied under such men as Sakuma Shozan. He also established connections with the Mito scholars. In 1854 he tried to stow away in one of Perry's ships with the intention of studying abroad, but he was caught by Bakufu officials and imprisoned for a time before being sent back to Choshu for punishment. There he was sentenced to house arrest, but allowed to continue teaching, his students including several of Japan's outstanding later leaders. To them he expounded a doctrine of revolution. It was based on the premise that Japan's existing rulers had sacrificed their right to power by the weakness and incompetence they had shown in the face of foreign threats; and that the country's only chance of salvation was therefore a rising of those close to the soil, men untainted by wealth or office, who would find leadership among a resolute minority of the samurai class and unity in their loyalty to the emperor.

In 1858 Yoshida turned from theory to practice, planning to assassinate Manabe, the Bakufu's emissary to Kyoto, as a stimulus to the anti-Tokugawa movement. He was detected, however, brought to trial and executed in the following year, a fate that served considerably to enhance his reputation. Many sought to emulate him in various ways. Some did so—in action —more successfully. Thus on March 24, 1860, a group of samurai, mostly from Mito, cut down Ii Naosuke outside Edo castle, achieving by far the most important political murder of the times and opening a new phase in Japan's political history. For Ii had no successor; and his death not only ended his dictatorship, it also removed the one man who had the ruthlessness to achieve a Bakufu revival. It thereby left the way open for a series of challenges to the Shogun's power which were to become steadily more effective with the years.

CHAPTER V

THE FALL OF THE TOKUGAWA
1860-1868

External relations—disputes with Britain—revival of Hitot-subashi party—Satsuma and Choshu—Meiji Restoration

THE ASSASSINATION of Ii Naosuke left the Tokugawa government without firm leadership at a time when its problems were growing rapidly more serious. Already by 1860 it was becoming clear that neither the treaty negotiations of 1858 nor the Court's half-hearted acceptance of them had solved the questions raised by the coming of Western diplomats and traders. The foreigners for their part soon found that privileges were of little use unless they could be enforced, enforcement being something which the Bakufu tried usually to prevent. On the other hand, their mere presence in the open ports was enough to arouse hostility in Japan. As this grew in vehemence, Edo's new leaders tried to meet the threat by playing off foreign against domestic enemies, a policy which led in the end to their own destruction.

An early move was to build facilities for trade at Yokohama, a fishing village, instead of nearby Kanagawa, as specified by treaty, isolating the foreign community from the main road between Edo and Osaka and making possible greater official control of access to it. Western diplomats accepted the change, but under protest. Yet within a year the newly-built town was handling the bulk of Japan's foreign trade and had become a focal point of the country's foreign relations. By comparison business elsewhere was negligible, though Nagasaki occasionally had a good year, since the domains of Satsuma, Tosa, Hizen and Fukui all traded there. As to commodities, the

staple of exports was silk. Silkworm eggs also played a significant, if temporary, role, because French and Italian crops were
hit by disease. Tea found a steady market, mostly in America,
while in 1862-5 there was a cotton boom, due to world shortages arising from the American civil war. Imports, as one would
expect, were mostly manufactured goods. Textiles were in
regular demand, but there was a growing emphasis on the
purchase of ships, weapons and machinery, which by 1867 had
turned Japan's small favourable trading balance into an import
surplus.

From the very first, official attitudes towards trade were
those of restriction and control. Japanese currency was given
an artificial value in terms of the Mexican dollar—the coin in
normal use on the China coast—and the amount of it made
available to foreigners was severely limited. Attempts were
also made to prohibit or restrict the export of certain goods,
until Western protests forced relaxation of these controls at
the end of 1859. The Bakufu's main recourse, however, was to
monopoly. In May 1860 a decree was issued granting monopoly
rights in all export consignments of grains, rapeseed oil, wax,
dry goods and raw silk to certain Edo wholesalers, through
whose hands shipments destined for Yokohama were to pass.
Since Yokohama was the main trading port and the mono-
polists were under Bakufu patronage, this seemed likely to give
the government control over all principal items of export,
except tea. But in practice the decree proved impossible to
enforce. It was widely evaded and for some time was a dead
letter, before being revived in November 1863 in support of
the Bakufu's efforts to secure the closing of Yokohama, when
it was directed against the silk trade, which it cut to negligible
proportions for most of the season. The embargo ended only
when the powers threatened serious consequences if Edo's
commercial policy were not changed and it was not until
October 1864, in fact, that the Bakufu bowed at last to the
inevitable, abolishing the monopoly and leaving trade to
develop in comparative freedom.

Throughout this period, the total value of trade fluctuated
widely. Accurate figures are impossible to determine, but exports appear to have reached a total of about 10 million dollars
by 1864, almost doubled in the next two years, then dropped

back again to about 11 million, while imports rose more steadily to nearly 7 million dollars in 1864 and over 18 million in 1867.[23] This was hardly enough to have any great impact on the Japanese economy, though concentration on a few commodities made the effect seem greater than it was. Thus foreign demand for silk and tea undoubtedly raised prices of those items, despite increasing production, and a short-lived export of gold coins in 1859, which was made profitable by the disparity between world gold: silver ratios and those of Japan, was also an inflationary stimulus.

Yet there were other results of relations with the West which were much more serious in their economic consequences. The Bakufu, it is true, received a revenue from customs duties and profits from monopoly trading, but it has been estimated that in the ten years 1859 to 1868 these came to less than half the increased expenditure on foreign affairs due to higher administrative costs, defence works, and indemnities paid for attacks on Western ships and citizens. The Shimonoseki indemnity alone, as we shall see, was put at 3 million dollars. Since Bakufu financial manipulations had already made the currency fragile, it is not surprising that inflation followed. Rice prices, the most reliable index, rose about 50 per cent in the four years after the opening of the ports. In 1865 and after, with the added effects of civil war, they jumped to three and four times the earlier figure, sometimes more.

Among the worst sufferers were the samurai, especially those living on stipends. To all their other arguments against the treaties, therefore, arising from considerations of policy or from xenophobia, was added that of economic distress, which could, rightly or wrongly, be attributed to the foreigners' coming. This added fuel to the existing fires. The more reckless tried to take vengeance on individual foreigners whom they encountered in or near the treaty ports. 'Often drunk and always insolent', the British minister called such bravos, '. . . the terror of all the unarmed population'.[24] In Yokohama two Russians were killed in August 1859 and a Dutch merchant captain in February 1860, this in addition to attacks on several Chinese and Japanese who were in foreign service. Western envoys began to fear the same treatment in Edo, where their public appearances were often greeted with volleys of abuse or stones; and in January 1861 their fears were realized, for Townsend Harris's secretary was murdered, while in July of the same year came a night attack on the British legation in which two members of the staff were wounded and several marauding samurai were killed. The result was to bring part of Britain's China squadron to Japanese waters. From this time on, as self-appointed champion of the Treaty Powers—and much the largest participant in Japanese trade—Britain began to put greater pressure on the Bakufu to carry out its treaty obligations.

At the same time, however, Edo was under a very different kind of pressure from the Imperial Court. In May 1860, Ii Naosuke's successors had sought to strengthen their position by proposing a marriage alliance between the Shogun and the emperor's sister, Princess Kazunomiya. This was eventually agreed, but the anti-foreign nobles and their samurai supporters managed to get the bargain made conditional. Within ten years, the Bakufu was forced to promise, 'action will certainly be taken either to cancel the treaties by negotiation or to expel the foreigners by force'.[25] This made specific the vague promise offered earlier by Manabe. It also conflicted sharply with the demands being urged by Sir Rutherford Alcock, making it necessary for the Shogun's government to find some gesture which would simultaneously demonstrate its sincerity to the Court and ease its difficulties with Britain.

The method chosen arose from a suggestion made by Townsend Harris. In January 1861, only a week after his secretary's murder, he expressed a willingness to help the Bakufu pacify its enemies at home by agreeing to postpone the dates set for the opening of Edo, Osaka, Hyogo and Niigata, all of which were due to admit foreigners by the beginning of 1863. This idea was readily taken up, it being formally announced in March that a mission would be sent to Europe to secure the consent of the other Treaty Powers. The Bakufu's stated object in this was to gain time to overcome the unrest caused by foreign trade and residence so far, so that when further ports were opened the same problems would not arise again. The British minister, Sir Rutherford Alcock, whose government held the key to the success of any talks, at first found the argument unconvincing. Nor was he made any more co-operative by the attack on his legation in July. Gradually, however, his opposition weakened and he even put a British ship at the embassy's disposal when it left in January 1862, though he was still quite clear at this time that so important a concession could not be made without 'equivalents' on the part of Japan. The last of his objections were then removed by the attempted murder of Ando Nobumasa, senior Councillor of State, in the following month. This convinced Alcock of the reality of the Bakufu's dangers and hence of its honesty in seeking the delay, which led him to support its proposals in London when he went on leave soon after. Alcock's approval, in turn, satisfied Lord Russell, who authorized negotiations. The resulting agreement, signed on June 6, 1862, postponed the opening of the two ports and two cities until January 1, 1868, requiring of Japan only a promise that the treaties would be fully implemented at the ports already open; and the example thus given by Britain was quickly followed by Russia, France and Holland, who agreed to similar concessions later in the year.

Russell and Alcock had acted in the belief that it was to Britain's advantage to support the Bakufu. They argued, first, that it was the duly constituted government, responsible for providing the law and order without which trade was impossible; second, that it was the power in Japan most firmly committed to friendly relations with foreign states. Both assumptions were reasonable in the light of their existing knowledge, but both were soon to be called in question. At the end of June 1862 there was a further attack on the legation in Edo, leading to the death of two men from the British guard. In September came another murder near Yokohama, at a village called Namamugi, when Charles Richardson, a British visitor from Shanghai, was killed by members of a Satsuma force because he failed to give way to the procession which they were guarding. This produced an explosion of anger from the foreign community at Yokohama, but demands that men be landed from the warships in harbour to attack the Satsuma troops were rejected by Lt-Col Neale, *chargé d'affaires* in Alcock's absence, who refused to take a step which might lead to war. All the same, he protested vigorously to Edo and sent home urgently for instructions. Bakufu officials, recognizing the dangers which the situation held, tried to secure the surrender of the murderers from the Satsuma commander, but without success; and when in October the domain sent a formal reply, it said in effect that the escort had acted in accordance with feudal custom and therefore would not be handed over for punishment. This left the Bakufu no choice but to explain to the British *chargé* that it did not have the authority to intervene directly in a *daimyo's* territories and could do no more.

These events, especially the Namamugi affair, brought a distinct hardening of British attitudes. In December Russell drew up full instructions concerning the reparations to be demanded: from the Japanese government, a full formal apology and an indemnity of £100,000; from Satsuma, execution of the murderers and an indemnity of £25,000. In case of refusal, he said, the naval squadron was to carry out such measures 'of reprisal or blockade, or both'[26] as seemed appropriate. In other words, London now authorized the use of force on a considerable scale. And by the end of March 1863, when he received these orders, Neale already had it at his disposal. Twelve British warships were assembled at Yokohama when he communicated the terms to Edo as an ultimatum.

Thus only two months after the Japanese mission to Europe arrived back from concluding the London Agreement, the country's foreign relations were again in a state of crisis. It was made more acute by the fact that the Bakufu was simultaneously facing demands at home for the complete expulsion of foreigners from Japan.

The death of Ii Naosuke and the indecision which characterized the actions of those who succeeded him made possible a gradual revival of the Hitotsubashi party in 1861 and 1862. By the summer of the latter year, under the leadership of Shimazu Hisamitsu of Satsuma, it was ready to make another bid for power. Again, as in 1858, it comprised a number of great feudal lords who looked to the Imperial Court for backing. This time, however, they had to be prepared to pay a higher price to get it. For one thing, the influx of radical samurai into Kyoto had continued steadily since 1858 and the connections they had formed with the lower-ranking nobles of the Court gave the latter much greater political pretensions than in the past. These operated especially in the field of foreign affairs, where, as we have seen, Kyoto was now willing to take the initiative in urging policies on Edo. As a further complication, the Choshu domain, long Satsuma's rival, had recently emerged from a period of relative inactivity on the national scene and was seeking, quite independently of the Hitotsubashi group, to turn the disputes between Court and Bakufu to its own advantage. In the process—partly because anti-foreign extremists were numerous among its own samurai—it soon revealed a willingness to encourage the Court in its chauvinist ideas, so that for some months, at least, Satsuma and Choshu seemed to be bidding for imperial favour by vying with each other in an apparent enthusiasm to achieve expulsion.

In June 1862, at the urging of these two domains, the Court decided to send a special envoy to the Shogun's capital. He was given two main tasks. First, he was to demand that Hitotsubashi Keiki and Matsudaira Keiei, Shimazu's allies in Edo, be admitted to high office. Second—and this was at Choshu's suggestion—he was to insist that the Shogun visit Kyoto to discuss expulsion.

At the beginning of August, the first of these objectives was achieved, though only after the Satsuma men in the envoy's bodyguard had openly threatened the lives of Bakufu councillors. Keiki became the Shogun's guardian and Keiei assumed the powers, though not the title, of Regent, while another Tokugawa relative, Matsudaira Katamori of Aizu, was appointed to control of Kyoto. All three then joined in proposing political reforms, despite continued obstruction from Bakufu officialdom. One of their aims, in accordance with the wishes of their *daimyo* colleagues, was to reduce the financial burdens on domains and bring the great lords into the Shogun's counsels. This was partly secured in October, when the system of 'alternate attendance' (*sankin-kotai*) was revised by cutting down the time which feudal lords were required to spend in Edo and dispensing with the system of hostages formerly associated with it. Domain establishments in the city were also to be made smaller and *daimyo* were to have the right of giving 'advice' when they visited Edo castle.

That the mission's results were mostly a success for Shimazu is not surprising, in view of the fact that he provided the envoy's escort, but they were not much to the taste of Choshu or the Kyoto samurai. Moreover, in the absence of the Satsuma forces, the extremists had achieved an unchallenged supremacy over the Imperial Court. So much was this so that on his return to Kyoto at the end of September Shimazu found the situation completely out of hand. Senior Court nobles were helpless before threats of assassination and general turbulence. Everywhere there were inflammatory placards, with brawls between Bakufu guards and samurai bravos a regular occurrence. Nothing short of force to clear the Kyoto streets seemed likely to restore the position; and Shimazu, doubting the loyalty of some of his own followers and anticipating a clash with Britain—it was on his way back from Edo that his men had murdered Richardson at Namamugi—was reluctant to provide it. Instead, he withdrew to Kagoshima, leaving the capital to its own devices. By so doing he enabled a few samurai from Choshu, Satsuma and Tosa, known to each other from the periods they had spent in attendance on their lords at Edo and sharing an outlook derived largely from Yoshida Shoin and the Mito scholars, to establish a temporary control over imperial policy. In November, at their insistence, one of their allies at Court, Sanjo Sanetomi, was appointed the emperor's second envoy to Edo, this time to require immediate action to 'expel the barbarian'.

These continuous demands for expulsion had the effect of bringing disagreement among the *daimyo* leaders of reform. Shimazu was against compromise. He would have preferred to tell the Court that its policy was impracticable and to have used force to eliminate the groups which were putting it forward. On the other hand, he could not give his whole attention to politics because of the Namamugi problem and preferred to remain for the time being in Kagoshima. Matsudaira Keiei, by contrast, was to some extent under the influence of radicals in his own domain. He argued that for the sake of national unity the emperor's orders must be accepted and the treaties cancelled, though he added that diplomatic negotiations should then be reopened on a more equal footing. With this Hitotsubashi Keiki could not agree. Like most Bakufu officials, he accepted the necessity for a limited opening of Japanese ports and held that the Court should be persuaded to change its views. He objected, however, to any suggestion of coercion on the lines Shimazu proposed.

The result of these differences was that Hitotsubashi and Matsudaira, when they went to Kyoto early in 1863 in response to the Court's demands, were at odds with each other and without Shimazu's backing. Once there, moreover, they faced concerted pressure from Court nobles and hostile samurai, acting in the emperor's name, so that when the Choshu domain also threw its weight against them they capitulated with hardly a struggle. Despite protests from Satsuma and Edo, they agreed to set June 25 as the date on which action would begin to 'exclude' the foreigners from Japan. The wording of the document they signed did not make it clear whether this meant expulsion by force or foreign withdrawal by arrangement, but it was formally notified to the domains, together with a warning that coast defences must be ready in case the foreigners attacked.

It soon became evident, nevertheless, that the Shogun's officials had no intention of provoking war if they could help it. At the beginning of June they promised to pay the indemnity which Britain was demanding for the Namamugi murder. Soon after, when the first instalment of the money was handed over, they tried to open negotiations for the closing of the ports. This, it seems, is what Hitotsubashi and the Bakufu had meant by their earlier promise. Even so, it was a great deal more than any foreign representative was likely to concede, as Neale very bluntly told them. It was also far less than Choshu and Kyoto wanted, less, indeed, than they meant to have. On June 25, 1863, the day appointed for Bakufu action, Choshu steamers attacked an American vessel in the Shimonoseki Straits. Early in July, ships and shore batteries also fired on French and Dutch vessels in the same area, inflicting casualties and damage. By the end of that month, in spite of local punitive raids by the French and American naval commanders, it had to be recognized that the Shimonoseki Straits were closed to foreign trade.

It was not long before fighting spread to Satsuma, though for very different reasons. In August a British squadron entered Kagoshima Bay to complete the second half of Russell's orders about the Namamugi incident, that is, to demand justice and indemnity from the domain responsible. Dissatisfied with the reply the officials gave him, Neale eventually ordered the seizure of three Satsuma steamers to force compliance, but this led to an exchange of gunfire with the batteries ashore which resulted during the next few hours in the destruction of much of Kagoshima and the sinking of the steamers. The British squadron suffered heavy damage and withdrew. Negotiations were subsequently resumed at Yokohama, where the Satsuma envoys at last promised to punish Richardson's murderers, if they could find them, and pay an indemnity (which they then persuaded the Bakufu to provide).

The operations at Kagoshima and the Shimonoseki Straits were hailed by patriots as a victory over both the foreigners and Edo. They also intensified the rivalry between Satsuma and Choshu. Choshu continued to work through Kyoto, where plans had already been announced for forming an imperial army with levies to be provided by the 'loyal' feudal lords. During the summer, moreover, inflamed by success, the samurai radicals had begun to arrange for the emperor to take over in person the command of the expulsion campaign, a direct challenge to the Shogun in his military function. Violence and terrorism reached new heights as the time for this coup came nearer.

They were suddenly cut short by Satsuma and Aizu. The one freed from preoccupation with British gunboats, the other alarmed at the threat to Bakufu power, they showed themselves willing to act while Edo merely argued. On September 30, 1863, their troops seized the gates of the emperor's palace and within a few days the whole situation in the capital had changed. Sanjo Sanetomi and several other anti-Tokugawa nobles fled to Choshu for refuge. So did many of the samurai who had been shaping policy. Others escaped to the nearby countryside and raised the standard of revolt, though they were quickly killed or scattered. At Court, the emperor's assumption of military command was 'postponed', the plan for an imperial army was abandoned. Finally, to mark the rapprochement between Court and Bakufu, it was agreed that the Shogun should again visit Kyoto, though this time as a signal of victory, not in acceptance of defeat.

This achievement was in fact Shimazu's doing and he lost

no time in showing that he knew it. In November he arrived in Kyoto at the head of 15,000 men, followed shortly by Matsudaira Keiei and Hitotsubashi Keiki. At Satsuma's urging, all three, together with Matsudaira of Aizu, Yamanouchi of Tosa and Date of Uwajima, were admitted regularly to discussions in the imperial palace. This was a privilege quite without precedent in recent times. And when Iemochi arrived in February 1864, an imperial letter enjoined him, too, to let them take part in the making of decisions. The document's language was fulsome, its policy Shimazu's, leaving little doubt about his dominance at Court. It was even rumoured that one of his samurai was drafting the emperor's correspondence.

To Bakufu officials this situation was no more welcome than that of the previous year, when the Court had been acting at the bidding of Choshu. What is more, their jealousy and suspicions were conveyed to Hitotsubashi Keiki, with the result that the Shogun's visit to Kyoto, which had been planned as a means of consolidating a success, ended by provoking instead a quarrel between Satsuma and Edo. The occasion once again was foreign affairs. Shimazu, now more than ever, held that it was necessary to disillusion the emperor about the possibility of national seclusion. Hitotsubashi preferred a compromise, believing that for the Shogun's government to blow hot and cold at the dictates of whoever happened to dominate the Court would soon destroy what little prestige it had. He therefore proposed that Edo should continue to work for the closing of the port of Yokohama, in the hope that this would be a token of its sincerity in meeting the emperor's wishes, without being extreme enough to embroil Japan in foreign war. Shimazu was contemptuous of such shilly-shallying. Hitotsubashi, in turn, waxed indignant at Satsuma presumption. The culmination was an emotional scene on March 23, 1864, when the young man subjected Shimazu to a tirade of drunken abuse, which gained him his point, but broke up the *daimyo* coalition.

The various members of the group, except Keiki, withdrew to their own territories soon after, leaving the government to solve its foreign problems without their help. Nor was co-operation between them ever fully restored. Keiki became more and more a spokesman for Bakufu officialdom. Shimazu, by contrast, fell gradually under the influence of the anti-Tokugawa faction among his followers, while Yamanouchi, Date and Matsudaira Keiei shifted rather uneasily between the two. In sum, one might say that a common interest as great lords and a desire for moderation in reform had proved weaker than conflicting family and feudal loyalties, so that the Hitotsubashi party had dissolved at the very moment when it seemed to have victory won. From this point on, the chance of compromise between the opposing forces in Japan was very much less.

As it transpired, the foreign problems to which Edo now had to give attention centred not on the closing of Yokohama, which was brusquely refused, but on Choshu's closing of the Shimonoseki Straits. The Western representatives had waited throughout the winter of 1863–64 for instructions from home about this matter, only to find, when they received them, that the decision was left to themselves. Rutherford Alcock, now back at his post, was glad of it. The time had come, he said, to make an example of Choshu and put an end to anti-foreign demonstrations in Japan. In this his colleagues eventually concurred, so that at the end of May 1864 the French, Dutch, American and British ministers renewed their demands for the opening of the Straits, threatening to take action themselves if Edo failed to do so. The Bakufu, after some delay, again countered with a proposal that Yokohama be closed instead. This was unwise and not at all well received, the ministers beginning at once to make preparations for a joint naval expedition against Choshu.

They had no sooner assembled a squadron than their plans were delayed by new prospects of a settlement. In July two Choshu samurai, Ito Hirobumi and Inoue Kaoru, who had previously been smuggled out of Japan to study in London, arrived in Yokohama with an offer to mediate. Their efforts were unsuccessful, but took up a good deal of time. Then in August, just as the ships were ready to leave, a Japanese diplomatic mission returned from Paris, where it had been sent earlier in the year in the hope of repeating the London success of 1862. Since it had signed a convention in June—without authority to do so—which provided for the Bakufu to open the Straits, if necessary with naval help from France, matters were again held up while awaiting Edo's reactions. These were prompt in coming. On August 24 the convention was disavowed, the envoys dismissed and punished. A few days later the joint force sailed: seventeen ships (nine British, three French, four Dutch and one American) mounting nearly three hundred guns in all.

On September 5, 1864, after an abortive attempt by Choshu to negotiate, the ships carried out a heavy bombardment of the batteries in the Shimonoseki Straits. During the next two days they landed men to take the emplacements and dismantle their equipment, seizing a number of guns and destroying others. This brought Choshu to terms. By September 14 conditions for a truce were settled, including a promise that navigation would be uninterrupted and an agreement in principle to the payment of an indemnity. Discussions were then transferred to Yokohama and Edo. Here the Bakufu finally accepted responsibility for the costs of the expedition and a convention setting out the arrangements was signed on October 22. It provided for an indemnity of 3 million dollars, payable in six instalments. Instead of paying it, however, Japan was given the option of opening another port to trade, either Shimonoseki itself, or some other place in the Inland Sea. Thus, far from restricting trade, it was obvious that the Treaty Powers had every intention of increasing it—and the Bakufu was left with no illusions about its ability to resist.

After these experiences, indeed, it no longer sought to evade the demands of Western envoys. Convinced at last that the risk of foreign war was greater than that of civil commotion, it preferred to put pressure on the Court rather than to quarrel over treaties. This was made amply clear in the autumn of 1865, when the representatives of the Powers, led by the new British minister, Sir Harry Parkes, made fresh proposals concerning the Shimonoseki indemnity. They were willing, they said, to waive the remaining payments. In return they sought the immediate opening of Hyogo and a public acknowledgment by the emperor that the treaties had his consent, the latter being expected in any case as evidence of Japanese good faith. This was at the beginning of November. The argument was backed by a sizeable squadron anchored off Hyogo and led to a flurry of exchanges between Osaka castle, where the Shogun was in residence, and the Imperial Court. The latter at first refused all concessions and dismissed the two Bakufu ministers who had urged them. At this the Shogun threatened to resign, the ultimate gesture. So armed, Hitotsubashi Keiki and the Councillors of State were able to beat down Kyoto's objections, despite protests from Satsuma, and on November 22 they secured the emperor's formal sanction of the 1858 agreements. This ended expulsion as an official policy. Seven months later, in June 1866, the Bakufu signed a new commercial treaty, reducing import duties to 5 per cent and removing almost all the restrictions on foreign trade.

The events of 1863 and 1864 also contributed to a change of heart among samurai extremists. Some had expressed private doubts about the wisdom of expulsion long before, like Takasugi Shinsaku and Kido Koin of Choshu, for example, who had done so as early as 1862. Similarly, Okubo Toshimichi and Saigo Takamori of Satsuma, though impeccably patriotic, favoured trade relations with the outside world as a means of strengthening Japan. All these men were now becoming powerful in their own domains and capable of influencing general policy. Moreover, their realism was something which the guns of British warships helped to spread. For after the bombardments of Kagoshima and Shimonoseki, although there remained a good deal of anti-foreign sentiment, especially in Kyoto, and attacks on foreigners occasionally took place, more and more of the samurai became convinced that expelling the barbarian was not a practical ambition, 'The irrational extremists', Okubo wrote in 1865, 'have for the most part had their eyes opened; they argue the impossibility of expulsion and even recommend the opening of the country.'[27]

For all this there was no public disavowal of expulsion by the samurai leaders. This was partly because such action would have involved a personal risk—Takasugi at one time had to go into hiding to escape the vengeance of the xenophobes—and partly because anti-foreign sentiments could usefully be exploited in the struggle against the Tokugawa. The slogan 'expel the barbarian' continued to play its part in rallying opposition. So did that of 'honour the emperor', though its significance was fast becoming as amuletic as the other. The Satsuma and Aizu *coup d'état* of September 30, 1863, had demonstrated the impossibility of building a successful revolution round Court nobles and ill-organized samurai bands. Too many leaders, too little discipline, a lack of economic resources—despite the sympathy and hospitality of individual merchants—these nullified the advantages of courage and fanaticism when the conspirators found themselves confronting a coherent military force. The lesson was driven home in August 1864. In that month some 2,000 men from Choshu, with allies from other domains, tried to reverse the previous year's decision by seizing control of Kyoto in their turn. They were thrown back after bitter street fighting, in which many of the most famous loyalists lost their lives.

This was the last attempt by lesser samurai to bring down the regime by independent action and its failure brought a change in the nature of the anti-Tokugawa movement. Much of its original leadership had been removed: killed in the fighting, murdered in factional brawls, executed or imprisoned by authority. Those who were left, as well as many of the rank-and-file, were beginning to reconsider their ideas. For one thing, they were a little older, a little more experienced in affairs. For another, it had been made brutally obvious to them that unorganized, scattered violence, undertaken at individual initiative, was no more effective against the Bakufu than it was against the West. Even the substantial, if surreptitious, backing of Choshu, plus a campaign of political terrorism, had produced only short-lived success, which had ended as soon as Satsuma threw in its lot with Edo.

From these facts the more open-minded drew two conclusions: first, that opposition could not be successful unless it had the military and economic support of domain governments; second, that they should therefore concentrate attention on securing control, or at least influence, in those domains—like Choshu, Satsuma and Tosa—where their sympathizers seemed already strong. This led them to accept hereafter the leadership of samurai who instead of escaping to Kyoto or elsewhere had remained at work in official posts. These were usually men of rather more moderate anti-Tokugawa views, co-operation with whom was only possible on a basis of compromise. Yet what was lost because of this in terms of radical objectives was gained in terms of the new relationship which became possible with feudal lords and senior retainers. In substance, the samurai of middle rank who now took over direction of affairs were able to shape a much more formidable combination than any before it, embracing both remnants of the radical loyalist movement and members of the Hitotsubashi party disillusioned by their failure to achieve reform: *daimyo*, officials, Court nobles, renegade samurai, even commoners. The final stage in the story of the Bakufu's fall is that of the formation of this alliance and its harnessing to specific political ends.

Choshu remained for some time the most important centre. Its anti-foreign activities had made it a refuge for all those who had been driven out of Kyoto in 1863–4 or whose political movements in their own domains had been suppressed by conservative lords. In both Fukui and Tosa, for example, the loyalists had been imprisoned or expelled when their friends in Kyoto failed. Survivors made their way to Choshu, where their help in fighting the foreigner was welcome. Often they joined special military units, put under Choshu command. Working with them were units formed by Choshu men themselves, irregulars whose enlistment had been authorized by the domain government in September 1863 in anticipation of foreign attack. Most of them were raised and led by lesser samurai, often with money provided by rich landlords and entrepreneurs of the countryside, and were recruited from rural families on the fringe of the feudal class. Younger sons, lordless samurai and the impoverished comprised much of their total strength. This gave them greater mobility than the usual feudal levy, as well as making for more radical views. Moreover, discipline was strict and the quality of leadership high, since promotion went by ability, not by birth, while a preference for Western-style weapons and training made the whole into a formidable force. Its size is uncertain, but there seem to have been about 150 units, each of anything from 100 to 500 men, the most famous being the Kiheitai, organized by Takasugi Shinsaku, the man who was chiefly responsible for the military efficiency of the irregulars and eventually converted them to political use.

Defeat by the foreigners at Shimonoseki and by Satsuma in Kyoto during August 1864 had discredited the Choshu radicals and brought a temporary reaction, putting power into the hands of the traditionalist samurai of the castle-town. Their immediate task was to save the Mori house from the consequences of its followers' actions, for on August 24, at Bakufu prompting, Choshu had been declared outlaw by the Imperial Court and preparations had then been made for a punitive expedition against it under the command of Tokugawa Yoshikatsu of Owari, who assembled contingents from the Bakufu and great domains at Osaka in November. At this point the new Choshu leaders agreed to negotiate a settlement. In December they admitted their fault and accepted punishment. In January the Bakufu forces were ordered to disband. Before the agreements could be carried out, however, Takasugi Shinsaku and Kido Koin, aided by the irregular units under their command, once again overthrew the so-called pro-Bakufu party within the domain and made the *daimyo* their prisoner. By March 1865, with the help of moderates whose loyalty to Choshu was greater than their respect for Edo, they had formed an administration and were able to dictate policy. Thereafter it was aimed singlemindedly at the destruction of the Tokugawa house.

Satsuma took longer to reach the same conclusion. The first effects of bombardment there had been an intensification of naval and military reform, new educational provision for samurai on Western lines, and the sending of students and envoys to Europe. The domain was even separately represented at the Paris Exposition of 1867, much to the Bakufu's annoyance. All this, however, was no more than an extension of activities which had begun under Shimazu Nariakira before 1858. In politics, change, if slower, proved in the end more drastic. The events of 1864, which had spelt failure for Shimazu Hisamitsu's plans, led to a lessening of his influence in Kagoshima—he was, after all, the *daimyo's* father, not the feudal lord himself—and pressure was brought to bear on him to give greater heed to those samurai of his entourage, especially Saigo Takamori and Okubo Toshimichi, who were known to be sympathetic to the loyalist cause. These two soon became the domain's chief agents in Kyoto and it was not long before they were making policy, as well as carrying it out.

The major question to engage their attention was that of

the Bakufu's relations with Choshu. Saigo had already acted as mediator in the attempts to reach a compromise at the end of 1864, but after the victory of Takasugi and Kido early in the following year it was obvious that Choshu was no longer willing to keep the bargain. Nor, for that matter, were the Bakufu's officials. In May 1865 they announced a second punitive expedition, to be under the Shogun's personal command. Several of the great domains protested, urging the importance of unity in the face of foreign danger and objecting to the cost, which none of them could afford; but Edo was by this time convinced that there was more at stake than a factional quarrel. Failure to assert its authority over Choshu, the Bakufu maintained, would destroy that authority entirely. By the autumn, therefore, it was clear that a trial of strength was not to be avoided.

Meanwhile, Satsuma and Choshu had been gradually overcoming their suspicions of each other with the help of refugees from Tosa. In September, Ito and Inoue, the samurai who had tried last-minute negotiations to save Choshu from bombardment in 1864, were sent to Nagasaki to arrange imports of weapons from a British firm. They were offered the hospitality of the Satsuma agency and a Satsuma ship delivered the consignment. Thereafter Satsuma regularly acted as the channel through which the highly illegal cargoes of armaments reached Choshu, a form of co-operation which did much to counteract the generations of rivalry that had so far kept the two domains apart. It soon gave place to a formal alliance, concluded secretly by Kido and Saigo at Osaka in March 1866. Satsuma agreed to use its influence at Court to restore Choshu to favour. Both bound themselves to overthrow the Tokugawa and restore the emperor to his former dignities. As a result the anti-Tokugawa movement acquired for the first time a solid core of military strength which made it possible to meet the Bakufu on equal terms.

The first evidence of this was given by Choshu. In March 1866 the Bakufu issued an ultimatum setting out the terms on which it would accept Choshu's submission: a reduction of the fief's territory by 100,000 *koku* and the retirement of the *daimyo*, Mori Yoshichika, who was to be succeeded by his grandson. The ultimatum was ignored. Military operations, now inevitable, began in July with attacks launched down the Japan Sea coast, along the Inland Sea from Hiroshima and across the straits from northern Kyushu, but all were held, the one from the north being decisively repulsed. The Bakufu's greater numbers—this despite the refusal of Shimazu and several other lords to send contingents—were matched by Choshu's superior technique, largely the product of Takasugi's training. Within two months Bakufu forces were being driven back on every front. At this point there came news that the Shogun Iemochi had died on September 19, giving pretext for a truce which Edo thankfully accepted.

The death of Iemochi made Hitotsubashi Keiki Shogun, with the unenviable task of saving the Bakufu from the consequences of an outstanding military failure. He turned to administrative reform, this time under foreign guidance. That he could seek such guidance was something new, stemming from the changes induced in Japan's relations with the West as each side came to know more about the other. Britain, for example, brought into direct contact with Satsuma and Choshu by the negotiations which followed bombardment, had learnt something of their outlook, even to the extent of sympathizing with it. Having defeated them, as one British diplomat put it, 'we had come to like and respect them, while a feeling of dislike began to arise in our minds for the Tycoon's people on account of their weakness and double-dealing'.[28] Thus during the fighting between the Bakufu and Choshu in 1866 Britain seemed often to favour the latter. Certainly Parkes and his young interpreters were becoming frequent visitors at the establishments maintained in Edo and Osaka by the anti-Bakufu domains, sometimes to their territories as well. This made them suspect to Bakufu officials.

By contrast, the activities of the French minister, Leon Roches, were more to Edo's taste. He preferred to support the established government, hoping to use its suspicions of Britain as a means of furthering French influence and trade. During 1865 this policy brought him a number of successes: a small shipyard and iron-foundry was built at Yokohama with French help; a school was established there with French teachers; and a major contract was signed for the construction of a dockyard at Yokosuka, work on which began towards the end of the year, though it was still unfinished when Tokugawa rule ended in 1868. Plans were also drawn up for a Franco-Japanese trading company, to deal chiefly in silk under government patronage, though these did not materialize until September 1866. Finally, agreement was reached in November of that year for the dispatch of a French military mission to reform the Shogun's army.

In these circumstances it was natural that Keiki should turn to Roches for advice about reform. In March 1867 the two men had a meeting in Osaka at which Roches put forward proposals for a complete reorganization of the Bakufu on Western lines. The council, he recommended, should be remodelled in the manner of a cabinet, controlling specialist departments of the army, navy, foreign affairs, finance and so on. Central control should be imposed on the domains and cash levies required from them instead of military service. A regular system of taxation would also be essential. Moreover, the government should sponsor new industries, mines and commercial undertakings.

This was much too radical a plan for Keiki and only a few of the measures were ever put into effect, chiefly the ones relating to military organization, though attempts were also made to introduce a degree of specialization into the higher offices of government, while old rules about status were sufficiently broken through to enable a number of able men to be raised to senior posts. What was done certainly fell far short of creating the authoritarian modern state which Roches seems to have had in mind. But it brought enough improvement to alarm the opposition. Satsuma and Choshu began to fear that they must act quickly or lose their chance, a fear that was confirmed by the events of June 1867, when the great lords and Keiki, now Shogun, again assembled in Kyoto for discussions of policy.

There were two matters to be decided: the opening of Hyogo and the 'punishment' of Choshu. About the necessity for the first of these, since it was required by treaty, there was no great difference of opinion, though there remained the task of overcoming the Court's reluctance. About the second the lords and the Shogun were sharply divided. Technically, Choshu was still a rebel. The Bakufu emphasized this point and clung to its demand for a reduction in Choshu territory. By contrast, the great lords, led by Shimazu, pointing to military realities, urged that the domain's *daimyo* receive no more than formal punishment and went so far as to refuse their consent to the opening of Hyogo unless they had their way about Choshu. Even when this was conceded they continued to quibble over forms. Finally Keiki lost patience and forced the Court to give its sanction to a compromise decision, announcing on June 26 that Hyogo was to be opened when the due date came and that 'lenient treatment' would be accorded to Choshu.

This demonstration that the Bakufu could still get its own way at Court was a blow to the hopes of Okubo and Saigo. With the help of the Court noble, Iwakura Tomomi, they had been busy extending their influence over the young emperor, Meiji, who had succeeded Komei in February and was more pliable in these matters than his father. It now seemed that this work might be wasted unless it were backed by force. However, the prospect of yet another armed intervention in Kyoto politics spelt danger to the moderate reformers, led by Tosa, who saw that whereas success would leave power in the hands of Satsuma and Choshu, failure might confirm the Bakufu's authority. In either case the uncommitted domains were likely to find themselves excluded from the making of decisions. Tosa therefore began to press for the formation of an imperial council of *daimyo*, presided over by Keiki, as a solution which would meet the wishes of the domains without entirely destroying the prestige of the Tokugawa. In October 1867, Yamanouchi and his chief adviser, Goto Shojiro, urged Keiki to resign in order to make such a council possible. Since this conformed well enough with his personal inclinations and seemed the only step that might avert another civil war, Keiki accepted the advice and submitted his resignation to the Court on November 9.

Implicitly, only the office of Shogun was at stake, not the Tokugawa lands and strongholds; but Satsuma and Choshu, though agreeable to the idea of a *daimyo* council, would not accept Keiki as its president nor his retention of the Shogun's vast estates. To do so, they held, would give him a decisive advantage in later disputes. Indeed, even before Keiki's offer to resign they had obtained in secret an imperial letter which pardoned Choshu and approved the use of force against the

Tokugawa. They had also brought Satsuma troops into the capital in substantial numbers. Resolved now not to turn aside or compromise, Okubo and Saigo told Goto on December 28 of their determination to act within the next few days. On the 29th Iwakura gave the news to representatives of Owari, Tosa, Fukui and Hiroshima. Recognizing that there was nothing they could do to prevent an attempted *coup d'état*—and conscious that joining it was less dangerous than letting it succeed without them—the four domains promised their help, playing a minor supporting role when five days later the much-canvassed plot was carried out. On the morning of January 3, 1868, troops under the command of Saigo Takamori seized the palace gates. A council was summoned, from which known opponents were excluded, and a decree was approved stripping Keiki of his lands and office. A decision was also taken to return formally to the emperor the responsibility for administration. It was this which gave the event its name: the Meiji Restoration, the restoration of power to the emperor Meiji. To all appearances it was no more than another palace revolution —as many of the participants must have thought it—but it was to prove the beginning of far-reaching change.

CHAPTER VI

NEW MEN AND NEW METHODS
1868-1873

Organization of new administrative machine—the Meiji oligarchy—abolition of feudal domains—land tax reform—centralization—the Iwakura mission

THE DECISIONS taken on January 3, 1868, after Satsuma and its allies had seized control of the imperial palace were not immediately made public. Nor did the emperor's new champions possess means of carrying them out. It was all very well to inform the Shogun that he was stripped of his lands and office, but none knew whether he would accept the decree or whether, if he rejected it, he could be made to submit by force. Accordingly, the next three weeks were a time of rumour and speculation, when only an inner circle of Court and Bakufu officials had any idea of what was going on. Choshu, pardoned by the Court, moved troops to Kyoto, which greatly strengthened the hand of the conspirators, while the Shogun, Keiki, withdrew to Osaka, where he had a substantial body of men at his command. Despite this he gave the impression of having abandoned all attempts to control the situation, though his chief supporters, the lords of Aizu and Kuwana, clearly wanted him to fight. Meanwhile Owari and Fukui, both of whom were Tokugawa relatives, were working to bring about a compromise, proposing that Keiki should surrender only his Court titles and such part of his lands as would provide the emperor with an adequate revenue. Keiki agreed. However, he reckoned without the growing hostility between Satsuma and Aizu. On January 26, apparently without the Shogun's authority, Aizu and Kuwana troops marched on Kyoto. Next day outside the city they clashed with those of Satsuma and Choshu. The latter, though heavily outnumbered, drove them back on Osaka, whence Keiki fled to Edo, and with this as pretext the Court was persuaded to proclaim him rebel. Japan again faced civil war, this time with the roles of Edo and Choshu reversed. In practice the worst was avoided. During the weeks that followed the imperial forces moved steadily eastward, but there was little fighting. Most *daimyo* along the route submitted even before the advance-guard reached them. Eventually Keiki reasserted his authority over his own advisers to the point of forbidding resistance, with the result that Edo was occupied early in April and formal surrender terms were negotiated soon after. They were comparatively generous. Keiki himself was to go into retirement, but his successor as head of the Tokugawa house was to retain lands of 700,000 *koku*—about the same as Satsuma, nearly twice as much as Choshu—and this, together with the promise of pardon to all Tokugawa vassals who swore allegiance to the new government, prevented hostilities on a national scale. Aizu rejected the settlement, resisting stubbornly for another six months in the mountains round Wakamatsu, but when its lord yielded with his castle and its garrison at the beginning of November, the whole of the north surrendered too. Thereafter, the only Tokugawa adherents still at liberty were a few who had escaped to Hokkaido by sea. They managed to hold out till June of the following year.

The relative ease with which the Bakufu was overcome was a great relief to the Satsuma and Choshu leaders, whose position had at first been exceedingly precarious. Though they had the enormous advantage of control over the emperor's person, many senior Court nobles were against them and had to be dismissed, while most of the great lords remained watchful rather than friendly. Even the domains which belonged to the victorious coalition had different interests and different viewpoints, so that there was always a danger of disruption. Certainly they were not capable of giving unified direction. Nor was the Court, for it had prestige without power: no lands, no revenue, no military force of its own, no officials outside the immediate area of the capital. Decrees issued in the emperor's name could be enforced only where the imperial army happened to be fighting—an army which comprised contingents from several domains, each under its own commander. Over much of the country, in fact, enforcement was at the pleasure of the individual feudal lord. Since the Bakufu's administration had come to a standstill as well, it is fair to say that in the first few weeks of 1868 Japan had no central government at all.

One solution might have been to found a new line of Shogun, as many contemporaries thought would happen. Yet there were obstacles which made this course unlikely. Neither of the obvious contenders, Satsuma and Choshu, could establish a clear superiority over the other, while both were cordially disliked by a majority. Moreover, the position of the two *daimyo* within their own domains was not such as to allow a personal rule of the traditional kind, still less its extension to the country as a whole. This being so, it was necessary to find a new institutional framework to make government effective. Habit, sentiment and the fact of Bakufu resistance combined to ensure that it should centre on the Imperial Court. Beyond this, all remained to be decided: the name and nature of political institutions, the men who should control them, the policies they would carry out. Decision of these matters was to be the main strand of Japanese history for the next five years.

The process began with an attempt to maintain as wide as possible an alliance against the Tokugawa. If the civil war were to be successfully prosecuted, the government had to make room for all the elements which had contributed to the Bakufu's downfall, or at least as many of them as qualified by status: Court nobles, great lords, samurai officials of the domains, even representatives of the radical movement. This was reflected in the early stages of constitution-making and appointment. On January 3, 1868, an imperial council took the first step by appointing new Court advisers to replace those who had been dismissed. At the head of the regime was an imperial prince, a choice which resolved conflicting claims among the active participants in the *coup d'état*. He was given as deputies two Court nobles who had played a distinguished part in anti-Tokugawa politics, Sanjo Sanetomi and Iwakura Tomomi. Three other nobles were rewarded for similar services by appointment as senior councillors (*Gijo*), being joined as such by two more imperial princes and the five feudal lords whose troops were manning the palace gates, those of Satsuma, Tosa, Hiroshima, Owari and Fukui. As junior councillors (*Sanyo*) were several more Court nobles of minor rank and three samurai from each of the same five domains, Choshu being added to their number later. In February the pattern was extended by the creation of administrative departments. At their head were *Gijo*, with *Sanyo* as their deputies or assistants, the latter being responsible in each case for the actual work of the department. This change made necessary an increase in the number of councillors, as also did the accession to the alliance of domains like Uwajima, Kumamoto and Tottori, so that by the beginning of June over one hundred *Sanyo* had been appointed. Since their duties were ill-defined and there was virtually no machinery to carry them out, this was clearly a move designed to influence opinion.

Two other devices were also designed to serve this end. The first, which was announced in March, was the summoning of delegates from all the domains to act as a consultative assembly. This proved a useful means of gauging feudal opinion and rallying support. The second, known as the Charter Oath of April 6, 1868, was a public statement in the emperor's name of the government's intentions, which promised that policy would be formulated only after wide consultation and that 'base customs of former times shall be abolished'.[29] The implication was that the old exclusiveness of Bakufu rule was not to be repeated, nor a new Bakufu established. This was to reassure those who were suspicious of Satsuma and Choshu. It was also to provide a basis for reconciliation with the defeated Tokugawa and the trained officials in their service, whose help was urgently needed if the national administration were to operate smoothly.

Once Edo had surrendered there was less need to maintain an appearance of universal support for the new regime, even though fighting still continued in the north. Moreover, the prospect of acquiring the bulk of the Tokugawa lands meant that Kyoto would shortly have something to govern, making it desirable that the administration contain fewer nonentities in high office. In June 1868, therefore, came a major reorganization. It was designed ostensibly to put into effect the principles of the Charter Oath; and in its enunciation of a separation of powers—nullified in practice by an interlocking of both men and functions between legislature, executive and judiciary —it gave evidence that study was already being made of Western constitutions. Its most important feature, however, was the re-distribution of posts. This was especially marked at the level of junior councillor and vice-minister of department, where there was a sharp reduction in total numbers, effected by cutting the representation of Court nobles (to three from over forty) and excluding many of the domains. The nineteen samurai nominated in the fourteen months for which the system lasted came from only seven territories: Satsuma, Choshu, Tosa, Hizen, Hiroshima, Fukui and Kumamoto. Two-thirds of them were men of middling rank and nearly all had held office in domain governments.

This tendency towards concentration of power in fewer hands increased as the controlling group gained confidence and strength. In August 1869, when all the fighting was over, the administration was again revised, taking this time the shape which it was to retain until the introduction of a Western-style cabinet sixteen years later. The Executive Council (*Dajokan*) became clearly the strongest arm of government. At its head was Sanjo, supported by a number of advisers of varying rank who together supervised the six executive departments: Civil Affairs (reorganized as Home Affairs in November 1873), Finance, War (divided into Army and Navy separately at the beginning of 1872), Justice, Imperial Household and Foreign Affairs. The high-ranking dignitaries who were ministers of these departments were all, except in the Imperial Household department, given samurai assistants. Moreover, only samurai were appointed to the key position of councillor (*Sangi*) to the Executive Council. A few Court nobles—Sanjo, Iwakura and perhaps half a dozen more—still held offices of some consequence. Two former *daimyo*, Date Muneki of Uwajima and Nabeshima Naomasa of Hizen, retained official standing, the first for almost two years, the second for a little less. But for the most part authority now passed into the hands of a small group of samurai from Satsuma, Choshu, Tosa and Hizen, other domains being excluded from all but subordinate posts. Even the consultative assembly of samurai, though it continued in a modified form, was allowed to fall into disuse. Its discussions were adjourned in October 1870 and it never met again, sure sign that the government no longer felt the need to win friends in the country at large.

From this time on, each crisis successfully weathered meant a more open assumption of power by the inner group. In the summer of 1871, when the old domains were abolished (*see below*), samurai took over as heads of two vital departments, Finance and Foreign Affairs. In October 1873, after a dispute over priorities which split the councillors into two hostile factions, the victors took direct responsibility for the formulation, as well as the execution, of government policy. Figureheads were no longer needed. Appearance and reality were one. In other words, the men who had first learnt to manipulate their own feudal lords, then their emperor and his courtiers, had at last achieved a position in which they could dispense with camouflage and avow their power. The 'Meiji oligarchy' was taking shape, with samurai from the south and west as its leading figures.

The senior member of the group was in fact a Court noble, Iwakura Tomomi (1825–83). Shrewd and capable, exercising great personal influence over the emperor and the Court, he served first as councillor, briefly as Foreign Minister in the autumn of 1871, then as senior minister until his death in 1883. Of the samurai, Saigo Takamori (1828–77), who had commanded the Satsuma troops in the civil war and negotiated the Tokugawa surrender, was at once the most popular and most contradictory. Acclaimed as champion and exemplar of the samurai class, he tried after 1868 to hold aloof from politics, only to find himself, because of his reputation and sense of duty, involved in every crisis. A conservative become revolutionary against his will, he ended as a rebel under arms. In sharp contrast was his boyhood friend, Okubo Toshimichi (1830–78). Okubo was by nature a politician, a ruthless and clear-sighted one, with an instinct for governing. In 1871 he became Minister of Finance and from November 1873, as Home Minister, emerged as the administration's strongest personality. He was responsible more than any other for the fact that its critics, including Saigo, were unable to divert it from its chosen course, a role which eventually cost him his life at the hands of Saigo's followers. Less incisive, but more flexible and open to new ideas, was Kido Koin (1833-77). The premature death of Takasugi Shinsaku in the spring of 1867 had left Kido almost unchallenged in his control of Choshu politics and hence the domain's chief representative in the central government. There he became an advocate of radical change, especially in political institutions, arguing persistently and often successfully against the more traditional outlook of the majority of his colleagues.

For all their differences of temperament, these four men had much in common. They were of the same generation and in origin of similar social standing. Iwakura, as a Court noble, was in theory vastly above the other three, but he came from the middle levels of his own class, just as they did from theirs. Saigo, Okubo and Kido were from families of full samurai rank, though with little pretension to wealth. They were respectable enough to quality for office even under the old regime, but had had to win promotion in the only way open to them in a society where status and authority were closely linked, through the household or entourage of their feudal lords. Iwakura had broken through barriers at Court in much the same manner by using the emperor's personal favour. Their colleagues, too, were men very like themselves, able but relatively junior members of the feudal ruling class, who were increasingly chosen for appointment by criteria of efficiency and experience. Those whose only claim to consideration rested on radical views and a record of anti-Tokugawa violence found honours easier to come by than responsibility, while some who had served the Bakufu found even this no disability once a year or two had passed and wounds were healed. Katsu Awa (1823-99) is a good example. A samurai of modest rank, formerly serving Edo as a naval expert, he was the only councillor appointed between 1869 and 1885 who did not come from one of the four paramount domains.

Within these domains there was emerging also a slightly younger generation, already important and destined to survive into the twentieth century. From Satsuma there was Matsukata Masayoshi (1837-1924), a man of semi-samurai descent, who was to become Finance Minister in 1881 and to hold that office for over fifteen years. From Tosa came Itagaki Taisuke (1837-

1919), a loyalist, military expert and eventually political party leader. Okuma Shigenobu (1838–1922) was from Hizen, where he had studied both Dutch and English before the Restoration, as well as supervising the fief's foreign trade. In 1869 he was made deputy in the two departments of Finance and Civil Affairs, Minister of Finance from 1873 to 1880, later party politician, founder of Waseda University, Foreign Minister. Two Choshu men, both of whom were of something less than full samurai rank by birth, achieved even greater fame. Yamagata Aritomo (1838–1922) was soldier more than politician, at least until his middle years. Ito Hirobumi (1841–1909) was, like Okuma, a modernizer with more than average knowledge of the West, having studied in London during 1863–4, in America during 1870–1. The training stood him in good stead when he was Minister of Public Works from 1873 to 1881. Thereafter, with the help of Iwakura, he succeeded Okubo as the government's outstanding leader, to be succeeded in his turn by Yamagata when the century ended.

It is true that these men were younger than Kido, Saigo, Okubo and Iwakura, as were six or seven others of similar background who served with them in the cabinets of 1885 and after. Yet they were old enough to have shared in the political struggles of 1860–68, as well as to have experienced the life of Edo, Kyoto and castle-town under the Tokugawa. This created a certain community of outlook which persisted despite quarrels and factional strife. For forty years after the Restoration, Japanese policy was determined by men from only four domains, forming a group which was homogeneous in age, social origin and political experience. This fact was vital to the success of the new government, for it gave a consistency and continuity to its actions which enabled fresh habits to become deep-rooted before another generation rose to challenge them.

Before this oligarchy could be said to rule Japan there had to be an authority it could wield. In 1869 this was yet to be created. The central government still depended on the domains for its military force, on former Tokugawa lands for most of its revenue, on the emperor's prestige for what obedience it could command. In fact, before any major decision could be taken and carried out, Kido, Okubo and Iwakura had to conduct a series of difficult negotiations. They had first to secure the support of Satsuma and Choshu—and the two *daimyo*, to say nothing of their senior retainers, did not always co-operate willingly—then that of the Imperial Court. This done, a combination of exhortation and intrigue would be employed to get the concurrence of the other feudal lords. It was all very complex and unsatisfactory. To samurai who were conscious of their ability and had been brought up in an authoritarian tradition, it seemed far better that the imperial government should possess real power. Moreover, as individuals they had little to lose by transferring their allegiance to it. What they might lose by way of feudal influence and standing would be more than balanced, if they were successful, by the rewards of office in an administration which really governed on a national scale.

Several steps taken during 1868 had indicated a desire to weaken feudal separatism. For example, the Court re-issued in its own name many of the old Bakufu restrictions on the activities of *daimyo*, such as the ban on issuing coinage or forming marriage alliances. It also ordered samurai who accepted office in the central government to sever relations with their original domains. In December came direct intervention, in the form of a decree which specified the titles to be held by senior domain officials, described them as 'subject to the Imperial authority' and ordered feudal lords to choose them from 'the fittest and ablest . . . irrespective of any other considerations'.[30] The implications of this were far-reaching, though the immediate effect was small. Also significant, perhaps, was the fact that confiscated Tokugawa estates were put under imperial officers, not re-distributed by way of reward to loyalists.

To several of the new leaders this was not nearly enough. As Ito put it many years later, 'the whole fabric of the feudal system, which with its obsolete shackles and formalities hindered us at every step . . . had to be uprooted and destroyed'.[31] Kido had advanced this view early in 1868, but it was far too radical for his colleagues and his proposals had been rejected. This did not stop him. In June he returned to Choshu and tried to persuade Mori to set an example, urging him to offer his lands voluntarily to the emperor. The plan aroused much hostility within the domain, but it was eventually adopted, with the proviso that Satsuma must be willing to act in similar fashion. This left Kido to try his arguments once again in Kyoto. In November, Okubo rather guardedly agreed. By February 1869 other Satsuma samurai had been won over, as had Itagaki of Tosa and Okuma of Hizen, and together they overcame the objections of their lords. On March 2 the four domains submitted a joint memorial putting their lands and people at the emperor's disposal.

It has never been quite clear what this document was intended to imply. Superficially, it was an offer to surrender feudal rights entirely, as some obviously meant it to be. On the other hand, its wording was capable of a different interpretation. Whether intentionally or not, references to the desirability of creating a single source of authority could as easily have been a condemnation of Court-Bakufu dualism as a plea for abolishing the autonomy of the feudal lords. Equally, the request that the emperor dispose of feudal territories at will, 'giving what should be given and taking away what should be taken away',[32] has something of the air of seeking confirmation of existing privileges, as was customary when one feudal regime succeeded another. There were certainly a good many who read it in this light, to judge by later reactions. Even within the inner circles of government the enthusiasm of Kido and Ito was by no means universal. Okubo felt that it was too soon for a trial of strength, especially as the samurai assembly gave the proposal no warm welcome. He supported a compromise, the terms of which were agreed after long debate and in July 1869 were at last put into effect. The memorial was accepted and all *daimyo* who had not already done so were ordered to follow the example of Satsuma, Choshu, Tosa and Hizen; but the lands surrendered were not brought under direct imperial control. Instead, the feudal lords were appointed governors in their own domains, with the right of choosing their subordinates. In principle, they became imperial officials. In practice, their position seemed likely to be much what it had been before. Most of them, after all, had inherited titles derived from just such offices as these, which their predecessors had usurped several centuries earlier.

That the government did not mean the change to be one in

name alone was made apparent by orders which were issued shortly after. Domain revenues were re-allocated, part to the former *daimyo*, part to specific administrative expenses, while reports were called for concerning levels of taxation, military force, population and similar matters. Samurai stipends were to be reviewed—many were in fact reduced—and some simplification made of the multitudinous subdivisions in samurai rank. All this accompanied the administrative reorganization of August 1869, which narrowed the basis of recruitment for the central government. The result was widespread criticism from those sections of the feudal class which felt their position threatened. It was of greatest importance, of course, in Satsuma and Choshu, without whose support the regime might easily have collapsed. In both, the feudal lord was hostile, as also was Saigo Takamori, and attempts to win them over early in 1870 failed. It therefore became necessary to postpone any further attack on domain privileges until unity had been restored.

By this time Okubo was convinced of the need to finish what had been begun, but neither he nor Kido wished to act without Saigo, since Saigo held the loyalty of the Satsuma troops. In March 1871, convinced that further delay would be dangerous, they made another effort at reconciliation. Iwakura was appointed special imperial envoy to Satsuma and Choshu. Kido and Okubo took the opportunity of bringing moral pressure to bear on their fellow-clansmen under cover of the ceremonies that this entailed, this time with success, for Saigo returned with them and entered into their plans for the total abolition of the feudal structure. In April they reached agreement with Itagaki of Tosa and in June troops from all three domains began to move into the capital. August 1871 saw the preparations completed. Okubo took over as Minister of Finance; Kido and Saigo became councillors, the other samurai resigning to make way for them; then Itagaki and Okuma joined the council as representatives of Tosa and Hizen. On August 29, having thus ensured control of the administration, the decisive step was taken. The emperor summoned to his presence those feudal lords who were available in the city and announced the abolition of the domains. All land was to become imperial territory, he told them. Local jurisdiction was to cease at once. A month later the domain armies, except those serving under imperial command, were ordered to disband, leaving the central government as the only legal possessor of military force.

This kind of treatment was a far cry from the blandishments which had been lavished on the *daimyo* only a year or two before. All the same, it was not dependent for its success only on the use of threats. A financial inducement was involved as well. Since the summer of 1869 the feudal lords had been receiving as governors one-tenth of the revenue from their domains and this sum was now to become for each of them a private income. It was a generous price for an office which had given more worry than power. The samurai, by contrast, did not fare so well. They were promised that their stipends would continue, but it was to be at the levels introduced as part of an economy drive in the past two years, so that a man who had held 100 *koku* before the Restoration might now receive as little as 60 *koku* or even a good deal less. The exceptions were the loyalists, who had been granted additional stipends, sometimes large ones, for their part in overthrowing the Tokugawa.

In abolishing the domains Kido and Okubo had gambled for high stakes and success marked a new stage in their fortunes. It brought them jurisdiction over the whole of the country's land and population, together with control of all the former revenues of the domains, so that the central government at last possessed the basic requirements for the creation of a modern state. At the same time, it had inherited a number of financial problems. One was the enormous burden imposed by the payment of stipends. Another, the first to be tackled, was the inefficiency in revenue collection which was caused by local differences in tax level and feudal custom.

As a first step to clarifying the tax position it was necessary to settle the question of land ownership. The feudal ban on the transfer or sale of land—which had been in existence, though often evaded, since 1643—was abolished in February 1872 and a start made on issuing certificates of title. By the following year this was well advanced and Okuma Shigenobu, as Vice-Minister of Finance, had worked out the details of a new land-tax system. They were announced on July 28, 1873. All land was to be valued—at its market price if it had recently changed hands, at an estimated price if not—and the owner of it was to pay an annual tax of 3 per cent of its value, which, it was calculated, would yield on average the same amount as had been paid in feudal dues. To the government, the advantages would be considerable: the amount of revenue would be predictable, both because it would no longer vary with the harvests and because it would be paid in cash; and there would not be the same sharp differences between place and place. To the owner and cultivator the system was less attractive, if only because it left fewer loopholes for evasion. It became, as we shall see, a major cause of rural unrest.

It was four years before the land-tax regulations of 1873 had been applied to all arable land and another four years before their extension to mountain and forest, but once this was done Japan had been given a modern system of taxation. This was true, at least, so far as concerned the land, which still provided far and away the largest part of the country's revenue. During the same period, moreover, the government had turned its attention to the samurai stipends. At the end of 1871 samurai had been given permission to enter farming, commerce and other occupations, but many had soon found themselves in difficulties for lack of capital. For this reason—avowedly—those whose stipends were less than 100 *koku* were informed in December 1873 that they would be allowed to commute them for cash. Relatively few chose to do so. Accordingly, on August 5, 1876, what had been optional for some was made compulsory for all. A scale was published showing the amount in government bonds which would now be granted instead of the annual allowance, all being required to accept the transfer. For the very largest pensions, those of the great lords, bonds were to be issued equal to five years' purchase, bearing interest at 5 per cent. For the very smallest it would be fourteen years at 7 per cent, with a series of gradations in between, stipends which were only tenable for life being redeemed at half these rates. The result was to provide former *daimyo* with substantial capital sums, whereas the poorest samurai received in interest a good deal less than they could live on; while for its own part the government achieved the economy it desired, reducing annual expenditure on this item to about half the cost of the stipends of 1871. At some loss to their reputation for good faith, the oligarchs were making their regime not only centralized but solvent.

They were also beginning to make it modern. The process of modernization will be discussed more fully in a later chapter, but it is important to note here that the Meiji leaders were from the start engaged in building a new Japan, not merely a new regime. Their motives stemmed partly from personal ambition, but even more from their views on the international situation. Again and again they had been told about European encroachments elsewhere in Asia. They had seen evidence of aggression, or so they regarded it, in bombardments of the Japanese coastline, events in which several of them had taken part. They had been given visual evidence of the West's superiority in arms and military organization, enough to convince them that Japan could only hold her own by adopting similar methods. They were, in other words, the heirs of Sakuma Shozan, Sato Shinen and Yoshida Shoin. There was the difference, however, that after 1868 such men were able to act, not merely recommend. Especially was this true after the abolition of the domains in 1871, which removed the greatest political obstacle from their path and opened the way for any number of reforms.

Even before this there had been indications that the new order was to be quite unlike the old. In 1868, for example, the government had been transferred to Edo, which was renamed Tokyo, and in November the emperor had taken up residence in the Shogun's former castle. In the following year, after the surrender of domain registers, changes had been made in class nomenclature. Court and feudal nobles were made members of a single peerage (*kazoku*), their retainers became gentry (*shizoku*), the lesser feudal ranks were combined under the label *sotsu*—abolished early in 1872—and the rest of the population became commoners (*heimin*). This did away with the functional groupings so beloved of Tokugawa scholars: the hierarchy of samurai, farmer, artisan and merchant. More important, it made a start on creating the sense of national unity for which the Mito school had pleaded. The attack, after all, was not only on class distinctions, but also on those lines of division which had split Tokugawa society between Court and Bakufu, *tozama* and *fudai*. It led logically to the abolition of the domains in August 1871, with its implied destruction of regional loyalties, or at least of their institutional focus. A month later came three measures which foreshadowed also the end of social status in its traditional forms. Commoners were given permission to intermarry with members of the peerage. Samurai lost the right of *kirisute-gomen*, that is, of using their swords on the lower orders with impunity. Last, and most ominous, they were to be permitted not to wear a sword at all. After this, it was not unduly surprising that in March 1876, when the government felt more confident of its position, a law was issued banning the wearing of swords entirely.

Samurai were also the chief sufferers from attempts to modernize the military establishment. It was obviously unsatisfactory that the imperial army should consist of units placed at the emperor's disposal by the domains, even when the domains were loyal. The arrangement became impossible once the domains had ceased to exist. The chosen substitute was conscription, a concept for which there were classical precedents both in Chinese and Japanese history, though feudalism had long since replaced it in Japan. The first regulations concerning it were published in January 1871, to come into force the following year, but the abolition of the domains made them largely out of date and little was done about putting them into practice. In December 1872 a new system was announced which provided that all men reaching the age of twenty might be required to serve three years with the colours. Six home depots were established and the peacetime force was fixed at 36,000 men. The result, once the first recruits were trained, was to deprive the samurai of their monopoly of arms and military skill. It also helped the government to indoctrinate a rising generation in its own ideas, contributing thereby to the shaping of loyalty and national unity.

So, too, did education. It was in September 1871 that a separate Department of Education (*Mombusho*) was created, almost exactly a year later that plans were announced for a compulsory system of primary schools. Similarly, much was being done to modernize Japan's communications, most matters pertaining to this being put under the supervision of a Department of Public Works in December 1870. By that time telegraphs were already in use in the Tokyo-Yokohama region.

In 1871 Japan was linked by cable with Shanghai and Vladi-vostock. On British advice plans were also drawn up for a railway to link Tokyo with Kyoto, Osaka and Kobe, the Tokyo-Yokohama section being completed in September 1872 after a little over two years work. Meanwhile, a government mail service had been instituted, first between Tokyo and Osaka in the spring of 1871, then for the whole country in 1872. All these developments helped to increase the authority and prestige, both national and international, of the central administration.

Some members of the government entered into the reform programme with enthusiasm, notably Okuma and Ito in the departments of Finance and Public Works respectively. Others accepted it as a necessary ingredient of national strength, though the details were not always to their taste and some of the social implications filled conservatives with horror. On balance, however, one can say that thus far the government's domestic policies seemed to have adequate support. By contrast, the handling of foreign affairs soon revealed differences that led directly to a quarrel.

In 1868 Okubo and his colleagues had lost no time in dis-avowing the expulsion policies with which the anti-Tokugawa movement had been linked in earlier days. They continued their association with the British minister, Parkes, who per-suaded the foreign envoys to declare neutrality in the civil war; and they took prompt steps to suppress those of their own followers who found the change of front too sudden to com-prehend. Various attacks on foreigners in the first few months after the Restoration, including an attempt to assassinate Parkes in March, brought forth all that could be desired by way of punishment and apologies. For all this, the Meiji leaders made it clear that in Japanese eyes the existing treaties were anathema. As soon as political stability had been achieved, they said, it was intended to revise them. Especially unpopular were the provisions concerning consular jurisdiction and the limita-tion of customs dues, the first being detrimental to national sovereignty, the second to government finance.

An opportunity to act on these ideas did not come until after the abolition of the domains, but in the autumn of 1871 it was at last decided to send a diplomatic mission to the United States and Europe to seek revision of the treaties. It was to be impressive in its size and composition, far more so than the embassies which the Bakufu had dispatched in previous years, since Iwakura was to lead it, supported by Okubo, Kido, Ito and a number of other senior officials, while the whole, with students, secretaries and interpreters, amounted to over fifty men. They left Yokohama in December 1871 and were received ceremonially both in San Francisco and in Washington. They were told, however, that talk about treaty revision was still premature. London's attitude was the same when they went there later in 1872 and the lesson was repeated by Bismarck in Berlin during March 1873, leaving no doubt that a variety of reforms, including a complete revision of Japan's legal system, would have to be carried out before the powers would accept a new relationship. Indeed, the envoys had the evidence of their own eyes to show them that Japan had far to go before she would be in a position to negotiate on equal terms. In eighteen months abroad—the first time for Iwakura, Okubo and Kido—they saw much of the West's economic and military progress; and it convinced them that their main task on returning home would be to step up the pace of modernization.

Unhappily, the caretaker government which they had left in Tokyo had meanwhile taken decisions of a very different kind, arising from Japan's relations with Korea. These had been uneasy ever since 1868, for Korea insisted on maintaining a traditional seclusion, which both Japan and China had abandoned, and rejected all overtures from Japan's new government on the grounds that they departed from established ways. Many Japanese were genuinely indignant at this, among them the Foreign Minister, Soejima Taneomi. Others, inspired by the expansionist ideas which had been taught by men like Yoshida Shoin, regarded Korea as a proper field for the growth of Japanese influence. They demanded military action, both to avenge insult and to extend their country's power. What is more, several of the government leaders were willing to back them, though it was for reasons which sprang from domestic rather than from foreign issues. War with Korea, they thought, might distract the advocates of expulsion from the dangerous subject of Japan's relations with the West. It might also serve as an outlet for samurai frustration, while a victorious campaign would provide rewards in land which could do much to relieve samurai distress. At one time such arguments were advanced by Kido. Saigo Takamori also used them, with increasing vehemence as it became obvious that the samurai class was losing its privileged position in Japanese society. He was supported, partly out of conviction, partly out of a desire to weaken the solidarity of Satsuma and Choshu, by Goto and Itagaki of Tosa, Soejima and Eto of Hizen.

Trouble came to a head with the rebuff of another Japanese envoy to Korea while the Iwakura mission was in Europe. Saigo, seeking a solution to personal as well as national problems, offered himself as next to go, in the expectation that he would be killed and so provide an excuse for war. The plan was agreed by the Executive Council in the summer of 1873, but before it could be carried out Iwakura and his colleagues were back from Europe and demanding that the decision be reversed. In October Okubo with some reluctance became their spokesman. He argued, first, that Japan's finances could not stand the strain of war; second, that all the country's energy and resources were needed for the task of reform; and third, that a Japanese-Korean struggle would make it all too easy for the powers to fish in troubled waters, to the evident disadvantage of Japan. Saigo's convictions were unshaken by this, but he could not withstand the pressures that were brought against him. Iwakura secured the emperor's support, Okubo and Kido that of most samurai officials. As a result the Korean expedition was abandoned and it was decided, instead, to concentrate on development at home.

The price was the unity of the ruling group. Saigo, Soejima, Eto, Goto and Itagaki all resigned, followed by many of their juniors, while those remaining in office closed their ranks. Ito, as Minister of Public Works, became a councillor on October 25, the day after Saigo's resignation, and Okuma took over as Minister of Finance. Okubo became the first Minister for Home Affairs in the following month. These three, with Iwakura, became the chief architects of a modernization policy which had for the first time been debated and resolved in general terms. Plans which had been piecemeal were now made coherent and purposeful. They were also lasting: Japan was to remain committed for twenty years to reform at home and peace abroad. All the same, neither the policy nor the men who administered it were to go unchallenged. The divisions which made one part of the leadership so powerful made the other into a new and effective opposition, in which Eto and Saigo turned to force, the rest, more dangerously, to political organization, with the result that the dispute over Korea in 1873 settled the pattern not only of policy, but also of politics, for best part of a generation.

CHAPTER VII

GOVERNMENT AND POLITICS
1873-1894

*The Korean crisis—movement for representative government—
Press Law—repression of liberalism—the bureaucracy—the
Meiji constitution*

THE DISPUTE over policy towards Korea, which split the
Meiji leadership towards the end of 1873, had far-reaching
repercussions on Japanese politics. Several of those who resigned office proved irreconcilable, despite conciliatory gestures
from the government, and some had recourse to armed revolt.
Eto Shimpei, for example, led an uprising in Hizen early in
1874, though it was easily suppressed. His colleagues from
Satsuma and Tosa proved at first more cautious, but they, too,
began to organize the discontented samurai in their former
feudal territories, a process made all the easier by the moves
towards commutation of stipends which soon followed the
Korean crisis. In Tosa this brought the formation of political
parties and a demand for representative institutions. In Satsuma
it led eventually to a major rebellion under the leadership of
Saigo Takamori.

Saigo was a romantic figure, almost destined, one might
think, to be a leader of lost causes. He was more powerfully
built than most Japanese, an excellent swordsman, an enthusi-
astic hunter and fisherman, a man with all the samurai virtues:
courage, generosity, lack of ostentation, a contempt for money.
With them went an impatience with routine that made him a
poor administrator, a loyalty towards his subordinates that
made it easy for them to sway him. He was traditional in outlook, if not always in policy, and was pledged above all to the

interests of Satsuma and the samurai class, a fact which brought him inevitably into conflict with men like Okubo and Kido, whose centralizing activities constituted an attack on Satsuma's local independence and whose search for national unity involved the destruction of samurai privilege. The clash of interests became abundantly clear in 1873 and thereafter Saigo held aloof from politics, manifestly disapproving. He devoted his energies instead to the affairs of his home province, where he founded a network of so-called 'private schools', aimed at training samurai in the military skills and providing them with a means of livelihood in what was fast becoming a discouraging environment. As the number of his 'pupils' grew—they were said to have totalled 20,000 in 1877—so did his influence. Before long Satsuma was outside the jurisdiction of the central government in all but name, for it had become an area in which no official appointment could be made without Saigo's tacit approval and no official policy could be implemented if he opposed it. It was a situation that could not be tolerated indefinitely by a government careful of its authority.

In 1876 came three actions that exacerbated the samurai sense of grievance. Early in the year the government concluded a treaty opening Korean ports to trade, a diplomatic victory achieved by methods that had been used on Japan herself only twenty years earlier, but none the less anathema to those for whom negotiation was only of value as providing a pretext for war. At home, in March the samurai lost their right to bear swords, the last surviving symbol of superior status. In August they lost their stipends, compulsorily commuted for cash or bonds at rates which represented a considerable loss of income. The result was an increasing, though local, turbulence. In October a small force of samurai attacked Kumamoto and a month later Maebara Issei led several hundred in revolt in Choshu. Saigo made no move; but Satsuma was clearly restless and the government played for safety by trying to remove stocks of arms and ammunition from Kagoshima, the provincial capital, late in January 1877. The attempt was anticipated by Saigo's followers, who seized the munitions themselves and claimed simultaneously to have uncovered a plot against Saigo's life, supposedly originating with Okubo in Tokyo, and in the ensuing uproar Saigo found his men were out of hand. He was forced to put himself at their head to seek redress by marching on the capital, a decision which on February 20 brought a proclamation declaring him a rebel.

What had been planned as a triumphal march met with unexpected resistance from the garrison at Kumamoto. This confined the rebellion to southern Kyushu and doomed it to failure, for the government was thereby given time to marshal its forces. Even so, it took over 40,000 men—the whole of the standing army and reserves—and some six months of steady campaigning before Saigo was driven back to make his last stand at Kagoshima. The end came in September 1877, when he and his chief followers died there in the face of overwhelming odds. They left behind them a legend which still haunts the city. More important, they had demonstrated that the samurai with his sword was no match for a peasant conscript army trained in Western methods and backed by a modern system of communications.

This proved to be the last of the feudal risings against the Meiji government. It was not, however, the end of samurai opposition. Members of the former feudal class in other areas had not been sufficiently at one with Saigo to rally behind him, but he had many sympathizers among them and they continued to advocate his policies for many years. Especially was this so of his plans for Japanese expansion on the mainland, which were taken up by men who formed the first patriotic societies of the period, some of whom were not averse to using force at home. Indeed, one result of the Satsuma Rebellion was to reinforce the connection which had earlier been established between foreign policy and assassination, ranging from the murder of Ii Naosuke in 1860 to an abortive attempt on Iwakura's life in January 1874. Okubo himself was a victim, killed in May 1878, and intermittent attacks on public figures continued for the following forty years: on Okuma in 1889; on Li Hung-chang in 1895, during the negotiations at Shimonoseki; on Ito in 1909; on Hara, as premier, in 1921. Not all these incidents involved ex-samurai, of course. Yet most were connected in one way or another with organizations that grew originally out of samurai discontent and continued to look back to samurai traditions of violence, both in domestic and in foreign affairs.

Violence was not entirely absent even from party politics, for these, too, owed their origin to samurai, specifically, in the first instance, to groups led by Itagaki Taisuke and Goto Shojiro of Tosa and Soejima Taneomi of Hizen. Like Saigo, they had resigned in 1873; and, like him again, it was not merely because of differences over foreign policy. For them, however, the additional motive was resentment of the monopoly of office by Satsuma and Choshu, not opposition to the process of modernization, so their subsequent actions took a different course. Soon after the Korea dispute they set out to marshal samurai opinion, especially that of Tosa and Hizen, behind demands for a constitution on Western lines. The choice was partly determined by a genuine interest in Western political institutions, which as early as 1868 had led Goto to question an English diplomat concerning 'the working of our executive government in combination with the parliamentary system, the existence of political parties and the election of members of the lower house'.[33] Many Japanese in those early days saw some kind of representative assembly as the solution to the problem of replacing a Tokugawa Shogun by a coalition of domains. Thus when Itagaki, Goto and Soejima petitioned for the creation of an elected legislature early in 1874, they could legitimately claim to be speaking for a considerable segment of informed opinion: in their own words, for 'the samurai and the richer farmers and merchants . . . who produced the leaders of the revolution of 1868'.[34] There was even backing for their ideas among members of the oligarchy still in office.

Nevertheless, it was not the theoretical attractions of parliamentary government that gave the movement its political strength. Rather, it was the continued existence in Japanese society of a variety of discontents. There were many, not only among samurai, to whom change was not always pleasing, from misfits who found that they lacked the ability to achieve in the new order the status which birth had given them in the old, to the simply ignorant who regarded newfangled devices like the telegraph and the railway with a superstitious dread. There were also the disappointed, men who had given their services in the Restoration movement, only to find their interests apparently disregarded by the Meiji rulers. Especially was this so in the countryside. The abolition of feudalism had given a new class of landowners a formal title to their land and a measure of social equality with those who had been their betters, but it had not as yet given them a voice in the running of affairs. The poorer farmers fared even worse, for the change of masters had in no way relieved them of their debts, while the new tax-collector—regular, impersonal, and demanding cash—was often more difficult to deal with than a feudal lord. Land tax, in fact, was a general grievance, affecting the whole village from landlord to tenant farmer. Not only was it as heavy a burden as feudal dues had been, but it was also demonstrably heavier than the taxation levied on industry and commerce.

Many of the aggrieved came to see in the demand for representative institutions, or 'popular rights', as contemporaries called it, a solution to their various ills, so that the movement soon became something much wider than a protest by the samurai of Tosa and Hizen. In its composition and complexity it resembled rather the pre-Restoration loyalist movement, shorn of those who had achieved office in later years. There were even certain similarities of doctrine. The establishment of a constitution was urged as a means of controlling the emperor's advisers, not of limiting the emperor's power, and was justified as necessary for the attainment of unity in the face of foreign threat. There were echoes here of 'honour the emperor and expel the barbarian', betraying the authoritarian and military backgounds of those who were the movement's leaders. As a modern scholar has put it, 'a warrior spirit shone through the liberal garment'.[35]

Such ideas gave the demand for popular rights a certain colouring of respectability, but they did nothing to make it acceptable to the Meiji government, whose members were perfectly capable of recognizing an attack upon themselves, whatever the theoretical framework in which it was put. On the other hand, the argument about national unity was cogent and had a powerful advocate in Kido. During his travels abroad in 1872–3 he had been convinced that the creation of an elected assembly would be the best device for gaining widespread support for the government's objectives, a view which he strongly urged on his colleagues on returning to Japan. He added, however, that the time was not yet ripe for anything revolutionary. With this, at least, Okubo agreed, though he differed from Kido about the powers which an assembly should be given. The matter was accordingly passed to a committee for detailed study and nothing more was done till a draft was made ready for discussion. This was in 1878; and in the meantime major changes had taken place in the structure of government leadership. Kido had died in May 1877, Saigo and Okubo within the year thereafter, leaving Iwakura as the only survivor of the original senior group. Three younger men now joined him in the inner circle: Okuma Shigenobu of Hizen, Minister of Finance since 1873 and largely responsible for implementing the new taxation system; Ito Hirobumi of Choshu, in charge of Public Works during the same period and hence controlling much of the modernization programme; and Yamagata Aritomo, also of Choshu, chief architect of Japan's new army. It was these three, with Iwakura, who had to settle the matter of the constitution.

During the next two years, Ito, Yamagata and Iwakura reached agreement on a number of propositions. First, they recognized that there was a good deal of criticism in Japan concerning the government's actions. Second, they admitted that the creation of a popular assembly on Western lines would be the most effective means of preventing opposition from becoming dangerous. Third, they showed themselves determined that such an assembly should not be given the power to challenge their own control of policy, not, at least, until several years of training and experiment had provided it with a suitably amenable membership.

Okuma made no contribution to these decisions. He knew, as did the others, that the constitutional movement was rapidly gaining strength in the country, but it was not until March 1881 that he made his own views known. When he did so, it was as a move in his struggle for power with Ito. The two had long been rivals, with Okuma getting rather the better of the early exchanges and securing the more influential posts, but in 1878 Ito had succeeded Okubo in the key office of Home Affairs. With the help of Iwakura and the powerful Choshu faction, he showed every sign of becoming Okubo's successor in something more than name, a prospect that seems to have determined Okuma's subsequent actions. His memorandum of

March 1881 was an attempt to redress the balance by putting himself at the head of the popular rights movement and securing the type of constitution which would give the leader of the elected representatives—in anticipation, himself—real authority. This would involve, he said, party governments and a cabinet responsible to parliament in the English manner, matters far more important than a sterile analysis of forms. Moreover, he demanded early action: framing of a constitution in 1881, an announcement of it in 1882, the first elections in 1883.

Okuma's more conservative colleagues took up this challenge. His proposals were formally rejected in June; and when he responded by associating himself with public criticism of certain supposed scandals concerning the sale of government undertakings in Hokkaido, they decided to oust him from office altogether. This was done in October 1881 with the emperor's consent. Simultaneously, in an attempt to disarm opposition, especially that to be expected from Okuma, they announced that the decision to grant a constitution had been taken in principle and would be implemented in 1890. Meanwhile, the imperial edict warned, 'those who may advocate sudden and violent changes, thus disturbing the peace of Our realm, will fall under Our displeasure'.[36]

There were a good many who were prepared to run this risk. Within a few days, Itagaki and Goto had formed a political organization called the Jiyuto, or Liberal Party.[37] Before long Okuma followed suit with his Progressives, the Kaishinto. Both groups hoped to influence the drafting of the constitution and to prepare for the day when they could take advantage of its provisions. Yet in other respects they were most dissimilar. The Liberals were linked regionally with Tosa, ideologically with French radicalism, and drew most of their support from rural areas. The Progressives, by contrast, looked to the city, English liberalism, and Hizen, their nucleus being a number of disaffected bureaucrats and intelligentsia, backed by wealthy merchants and industrialists. Moderation was their watchword, though this did not save them from persecution. Both parties, in fact, soon found that the government's threats were seriously meant.

Some years before this the government had taken powers to

:ontrol or suppress expressions of opinion hostile to itself, especially those that appeared in the rapidly expanding daily press. The first Japanese newspapers, dating from the closing years of Tokugawa rule, had been noted for their lack of editorial comment, but this omission was soon repaired by their successors after 1868. Most, moreover, tended to be anti-government, like the *Mainichi* and Okuma's *Yubin Hochi*. It was partly for this reason, partly because journalistic standards were universally low, that the Press Law was enacted in 1875. It required that owner, editor and printer be registered; that all comment be signed and pen-names prohibited; and that the editor be held responsible for any subversive or slanderous articles published, including any matter that 'reviles existing laws, or confuses the sense of duty of the people to observe them'.[38] Penalties included imprisonment as well as fines and were imposed freely in the next two years. Then in July 1877 the law was revised to give the Home Minister even greater powers. Thereafter he had the right to prohibit or delay publication of any offending paper, a measure of authority that was used extensively to muzzle public discussion of the promised constitution.

In April 1880 the range of controls had been extended to include the activities of political parties and similar organizations. Political meetings were put under police supervision; members of the armed forces, police, teachers and students (whether in public or private schools) were forbidden to attend them; and associations formed for political ends were forbidden to advertise meetings, to solicit membership, and to combine or correspond with similar groups in other parts of the country. This might have seemed sufficiently comprehensive, but more was yet to come. In December 1887 the Peace Preservation Regulations were announced, again strengthening the hand of the police in suppressing secret societies and political associations. They were now authorized to 'exile' from the immediate area of the capital city any person plotting or inciting a disturbance, 'or who is judged to be scheming something detrimental to public tranquillity'[39]; while a few days later the Home Minister was given powers to suspend or prohibit the publication of books, periodicals and newspapers on pretexts that were equally flimsy.

Regulations of this kind were ostensibly of general application, but in practice they were directed against the advocates of parliamentary rule. Arrests, both of editors and politicians, became frequent. The effect was to discourage the faint-hearted and anger the extremists, thereby helping to emphasize differences within the opposition ranks; while the resulting disunity was accentuated by the ban on combination and correspondence, which prevented the political parties from becoming national organizations with centralized control, since they made it necessary for each local group of sympathizers to remain—at least legally—distinct. As a consequence, such groups tended under pressure to go their separate ways, tearing the movement to pieces as they did so.

It was the Jiyuto (Liberal Party) which suffered most severely. As leadership became local rather than national, so the conflict of interest between two of its elements, the landlords and the farmers, became more accute. For the political crisis coincided with the adoption of deflationary financial policies in 1881, which checked the rise in farm prices, especially of rice, and brought much hardship in the countryside, its impact being greatest on those with least reserves, namely, the tenants and poorer owner-cultivators. Friction between them and the relatively wealthy landlords had in any case been growing throughout the century, as the commercialization of agriculture tended more and more to thin the ranks of the middle farmers, enriching a few, impoverishing most; and the process quickened after the reforms in land tenure and land tax during the years 1871-3. In the past, the peasant's ultimate appeal in such a situation had been to force. This, however, was becoming increasingly difficult as the state, now provided with modern police and a conscript army, gained strength. Accordingly, many farmers had found an outlet for their discontent through support for the new political parties, looking to them for redress much as they had done—briefly—to the anti-Tokugawa movement fifteen years before. But this time the government proved stronger than its opponents. When this became apparent, the more desperate turned once more to violence, directed, as it had nearly always been, against the nearest enemy, the village landlord. Riots of this kind became widespread in 1884, the immediate effect being to alarm most landlords, as well as moderate samurai leaders, into with-drawing from the organization in whose name much of this activity was being carried on. This was the final blow, bringing formal dissolution of the Jiyuto in October 1884. Okuma and several of his friends left the Kaishinto soon after.

Thus the government's efforts to weaken its opponents by censorship and police action clearly paid good dividends. They were not, however, its only recourse. Apart from an unsuc-cessful and short-lived attempt to create a government party, the Teiseito, it also developed a more constructive policy aimed at establishing new political institutions. This was designed partly to consolidate the hold which the ruling group had already secured over the principal organs of the state. Yet it was also a continuation of the progressive centralization of authority which had begun with the abolition of feudalism, training the people, in Ito's words, 'to extend their vision beyond the pale of their village communities, to look upon the affairs of their districts and prefectures as their own, until finally they could interest themselves in the affairs of state and nation as strongly as, or even more strongly than, in the affairs of their own villages'.[40]

It is convenient to look first at the administrative aspects of this process, which had given evidence of the oligarchy's intentions even before Okuma had challenged it in 1881. When the domains were abolished in 1872 they had been re-named prefectures (*ken*), making, with those already formed from the Tokugawa lands, 302 in all, in addition to the three cities (*fu*) of Tokyo, Kyoto and Osaka, which were separate local govern-ment areas. At the beginning of 1872 the prefectural boun-daries were re-drawn and their total number reduced to 72 (dropping to 45 by 1890). In them, during the next few years, a system of local officialdom was gradually built up, codified in November 1875 by the issue of regulations defining the titles, functions and authority of its members. The range of their activities was wide. It included: supervision of shrines and temples; maintaining schools and public buildings; control of patents and copyright; tax re-assessment after local calamities; reclamation of forest land; riparian and harbour works; the maintenance of roads and bridges; census returns and land registration. Most important of all was the fact that the

prefectural governor had control of the police and was therefore responsible for carrying out the various laws against
political association.

This system of local administration was tied to the central
government through its subordination to the Home Ministry,
established in November 1873. In view of the strong tradition
of provincial autonomy inherited from feudalism, it was at first
necessary to provide specifically for the ministry's right to
intervene in local matters, but under Okubo's strong guidance
this phase did not last long. By 1876 the prefectural authorities
not only looked to Tokyo for appointment, but had also been
made subject to a system of rewards and punishments. They
thus became part of a national bureaucracy which depended
for its power on central, not local, connections and drew its
personnel from a variety of sources: former samurai officials of
the domains, including those of the Tokugawa; Japanese who
despite relatively low birth had acquired special knowledge
by travel or study abroad; and some, though they were few as
yet, who qualified by possession of commercial and industrial
expertise. That most were ex-samurai reflected the limited
educational opportunities of the old order as much as it did
the prejudices of the new. What is more, despite the assertions
of the government's critics, it does not appear that the men of
Satsuma and Choshu had any overwhelming advantage, except
at the very top. For the majority, the determining factors were
ability, experience and loyalty, not geography or inherited
status.

Under Ito's influence, bureaucratic practice was reduced to
written rule. In December 1880 regulations were issued for the
conduct of business in the chief ministries: Foreign Affairs,
Home Affairs, Finance, Army, Navy, Education, Public Works,
Justice, and Imperial Household. The powers and duties of
the minister and his subordinates were defined and those matters listed in which the Council's authority was needed before
action could be taken. Nevertheless, this did not prevent
the re-appearance of administrative abuses which had been a
familiar feature of the Tokugawa period. There were some new
ones, too. Lack of a proper budgeting procedure and of a
fixed establishment in the lower ranks enabled men to put their
friends on the pay-roll, increasing the government's salary bill

by 60 per cent between 1873 and 1884 without any commensurate increase in work done. Indeed, the work done seemed to grow less, as government business became submerged in a sea of paper. Insistence on centralized control involved constant appeals from juniors to seniors, bringing delays, a loss of confidence and initiative, a proliferation of memoranda. All these points were made by Ito in a circular to departmental heads in December 1885. He called on them to remedy the faults and re-impose a proper discipline. Two months later came a new set of civil service regulations, designed to close the loopholes he had noted. They created a system of examinations to decide appointments and promotion; prescribed the limits of departmental budgets; laid down with precision the number of posts to be filled; and dealt with a host of details concerning the keeping of archives and accounts, such as the issue of warrants to authorize payment, the use of entry books, the numbering of letters, the circulation and approval of drafts. One may question whether this was the best way of restoring a sense of responsibility to individual members of the government machine. Nevertheless, there is no doubt that it took Japan a step nearer to being a modern state.

So did the other institutional changes of these years, those which involved advisory and policy-making organs. In July 1884 a new peerage was established, providing for five ranks, those of prince, marquis, count, viscount and baron. The new titles were not territorial—a further departure from the feudal pattern—but of the 500 created in the first instance all but about thirty went to families of the old nobility. Sanjo and Iwakura were made princes, the latter posthumously, since he had died in 1883, while Okubo and Kido, also posthumously, were given the rank of marquis. Of more direct importance were the counts, whose numbers included fourteen members of the ruling oligarchy, mostly ex-samurai. Among them were Ito and Yamagata. Of the viscounts, twelve (out of 321) were generals and admirals of the new armed forces. Thus rewards were granted sparingly. Still that very fact made them the more impressive and helped to reconcile the former ruling class to the intrusion of powerful upstarts. It also underlined the dangers of nonconformity. Goto, Itagaki and Okuma had done as much as any to deserve recognition in the early days of the Restoration, but their names were pointedly omitted from the list of honours.

Another step was taken in December 1885, at the same time as Ito's move to reform the civil service. This was the creation of a cabinet on European lines to replace the Executive Council (Dajokan), with its unwieldy mechanism for controlling the administration. Ostensibly this was intended to increase efficiency by making it clear where the responsibility for any major decision rested. In practice it marked the open emergence of Ito to a dominant position, giving him as Premier powers of overall supervision, while the eight ministers who made up his cabinet were each responsible only for their own departments.

Both the peerage and the cabinet were important as preliminaries to the granting of a constitution, the former because it made possible an Upper House with a well-nigh handpicked membership, the latter because it established in advance the principle that ministers were responsible to the Throne, not to an elected legislature. The coping-stone was set on this edifice by the creation of a Privy Council in April 1888. It was to be the highest advisory body of the state, consulted, among other things, on all matters pertaining to the interpretation or revision of a constitution. Since appointments to it were controlled by the existing government and it was forbidden to receive petitions from the public, there was little chance of it succumbing to opposition pressure. In the circumstances it seemed a work of supererogation to provide that 'it shall not interfere with the executive'.[41]

Nothing, in fact, was to be allowed to interfere with the executive, least of all the elected representatives of the people. This had first been made clear in the local assemblies, created for prefectures in 1878 and for towns and cities two years later, in which electoral rights were limited to substantial citizens and business was restricted to debate. Officialdom, in the persons of the local governor and the Home Minister, retained the power to initiate bills, to veto recommendations, and to suspend or dissolve an assembly's sittings, a degree of authority which the government hoped to secure for itself over any national legislature created at a later date. This ambition was made manifest in the outline constitutional provisions which

Ito and Iwakura worked out in the summer of 1881. They were embodied in a memorandum by Iwakura in July and accepted by the inner council in October, thus providing an unpublished but authoritative sketch of what was meant by the promise that the emperor would grant a constitution: a cabinet responsible to the emperor; a bicameral assembly with an elected lower house, but without the right to initiate legislation or, in the last resort, to deny the government money; and an electorate based on a property qualification. Despite Iwakura's death in 1883 this plan was closely followed.

In March 1882 Ito left on a visit to Europe which was to last almost eighteen months. His avowed aim was to study European constitutions with a view to advising the emperor concerning that which was to be issued in Japan, but, as we have seen, he was already fairly sure what it was he wanted. Accordingly, he went straight to Berlin and Vienna, where he expected to find it, and only later paid visits to Paris and London, whose traditions were alien to his purpose. Most of his time was spent studying under men like Rudolph Gneist and Lorenz von Stein, whose views confirmed Ito's existing predilections and were later injected directly into the drafting of the constitution by two German participants, Alfred Mosse and Hermann Roessler. A brief excursion into the theory of parliamentary government under the guidance of Herbert Spencer did little to reduce the predominantly German tone of the expedition.

For some time after his return to Japan Ito was preoccupied with establishing the peerage, cabinet and civil service, so that it was not until 1886 that detailed work was started on the constitution itself. When it was, the discussions were held in secret and under Ito's personal supervision, mostly in the Imperial Household Ministry and at Ito's summer residence. Thus it is not surprising that the pace was leisurely, little affected by the occasional outbursts of popular agitation. Nor is it to be wondered at that the principles observed did not differ fundamentally from those laid down in 1881, since only men of Ito's own choosing had any part in the deliberations. Indeed, the document laid before the Privy Council in May 1888 and promulgated at a short private ceremony within the palace on February 11, 1889, might well be described as little more than an expansion of the points originally made by Iwakura. Certainly it perpetuated the authoritarian tradition, begun by Okubo, which came naturally to men who had spent their youth under a form of feudal autocracy. To the oligarchs, after all, the prime object was to create a strong Japan. Effective government was an essential part of this process, as was the suppression of opposition, which was seditious because it might weaken. To quote Ito again, the administration had to be safeguarded against 'the onslaught of extremely democratic ideas, which showed symptoms of impatience at every form of administrative activity, whether justifiable or not—for, in such a country as ours, it was evident that it would be necessary to compensate for its smallness of size and population by a compact solidity of organization and the efficiency of its administrative activity'.[42]

Such arguments, as embodied in the constitutional provisions, did not appeal greatly to the political parties, which had been revived in anticipation of the document being put into effect. Many powers were reserved to the emperor, to be exercised in fact by his advisers, including declaration of war, conclusion of treaties and supreme command of the armed services. In addition, the emperor had extensive ordinance rights, while he could freely adjourn or prorogue the assembly, which was to be called the Diet. As regards finance, some important items of regular expenditure were excluded from the Diet's consideration altogether. More significant, it was laid down that should the assembly fail to pass the budget the government was entitled to carry out the budget of the previous year. Thus parliamentary control went no farther than the right to deny new taxes; and though this could be a potent weapon in harassing a cabinet, as the next few years were to show, it did not provide a sufficient means of exercising influence over general policy. What is more, it was by no means certain that the lower house could even control the policies of the Diet. The House of Peers, after all, had equal authority with it and a membership that tended naturally to support the regime. When one adds to this the fact that the initiative for constitutional revision could come only from the emperor, there seemed little chance that the political parties would be able to secure real power.

On the other hand, although the Meiji Constitution imposed serious disabilities on any opposition, it did not follow that these must prove enduring. Other men at other times and places had faced institutional obstacles just as great and had overcome them. It is true that there was bound to be a struggle in Japan between parties which upheld the principles of parliamentary rule and oligarchs who believed in government that was 'transcendental', that is, above sectional interests and therefore above party; but in that struggle, victory would go to the side which was stronger. It was not certain that this would be the side which the constitution favoured. Only when the Diet opened, in fact, would the time of testing begin, to see whether Ito's judgment as a politician equalled his skill as a constitutional draftsman.

As a preliminary, Yamagata Aritomo became Premier in December 1889, supported by Ito, though the latter was not a member of the cabinet. In the following July they carried out the first elections for the lower house. Only about 500,000 electors were qualified to vote (out of a population of forty million), but most of them did so and proceedings were generally orderly. Less successful, from the government's point of view, were the returns. Goto's party gained sixty seats and those of Itagaki and Okuma fifty each, while many of the 140 independents who made up the rest of the representatives were equally hostile to the administration. The result was a clash as soon as the session opened in November, with the Diet demanding heavy cuts in the budget and accepting a compromise only after Yamagata had made extensive use of threats and bribery. In the interval between sessions, Yamagata handed over to Matsukata Masayoshi, famous as Minister of Finance since 1881, but this did nothing to save the next budget. Matsukata was forced to dissolve the Lower House in December 1891 without having got it through.

The elections of February 1892 were notorious for the government's attempt to use the police to dictate the voting, an attempt which left twenty-five dead and nearly 400 injured to mark the campaign. Nor did it in any way reduce the Diet's hostility to the men in office. The session, which started in May, was as stormy as ever and brought Matsukata's resignation, Ito following him as Premier in August, with Yamagata at the Ministry of Justice. They in their turn were faced with a vote of impeachment in February 1893. Ito now tried a new technique: direct imperial intervention on the cabinet's behalf, which worked for the moment, but did not save him from having to seek a dissolution in December. The resulting election was held in March 1894; the session opened in May; and the Lower House was dissolved again at the beginning of June. It began to look as if the constitution was unworkable altogether.

Yet the frequent clashes were slowly tending to the government's advantage. Elections were expensive and their constant repetition cured many politicians of a taste for electioneering. Moreover, party leaders were becoming convinced that the deadlock could not be broken in the Diet's favour. This implied that it might be in their own interests to seek a compromise with those in power; and as ex-oligarchs they would not find it difficult to do so. Goto, indeed, had held a cabinet post for the past three years. Ito, for his part—though over Yamagata's protests—was willing to conclude an alliance with them, in the hope of securing votes for the government in the Lower House without sacrificing its ultimate control of policy. He had actually begun discussions with Itagaki on this basis in 1893 and within a year or two was to consider forming a party of his own. Thus events were moving towards a new phase, one in which the Diet was to become the scene of a struggle, not between parties and government, but between party and party, with office, though not power, as the prize. Adversity and self-seeking, in fact, had broken the unity of the constitutional movement. It was not until the twentieth century that social and economic change was to give the political parties fresh sources of strength and thereby revive their will to challenge the established order. Before turning to this part of the story, hower, it is desirable that we should examine other aspects of Meiji history to see how Ito and his colleagues used the authority they gained.

CHAPTER VIII

MODERNIZATION 1873-1894

Reorganization of army and navy—law—national education system—agricultural development—transport—state factories —textiles—knowledge of the West

---

ON JANUARY 1, 1873, a new calendar was brought into force in Japan: the Gregorian calendar, as used in western Europe, which replaced the lunar calendar originally derived from China. The change affected much that was familiar. Dates for festivals, the beginning of the four seasons, the New Year itself, all now fell on different days. The farmer had to learn new designations for his times of planting and harvesting, the merchant for his debt-collecting, the priest for his ceremonials. Even though many preferred to go on using the old system side by side with the new, the decision had repercussions which struck deep into Japanese life. Equally, it symbolized an important aspect of the government's policy, its determination to turn away from the traditional and towards the modern, away from China and towards the West, at least in those matters on which the building of a powerful and well respected state depended. The policy was not entirely new, either in concept or in method. Nevertheless, the Meiji leaders gave it a breadth and drive that were to revolutionize society. Indeed, by 1904 they had transformed a backward, largely feudal, Japan into one which was capable of winning a modern war, an achievement that made them the envy of all Asia.

Some of the foundations for it had been laid before the Restoration. For several generations Japanese scholars had been studying the West, especially its military science, and after Perry's arrival their efforts had received official support. In 1855 the Tokugawa council established a bureau for the translation of foreign books. In 1860 it sent its first students abroad to study, attaching them to a diplomatic mission to the United States, an example which was followed, whenever opportunity offered, by a few of the great domains, though for the latter it was action which had sometimes to be taken illegally and hence in secret. Moreover, natural curiosity soon extended the field of interest to include geography, politics, economics and much else, so that by 1868 Japan had already at her disposal a nucleus of men trained in Western skills. Others had acquired experience at home, running the Western-style plants which had been set up in different areas—the Saga cannon foundry, a cotton-spinning factory at Kagoshima and several more—or learning to navigate and maintain the steamers which their feudal lords had purchased. It was the existence of such men, most of them young, that made modernization possible.

Equally important were the qualities of leadership shown by the Meiji government. Its members, as we have seen, were convinced that their country was in danger of foreign attack, that it could be saved only by strong rule and an efficient military machine. To achieve these quickly was therefore the task to which all other considerations were made subordinate. Ideas of social welfare were never allowed to divert policy from the chosen ends. Opposition that threatened those ends was crushed. It is true that political and personal ambition played a part in this, but it was not a controlling part: the oligarchs, as their record shows, were patriots as well as politicians. And they were capable of a surprising degree of detachment in their patriotism, a ruthlessness in sacrificing the picturesque to the efficient which offended traditionalists at the time and has provoked critics since. It mattered little to Okubo and Iwakura and their like that a foreign observer in 1868 described their troops as 'horribly untidy soldiers'.[43] It mattered much that the soldiers were winning a civil war. A similarly pragmatic outlook was to govern their attitude towards telegraph wires, railway lines and factory chimneys, however much these might be thought to mar the beauty of a Japanese landscape.

Politics came first in the regime's calculations because it was on this that all else depended. Thus the earliest reforms were directed towards increasing the government's authority: the abolition of feudalism, new methods of taxation, even the improved communications which were developed by the Department of Public Works in 1871-3. Other aspects of modernization, too, had a political function. The conscript army, for instance, provided a loyal force capable of quelling unrest at home, as it demonstrated in 1877 with the defeat of Saigo's rebels. It was also used to end the peasant revolts to which Japan had been subject for over a century and it later became a means of indoctrinating a substantial number of young men in their duties to an authoritarian state.

All the same, the army's main role was to defend Japan against a possible enemy attack. Already in the late Tokugawa period feudal rulers had done what they could to prepare for this, with the result that the new government inherited some useful military establishments, a number of gunnery and naval specialists, and a varied knowledge of Western military techniques. There was an arsenal at Osaka and a naval dockyard at Yokosuka. There was a valuable fund of experience gained when the Bakufu, albeit belatedly, had tried to reorganize its army under the tutelage of France; more still derived from the experiments of Satsuma and Choshu, the first in the creation of a naval squadron, the second in arming and training a land force in the European manner. Against this background, it is not surprising that military reform was given high priority in the Meiji government's plans. This was so even in the early days, when preoccupations were political, and its importance increased as the danger of successful insurrection passed. More and more, attention was concentrated on Japan's ability to fight a foreign war.

In 1878 Yamagata carried out a reorganization of army administration on German lines, including the creation of a General Staff, and in the following year increased the period which a conscript had to serve in the reserves. He raised it again in 1883 to make a total of twelve years' service, three of which were with the colours. This provided a peacetime establishment of 73,000 men and a total wartime strength of 200,000 more, the whole force being equipped by 1894 with modern rifles and artillery, mostly of Japanese manufacture. The decade after 1883 also saw the opening of a Staff College;

greater specialization of function (infantry, artillery, engineers, supply); an improvement in training methods; and a sharp rise in the army budget.

The navy shared in the expansion, too, though its growth relied more on foreign help. In 1872 the newly-formed Navy Ministry had possessed seventeen ships, totalling almost 14,000 tons, of which only two were ironclads. Two Japanese-built steamers of moderate size were added in 1875-6, three much larger vessels were bought from England in 1878, and further building or buying programmes were announced in 1882, 1886 and 1892. At the outbreak of war with China in 1894 the fleet included twenty-eight modern ships, aggregating 57,000 tons, plus twenty-four torpedo-boats. Dockyard facilities were by that time sufficient for full repairs and maintenance, while training was thoroughly up-to-date. What is more, Japan was able to make her own torpedoes and quick-firing guns.

All this is evidence of a strong military emphasis in the government's policies, confirmed by the fact that at the end of the period one-third of the national budget was being spent on the army and navy. Military industry was kept under close official control, as were other installations that had a military use, like the telegraph system. Telephones were made a government monopoly when they were introduced for public use in 1890, while the railways, about 30 per cent of which were government-built, were nationalized in 1906 to ensure their proper development for strategic purposes. In other words, one is conscious of military considerations underlying many phases of the modernization process.

Yet modernization was by no means confined to things political and military. It extended also to the law, to education, to the economy and much else, affecting in the end almost every part of Japanese society. Indeed, it is the very comprehensiveness of reform that justifies the application of the label 'modernization' to it. China, after all, also adopted something of the West's military methods in the nineteenth century and learned to use the telegraph and railways, but the Chinese did not thereby achieve a revolution in their way of life. That the Japanese did so was due in large measure to the readiness of their leaders to reform radically and fundamentally in every field. For this they had to be imaginative as well as ruthless.

Some changes stemmed from a desire to achieve respectability in Western eyes, this being a step on the road to full equality. For example, the Iwakura mission had learnt in 1872–3 that neither America nor the European powers would contemplate revising the legal provisions of the existing treaties—those which put foreign residents in Japan exclusively under the jurisdiction of their own consuls—until they were convinced that Japan's judicial practice was up to Western standards; and recognition of this fact brought a complex series of law reforms, largely under foreign guidance, which lasted twenty-five years. They began at the end of 1873 with the appointment of a French lawyer, Gustave Boissonade de Fontarabie, as adviser to the Ministry of Justice. In this capacity he at once set about drafting a criminal code based on elements of Japanese feudal law and the Code Napoléon of 1810, the draft being completed in 1877, reviewed at length by the politicians, then promulgated so as to come into force at the beginning of 1882. His proposals for a civil code, however, had a rougher passage. The first version was rejected in 1878 as being too French and it took a series of committees twelve more years to produce something to the government's satisfaction. Even so, the code's promulgation in 1890 aroused a storm of protest, led by those who had been trained in English law, with the result that the Diet voted to postpone the date of its enforcement. A similar fate overtook most sections of the new commercial code, which had been devised under Hermann Roessler's supervision in the period 1881–90. Both documents were therefore reviewed again and did not receive final approval until 1898–9, when they were submitted in a form which revealed signs of increasing German influence.

Some provisions of the new legal system, such as the abolition of torture, the creation of a trained judiciary and the setting out of rules of evidence and procedure for the courts, were generally admitted to be necessary, but there were many who felt that in matters affecting property and the family the codes had departed too far from Japanese tradition. Much of the political excitement concerning this subject in and after 1890 was due to feelings of this kind. Similar hostility was also aroused from time to time by other results of government sensitivity to foreign views, especially where these were aimed at achieving a degree of social respectability in Western eyes. Often the action taken was thought to be trivial or degrading, like the holding of balls for the diplomatic corps or the use of Western dress at Court. Often it was merely alien and inexplicable. Thus the attempts which were made to prevent mixed bathing in Tokyo's public bathhouses, to establish censorship of stage jokes, to prohibit the sale of pornographic art—of which a great amount had been produced in the Tokugawa era—and in other ways to provide an atmosphere which Victorians might find congenial, met with little sympathy or understanding among large sections of the Japanese public. As a result the government's efforts were not entirely successful. As late as 1907 there were still pitfalls for the sensitive and unwary traveller, as witness this passage from a tourist handbook of that year:

'Europeans usually avail themselves of the first-class railway cars whenever such are provided, and ladies in particular are recommended to do so, as . . . the ways of the Japanese *bourgeoisie* with regard to clothing, the management of children, and other matters are not altogether as our ways.'[44]

There is no doubt that in these social matters Japanese officials were under some pressure from foreign missionaries and other residents. Many foreigners, however, also offered help and advice in fields where it was better received and more effectively carried out. This was notable in education, where much that was new in both content and administration derived from foreign advisers, and much that was taught depended on American and European teachers. Nevertheless, it was the Japanese themselves, in the last resort, who had to make the system work. For their success in doing so, the credit must be shared: by the Meiji government, because of its energy and farsightedness; and by members of the ruling class as a whole, in whom an essentially Confucian training had bred a respect for learning that was reflected, *inter alia*, in an enthusiasm for the founding and running of schools.

The government's plans, as announced in September 1872, envisaged dividing Japan into eight educational regions, in each of which there were to be one university and thirty-two secondary schools. Each secondary school district, in turn, was to include 210 primary schools—one for every 600 of the population—where all children after reaching the age of six were to receive sixteen months of compulsory education. The scheme was ambitious, almost too ambitious for a country that had abolished feudalism only a year before, but progress under it was astonishingly rapid. By 1880 there were 28,000 primary schools with over 2 million pupils (about 40 per cent of the children of school age) and it had become possible to increase the compulsory period to three years. In 1886 attendance was 46 per cent and the period was increased again, by a further year. Thereafter, attendance continued steadily to rise. It was 60 per cent by 1895, 90 per cent by 1900, 95 per cent in 1906. In the same period secondary education was becoming specialized, with the creation of normal schools (1872), middle schools (1881), higher middle schools (1886) and girls high schools (1889). To complete the pyramid, various government institutions of higher education, which had been amalgamated in 1877, were reorganized as Tokyo Imperial University in 1886.

A key part in this development was played by Mori Arinori, a former member of the Iwakura mission, who was Minister of Education from 1885 to 1889. It was his ordinances, issued in the spring of 1886, that gave the system the shape it was to retain for twenty years: an eight-year period of primary schooling, half of it compulsory, involving attendance for five hours a day, six days a week; a middle school course of four years with similar hours; then a range of higher levels, reaching to the newly-created university. He also ensured close government control, thereby confirming a tendency that had existed since 1880. From this time on, the Ministry prescribed all textbooks, while exercising general supervision of the schools through the workings of local government, that is, by its influence with the town and village authorities to whom the details of administration were entrusted. Private foundations were made subject to official licence and inspection. Thus the whole of education was made subservient to the state's own needs, providing on the one hand a practical training, through a curriculum on Western lines, on the other a moral education based on Confucian ethics and an emperor-centred nationalism. Together the two elements were to produce good citizens:

good in that they were loyal to the regime; and good in that they had acquired the basic skills which modern life demanded.

In the twentieth century this education system was to prove an essential unifying force in the Japanese body politic. It was also fundamental to the emergence and full development of an industrial society. In the earlier stages of economic growth, however, such as took place in the years before 1894, education was less vital than other features of government policy, those that were directly designed to stimulate the increase of national wealth. It is to this aspect of Meiji history—a new and more sophisticated application of the slogan *fukoku-kyohei*, 'rich country, strong army'—that Japan owed most of her initial success.

Economic modernization began, not with the factory, but with the farm. To men who had begun life as feudal retainers, it was axiomatic that land was the chief source of government revenue and that the encouragement of production on it was the first task of an official. The difference was that they could now draw on the experience and technology of the West, as well as of Japan. They lost no time in doing so. Agricultural students were sent abroad; foreign experts were invited to advise on specific projects, such as the opening up of land in the island of Hokkaido; new strains of plants and seeds were imported; Western farming implements were bought and tried. All this was done on government initiative, sometimes with more fervour than understanding. Attempts to plant vineyards and introduce sheep-farming, for example, were among the early failures. By contrast, the innovations in irrigation and the use of fertilizers proved generally successful, while the greatest advances of all in the long term were achieved by the founding of experimental stations and agricultural colleges. The most famous of them were established in Hokkaido in 1876 and in Tokyo in 1877, but others soon appeared throughout the country. The results of their work, moreover, were made widely available by travelling instructors, appointed to advise farmers on new techniques.

In some ways agriculture was little changed by these developments. Plots remained small—just over an acre was a typical holding—and cultivation remained intensive, for these things were part of the fundamental pattern: Japan's villages had little land, much labour, and grew rice as their staple crop. On the other hand, the commercialization of agriculture, which had begun under the Tokugawa, increased with the removal of feudal controls, thereby bringing still greater concentration in landholding and a steady growth of tenancy. About 40 per cent of the land was held by tenants in 1890, compared with an estimated 20 per cent at the time of the Restoration; and since rents were high and paid in kind, half the crop being a not uncommon rent for rice paddy, the change brought much distress in rural areas. All the same, it cannot be claimed that the village as a whole suffered a decline in standards. Total rice yield grew over 30 per cent between 1880 and 1894, partly because the area under cultivation was enlarged, but mostly because new farming methods gave a 20 per cent increase in yield per acre. Lesser crops, like wheat and barley, showed a similar improvement. As a consequence, agricultural production not only kept pace with a considerable growth in population, but also made possible an increase in *per capita* rice consumption, which rose in the same period from four bushels a year to five. This was a national gain, not a merely rural one, but one can hardly suppose that the countryside did not share it. Indeed, since there was no substantial price move against farm products, landlords and owner-occupiers, if not tenants, can be said to have enjoyed a measure of prosperity.

Apart from cereals, economic change also affected other items to which the Japanese farmer looked for income. In coastal villages, where farming was often combined with fishing, better boats and equipment tipped the scales in favour of the latter and eventually—after 1900—made fishery a major industry. Elsewhere, greater demand for cotton textiles and the growth of a native spinning industry brought a steady increase in the quantity of cotton grown. By 1887 Japan was almost self-sufficient in it. However, imports tended to rise thereafter as competition came from India, and by the end of the century home production had dropped sharply on this account. Of the cottage industries, some, notably the spinning, reeling and weaving processes for textiles, declined at about the same time, unable to compete with the price and quality of factory-made materials. A modest call for handicrafts like fans and lanterns gave some compensation, but it was silk, above all, that now became the farmer's stand-by. An export market was first created for it in the 1860s because of silkworm disease in Europe. Subsequently the high quality of the Japanese product maintained and expanded the demand, so that more and more families entered the business, while increased scale made possible a number of technical improvements. By the nineties, even double-cropping was becoming common, giving a summer-autumn crop as well as one in spring. As a result, annual production of raw silk easily topped a million *kan* in 1900 (1 *kan* = 8·27 lbs.), as against 278,000 *kan* in 1868 and 457,000 in 1883. Exports, at an annual average of 27 million yen[45] for the years 1889–93, accounted for a third of Japan's export trade by value.

These figures give some idea of the importance of agriculture to the country. And one could easily add more. For example, agriculture was, and long remained, Japan's commonest occupation: something like three-quarters of the population earned their living by it in 1872 and a fraction over half did so as late as 1920. Moreover, it provided about 80 per cent of total tax revenue up to 1880, still over 60 per cent in 1894. This made it as much a factor in the formulation of government policy as it was in the daily life of the Japanese people. Indeed, it is clear that industrialization itself could not have been achieved so quickly—even, perhaps, at all—had it not been for the rise in agricultural productivity and the changes associated with it. The increase in rural cash incomes created a home market which was essential to industrial growth. Equally important, the poverty and large families of the tenant-farmers drove cheap labour from the village to the towns. Finally, agricultural exports paid for much of the industrial machinery and materials that had to be bought abroad, while agricultural taxes became capital that the government could invest.

That the government chose by its taxation policy to penalize the farmer to the advantage of the merchant and industrialist is further evidence of the determination it showed in pursuing its ends. The decision was not without risk, as the constant unrest in rural areas showed. Yet it was a necessary one, if the non-agricultural sector of the economy were to be developed. This was a matter in which the Meiji leaders had little choice, unless they were prepared to abandon their international and political ambitions, for high population density—already in 1868 some 2,000 persons to the square mile of cultivated land —put limits on agricultural development, while other factors, such as good sea communications and nearby Asian markets to be exploited, promised advantages for industry and trade. All the same, it is doubtful whether such considerations were decisive in Japanese thinking, however much they may have been determinants of success. More compelling was the belief, to which foreigners themselves so obviously subscribed, that trade and industry were the pillars on which Western greatness rested. The spirit of emulation, if nothing else, drew Japan towards them.

In many ways the Meiji government contributed usefully to their development by policies that were not specifically directed to that end. The abolition of feudalism gave freedom of occupation to millions of peasant families, thus making possible the emergence of a mobile labour force; and the breaking down of local separatism, to which it also led, completed the process of creating a national market. Thereafter, by maintaining political order and financial stability, by ensuring security of property and person, the politicians provided an environment which was favourable to all forms of economic growth. The new communications network, too, had economic as well as administrative value. But in addition to all this, the government took steps to foster the particular kinds of activity of which it approved. By engaging in foreign trade on its own account it obtained funds to import goods and machinery, lending some of them to local authorities to serve as models for Japanese manufacturers, selling others on an instalment plan to those who needed capital equipment. It organized trade fairs, set up technical schools, sent students for training to Europe and America. Foreign instructors, advisers and engineers were brought in to run a number of the new concerns and train the technicians who were to run them in the future, as many as 130 being employed by the Department of Public Works alone by 1879. Official policy, however, was to replace them as soon as possible by Japanese, whose salaries were smaller, an attitude which led one British resident to observe that 'the Japanese only look upon foreigners as schoolmasters. As long as they cannot help themselves they make use of them; and then they send them about their business. . . .'[46] It was precisely this, of course, that eventually made Japan's industrial technology self-sustaining, in contrast to that of other Asian countries, which remained for the most part dependent on foreign help.

Another vital field of government action was the provision of capital in those sections of the economy where private investment was slow in coming. Much of the accumulated wealth of Tokugawa merchants—which was in any case too small, because of the restricted nature of their operations, to have financed the modernization programme on its own—had been put to use in various financial and commercial schemes of the Bakufu or domains and had therefore been lost when those institutions were destroyed. Much else was invested in usury or land, outlets that continued, because of high rents and interest rates, to attract a large proportion of the country's savings. By comparison industrial ventures, involving greater risks and slow returns, seemed best avoided. Even the private capital created by the commutation of samurai stipends in 1876, often in substantial units, found its way mostly into banking rathei than industry, while such investors as did turn to the latter were inclined, at least in the early stages, to put their money into businesses that were small-scale and relatively familiar, like handicrafts or textiles. As a result, plans needing heavy, long-term investment had usually to depend on state finance.

This can be seen in the history of modern transport. Coastal shipping was the easiest form to develop, both for geographical reasons and because it had become the commonest means for the bulk movement of goods in the Tokugawa period, so that some of the necessary commercial facilities and organization already existed. There were even one or two Western-style shipyards, built before the Restoration at places like Uraga and Nagasaki. Hence the main need was for better ships; and this was met partly by using those which had originally been bought from foreigners by various feudal lords, partly by government help to some outstanding entrepreneurs of the Meiji era. The former Tosa samurai, Iwasaki Yataro, whose firm became known as Mitsubishi in 1873, is a notable example.

He began with a few ships acquired from his domain at its dissolution. Soon after he absorbed another concern, operating between Tokyo and Osaka; he ran (and then took over) vessels bought by the government for use as military transports; and he established a foreign service, with routes to Hong Kong (1879) and Vladivostock (1881). In 1885 his line amalgamated with some of its rivals in the coastal trade to form the Nippon Yusen Kaisha (NYK), with fifty-eight ships totalling 65,000 tons. Dividends were guaranteed by the state at 8 per cent for fifteen years. Moreover, like others in the business, the company continued to receive subsidies, mail contracts and similar forms of government help, accepting in return government supervision of its routes and operations.

In railway building, a quite new form of enterprise, the role of government was at first much greater. It controlled all construction up to 1877, by which date three short sections of the planned Tokyo-Kobe line had been completed: those between Tokyo and Yokohama (1872), Kobe and Osaka (1874), Osaka and Kyoto (1877). The slow progress was due in part to political unrest, in part to lack of experience, but after the Satsuma Rebellion work speeded up, with private companies also beginning to participate. The latter, indeed, soon owned more mileage than the government. From 130 miles in 1885 they expanded to over 1,500 miles ten years later, while government track in the same period increased only from 220 to 580 miles. At this stage, the main line ran along the Pacific coast from Aomori in the north to Kobe on the Inland Sea, with plans already made for extending it to Nagasaki. A spur had also been built across the mountains from Tokyo to Naoetsu. Since freight traffic was heavy and profits high, the investors who had followed the state's lead in putting capital into these lines, mostly former samurai and feudal lords, found themselves well rewarded.

The development of manufacturing industry followed a similar pattern: of state initiative at first and private investment later, with the year 1881 marking a watershed between the two. In the first phase government activity took the form of establishing and operating factories, some of them designed as models to encourage the introduction of new techniques, some to fill needs which, though important, were unlikely to be a source of profit. Thus silk-reeling plants of the French and Italian type were opened at Tomioka and Maebashi in 1870, in order to stimulate the export trade by standardizing quality. A cement works was established in 1872, partly to reduce expensive imports at a time of trade imbalance. The manufacture of tiles, glass and chemicals was also started. Modern cotton-spinning was introduced in the Nagoya area in 1878, this with the double object of diverting traditional skills into new channels and providing employment in a region which had been badly hit by foreign competition, while other attempts to simulate regional development brought, for example, a brewery and a sugar factory to Hokkaido. Altogether such government-owned concerns numbered fifty-two by 1880, to say nothing of three shipyards, ten mines and five munitions works.

The cost of investment in these various undertakings was considerable, averaging more than 5 per cent of ordinary revenue for the years 1868–80. Heavy expenses were also incurred towards the end of the period for the payment of samurai stipends and suppression of the Satsuma Revolt, so that the Treasury's problems, complicated by a drain of specie arising from the persistent excess of imports over exports, began to seem alarming. By the late 'seventies recourse to further note issues had brought inflation, despite an expanding economy's greater need for cash. The value of government paper dropped sharply. Rice prices jumped from Y5·7 per *koku* in 1877 to Y9·4 in 1879, Y12·2 in 1880. Farmers found the change much to their advantage; but for the government it had serious implications, since it not only reduced the real revenue to be obtained from land tax, but also put in jeopardy the income which ex-samurai received from bonds, thereby adding to their discontent. The crisis, in fact, was political as well as financial and was grave enough on both counts to endanger the regime.

In the course of 1880 and 1881 the government sought urgently for remedies, but it was not until November of the latter year, with the appointment of Matsukata Masayoshi as Minister of Finance, that its policies can be said to have become effective. Under Matsukata's guidance, strenuous efforts were made to balance revenue and expenditure. New taxes were imposed on rice-wine and tobacco; government grants and subsidies were much reduced; and stringent economy was observed in administration. The result was a gradual restoration of stability. By 1886 it proved possible to redeem government bonds bearing interest at 8 to 10 per cent by a conversion issue at 5 per cent, while by 1894 parity had been restored between yen notes and silver.

Towards the end of 1880, in the early stages of this economy drive, it had been decided to dispose of the government's factories. Those which were engaged in the manufacture of munitions were excepted, but the rest, it was announced, would be sold to the highest bidder, a decision that was to have important repercussions. It was not due to a sudden change of heart about the role of private enterprise in industry. Nor was it, as has sometimes been alleged, part of a conspiracy to transfer valuable plants at bargain prices to the oligarchy's friends among the businessmen, though this, it is true, was often the effect. Rather, it was a financial measure, aimed at reducing calls on revenue and recouping some part of the funds that had been invested. Even this was not easy to accomplish. The shortage of capital, which had been a factor in producing state initiative in the first place, still persisted. The prices offered were accordingly low; and that they came from friends of those in power was often because such men were in a better position to assess long-term advantages, not because they were given an opportunity for rapid profit. Most of the concerns, after all, were running at a loss, which is why they were for sale. They continued to do so for some time afterwards. It was not until Japan had a far more highly developed domestic market that the yields from industrial pioneering could be counted in substantial sums. When this did happen, however, it contributed largely to the dominant position which a few great firms were able to win in the Japanese economy. Outstanding among them were those who bought government plants in the early 'eighties: Iwasaki's Mitsubishi company, which acquired the Nagasaki shipyard in 1884; the house of Mitsui, one of the very few great merchant families of Tokugawa times that continued to thrive and expand in the modern era, now purchaser of the Tomioka silk-reeling mill; and others like Asano and Furukawa, investors, respectively, in cement and mining.

The sale of government undertakings marked the beginning of a new phase in economic policy, one in which subsidies and contracts awarded to private firms replaced state ownership and operation. With such encouragement heavy industry continued slowly to increase. New shipyards were opened in 1881 and 1883. The Shibaura Engineering Works was founded in 1887. In 1892, like several others, it began to produce electrical equipment and machinery, while the same year also saw the appearance of the first Japanese-built locomotive. In mining, application of modern methods maintained a steady rise in output. Annual coal production, for example, actually reached 5 million tons (metric) in 1895. By that time it was an export item, as was copper, though industry still relied on purchases abroad for most of its iron and almost all its steel.

Striking as many of these achievements were, they were still far from altering the character of the Japanese economy. Engineering, shipbuilding and similar trades were in their infancy, important because of their promise for the future, but having less effect in the short term than the many smaller innovations that contributed to economic growth: 'the ricksha and the bicycle; the rodent-proof warehouse; elementary sanitation; better seeds and more fertilizer; the kerosene and then the electric lamp; a simple power loom; the gas engine in the fishing boat; the divorce of personal from business accounts; the principle of limited liability'.[47] It was through such unspectacular changes in the first place that the national wealth increased. This in turn, by virtue of the purchasing power that it created, made possible the profitable development of large-scale manufacture.

One field in which modest improvements brought notable results was textiles. Spinning, reeling and weaving required less capital outlay and less technical knowledge than trades like heavy engineering; they could be successfully carried on in small workshops, as distinct from large factories; and they made use of a type of labour which Japan's farm households could easily provide. For these reasons the textile industry was the first to attract private entrepreneurs and to free itself from dependence on government aid. Silk textiles were least affected at this stage, probably because the bulk of the demand was for exports of raw silk, not for thread or fabric, so that few firms were using power-driven filatures or looms in 1894. Modernization in the cotton industry, by contrast, was by then much more advanced. In spinning, the number of spindles rose from 8,000 in 1877 to 77,000 ten years later, this being no more than the equipment of a fair-sized Lancashire mill, but with 382,000 spindles in 1893 the annual output of yarn increased to 88 million pounds. Significantly, this was accompanied by a sharp rise in imports of the raw material, nearly all from India. The market for the yarn was largely domestic and the piecegoods into which it was made were woven for the most part on narrow handlooms, but the rapid expansion of output that began about 1890 soon led to the increased use of power. Installation of power looms had already been undertaken here and there, but it was not until the great growth of exports after 1895 that it was to become widespread. Meanwhile, enough had been achieved in the adoption of modern machinery and techniques to enable the export opportunity, when it came, to be exploited.

This, indeed, is true of the economy as a whole, not just of textiles. Statistics of industrial activity on the eve of the war with China, though small by contemporary Western standards, are impressive when compared with those of a decade earlier— a sixfold increase in factory consumption of coal, for example, and an output of cotton yarn that had been multiplied by more than twenty—and even seem considerable in absolute terms for a country where development was so recent. Coal consumption in factories was a million tons, yarn output a hundred million pounds, in 1894. Foreign trade, too, though as yet on a modest scale, with annual averages for both imports and exports at less than 80 million yen in 1888–93, was beginning to change its character. Between 1878–82 and 1893–97, purchases of finished goods dropped from 48·6 per cent of imports as a whole to 35·1 per cent, while imports of raw materials rose from 3·5 to 22·7 per cent. Similarly, exports of finished goods increased—chiefly because of textiles—from 7·2 to 26·2 per cent. For the first time, moreover, the country had an export surplus. This was still not the pattern that one associates with a fully industrial state, such as Japan was to develop in the twentieth century. It implies, however, that this was the direction of change, that industrial growth was now great enough to have a substantial effect on foreign trade. In other words, some twenty years of effort were bearing fruit.

So far in this chapter the emphasis has been on the actions and policies of government. This is reasonable enough, for in this first stage of modernization it was the Meiji government that provided the leadership, the framework and many of the stimuli without which success could not have been achieved. But it must not be thought because of this that the Japanese people were entirely passive. Not everything was planned and centrally directed, not all change happened where and how the government wished. Indeed, once the years of preparation were over and those of reward began—something which in most fields of activity came soon after the war of 1894-5—it transpired that expansion was often greatest in those areas where government action had been least, like textiles. Certainly modernization could never have succeeded had it not been for the many thousands of Japanese who showed themselves willing, sometimes more than willing, to try new ways of earning a living, to study (and let their children study) foreign books, to adopt habits that were alien to their own upbringing and traditions.

Many of the men who set an example in these matters were former samurai, like Iwasaki Yataro, with an outlook and interests that followed closely those of the Meiji leaders. Others were of merchant stock, like the Mitsui. Others again came from the richer farming families of central and west Japan, usually claiming some kind of samurai background, whose members had already shown themselves interested in various forms of non-agricultural enterprise before the Restoration. It was from these elements that the new ruling class was formed. They provided the bureaucrats as well as the entre-preneurs, the educators as well as the soldiers, thereby achiev-ing a social coherence that does much to explain the single-mindedness with which Japan sought self-improvement. Men of humbler origin pursued similar goals in the hope of gaining wealth and recognition, as many of them were able to do in the more open society that emerged after 1868. Sometimes they succeeded because of ability in trade. Sometimes it was because of a more or less accidentally acquired knowledge of the West, which gave them the ear of those in office. Nearly always it was in the context of what was new in Japanese society, not what was old, for this meant both conformity and advancement.

Among the most famous of the modernizers were the writers, whose books on Western customs and behaviour became for many the only reliable guide in an otherwise uncertain world. Fukuzawa Yukichi (1835–1901) is an outstanding example. As a young man, a samurai of low rank in a Kyushu domain, he was sent to study gunnery and Dutch at Nagasaki. Later, on his own initiative he added medicine and English. By 1862 he had already visited both America and Europe as interpreter to diplomatic missions, but thereafter fear of assassination in an age of frequent anti-foreign violence turned him away from politics and public office to a life of teaching, writing and translating. His first book, *Seiyo Jijo* (Conditions in Western Lands), achieved immediate success. A compendium on European countries, their governments and their economies, it was the forerunner of many more in which he dealt with subjects as apparently remote from each other as food and clothing, elementary science, parliamentary procedure. All, to him, were relevant as parts of Western life. The earnings from these publications, which were considerable, were devoted to a school that he established in 1863 to teach a Western-style curriculum. It eventually became Keio Gijuku, one of the two earliest and greatest of Japan's private universities (the other being Waseda, founded by Okuma Shigenobu in 1881).

Reading Fukuzawa's autobiography one gets the impression of a man not always likeable but of a formidable purpose. As a liberal he insists on the importance of merit, rather than birth, but this is coupled nevertheless with an eagerness for recognition from those whom he knows to have influence and standing. As an educator he is a constant critic of things traditionally Japanese, praising the Western alternatives to them. In this, at times, there is more than a trace of smugness and pomposity. Yet through it all comes the conviction that his enthusiasms are genuine, his desire to educate sincere. Above all, his aims are patriotic: 'the purpose of my entire work', he writes, 'has not only been to gather young men together and give them the benefit of foreign books, but to open this "closed" country of ours and bring it wholly into the light of

Western civilization. For only thus may Japan become strong in both the arts of war and peace. . . .'[48]

In this task Fukuzawa, like others, was helped by a spate of translations from books in Western languages, which often ran as serials in newspapers and magazines. Among the most influential was Samuel Smiles' *Self-help*, published in 1871. Bulwer Lytton's *Ernest Maltravers*, translated in 1878–9, was much imitated as a novel and much valued for its information on Western manners; Jules Verne's *Round the World in Eighty Days* (1878) had great vogue as a sort of annotated handbook on foreign travel; while translations also appeared of *Robinson Crusoe*, *Aesop's Fables*, *The Arabian Nights* and *Pilgrim's Progress*, to say nothing of Moore's *Utopia* and Rousseau's *Contrat Social*. All these were available by 1880. A decade later attention had turned to the moderns: Turgenev, Dostoievsky, Tolstoy, Victor Hugo, Ibsen. And there was even a version of *Little Lord Fauntleroy* in 1892.

One result of the flood of information derived from these and other sources was to bring changes in Japanese literature and art. Novels became more realistic, though very dull, with themes that were thought to be attractive to the 'modern' public, such as politics, history and world affairs. Among the most popular, for example, partly because of its 'beautiful Chinese style, suitable for chant reading',[49] was one called *Kajin no kigu* (Strange Encounters of Elegant Women). In it the reader was taken through a survey of world revolutionary and independence movements, escorted by two female beauties, one from Ireland and one from Spain—an exercise that was of doubtful value as literature, but enabled the author to exploit contemporary interest in the liberal movement and international problems. Not unnaturally, the book is now more an object of curiosity than of admiration. One could be equally disparaging about the first examples of the Meiji period's drama, or the attempts to write rhyming verse; but since these, like the political novels, were no more than experiments, which eventually made way for something very much better, it is more charitable to avoid discussing them at all.

A similar discretion is appropriate in commenting on some other aesthetic imports from the West, like painting, new forms of which were stimulated by the founding of a government art school in 1876, or architecture, which was regarded as so severely practical a subject that at the imperial university it was included under engineering. In these matters, perhaps, it would have been better had Japan come under Europe's influence at a different date. Certainly the gulf that existed between the artistic criteria of traditional Japanese society and those which were now acquired proved too great to be bridged, at least for another fifty years. The country was left with two quite different standards. One, reflecting the taste of late nineteenth century Europe, applied to the architecture of government offices, banks and railway stations, to the design of goods for export, to furniture and interior decoration in the Western manner. The other, which maintained the inherited emphasis on line and texture, rather than on colour, continued to determine the appearance of such buildings as shrines and the majority of private dwellings, as well as that of articles and utensils made for everyday use. The dichotomy between the two became one of the unmistakable features of modern Japan.

The catalogue of items illustrating this divorce between old and new could be extended to include food, dress, hair-styles and much else. To some of them we shall need to return in a later chapter. This one, however, should end with the observation that not all Japanese reactions to things Western were those of unqualified enthusiasm. Quite apart from the hostility that was aroused in defence of vested interests, there were many Japanese who came to oppose the whole process of modernization, on grounds of cost, of religious prejudice or of simple conservatism. A good deal of such sentiment found an outlet in opposition to the Meiji government. Much more went to swell the rising tide of nationalism which, towards the end of the century, helped to decide what aims Japan's newly acquired skills should serve.

CHAPTER IX

NATIONALISM AND FOREIGN
AFFAIRS 1890-1904

*Political indoctrination and traditionalist sentiment—war with
China—the Triple Intervention—military build-up—Anglo-
Japanese alliance—war with Russia*

IN THE twenty years of social, political and economic reform
that followed the Restoration, Japanese attitudes towards the
outside world underwent a gradual change. On the one hand,
greater knowledge of Western habits and institutions brought
the Japanese people a new awareness of what was individual
about their own. On the other, the frustrations which arose
from a sense of inferiority in dealings with the West, an inevitable concomitant of diplomatic weakness and cultural borrowing, not only gave emotional impetus to policies aimed at
increasing national strength, but also became linked with specific objectives in foreign affairs. The result was an upsurge of
nationalism and a decade of military effort. At the end of it,
Japan had achieved the equality of status for which she longed
and had begun to lay the foundations of an empire, so marking
the end of the first stage of her modern growth.

The beginnings of this process can be traced to the handful
of samurai publicists of the century's middle years, whose
patriotism was communicated in the 1860s to most members of
their class and helped to give a constructive turn to what began
as an anti-Tokugawa movement (see Chapter III). Subsequently
the prevalence of samurai at all levels of early Meiji leadership
ensured patriotism a continued importance in political debate.
Okubo and Ito, when the Iwakura mission ended, gave it as a
reason for concentrating on reform at home, rather than expansion abroad. Saigo used it to justify his plans for attacking

Korea and opposing a government that refused to carry them out. Itagaki and his followers claimed it for the political parties. Thus by 1880 'love of country' (*aikoku*) had assumed something like the place in politics that 'expulsion of the barbarians' (*joi*) held twenty years earlier: a symbol of respectability to which appeal could successfully be made because it touched emotions shared by all. What is more, its most vociferous expression came from the opponents of the men in power —as had been true also under the Tokugawa—for it was one of the few weapons that could be safely used against an authoritarian regime that had declared for a foreign policy of moderation.

A number of factors operated to spread this patriotic sentiment throughout the population and thereby establish a basis for nationalism in the modern sense. The government's efforts at political unification, its attempts to marshal support by the creation of local elected councils and assemblies, its development of an efficient system of communications, all these helped indirectly to foster a sense of national consciousness. So did compulsory education, both by reducing regional differences of speech and manners and by enlarging the reading public. Nor was any opportunity lost of bombarding the literate with political propaganda. Newspapers of the period tended to be political and scurrilous, novels political and dull, and both were written in a language much closer to the vernacular than had been fashionable hitherto, which made them accessible to a wider circle. Accordingly, more and more Japanese were encouraged to have views about their country's politics and future.

The Meiji government did not object to this, providing the views themselves were such as it approved. And it took steps to make sure they were. One means to this end was an extensive use of powers of censorship, especially of the press. Another was a programme of political indoctrination, aimed at making the emperor a focus of national unity. It owed much to official sponsorship of the Shinto faith, for it was Shinto, after all, that rationalized the emperor's authority as deriving from divine descent and gave him quasi-sacerdotal functions. It is not surprising, therefore, that Shinto was given a place of honour in the constitutional arrangements of 1868–9 and became for a time something very much like a State religion. Later the army also played its part: a conscript's training naturally laid stress on loyalty towards the man who was both ruler and commander-in-chief. The generality of Japanese, moreover, acquired the proper sentiments at school. The compulsory course in 'ethics', worked out with much debate in the 1880s, emphasized in about equal proportions the Confucian obligation of filial piety and the national one of loyalty, the two going hand in hand with military drill, also introduced into the curriculum at about this time, as determinants of the future citizen's attitude towards his civic duty.

The trend was given formal expression in the Constitution of February 1889 and the Imperial Rescript on Education of October 1890. The first defined the subject's relationship to his monarch, putting traditional concepts in modern dress. The second made it clear that education was to be subordinate to the service of the State, outlining the substance of what was to constitute 'ethics' and providing for ceremonial expressions of loyalty in the daily life of schools. Though some objected—mostly Christians—that this was to give official sanction to an essentially religious act, they were overruled. Education and patriotism remained thereafter in close alliance.

Patriotism, of course, was in this context equated with loyalty to the emperor, as was to be expected from a regime which depended largely for its authority on control of the emperor's person. But it was already acquiring other connotations, too. Many Japanese, offended by the uncritical enthusiasm for Western dress, customs and gadgets which had characterized the first decade of Meiji history, came to think it patriotic to eschew them altogether when one could. Others, less consciously or less militantly anti-Western, began to rediscover arts and pastimes which preoccupation with the West had made neglected. In 1881, for example, a society was formed to revive interest in Japan's own traditions of painting and fine art, as distinct from those more recently brought in from Europe. Iwakura, with some of his friends, sponsored performances of the classical Noh drama and helped to raise the funds to build it a new theatre in Tokyo's Shiba Park, this also in 1881, while the following decade saw a modest renewal of interest in such minor arts as flower arrangement (*ikebana*) and the tea ceremony (*cha-no-yu*), often under the patronage of newly-rich merchants and industrialists, who were in this the natural successors of feudal lords. Such men also became patrons of Japanese-style wrestling (*sumo*), which by 1900 rivalled baseball as a national sport. Other sports of Tokugawa times, like fencing (*kendo*), were kept alive by the armed forces and police, to find renewed popularity in the end in the more nationalistic atmosphere of the twentieth century.

This atmosphere, indeed, was being heralded as early as 1890. Japanese taste in Western music, which had already shown itself martial both in theme and in performance, was now being exemplified in patriotic songs, bearing titles like 'Come, foes, come' (*Kitare ya kitare*, published in 1888) or 'Though the enemy be tens of thousands strong' (*Teki wa ikuman ari totemo*, published in 1891), which were performed for schools, military units and other audiences throughout the country. The Meiji leaders, in fact, with the unconscious help of their political rivals, had created a public opinion more actively interested in Japan's international position than was entirely comfortable. Exhortations designed to increase loyalist fervour, made for the sake of political unity, and criticisms of government 'weakness' in foreign affairs, made as moves in a struggle for power, had persuaded large sections of the population to hold views on policy which did not altogether accord with what was practical. Specifically, men looked for radical revision of the old 'unequal' treaties and for some sort of military action on the Asian mainland. These were hopes that the government shared. However, it found it necessary to move more slowly towards achieving them, and to choose its methods of doing so with greater circumspection, than the press and public seemed sometimes ready to approve.

The earliest manifestations of this difference in outlook arose over treaty revision, a subject which Japanese diplomats approached with two main objects in mind: first, to abolish or modify the system of extra-territoriality, by which foreign residents in Japan came under the legal jurisdiction of their own country's consuls; second, to secure the right of adjusting Japan's tariffs on foreign goods, most of which were fixed by treaty at 5 per cent. In view of the two sides' disparity in strength, these aims were only likely to be attained by patient negotiation, as had been demonstrated in the Iwakura mission's talks in 1871-3. The lesson, moreover, was underlined by the experiences of the next few years. Thus in 1878-9, when the United States agreed to tariff autonomy for Japan, Britain refused outright. Again in 1882 Britain proved adamant over extra-territoriality. Thereafter Japanese officials recognized the need for compromise, but the first attempt at one, involving a proposal for mixed courts under Japanese and foreign judges, was wrecked by an outburst of popular criticism in 1886. In these circumstances it required some courage for Okuma, as Foreign Minister, to reopen the talks in 1888, but he chose to negotiate in the calmer atmosphere of the Western capitals and by the following autumn had won general acceptance for the abolition of extraterritoriality, subject only to the creation of mixed courts for cases of appeal. At this point the news was again made prematurely known. A storm of opposition was aroused in Tokyo, where feeling now ran very high on questions of national sovereignty, and in October Okuma himself was wounded by a bomb thrown at his carriage by a nationalist fanatic. As a result, the negotiations were dropped and the Kuroda government resigned.

With the opening of the Diet in 1890 the issue became more deeply involved than ever in domestic politics, in that the opposition parties, seeking desperately to break the grip of an entrenched oligarchy, made every use they could of popular feeling on foreign affairs. This was sometimes an embarrassment—on one occasion statements in the Diet brought a sharp protest from Great Britain—and uncertainty about their political future made it difficult for ministers to negotiate with confidence. On the other hand, it also gave them an argument they had not before possessed. When Mutsu Munemitsu, as Foreign Minister in Ito's cabinet, decided to resume talks with London in the summer of 1893, he was able to point out that Japanese public opinion would be satisfied with nothing less than the complete abolition of extra-territoriality, even to hint that if the treaties were not revised they might be renounced. Since the veiled threat was accompanied by an offer of commercial advantages, it sufficed as a basis for discussion and brought eventual success. Details were worked out during the next few months, providing that extra-territoriality should end after Japan's new civil code came into force (ultimately this was in 1899) and that foreign merchants, in exchange, should for the first time be given access to Japan outside the treaty ports. An agreement embodying these terms was signed in July 1894. Similar ones with the other powers came soon after, for in these matters Britain's example was decisive.

The event, unhappily, gained less applause than it might otherwise have done, because it came at a time when attention was concentrated on another aspect of the country's foreign affairs, its relations with the neighbouring mainland. These had long been a matter of vital interest to Japan. Writers throughout the century, as we have seen, had looked to China, Manchuria and Korea as the natural outlet for Japan's ambitions. Even in the dark days after the signing of the treaties, when realization of national weakness had induced a defensive attitude in nearly all, there were still some, like Yoshida Shoin, who had thought survival impossible without a continental foothold. A number of the Meiji leaders, several of them Yoshida's students, shared this view. They were strengthened in it by the activities of Saigo Takamori. In 1881, after Saigo's death, survivors of his rebellion and others sympathetic to them formed a patriotic society, the Genyosha, designed to promote such expansionist ideas, to which end they took every opportunity of bringing pressure to bear on government leaders and stirring up nationalist opinion. Korea became an important focus of their efforts, as it did also for pamphleteers and politicians. As a result, Korea, like the treaties, was made a subject of debate; and many Japanese in all walks of life became convinced of the need to intervene there, either from a belief that Korea should be made to follow Japan's example of reform and modernization, under Japanese tutelage, to make her a worthy ally against Western dominance, or in the conviction that Japan must create an anti-Western league, which China and Korea must somehow be made to join, as a means of saving both herself and her neighbours from continued exploitation.

Such reasoning was not in itself unwelcome to the Meiji government. It did conflict, however, with the policy of restraint laid down in 1873. For although this had not entirely precluded territorial advances—in 1874, for example, Japan won tacit Chinese acceptance of her control of the Ryukyu islands and in 1875 took over the northern Kurile chain from Russia, in return for waiving her claims to Sakhalin—it had certainly implied a resolve to follow the paths of compromise and negotiation. Yet where Korea was concerned this proved difficult to do. The formal establishment of relations between the two countries, a treaty which opened two Korean ports to trade in 1876, was only made possible by the threat of force. Once completed, moreover, it was immediately challenged by China, on the grounds that Korea was a Chinese vassal state, incapable of concluding such an agreement with another country. The claim initiated an era of intrigue in which both China and Japan entered into a struggle between factions at the Korean court, their rivalry culminating in an armed clash between Chinese and Japanese forces in Seoul at the end of 1884. It took direct negotiations between Ito and Li Hung-chang the following spring to avert hostilities.

Both sides on this occasion agreed to withdraw their troops, but this did not mean that either had yielded its position. Inevitably there came another crisis. In June 1894 a number of local revolts broke out in Korea, organized by anti-Western groups called Tong-haks, and the king, acknowledging his vassal status, called for Chinese help. This was quickly given. Japan, however, held that the action was contrary to the 1885 convention. She therefore sent forces of her own, so shifting the emphasis from the Tong-hak revolts, which were in any case soon suppressed, to the much more dangerous issue of Sino-Japanese conflict.

Several factors contributed to making the situation more serious than it had been in 1884. For China's part, French and British encroachment along the frontiers of Tongking, Tibet and Burma had induced a stiffer attitude concerning her rights in border areas, an attitude made all the more uncompromising by the greater self-confidence with which she could approach a struggle against Japan. The latter, on the other hand, was also confident, for the previous decade had seen a considerable growth in the size and efficiency of her army and navy, as well as a solution to her most pressing financial problems. Hence caution in her international dealings seemed less needed than it had been before. Indeed, too much caution would provoke the parties and public opinion, as the Diet's vociferous comments on treaty revision had already shown. This being so, the specific considerations making for action in Korea gained greater weight. These were partly economic, arising from the trade recently established between the two, and partly strategic, in that Korea was Japan's obvious route of access to north-east Asia. Both would be threatened if Korea fell under another power's control. From Japan's viewpoint, therefore, whether one saw the danger as coming from China, seeking to make her suzerainty effective, or from Russia, who had just announced plans for building a railway to her Siberian possessions, there seemed good cause for taking action before the threat developed.

It is impossible to tell how much of this reasoning Ito accepted in 1894. It is certain, nevertheless, that his actions had an air of purpose which had been lacking hitherto. At the end of June, far from withdrawing Japanese troops, he announced his intention of keeping them in Korea until the Korean government had carried out an extensive catalogue of reforms, one effect of which would have been to substitute Japanese for Chinese influence and end all Chinese pretensions to special rights. In July he warned China to send in no more men, while shortly after his own took over the Korean royal palace. This left China no choice but to submit or fight. Since she refused to relinquish her rights without an effort to defend them, there was from this point no hope of avoiding war.

Its formal declaration came at the beginning of August and was followed by a series of startling Japanese victories. In fact Chinese resistance was so weak, Yamagata commented later, that 'Japanese officers did not encounter any serious problems worthy of careful consideration'.[50] By the end of September the Japanese army controlled most of Korea and the navy had command of the Yellow Sea. In October, two divisions under Yamagata moved into South Manchuria. Three more under Oyama moved against Liaotung, capturing Port Arthur the following month, and then took Weihaiwei in February 1895. The road was now open for an advance against Peking. With seven Japanese divisions poised to take it, China was forced to come to terms, sending Li Hung-chang to negotiate with Ito in Japan and agreeing to virtually any conditions he chose to state. Not unnaturally the peace treaty, signed in April at Shimonoseki, was harsh. It recognized the independence of Korea, thus ending Chinese claims to suzerainty; it ceded to Japan the island of Formosa (Taiwan) and the Liaotung peninsula, including Port Arthur; it opened four additional Chinese cities to foreign trade; and it provided for the payment by China of a substantial indemnity in cash. To the Japanese, both government and people, the fruits of victory seemed very sweet.

1895

Japan's victory over China had a number of repercussions. It demonstrated that China's weakness was more than had been thought. It also revealed that Japan's modernization had been remarkably successful. Together these pieces of knowledge were to change the international scene. Japan, moreover, gained a new sense of satisfaction and achievement, to say nothing of more practical rewards: scope for her activities in Korea; status as a 'treaty power' in China's foreign trade; the acquisition of a useful colony, Formosa.

Yet not all was to the good, as the country was quickly to discover. International prestige also brought with it responsibilities and dangers. By making herself a factor to be reckoned with in Far Eastern affairs, Japan had involved herself more closely in the rivalries of the powers, not always to her own advantage. The first proof of it came within a week of the signing of the Shimonoseki treaty. On April 23 the representatives of Russia, France and Germany informed Tokyo that their governments viewed with concern the prospect of the Liaotung peninsula being transferred to Japan. They advised its return to China. Ostensibly they did so because Japan's control of the peninsula would be a threat to China and to the peace of the area. In fact the motives were less altruistic: Russia aimed at preserving her own opportunities for expansion; France, her ally, hoped to gain Russian support for French ambitions in the south; and Germany sought to edge Russia away from European politics. None of this, strictly speaking, involved Japan; but it was Japan, because of the new relationship she had established with China, that gave the three powers their opening to act.

The information available to Ito's cabinet was that Russia,

at least, was willing to back her demands with force. Nor would she modify her terms. What is more, although feelers put out to other capitals revealed a certain amount of sympathy for Japan, they brought no definite promise of support. Since the country was exhausted by the war with China and could not hope to resist alone, the cabinet had no choice but to communicate to the governments concerned its formal decision to submit, this being on May 5, three days before ratifications of the treaty were exchanged. All that Japan could get to salve her pride was an increase in the size of the indemnity.

Pride, there is no doubt, was at the heart of the matter. The loss of Liaotung did not by any means rob the treaty of all its value, but the manner of the loss affected Japanese opinion as if it had. The war had brought a tremendous wave of enthusiasm in Japan, silencing even the government's critics in the Diet. Victory was hailed with exultation. Then, without warning, came humiliation, a savage reminder that half a century's work had still not put Japan in a position to ignore or reject the 'advice' of one of the powers. It is no wonder that the shock was great and that it brought a mood of bitterness. For years thereafter the Japanese public remained resentful, more open than ever to the persuasions of nationalist extremists, more anxious than ever that its own government's policies should be such as would bring prestige. In this sense the Triple Intervention, as it was called, served to rally Japan for another advance, despite the further measure of hardship that this entailed.

The government's own immediate reactions were military, devised to ensure that next time indignity could be properly resented. Thus in 1896 six new divisions were added to the regular army, bringing its total to thirteen and doubling its first-line strength. In 1898 both cavalry and artillery were organized as independent brigades. Meanwhile every effort was being made to improve equipment, especially to provide better rifles for the infantry and quick-firing guns for the artillery, as well as to set up facilities for their manufacture in Japan. By 1904 this had been achieved. Similarly, the country was made self-sufficient in naval armaments and the navy was greatly increased in size. A naval building programme, starting in 1896-7, budgeted for the addition of four battleships, sixteen cruisers, twenty-three destroyers and over 600 other craft to the existing fleet, bringing the total of major war vessels (destroyers and above) to seventy-six, aggregating 258,000 tons, by the end of 1903.

The cost of these developments was heavy. Army expenditure, just under 15 million yen in 1893, rose to 53 million in 1896 and remained at about that level till the Russian war. Naval expenditure was more variable, but was still appreciably higher than before: 13 million yen in 1895, rising to over 50 million in 1898, then declining to 28 million in 1903. Most of this was met by the government from its own resources, by means of an increase in taxation on business and personal incomes, the levy of a tax on rice-wine, and the creation of official monopolies in camphor and tobacco. To these were added a number of foreign and domestic loans which doubled the national debt within a decade. Even so, government debt was only a little over 500 million yen in 1903, a figure which the rising national income, now showing the effect of industrial growth, made quite admissible.

Direct measures of rearmament were supplemented by policies designed to channel investment into heavy industry, in particular those sectors of it which had a military importance. Thus the paid-up capital of the engineering industry rose from 2·6 million yen in 1893 to 14·6 million ten years later. Shipping and shipbuilding received substantial subsidies, dating from 1896, which had it as their object to increase both the use and the construction of vessels of a modern type. This they did, bringing a sharp rise in total merchant tonnage—35 per cent of ships entering Japanese ports in 1903 flew the Japanese flag, compared with 14 per cent in 1893—and a modest but respectable development of yards able to build steel ships. The government also decided in 1896 to establish an iron and steel industry. Its great Yawata works, founded as a result of this decision, began production in 1901 and was largely responsible for raising the annual output of pig-iron to 243,000 tons and of steel to 255,000 tons (metric) by 1913. Coal output, too, rose rapidly, from 5 million tons in 1895 to 13 million tons in 1905. More significant, perhaps, was the fact that much of the coal was being used by factories.

The economic implications of these developments will be

discussed in a later chapter. Here it is sufficient to underline their importance for foreign affairs: first, as a measure of the government's determination; second, as one explanation of its growing self-confidence after 1900. Nevertheless, any examination of Japanese policy in these years must begin by emphasizing not its confidence but its caution, a quality due not only to memories of the Triple Intervention, but also to the very real difficulties with which Japan was faced.

They arose chiefly from the change that was taking place in Europe's relationships with China. The exclusive concern with trade, which had determined China's earlier relations with the West, was being supplemented in the last quarter of the century by a rising volume of investment, involving railway-building, the exploitation of mineral resources, sometimes the establishment of industrial plants. These gave the powers new rights which they thought it their duty to protect. What is more, the distribution of investment tended to fall into regional patterns, so that each power had greater interests in some areas of China than in others. The result was greatly to increase the dangers of partition, the more so because several of the powers were already established on the Chinese frontier: Russia in the north, France and Britain in the south, all looking for special privileges in the regions contiguous with their existing holdings.

Matters came to a head with Japan's victory over China, partly because it raised doubts about the ability of the Chinese government to protect foreign investments and therefore tempted the powers to take action on their own, partly because it enabled Russia, France and Germany to seek rewards for their intervention. In 1896 Russia made the first move, securing the right to construct a railway, the Chinese Eastern, across Manchuria, to link Vladivostock with Russian territory farther west. In November 1897 the murder of two Roman Catholic priests gave Germany in her turn an opportunity to present demands, these resulting in a treaty (March 1898) which gave her a naval base at Kiaochow and extensive economic rights in the province of Shantung. News of it precipitated a scramble for concessions by the other powers. Within a few days Russia received a lease of Port Arthur and recognition of her special position in Manchuria. France, a month later, acquired a base at Kwangchow-wan, railway rights in Yunnan, and China's promise that she would not alienate Yunnan, Kwangtung or Kwangsi to any other power. This led Britain to safeguard her own strategic and economic interests. By July she had obtained a non-alienation agreement concerning the Yangtse valley, an extension of territory opposite Hong Kong, and the lease of a base at Weihaiwei.

These events caused Japan considerable concern. It was bad enough to see those who had checked her own ambitions engaged in rewarding themselves in the manner which they had described, when Japan had tried it, as a threat to peace. It was worse still to realize that she could neither prevent them from doing so nor effectively share the spoils. To be sure, she was able to secure a pledge of non-alienation for Fukien, the province opposite Formosa. But for the most part she could only watch and wait, hoping that Britain and America would serve both Japan's ends and their own by preventing the complete dismemberment of China.

The Yamagata government, which took office at the end of 1898, was able to do something more constructive. During 1899 Chinese resentment of foreign actions was manifested in widespread anti-foreign outbreaks, the most serious of which, in Shantung and the north, were led by groups called Boxers. In the spring of 1900 they seized the approaches to Peking and laid seige to the foreign legations, thus making necessary an immediate military intervention by the treaty powers. Japan alone was in a position to send substantial reinforcements quickly. She therefore played a leading part in the operations that followed, providing nearly half the troops that relieved the legations in August and occupied Peking. Yet for all this she acted with circumspection, showing a studious care for her allies' susceptibilities—even at some risk of delaying the expedition—and observing all proper military and diplomatic etiquette. Her behaviour, in fact, much enhanced her international reputation. It also gave her a voice in the negotiations by which a settlement was reached in 1901 and a share in the huge indemnity required from China.

To set against this was a deterioration in her relations with Russia. These had improved slightly after 1895, despite the growth of direct rivalry between the two in Korea, for Russia was too preoccupied with China and Manchuria, Japan too conscious of her recent rebuff, to push matters to extremes. In 1896 they agreed to co-operate in Korea's development and in April 1898 Russia even recognized Japan's greater claim to economic preference in that country. This eased the tension, at least till Manchuria brought it back, a development that occurred as a by-product of the Boxer troubles. Russia held conspicuously aloof from the plans to relieve the legations at Peking. By contrast, she used the spread of the outbreaks to the north-east provinces as an excuse to occupy Manchuria entirely. Nor would she evacuate the area until China came to terms. Since the terms, as stated in February 1901, would have made Manchuria a Russian protectorate, they brought urgent protests from the powers, most vigorously from Japan, forcing Russia to deny any territorial ambitions. At this the crisis died, becoming submerged for a time in the acrimonious exchanges about allocation of the Boxer indemnity between its various claimants.

One result of these manoeuvres was to bring Britain and Japan together, since they had a common interest in opposing Russian expansion. Britain feared for her influence in China if the Russian occupation of Manchuria were to prove permanent. Japan saw it as blocking her own best route to the mainland and also as a threat to Korea. Neither could afford to let it pass unchallenged. Yet a formal agreement to oppose it was not an easy step to take. For Britain it would involve a break with the diplomacy of 'splendid isolation'. For Japan it might well mean abandoning hope of a local compromise with Russia, though many in Tokyo, including Ito, still saw such a compromise as the country's wisest course. On both sides, therefore, the approach to an agreement was cautious and its outcome by no means inevitable.

The possibility of alliance had been widely canvassed in both countries since 1895, when Britain's refusal to join the Triple Intervention—because she approved the commercial provisions laid down at Shimonoseki—had done something to wipe out the memory of her earlier opposition to treaty revision. Still, this seemed a slender base on which to found a diplomatic and military arrangement. More important, in fact, were the personal links established between the two countries by Britain's role as a tutor in modernization. By the training of naval officers, the education of students, the provision of experts in many fields, she had helped to create a group in Tokyo that favoured closer ties. It was strengthened by the unobtrusive but effective co-operation between British and Japanese officials over details of the Boxer expedition and indemnity. Publicly, the case for alliance was urged by a number of propagandists. Two in particular, Captain Frank Brinkley, owner of the *Japan Mail* and Tokyo correspondent of *The Times*, and Edwin Arnold of the *Telegraph*, were able to influence opinion in London, while the approval of Okuma was enough to bring favourable comment from the *Mainichi* and *Yomiuri* in Japan.

It is probable that none of this would have done more than create a friendly atmosphere, had there not been a practical issue for cabinets to resolve, such as was provided by the Russian moves in China. Indeed, it was not until the summer of 1901 that private feelers and unofficial talks gave way to negotiation proper. In July, Hayashi, Japan's minister in London and long an advocate of alliance, had a meeting on the subject with the British Foreign Secretary, Lord Lansdowne. This resulted in Hayashi seeking formal instructions from his government and, when these proved encouraging, in an exchange of views about the terms which alliance might involve. Two difficulties rapidly became apparent. Both sides wished to guarantee the *status quo* in China and prevent Russian annexation of the Manchurian provinces. Britain, however, wanted any promise of mutual support to apply also to the defence of India. To this Japan objected on the grounds that it would weight the bargain heavily in Britain's favour. By the same token, Britain was hesitant about giving full support to Japan's position in Korea, since she had no desire to become involved in an exclusively Russo-Japanese quarrel. Discussion of these points, as well as of a difference about the distribution of naval forces, lasted into November.

There then occurred a short delay, occasioned by the activities of Ito. He had been succeeded as premier in June by Katsura Taro, a protégé of Yamagata, but he remained exceedingly influential and convinced of the need for talks with Russia. In mid November he persuaded the cabinet to hold up further discussions until he had made a private visit to St

Petersburg. This took place at the end of the month. Early in December, he had a number of meetings with Lamsdorff, Russia's Foreign Minister, and although they did not go well, Lamsdorff eventually offered some small concessions about Korea as a basis for formal exchanges. He expected in return a free hand for Russia in northern China. But the concessions, such as they were, had already been made abortive by events. Before Ito could report the result of his proceedings to Tokyo, British suspicions of possible duplicity—the visit to Russia was widely known—forced Hayashi to resume negotiations and Katsura to support his doing so.

An alliance was now inevitable, if the problem of its terms could be overcome. And after hard bargaining, this was at last achieved. The naval question was left for separate discussion by the naval staffs; Britain's demand that India be included in the scope of the agreement was dropped; and the difficulty over Japan's position in Korea was met by careful drafting. As finally signed on January 30, 1902, the treaty recognized that 'Japan, in addition to the interests which she possesses in China, is interested in a peculiar degree politically as well as commercially and industrially in Corea',[51] but it did not provide automatically for British help if Japan became on this account involved in war with Russia. Instead, each country agreed to remain neutral if the other became engaged in hostilities in the Far East area. This, at least, held good when only one enemy was concerned. If either was attacked by two powers or more, the military provisions of the alliance were to become effective.

The agreement, despite the care taken in its wording, meant something different to each of the parties to it. From the British viewpoint it was to be a warning to Russia, but not a provocation, as the public announcement of its contents took pains to show. To Japan it was a triumph, this not merely because it gave her an alliance on a footing of equality with the greatest of the powers, but also because it enabled her to treat with Russia on more even terms. There could be no repetition of the Triple Intervention, it was clear, while Britain held the ring. In this sense Japanese extremists saw the alliance as an invitation to aggression. Even the moderates, among whom the government must be numbered, were emboldened by it to refuse any unfavourable compromise about Korea.

The immediate results—or apparent results—were highly satisfactory to both Japan and Britain, for in April Russia agreed to withdraw her forces from Manchuria, the operation to be effected in stages at six-month intervals. The first, in October, was duly carried out, though the troops were only transferred elsewhere in the region. The second stage, however, expected in April 1903, did not take place. Instead, Russia gave every indication of preparing for another advance. In June, therefore, a Japanese imperial conference took the decision to propose a general settlement with Russia. It was to be on the basis of a joint undertaking to respect the territorial integrity of China and Korea, coupled with a recognition of Russian railway rights in Manchuria and Japanese interests, both political and economic, in Korea. To this Russia responded in October with counter-proposals as severe as if the Anglo-Japanese alliance had never been signed. She demanded a guarantee of territorial integrity for Korea only, excluding China (and hence Manchuria); a promise by Japan not to fortify the Korean coast; and recognition that Manchuria was outside the Japanese sphere of interest. Katsura, under pressure from a public opinion increasingly eager to fight, could not entertain such terms. It seemed better—and more practical, if his military advisers were to be believed—to gamble on a war which might resolve the question once and for all, rather than accept a line of containment drawn by Russia. Hence Japan's reply in January 1904 stated her minimum terms in the form of an ultimatum. When it was ignored she declared war.

This was on February 10, but diplomatic relations had been severed four days earlier and hostilities had already begun. Russian troops had crossed the frontier into Korea. Japanese naval units had attacked a Russian squadron. For Japan, indeed, the important task at this stage was to secure control of the straits across which her reinforcements had to move to enter Korea. It was accomplished on April 13 by victory over a Russian naval force outside Port Arthur. The Japanese First Army was now able to strike along the Yalu River, forcing a crossing on May 1 and moving into south Manchuria, while the Second Army landed in the Liaotung peninsula a few days later. Within a month General Nogi's Third Army had laid siege to Port Arthur itself, though the garrison's capitulation did not come until the following New Year, after some of the bitterest fighting of the war. Meanwhile in late August and early September Oyama's forces took Liaoyang and drove the Russians back on Mukden. Here a decisive battle was fought in February and March 1905, sixteen Japanese divisions, numbering some 400,000 men, being thrown in to achieve the capture of the city. As a final blow to Russia's hopes, her Baltic fleet, which had left Europe in November and sailed halfway round the world to break the blockade of Vladivostock, was met by Admiral Togo's forces in the Tsushima Straits on May 27 and practically annihilated.

These events made peace negotiations possible, especially as both sides had other reasons for wishing to end the struggle. Russia, although not admitting that her military resources were at an end, was in difficulties with political unrest at home. Japan was on the verge of financial exhaustion. Accordingly, when Japan asked for American mediation, a peace conference was arranged at Portsmouth, New Hampshire, and plenipotentiaries met there in August 1905. Japan's demands were stiff, as befitted an apparent victor. They included recognition of her supremacy in Korea; transfer to Japan of Russian interests in south Manchuria, including the railway and Liaotung; the cession of Sakhalin; and payment of a war indemnity. The last two Russia flatly rejected, giving every indication that she would break off the talks if Japan continued to press them. Even American intervention only succeeded in modifying her stand a little, to the extent of offering the southern half of Sakhalin. An indemnity she would not on any account consider. Disappointed, but unable to face the prospect of further fighting, the Japanese government gave way and on September 5 its representatives signed the Treaty of Portsmouth in its modified form.

Unsatisfactory as this was to the Japanese public, which had been led to expect a far greater return for its efforts and expressed its displeasure in riots that occasioned martial law, it was nevertheless a very great achievement. For the first time in modern history an Asian country had defeated one of the powers in full-scale war. By doing so, it had secured both real advantages and symbols of prestige: a paramount position in Korea and valuable rights in South Manchuria, to be added to

NATIONALISM AND FOREIGN AFFAIRS 1890–1904

Formosa and a share in the China trade. Indeed, if the Anglo-Japanese alliance had signified the attainment of equality, the Russo-Japanese war did more again. It brought revenge, self-confidence and a sense of mission, setting Japan on the road that was to make her in the following forty years an exemplar of Western civilization, transplanted; a champion of Asia against the West; and the megalomaniac builder of an empire overseas.

CHAPTER X

THE END OF AN ERA

*Annexation of Korea—political society—the economy—city life
—religion*

THE MEIJI emperor died on July 30, 1912, after a reign of
forty-five years which had seen astonishing changes. His own
status had been raised from that of an ineffective recluse,
regarded by foreign visitors as something akin to a pope, to
that of a semi-divine monarch of a vigorous nation state. His
country after years of international weakness had won two
wars and acquired the beginnings of an empire. His subjects
had learnt and put to use new ways of making wealth. They
were already beginning to show the effects of it in their standard
of living. They were also more efficiently governed, better
educated and more conscious of participating in national life
than they had ever been before. In sum, the first stage of
modernization had been successfully completed.

It is useful at this point to survey the effect of these achievements and the kind of society they had brought into being, for
Japanese history in the twentieth century was to be in many
ways an extension of them. Nor was it always a pleasing
one. Industrialization was to bring not only a higher level of
national wealth, but also a clash of interests between town and
country, manager and worker, reactionary and progressive,
arising from the pattern of its distribution. It was to contribute
to a weakening of the family and of the community in their
older forms. Again, the stresses which this introduced were to
be the greater because of a growing awareness of the dichotomy
between what was Japanese and what was foreign, what was
traditional and what was modern, in ideas, in politics, in social
custom and much else. Thus Japan under her next two

emperors became the scene of a new kind of quarrel, which threatened to disrupt society far more completely than it had been in the time of Meiji. It also turned, partly for the same reasons, to a career of expansion abroad, as the urge to achieve equality became chauvinism of a virulently racial type.

The revolution in Japan's international position, which made many of these later developments possible, had been one of the major objectives, as well as one of the greatest successes, of the Meiji leaders. It was certainly the most striking to contemporary observers. In a little over eleven years—from 1894 to 1905—Japanese diplomacy, backed on two occasions by military force, had secured revision of the unequal treaties, alliance with one of the great powers, colonies in Formosa (Taiwan) and southern Sakhalin (Karafuto), a preponderant position in Korea and important rights in South Manchuria, including Liaotung. Very soon these gains were confirmed and extended. In July 1905 the United States had given its blessing to Korea's subordinate status and in August the Anglo-Japanese alliance was renewed, its scope being extended to provide for the defence of British interests in India and a more precise recognition of Japan's hegemony in Korea. In September came the Treaty of Portsmouth, ending the Russian war. In November, Ito negotiated an agreement by which Korea became a Japanese protectorate, giving Japan control of the country's foreign affairs. A month later China acquiesced in the arrangements made about her various possessions, so that by the end of the year Japan was ready to exploit her gains with little fear of international interference.

The first step was the appointment of Ito as Resident-General in Seoul in February 1906. He had extensive powers, but they were not enough to overcome Korean opposition or to prevent a Korean appeal for help to the Hague conference in June 1907. Accordingly, the king was made to abdicate in July of that year and Japan assumed responsibility for domestic as well as foreign policy, though unrest continued to frustrate many of her plans until the date of Ito's resignation two years later. Outright annexation had by then become the Japanese aim and Ito's murder by a Korean fanatic at Harbin in October 1909 gave pretext for it. In the following May, General

Terauchi Masatake, War Minister since 1902, was appointed concurrently Resident-General, with orders to assert complete control of the country by police and army. This done, on August 22, 1910, he forced the Korean government to sign the annexation treaty.

Events in Manchuria meanwhile had gone more smoothly. In June 1906 exploitation of Japan's rights there was entrusted to the newly-formed South Manchuria Railway Company, in which the government held half the capital and had the right to appoint the two chief officers. Apart from running the railways and building more, the company was empowered to engage in mining, public utilities and the sale of goods, in addition to collecting taxes and conducting administration in the railway zone. It was designed, in other words, to be as much an organ of policy as a source of profit. Under its patronage and control, which were shared in the political and diplomatic fields with the Governor-General of Kwantung (Liaotung), first appointed in August 1906, Japanese investment proceeded rapidly. This was recognized as inevitable by the powers. A rapprochement with France and Russia in 1907, under the stimulus of Britain's example, and confirmation of the 1905 agreement with America, which came in the Root-Takahira notes of 1908, virtually insured international acquiescence in the special privileges being accorded to Japanese business in Manchuria. There were rumblings of protest from London, but not enough to prevent renewal of the Anglo-Japanese alliance in 1911. All in all, Japan had good reason to be satisfied with both her status and her opportunities.

Their maintenance and, if possible, improvement depended in some degree on social and political stability at home, something which in the first decade of the twentieth century the country seemed well on the way to achieving. The institutions created in the previous forty years had not been intended to destroy one ruling class and substitute another, with all the upheaval such a process would have entailed. Rather they had shifted the distribution of political authority within the ruling class and introduced new elements to it. Thus former court nobles and feudal lords, though no longer holding important office, were reconciled to the regime by wealth and dignity, the first deriving from bonds which the state had given them,

the second from their position in the peerage. The most able
of the ex-samurai, profiting from superior training and experience, had also found a satisfying niche in the established order.
Some became—or perhaps, one should say, remained—soldiers
and bureaucrats. Others became leaders of industry and commerce. Both groups were eligible for appointment to the
peerage, which underlines the fact that the new society, if it
retained much of the respect for place that had characterized
the old, had no intention of perpetuating privilege. For those
of comparatively humble birth but great achievement, power
and honours now ran together. The Meiji leaders, after all,
had won their way not only to the highest offices, but also to
the topmost ranks—Ito and Yamagata both held the title of
Prince—setting an example that was valid at every level. As a
result, a soldier or bureaucrat could look forward to becoming
baron or viscount, as well as general or vice-minister.

The services and the bureaucracy were in fact the most usual
and most respectable route to such advancement. Both were
alike in requiring discipline, professional efficiency and high
standards of personal conduct from their members, while their
insistence that appointment and promotion go by merit meant
that a career in them was open to all who could pass the
appropriate examinations. Since education was equally open,
it followed that any family which could put its sons through
the proper school and college training could hope to enter
them in the upper grades of government service. With few
exceptions, the poor were in practice excluded. But the prospect was a real one for many families that could not otherwise
have expected to be part of a ruling class: modest landowners
and well-to-do farmers in the countryside, the smaller merchants
and industrialists of the towns.

To all who had ambition, whether for themselves or for their
sons, education, especially higher education, therefore became
an important preoccupation. Primary schools already catered
for 97 per cent of the seven million children of school age in
1907, when the length of the compulsory course was raised
from four years to six. Secondary schools in the same year had
about 150,000 pupils. The numbers at university were also
rising and there was still a large unsatisfied demand for places.
To the three existing universities in Tokyo (the Imperial

University and the private foundations of Keio and Waseda) were added others elsewhere—Kyoto in 1903, Sendai in 1907, Fukuoka in 1910—whose graduates helped to fill responsible posts in the bureaucracy and other fields. Even so, competition for entry remained fierce, extending to the better high schools as well as the more popular university departments; and it is one of the more significant, not to say commendable, features of modern Japan that the vast majority of applications were decided by ability, not by birth or wealth, except in so far as a moderate degree of wealth was necessary to enable a family to maintain its sons in full-time study.

In many ways, in fact, Meiji Japan had done much towards realizing an ideal of the late Tokugawa reformers, that is, the promotion of men of ability regardless of inherited rank. By so doing it had reduced the dangers of subversion. Nevertheless, the existence of a career genuinely open to talent, while it made revolution unlikely, did not preclude political disputes. There were many, even among those who had helped to bring the regime about, who had been neither fortunate nor successful under its rule and who accordingly sought to change its policies. It was of such men that political parties had been formed: disgruntled oligarchs, who had fallen out with their fellows; landowners and farmers disgusted at fiscal discrimination against the village for the benefit of the town; merchants and industrialists who felt their influence to be less than their wealth deserved; and numerous ex-samurai who lacked the ability or the luck which would have let them preserve an earlier way of life in a changing world. These were not revolutionaries, in the sense of men wishing to overturn society. But they were hostile to the oligarchy which governed Japan and determined, if possible, to make it share its power.

All the same, by the end of the Meiji period the oligarchy was more strongly entrenched than ever. Its own senior members—Ito, Yamagata and Matsukata—had become Genro, men who because of long and meritorious service had been made permanent and personal counsellors to the throne, advising the emperor on his choice of a Prime Minister and consequently able to keep a large measure of control over both the composition and the policy of each new government. Through the years, moreover, they had put their nominees into most key positions outside the cabinet. Appointments to the Privy Council, the House of Peers, the high command of the armed forces and the upper ranks of the central bureaucracy were an imperial prerogative, which was exercised, of course, on the advice of the men in power. This implied an important limitation on the practice of promotion by ability. Though birth or wealth would not in themselves suffice, a man who wished to attain the very highest place, at least politically, needed to have or to establish 'connections' with the inner group, links of lineage or marriage or obligation which were a guarantee of his loyalty. One might recall Ito's description of the Japanese polity: that of an overgrown village, in which 'family and quasi-family ties permeated and formed the essence of every social organization', so that 'cold intellect and calculation of public events were always restrained and even often hindered by warm emotions between man and man'. This, as he said, was 'a healthy barrier against the threatening advance of socialistic ideas'. Equally, it produced a situation in which 'free discussion is apt to be smothered, attainment and transference of power liable to become a family question . . .'[52] The words were written of the days before the granting of a constitution, but they remained valid of the twentieth century, too.

To set against this close-knit monopoly of office, opponents of the Meiji government had two main weapons. The first was public opinion, expressed through a vigorous daily press and occasionally by riotous assembly, though the latter had the drawback that it was only effective at moments of crisis, usually after, not before, a decision was taken. The second was the elected lower house of the Diet and the political parties that were active in it. Between 1890 and 1894, as we have seen (see Chapter 7), the parties had fought, though unsuccessfully, to establish control of the budget and through it of policy as a whole, the struggle being marked by a series of dissolutions and elections and by the attempted use of force to decide them. Then came the war with China, submerging partisan feeling for a time in a wave of patriotism. After it, Japanese political life moved, if rather jerkily, towards a compromise. This depended on a realization by the oligarchs, on the one hand, that they could not make the constitutional machinery work if the Diet remained permanently obstructive, and by the politicians, on the other, that short of revolution the oligarchy's defences were impregnable. Since both sides were committed to ideas that made revolution out of the question—an emperor-centred state and a people united in pursuit of national strength—this eventually led the one to offer cabinet posts and minor concessions on matters of policy, the other to accept them.

The first sign of the change came in 1895, when Ito won the support of the Liberal Party (*Jiyuto*), the largest group in the lower house, and gave the Home Ministry to Itagaki. On the fall of Ito's government in 1896 his successor, Matsukata, made an alliance with Okuma's party on similar terms. However, neither arrangement worked very well, for there was much disagreement with it on both sides, notably from Yamagata, and Ito could not repeat the pattern when he became premier again in 1898. Yet without it he was unable to overcome the hostility of the lower house. He therefore took the initiative in bringing the Okuma and Itagaki groups together to form the first party cabinet in Japanese history. The two men took office on June 30, 1898, Okuma as premier and Foreign Minister, Itagaki as Home Minister, and they were backed by a newly-formed party which included the followers of both, the Constitutional Party (*Kenseito*), standing for loyalty to the throne, maintenance of the constitution and cabinet responsibility to the Diet. Unhappily, these were platitudes which only glossed over the differences between the party's two original components, adherents of Itagaki and Okuma respectively. They soon fell out over taxation policy, in which they represented different interests, and over the division of political spoils. Equally serious, they faced a united and unco-operative bureaucracy, for the effect of Ito's move had been to change the nature of the struggle only in the sense of making it a contest between cabinet and oligarchs, instead of between cabinet and Diet. In fact, the Diet played no part in the matter at all, since the government resigned on October 31, before the session had begun. It was replaced by that of Yamagata, who for the next two years secured parliamentary majorities for vital bills by the use of bribery.

The situation was complicated by a growing rivalry between Ito and Yamagata, partly personal, partly due to differences over foreign policy, partly reflecting a conflict between civil

1 Himeji Castle. A fine example of a
feudal stronghold of Tokugawa times, which
still dominates the modern city

Tokugawa Japan

2 A feudal lord and his escort, *en route* to Edo, at a river crossing

3 A feudal lord's escort entering the outskirts of Edo

4 Saruwakacho, a street in Edo, by moonlight. From a print by Hiroshige (1797–1858)

5 TOP RIGHT A timberyard at Tatekawa. From a print by Hokusai (1760–1849)

6 BOTTOM RIGHT. A waterwheel at Onden. Also from a print by Hokusai

7 Commodore Perry arrives to open negotiations at Yokohama, 1854

The Opening of Japan

8 Handing over the official presents brought by Commodore Perry, Yokohama, 1854

9 Saigo Takamori (1828–1877) **10** Ito Hirobumi (1841–1909)

Meiji Japan

11 Okubo Toshimichi (1830–1878) **12** Yamagata Aritomo (1838–1922)

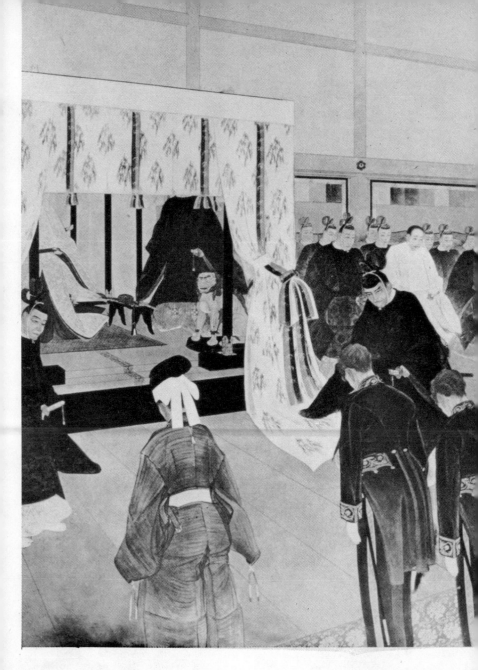

13 The Imperial Court, 1868. For the first time the Emperor receives the foreign envoys in audience

The Imperial Court, 1889. The Emperor announces the Meiji
Constitution

15 Modernization. A primary school, probably in the 1880s, with adult pupils as well as children. From a contemporary print

16 RIGHT: Modernization. Shimbashi Station in Tokyo, sometime before 1894. From a contemporary print

しんばし鐵道寮

17 Signing the peace treaty between Japan and China at Shimonoseki, 1895

18 TOP RIGHT: The Russo-Japanese War, 1904–5. Japanese infantry waiting for engineers to bridge the Tatung River

19 BOTTOM RIGHT: Tokyo's main shopping street, the Ginza, in 1904. Compare the illustrations of Edo fifty years earlier (no 4) and Tokyo fifty years later (no 36)

International Recognition

21 Saionji Kimmochi (1849–1940), Japan's chief delegate to the Versailles Conference, 1919

22 The Washington Conference, December 1921. The Japanese delegation is seated at the table to the left

20 LEFT: 'Allies'. *Punch* celebrates the renewal of the Anglo-Japanese alliance in 1905 after Japan's victory over Russia

Between the Wars

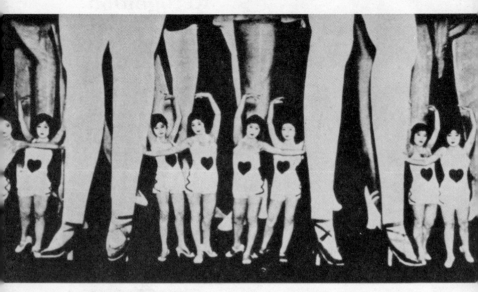

23 A scene from the 'Kajino Follies', Japan's first modern revue, presented at Asakusa in Tokyo in 1929

24 The beach at Kamakura, 1933

25 In the 1930s the school day starts with an obeisance to an
enshrined portrait of the Emperor

26 Factory girls marching to work from the company's
hostel in which they live

Victory and Defeat

27 The first Konoe cabinet, June 1937. Konoe is at the front (in overcoat), with Foreign Minister Hirota on his right

28 The First Division leaves Tokyo for service in Manchuria after the abortive military revolt of February 1936

29 Pearl Harbour, December 1941. USS *Arizona* sinking after the Japanese attack

30 Hiroshima, August 1945. The first atomic bomb casts its shadow over Japan

31 Surrender. The Japanese delegation aboard USS *Missouri* in Tokyo Bay, September 1, 1945

Surrender

32 Tojo Hideki (1885–1948), hanged as a major war criminal in 1948

33 Yoshida Shigeru (b. 1878), Prime Minister during most of the period of military occupation

34 LEFT: Industry. Part of Osaka in 1957

Postwar Japan

35 Agriculture. Terracing makes possible the maximum use of land

36 Tokyo. Part of the centre of the city in 1957

and military interests within the Meiji leadership. In September 1900 Ito tried to strengthen his hand by forming a party of his own, organizing what was left of the old Liberals into an Association of Political Friends (*Seiyukai*), but forcing them to accept as the price of patronage his own view that cabinets must be 'independent'; in other words, that party representation in the cabinet did not involve the cabinet's subordination to party. On this basis a government was formed, though it proved short-lived. Yamagata opposed it, exploiting the ascendancy he had established in the services and the House of Peers; and Ito could not entirely match this combination, even by invoking the emperor's intervention, a device he had earlier used against the Diet with striking success. In June 1901 he resigned again, after less than a year in office.

From this time on, Ito and Yamagata were represented in politics by their respective protégés, Saionji Kimmochi and Katsura Taro, who alternated as Prime Minister for the next twelve years. The later part of this period is known as that of 'the Katsura-Saionji truce', a phrase which fairly reflects the tacit understanding between the two main groups. Each possessed the power to obstruct the other, each realized that it was usually better to refrain from using it. Saionji, after he succeeded Ito as president of the Seiyukai in 1903, commanded a fairly docile majority in the lower house of the Diet and the support of Ito's friends in the bureaucracy. Katsura had the backing of Yamagata, the services and the House of Peers. Either could therefore govern as long as he had the other's consent, neither could do so without it. Their recognition of this fact gave Japan a spell of rather deceptive calm.

Katsura remained in office from June 1901 until the outcry over the Treaty of Portsmouth at the end of 1905 brought his resignation. Saionji followed him in January 1906. He included only two Seiyukai ministers in his cabinet, out of deference to Yamagata's views, but had to resign in June 1908 because he failed to reconcile the policies of his party with those of the Genro on the subject of finance. This brought back Katsura until the summer of 1908, when he, too, had difficulties over finance, which he preferred to let Saionji solve. Saionji's attempt to do so by a policy of retrenchment, however, incurred the hostility of both the services, as well as that of Yamagata, and the government was eventually forced out in December 1912 by its inability to replace the War Minister, who had resigned.

There then came a stormy interlude, lasting less than two months, in which Katsura tried to make himself independent of the Seiyukai by forming a party of his own and independent of the Genro by the use of imperial rescripts. He succeeded only in uniting all against him. In February 1913 the Seiyukai launched violent attacks on him in the Diet. Thousands rioted outside the building and stormed the offices of pro-government papers. With the situation completely out of hand, much as it had been in 1905, just after the Russo-Japanese war, Katsura resigned. He died soon after. Since Saionji now became a Genro, the truce was at an end and the men who had effected it made way for others.

Two factors had helped to make the truce possible. First, there was a general feeling of satisfaction in Japan, occasioned by victory in war, the acquisition of fresh territory and the knowledge of steady progress in development at home, which tended to blunt the edge of political passions. Second, there was the fact that the country's substantial citizens had acquired a vested interest in the society which the Meiji leaders had built. Through local assemblies and councils they had achieved standing in prefectural and municipal affairs. By providing recruits for officialdom they had begun to feel part of a national structure and to gain confidence that its outlook would reflect their own. Finally, as voters—the property qualification for suffrage remained in 1912 the payment of 15 yen a year in national taxes, despite several efforts to reduce or abolish it—they chose members of the Diet. It is not surprising that their representatives showed less enthusiasm for what seemed an unavailing and perhaps unnecessary fight to secure control of cabinet policy.

Yet all this was in some part misleading. Changes were already taking place in late Meiji Japan that were to make the political parties both more powerful and more militant, for it was by giving organization and coherence to those whose significance had not so far been fully realized, the Japanese of the city, that they were eventually to achieve a larger measure of success. In other words, their future depended on what was happening to the nation's economy.

Agriculture was still the chief sector of the Japanese economy in the early twentieth century, despite all the efforts to foster industry in the previous generation. It employed about 14 million people, and this, as late as 1920, represented just over half the occupied population. Production of the two main crops, rice and raw silk, was steadily increasing. Rice production, the annual average of which was some 30 million *koku* in 1880–84, became 40 million *koku* in 1890–94, almost 45 million in 1900–04, and 51 million in 1910–14, most of this being due to a fifty per cent rise in yield per acre. There were proportional increases in the yields of lesser crops like wheat and barley. Output of raw silk grew even faster: 11·5 millions lbs. in 1894, 16·5 million in 1904, 31 million in 1914. By the end of the period it accounted for exports valued at 144 million yen, nearly a third of the country's export total.

Over the same years, the process by which the farmer became involved in production for the market and the level of his money expenditure was raised had been completed. He now had to buy fertilizer, tools and seed as well as a variety of household goods, while taxation had also to be paid in cash, not kind. Thus subsistence farming had become impossible. Many owner-cultivators were unable to solve the problems which this situation posed and sank to the status of tenants. As a result two-fifths of the land was tenant-held by 1900. Others, the more successful, became landowners on a larger scale, marking the continued separation of the village into rich and poor. To the rich—a proportion of whom were absentees, since land remained a profitable investment for men who made their money in the towns—the new society gave opportunities of influence, education and good living rather greater than had been enjoyed by their predecessors in feudal Japan. To the poor it gave an opportunity of a different kind: that of finding employment for daughters and younger sons whom the family could no longer support.

For the most part this was in the textile trades, which were the most highly developed sector of Japanese industry. Silk reeling and weaving remained largely rural and provided a good deal of local employment, much of it in the large modern filatures that appeared after 1890. Cotton was even more important, though the location of its factories forced labour to leave the village for the town. As a crop, cotton had ceased to be of value, since the removal of duties in 1896 had made it impossible for home growers to compete with imports from India, but the spinning and weaving sections of the industry were entering a phase of rapid expansion. The number of factory spindles rose from 382,000 in 1893 to 2·4 million twenty years later, yarn output from 116 million lbs. to over 650 million lbs. in a similar period. At the end, between 30 and 40 per cent of the yarn was going to export. The rest went to domestic weavers, of whom a considerable proportion were still engaged in household industry, using handlooms. By 1913, however, there were 85,000 persons employed in concerns with at least five workers. Some of them were specialist weaving firms, producing mostly narrow widths for the home market and as often equipped with handlooms as with power. Others—and these usually the largest—were power-equipped weaving sheds attached to spinning mills, producing wide standardized fabrics for foreign trade. Their exports of piecegoods were valued at 33 million yen in 1913, compared with only 5·7 million in 1900.

Heavy industry, although it had received a great stimulus from government policies of subsidy and investment after the Sino-Japanese war, was as yet impressive for its rate of growth rather than its volume of output. In shipbuilding the annual average of tonnage launched reached 50,000 tons in 1909–13, when there were six yards capable of building steel ships of a thousand tons or more. Pig-iron and steel production had both reached substantial levels: about a quarter of a million tons of each in 1913, representing a half and a third of the country's needs, respectively. Progress had also been made in some types of heavy engineering, notably the manufacture of railway locomotives and rolling stock, while there were a few large firms engaged in making items like electrical equipment, cement, paper, china, glass and so on. Even so, much of the production of consumer goods, including many of Western type, like bicycle parts and other engineering components, was carried on in a host of small family workshops that were to be found in every industrial town.

The development of factories and workshops, whatever their size and type, depended a good deal on the provision of power and transport. In this much had been achieved. Coal output, 5 million metric tons in 1895, was 21 million tons in 1913, of which 40 per cent was used in industry. Electricity, both for power and lighting, had also become available since 1900, mostly from hydraulic plants. One of them gave Tokyo its first large-scale supply in 1907, another, reputedly the largest in Asia, did the same for Osaka four years later. In 1913 the total generator capacity in operation was over half a million kilowatts.

The railway network by that date served most parts of the Japanese islands. The main line, which in 1891 had stretched from Aomori to Kobe, with a spur from Tokyo to the Japan Sea coast at Naoetsu, had been extended by 1901 to Shimonoseki and Nagasaki. In 1906 the decision was taken to nationalize that part of the track which was owned by private companies— about two-thirds—on the grounds that private ownership had led to a lack of standardization and too great an emphasis on immediate returns. The result was to give the government control of all but about 10 per cent of the 5,000 miles of railway then in use. A map of it in 1907 shows, apart from the Aomori-Nagasaki route, on which sleepers and dining cars were now available, two fairly complex local networks round Tokyo and Kyoto-Osaka, with several extensions begun or completed in northern Kyushu and along the Japan Sea coast. Only Hokkaido and Shikoku were completely without a line. Over those elsewhere, 140 million passengers and 24 million tons of goods were carried in this same year.

Locally, the rail system was supplemented by roads, rough but adequate, which made possible the movement of a vastly greater number of carts and other vehicles. The registered number of horsecarts alone rose from under 1,000 to over 86,000 in the twenty years ending in 1897. At the ports the railways linked with coastal and foreign shipping services, of which an increasing proportion were run by Japanese. The merchant marine had grown to 2·4 million gross tons by 1913, sixty per cent being powered by steam or motor; and at this date it carried approximately half the cargoes entering and leaving the country, providing a daily steamer service between Yokohama and Kobe, as well as at least two a week to Nagasaki and Hakodate, and operating regular liner routes to Korea, China, the Philippines, Australia, India, Europe and North America. San Francisco could be reached in sixteen days. Passengers for Europe had a choice of several lines via Suez (P and O, Messageries Maritimes and Norddeutscher Lloyd, in addition to the Japanese NYK), all taking about forty days, or they could travel on the weekly service to Vladivostock and thence by the Trans-Siberian railway.

Japan, in fact, was nothing like so remote and isolated as it had been a generation earlier. Nor did it any longer look quite so oriental, at least in the principal towns. Two of these were large by any standards: Osaka with nearly a million residents at the 1903 census, Tokyo almost twice that size. They also contained much that was familiar to a Western visitor. Both by 1907 had a waterworks, local electric railways, the beginnings of a street electric tramway, and numerous public buildings, banks and offices in the Western style. Less sightly still was the network of telegraph, telephone and electric light wires overhead, while one traveller wrote of Osaka in 1901:

'What strikes the stranger at first glance is the large number of factory chimneys, which proclaim its great manufacturing interests. Hundreds of these smoke-begrimed tops look down upon him, until he begins to think the building of factory chimneys is the one occupation of the people.'[53]

Ironically, even the hundreds of rickshaws, which gave the streets an aspect so unlike those of Europe and America, were a modern addition, only a little older than the bicycles that were just beginning to replace them.

What was true of Tokyo and Osaka also held good on a smaller scale for Kyoto, Yokohama, Nagoya and Kobe, with their resident populations ranging between 250,000 and 400,000 in 1903, and the other nineteen provincial cities which had 50,000 people or more. All had their quota of modern facilities and of brick or concrete buildings to contrast with the traditional architecture of shrines and private homes. Sometimes one could find such things in the countryside, too. Government offices and schools, wherever situated, usually looked thoroughly un-Japanese. Moreover, although the traveller who wished to visit mountainous regions was advised by a guidebook of 1907[54] to take food, flea-powder, disinfectant, soap and candles, as well as bedding, and to be prepared to walk—'the Japanese pack-saddle is torture'—with baggage carried, in the absence of pack-horses, by a coolie—'not improbably a grandfather superannuated from regular work, or possibly a buxom lass'—there were also rural areas which could be easily reached and where a good deal of comfort could be had. Tourist hotels at Nikko and Miyanoshita, their very existence symbolic of change, advertised their possession of electric light, telephones and billiard-rooms; and local inns might well be found to provide chairs and tables, sheets and pillows, if not beds.

All this was symptomatic of something more than a mere desire to emulate the West. The character of the cities and the rate at which their facilities were growing indicated that the modern sector of the economy was at last becoming a significant feature of national life. The proportion of urban population was increasing: 16 per cent lived in towns of over 10,000 inhabitants in 1893, 21 per cent in 1903, 28 per cent in 1913. The number of factory workers, 420,000 in 1900, was twice as large a decade later. Foreign trade figures told a similar story. Exports of semi-manufactured goods, mostly silk, remained a fairly constant 40 to 50 per cent of the whole, but those of food and raw materials were declining, while those of finished articles grew. These last two groups reached equality in 1893–7, when each accounted for about 26 per cent of exports. After another ten years, the percentages were 21 for food and raw materials, 31 for manufactured goods. Similarly imports of raw materials, especially iron ore and cotton, were also getting larger, comprising 22 per cent of total imports in 1893–7, 44 per cent in 1908–12. The pattern is one that is appropriate to a period of steady industrialization.

Thus the first few years of the twentieth century mark a definite stage in Japan's economic history, dividing, one might say, the time of preparation from that of achievement. What is more, there were signs of what the latter might bring by way of benefits and problems. Statistics concerning wages for the period before 1914 are unreliable, but such as they are they indicate a rise in real wages in the twenty years after the China war of the order of 30 per cent. There had already been an increase in *per capita* consumption of rice in the 1880s, from 0·8 *koku* (4 bushels) a person every year to a fraction over a *koku* (5 bushels). This level was maintained, though not improved upon, for half a century. Since rice was very much the preferred diet of Japanese, this must count as better living. So must the greater consumption of textiles, for exports of these did not by any means take the whole of the increase in production.

On the other hand, the country's population had risen from 35 million in 1873 to 46 million in 1903 and the graph was still moving rapidly upward. There were therefore more people to share the available food and goods. Soon after 1890, indeed, Japan became a net importer of rice and by 1904 was buying nearly 3 million *koku* a year abroad, mostly from Korea and Formosa. Thereafter she faced the familiar problem of the densely populated industrial state, the need to import substantial food supplies and to export goods in payment for them, complicated in her case by negligible home production of raw materials like iron ore, lead, tin, petroleum, cotton and wool, large quantities of which had therefore to be imported too.

These circumstances, in conjunction with the government's resolve to maintain a large military establishment, helped to hold back the rate of increase in standards of living. And such increase as did occur was not evenly apportioned. The town profited more than the village, the owner and manager more than the urban worker. It is true that this was in one sense a stimulus to economic development, in that it made possible a high level of savings and investment, for example, and ensured ample supplies of cheap industrial labour, but it also threatened to bring political unrest. Entrepreneurs, acquiring wealth, sought influence, usually through the existing political parties. Workers, suffering from low wages and atrocious labour conditions, began to organize trade unions and parties of their own. They met with a sharp reaction from officialdom. In 1900 police regulations were issued making strikes illegal and in the following year a new Social Democratic Party was suppressed within a day of its formation. Moreover, attempts to introduce labour legislation, beginning as early as 1898, met with obstruction from vested interests represented in the Diet. In the cotton industry, especially—where young female workers, 'hired from the countryside by practices which bordered often on seduction'[55] and lodged in factory dormitories, were required to work a twelve-hour day or more in even the best concerns—mill owners fought stubbornly to delay the passage of a Factory Act prescribing a maximum of an eleven-hour day for women and children. It was 1911 before the bill became law and another five years to its enforcement. The story spoke eloquently of future troubles. Japan, it seemed, in acquiring a modern industry, was acquiring also a problem in industrial relations and the politics that went with it.

The influences that were changing the Japanese city were also changing the life of its inhabitants, not only in respect of where they worked and what they did there, or of the politics they argued, but also in terms of what they wore and ate and how they spent their leisure. An early sign of it was the disappearance of traditional hairstyles, chiefly among men, and the substitution of close cutting in the European manner. Official approval of the change was announced in September 1871. By that date Japanese were already to be seen in public wearing a fine array of international clothing—there are references to Prussian hats, French shoes and invernesses—and in 1873, it is said, Satsuma samurai appearing in Tokyo in the old costume 'were as much stared at as foreigners had formerly been'.[56] Thereafter the example of the Court (which had adopted Western ceremonial dress at the end of 1872), the cabinet and the diplomatic corps, to say nothing of the uniforms used by the services, police and railway officials, all helped to make the new clothing widely accepted. By the end of the century it was worn almost universally among the upper classes, at least on public and business occasions. The 1907 guidebook observes helpfully:

'Japanese officials now attend their offices in frock or morning coats, and Europeans visiting them should be similarly attired. At garden parties and special social functions, frock-coats and tall hats are expected.'[57]

If one adds that the use of visiting cards was general and that the smoking of cigars and cigarettes was becoming popular, it is clear that the visitor could soon be made to feel at home. In the towns he could get beer, which was successfully produced in Tokyo and Yokohama, and most varieties of Western food, though elsewhere he might find it difficult to obtain bread, meat or milk and might have to depend on the rice and fish, supplemented by chicken and eggs, of which the more expensive versions of the Japanese diet consisted.

All Western foods, of course, were still luxuries to Japanese, as were most of the country's imported pastimes and entertainments. Western music, for example, had first been performed in the 1880s at the Rokumeikan, a hall built in Tokyo to provide a place at which Japanese official society could meet foreign diplomats and other residents. The newly-formed services bands and some of the court musicians played there in concerts and also for dancing, lessons being given by a German instructor. Before long, as a result, Western music became a polite accomplishment. It was taught at the Tokyo School of Music, founded in 1887, which in 1903 helped to put on the first opera in Japanese, a translation of Gluck's *Orpheus*, with the help of a foreign conductor and pianist. Such pleasures were for the few, however. Popular taste remained wedded to martial music—also in the Western style—like the marches and military songs that were taught in schools, which from August 1905 could be heard at the new bandstand in Tokyo's Hibiya Park, where army and navy performed alternately. A few years later similar performances were begun in Osaka. The great acclaim with which they were greeted brought a multiplication of the concerts and a proliferation of bands, many of them under private auspices.

In the theatre the Japanese tradition proved better able to hold its own, for although the revival of Noh towards the end of the nineteenth century was a matter largely of aristocratic patronage, the Kabuki drama, with its melodramatic plots, coarse humour and vivid spectacle, continued to have a wide appeal. It was handicapped for a time by government insistence that its stories be useful and rewarding—and by attempts to perform translated Western plays, for which its techniques were quite unsuitable—but it nevertheless remained far more successful than performances in the Western style. These, too, relied heavily on translations at first, with Shakespeare, Molière and Ibsen all represented. What is more, it was not until late in the Meiji period that the acting and staging of them reached competent standards. That they did so was largely the work of Kawakami Otojiro, whose travels abroad between 1893 and 1903 enabled him to introduce modern stage lighting, scenery and other improvements for his Tokyo productions.

Concerts and the theatre in their new forms were for those who lived in, or could visit, one of the major cities. The rest knew of them by hearsay or by what they read. Indeed, much of what was new in Japanese life in general found an expression in its literature, not now because books had a didactic purpose, like those just after the Restoration, which had been concerned to introduce novelties of thought and custom to the uninformed reader, but because they reflected an environment in which the writer lived and worked. For example, Nagai Kafu's *Sumida-gawa* (The Sumida River, 1909), a novel about the passing of the old Tokyo, is full of references to things like night school, tramcars, gaslight in the theatre, an isolation hospital, and so on, an apparently random selection of modern trappings which yet form an essential background to the plot. The story and its characters depend on changes in society in a much more fundamental way. Central to them are the student, Chokichi, whose mother, a teacher of dramatic recitation, wants to put him through university in order that he may qualify for the security of a salaried job. He, however, is drawn to the threatre, a kind of disobedience which is also a turning back to a way of life his mother had rejected for him, though it was in a sense her own. The resulting conflicts, between duty, defined as respect for parental authority, and inclination, as well as between the traditional and the modern in Japanese living, are themes that were to be characteristic of many books, plays and eventually films in the twentieth century. Of a different kind, but equally contemporary in concept and setting, was Tayama Katai's *Ippeisotsu* (One soldier, 1908), a grimly realistic story of a private serving in the Russo-Japanese war, whom illness, loneliness and hardship drain of patriotism and courage until he can do no more than hide himself and die. The idea, the treatment, even the prose in which they were written, made novels like these a far cry from those of a generation earlier.

Yet literature had not entirely abandoned its past. There was a novel called *Takekurabe* (Growing Up, 1895) by the woman novelist Higuchi Ichiyo, about a group of boys and girls in their 'teens who lived on the outskirts of Tokyo's pleasure quarter, the Yoshiwara. Acute in observation, it had strong echoes of the better Tokugawa writing, like that of Saikaku, so much so that it makes one hardly aware of a changing world at all. Were it not for references to the new currency, the *yen*, the scene might easily be Edo. Nor is this due to mere nostalgia on the author's part. Rather, it is because she had chosen for her subject an aspect of Japanese society which had itself changed little, if at all.

This serves to emphasize something which an interest in the modern might easily lead one to overlook, the fact that there were many things in Japan which had been hardly touched by the Meiji reforms, at least in their essentials. The manners and outlook of the Yoshiwara and the Kabuki theatre, the seasonal rhythm of life on the farm, the social exchanges properly to be observed between families and persons, these remained much as they had been in 1800. So did a great part of Japanese religion. Buddhism, it is true, to some extent declined. Deprived of official support by the fall of the Tokugawa, it was sharply attacked after 1868 by the adherents of Shinto, who on a number of occasions used force against its priests and temples. Moreover, they were encouraged in their actions by the policies of the Meiji government. Dependent for their own authority on that of the emperor, the new leaders were naturally prejudiced in favour of a religion which asserted his divine descent. They therefore gave it a place of honour, not only in court ceremonies, where it had always been predominant, but also in administration, setting the Council of Shinto Religion above even the Council of State in the formal hierarchy of their first constitutional arrangements. When this plan was abandoned in 1872, Shinto still received direct government patronage through the appointment of official teachers to promote its spread.

Greater knowledge of Western practice, together with a

limited revival of Buddhism, brought a change in 1877. Thereafter government policy distinguished between two different kinds of Shinto: that which had a direct bearing on questions of state and that which was concerned only with religious belief, the first being put under the supervision of a department within the Home Ministry, which became responsible for classifying and financing most national, and many local, shrines, while the second became a matter for private organizations acting on their own. After a few years several of the latter received official recognition as separate religious bodies, that is, as Shinto sects. This gave them the same standing as the Buddhist sects with which they might be said to have competed.

Thus by 1900 State Shinto and Sect Shinto were clearly separated, the one concerned largely with the emperor and official ceremonial, the other with those elements of popular belief which had for centuries been the chief part of religion as the majority of Japanese knew it. Within the average household, in fact, religious observance had been little changed. It had long been eclectic, linked to the rituals of birth, marriage and death and to the festivals of local deities, rather than to broad concepts of faith and organization. Accordingly, a relative increase in the influence of Shinto on the national scene, and a relative decline in that of Buddhism, made little difference, for to the family it meant no more than a shift of emphasis within a common tradition.

The challenge to this tradition that came from Christianity, though radical, was no more productive of widespread change. It was not until 1873 that diplomatic pressure made Christianity legal and for some years afterwards the missionaries had to struggle against the heritage of Tokugawa anti-Christian propaganda. The frenzy of enthusiasm for all things Western, which engulfed Japan at the end of the 1870s, eventually helped them to overcome it, as did recognition of, and respect for, missionary achievements in medicine and education, but the churches suffered setbacks again a decade later from the growth of nationalism and a revival of anti-foreign feeling. The result, despite a great outpouring of funds and human effort, was a total of no more than 140,000 converts by 1907. Of these, 60,000 were Roman Catholics, with an archbishop in

Tokyo and bishops in Osaka, Sendai and Nagasaki; just under 50,000 were Protestants; and 29,000 were followers of the Greek Orthodox faith, which had been propagated with considerable success by a handful of priests from Russia.

Christianity was often more important in its influence on ideas than the number of its adherents would lead one to expect. Nevertheless, it was not strong enough to revolutionize the whole outlook of Japanese society. Indeed, if the Meiji era brought a challenge to the old beliefs at all, it was the threat to Confucian ethics and the patterns of behaviour based upon them that came from the temporal strand of Western thought, now embodied in the curriculum of schools throughout Japan and in much of the country's daily life. Institutionally, Confucianism had suffered severely from the Restoration, because of the abolition of the establishments for teaching it which had been maintained by the Bakufu and feudal lords. Moreover, the cosmological elements in Confucian philosophy, like those in Western religion, proved unable to survive the growth of science.[58] On the other hand, in matters of politics and ethics Confucian tenets remained the norm. They found their way habitually into government edicts and they played a vital part in shaping the education system's course in 'morals', so that Confucian virtues of loyalty, harmony and filial piety, in which schools had to provide instruction, became the basis of civic and social duty in the modern state.

This was a situation that greatly appealed to conservatives, who could console themselves with the observation that however much the mechanisms of government were of alien origin, the ideas that suffused its working were Japanese. Patriotism and a respect for the past for them went hand in hand. By contrast, radicals and reformers turned more and more to the West for inspiration, not only in science and technology—which were patriotic because they contributed to national strength—but also in questions of human behaviour and relationships. Christianity, for the most part, they rejected, just as they rejected the ancient religions and philosophy of Japan. Instead, they turned to the example of a new generation of Western thinkers for theories that were secular, pragmatic, even anti-religious, thereby initiating a conflict which, because it involved the emotions of nationalism as well as the traditions of family life, contributed largely to the turbulence of the following fifty years. The Meiji leaders had succeeded remarkably in their plans to make Japan strong and modern. In doing so, however, they had set up tensions whose results were nearly to destroy their work.

CHAPTER XI

JAPAN BECOMES A WORLD POWER
1914-1922

Japan and the mainland—declaration of war on Germany—the Twenty-one Demands—relations with the Allies—peace settlement—the Washington Conference

WHEN A MAJOR war broke out in Europe in August 1914, Japan, by virtue of the progress she had made in the previous fifty years, was for the first time in a position to intervene in European questions. By 1918, when the war ended, doing so had made her a world power, with a military and naval establishment capable of giving substance to the rights she claimed, as well as an economy far enough developed to support her forces, population and prestige. Thus at Versailles Japan's delegates ranked next in importance to those of Britain, France and the United States. In the League of Nations she had one of the permanent seats on the Council. Finally, at Washington in 1922 her activities became the subject of international agreements which sought to restrict the Japanese advance in China and elsewhere, an event that constituted a tribute, if an unwelcome one, to the speed at which her strength and influence were growing.

This was a situation very different from that which the Tokugawa had faced, or the Meiji leaders, yet the policies that brought it about were nevertheless a development of, rather than a departure from, those of the nineteenth century. The fear of Western encroachment still lingered in Japanese thinking on foreign affairs, bringing an almost universal acceptance of the need for national strength. Behind it lay the same ambivalence of reaction, paralleling, though in a new context, what an earlier age had labelled *kaikoku* ('open the country') and *joi* ('expel the barbarian'). There were men who argued, like the supporters of *kaikoku*, that the country must observe the rules of procedure that the West laid down and seek recognition, as well as safety, within them, forming alliances, exchanging goods, borrowing ideas. There were others, the uncompromising, who wished instead to turn away from the West entirely. They did not, it is true, urge seclusion or a war of liberation, as *joi* advocates had done; but by demanding for Japan a position of supremacy in East Asia, which would make her independent of Western help and able to repel any new attempt at extending Western dominance, they were appealing to the same prejudices and emotions.

Among both groups, preoccupation with the nearby mainland was as great as ever. Since 1894 the ties of geography and tradition had been reinforced by two successful wars and the acquisition of territorial possessions, giving Japan important interests to defend and a foothold on the continent from which others might rapidly be added. The result was to make China and her northern neighbours more than ever a focus of Japanese ambitions. One contemporary described these bluntly as 'a determination to be undisputed masters of Eastern Asia',[59] which war in Europe, distracting the attention of the powers, made practical. The description gains validity from the actions of Japanese governments between 1914 and 1922. On the other hand, Japanese policy was neither so consistent nor so easily agreed upon as this might make one think, for there were differences of outlook, even as regards China, which led at times to bitter argument.

In fact, one can identify three main strands in the debate on Far East policies:

First, exemplified in the demands for reform in Korea, which had precipitated the war of 1894-5, was the desire to create a defensive league of states, modernized and under Japanese leadership, which would free its members from subjection to the West. This concept helped bring about the annexation of Korea, a step justified as the sole means of overcoming Korean lethargy and reaction. It also led to much dabbling in the politics of China, undertaken in a search for men who would

lire Sun-Yatsen

co-operate if they were backed—and their reluctance occasionally overborne—by Japanese arms and money. There were,
however, contradictions: supporting revolutionaries overseas
might be a way to stimulate modernization, but there was
always the risk that it might encourage radicals at home; while
intervention designed to make China resist the West tended,
paradoxically, to arouse a nationalism which had as the target
of its hostility, Japan.

Second, alternative to such a league, were plans for an empire
on the continent from which Japan would gain strength enough
to defend the area singlehanded. This began as military strategy,
involving Korea, Manchuria and perhaps Mongolia, with
defence against Russia as its primary object; but in the twentieth century, when the region gained importance as a market
and source of raw materials, it had an economic side as well.
This was to culminate in the industrialization of North Korea
and South Manchuria, chiefly after 1930.

Third, was the application of a similar plan to China, though
with greater emphasis on trade and outlets for investment.
There were men, undoubtedly, who hoped to find in China
the kind of opportunities that Britain had found in India—
just as there were men who thought in terms more grandiose
still, of an empire stretching to the Indo-Chinese peninsula
and beyond—but for the majority, China, if not an ally, was to
be a source of Japanese wealth. As such, whether she wished
it or not, she would contribute to the area's security. Yet even
in this there were problems. Trade, if China proved obstinate,
would have to be supported by bases, sometimes by the use
of force. It might also, if Japan's rights were privileged or
exclusive, evoke the hostility of Britain and America. Economic expansion, therefore, for all that it was apparently
peaceful in intent, involved risks which not everyone was
prepared to take.

These plans and policies were not incompatible with each
other in one respect, for all could usefully contribute to the
increase of Japanese strength. They might thus be regarded as
different methods for the attainment of a single goal, divergent

rather than contradictory, with belief in one not necessarily a barrier to acceptance of the rest. On the other hand, they were not sufficiently alike to ensure unanimity in action. When the moment came for making practical decisions—drafting a diplomatic note, for example, or moving troops—a country with limited resources had to be clear what its immediate objectives were. Was it more important at a given time to placate Western opinion or to secure a vital base? Was it better to browbeat or to woo the Chinese leaders? Was action in China or Manchuria the more appropriate, taking account of the fact that different foreign powers might be concerned, according to the choice that was made? These were the sort of questions a government would have to ask. That its members were committed in general to a policy of expansion did not guarantee that they would arrive at identical answers.

The surviving Meiji leaders, now, as Genro, the emperor's senior advisers on matters of state, were inclined to caution. Yamagata Aritomo, much the most influential since Ito's death, has always been regarded as a militarist, but his comments on foreign affairs in 1914 and 1915 show a marked reluctance to approve provocative measures. He agreed that Japan must strengthen her position in China and Manchuria. At the same time, he identified two limiting factors: first, that nothing be done to provoke the powers; second, that China be won to an attitude of genuine co-operation. Only in this way could Japan consolidate her gains and retain them when the European war was over. For once the war ended, he thought, 'the various countries will again focus their attention on the Far East and the benefits and rights they might derive from this region', exacerbating 'the rivalry between the white and non-white races'.[60] In such a situation, Japan and China would have to co-operate to survive. This would be impossible if Japan had meanwhile acted so as to alienate China, driving her, perhaps, into America's arms.

In the army, many senior officers accepted Yamagata's views. Others preferred Japan to rely on her own efforts, as she had done against Russia in 1904, and concentrate on building up her military bases in the north. Diplomats, by contrast, were with few exceptions anxious to proceed by negotiation, not by force. Party politicians were attracted to the support of economic penetration by their links with businessmen, to a desire for quick successes by their need for votes. As a result, all variations on the theme of priority were represented in policy discussions. Moreover, the decision reached at any given time was likely to reflect the balance of political strength between these groups and individuals, not necessarily a reconciliation of ideas.

It might also be influenced by pressures from outside. Newspapers, popular and thoroughly nationalist in tone, could be counted on to demand 'strong' action whatever the issue. So might the mobs, the more easily incited on this question because of the loyalty they were taught at school or in a conscript army. Then there were the personal pressures, difficult to assess but certainly exerted, that were brought to bear on public figures. Not least were those that emanated from societies of patriots, the first of which, the Genyosha, founded by ex-samurai in Fukuoka in 1881, had a range of activities that ran all the way from espionage, agitation and murder in Korea, to the provision of strong-arm men for use in Diet elections and attempts at intimidating those whom it accused of 'weakness' in foreign affairs. The bomb attack on Okuma in 1889, for example, was by one of its members, the assassination of the Korean queen in 1895 by others. It was a Genyosha man, Uchida Ryohei, with the patronage of another, Toyama Mitsuru, who founded a still more famous organization in 1901, the Kokuryukai (the Amur River Society, more often called the Black Dragon Society). This carried on the Genyosha's work, but with emphasis on Manchuria instead of Korea. After 1905, anticipating the next stage of Japan's advance, it turned to China, establishing connections with men like Sun Yat-sen and acting as a semi-official intelligence corps for the Japanese army. Simultaneously it sought to bring Japanese leaders into conformity with its plans, sometimes by threats, sometimes by persuasion—Uchida and Toyama, as ex-samurai of manifest sincerity, had access to the very highest circles—and sometimes by public demonstrations. The plans themselves were outlined in a memorandum which Uchida sent to government officials in November 1914: Japanese agents were to incite their friends among the Chinese radicals to revolt;

the Japanese army would be sent to restore order, bringing its
protegés to power; and a defensive alliance could then be concluded between the two governments. It was the pattern of
Korea in 1894, repeated.

Though neither the Kokuryukai nor any other single group
was able to exercise a decisive influence on Japanese policy,
the effect of all these pressures, both within the government
and outside it, was to create a climate of opinion in which an
advance of some kind on the Asian mainland—whether military or economic, in China or Manchuria, with Chinese co-
operation or without it—became axiomatic. Despite the ebb
and flow, as first one faction gained the upper hand and then
another, and despite some changes of direction, there resulted
an overall movement towards Japanese domination of an area
comprising China, Manchuria, Korea and the adjacent islands.
This is the theme of the country's foreign relations between
1914 and 1922.

The European crisis of 1914 came at a time when Japan had a
government willing to exploit it. The Yamamoto cabinet,
which had succeeded that of Katsura in the previous year, fell
in March 1914 as a result of revelations that bribery had been
used to influence the placing of naval contracts. This brought
to power Okuma Shigenobu as Prime Minister, with Kato
Komei to handle foreign affairs. Both were party politicians.
Both were also supporters of the Anglo-Japanese alliance, but
they did not feel themselves committed on this account to
maintaining the *status quo* in China, notwithstanding the fact
that this was ostensibly a principal aim of the agreement.
Indeed, they were anxious that Japan's position in China be
strengthened by all possible means.

This became apparent at the beginning of August, when
Russia, France and Britain in quick succession declared war on
Germany. Their action raised the question whether Japan's
alliance with Britain, even though it did not apply specifically
to Europe, imposed on her any military obligations in such a
situation, an issue raised by Britain herself a few days later
when she sought Japanese help in protecting Hong Kong and
Weihaiwei, as well as in naval action against German commerce
raiders in the Pacific. Kato, in particular, felt that this was too

limited and too unprofitable a form of co-operation. He preferred war, arguing that the freedom of action which would come
with full belligerent status far outweighed the risk of being on
the losing side; and on August 8 he succeeded in persuading
the cabinet and Genro to his point of view. The news greatly
alarmed the authorities in London. Thinking, like most diplomatic representatives of the powers, that Kato's intentions
were to involve China in the war and so exploit Europe's preoccupation with its own affairs, they tried first to get Japan's
decision changed, then to secure an assurance that no action
would be taken against German bases on the China coast. But
both efforts failed. On August 15 Japan demanded that Germany withdraw or disarm her warships in Far Eastern waters
and surrender to Japan the leased territory of Kiaochow. When
the demand was ignored, a declaration of war followed it on
August 23.

Japan's military action was prompt and successful. On
September 2, 1914, her troops began to land in the Shantung
peninsula and advance towards Tsingtao and Kiaochow Bay.
By November 7 Tsingtao had fallen, marking the completion
of the campaign. Meanwhile, naval operations during October
had led to the occupation of the German-held Pacific islands
north of the equator. Thus in less than three months all German bases, railways and other installations in Japan's sphere of
interest had been taken over.

This left the way clear for action regarding China, or rather,
for an extension of the action that had already been begun in
the previous year. Many Japanese, especially members of the
Kokuryukai and their associates, had welcomed the success of
the revolution begun by Sun Yat-sen's supporters at Wuhan in
1911, which led to the creation of a Chinese republic in 1912.
Equally, they had been disappointed when the former imperial
official, Yuan Shih-k'ai, became its first president, instead of
Sun, whom they had expected to plan the modernization of his
country in co-operation with Japan. Hence there was much
sympathy for Sun when he led a revolt against Yuan in 1913.
Moreover, when a number of Japanese in Nanking were killed
or manhandled by troops under the command of Chang Tso-
lin, who had been sent to suppress the revolt, indignation
found a practical outlet. Protest meetings, newspaper editorials

and the assassination of a Foreign Ministry official all contributed to persuading the Japanese government to present demands in October for an indemnity and the dismissal of Chang Tso-lin. Yuan had little choice but to grant them, together with fresh railway rights for Japan in China.

Okuma, it was thought, when he succeeded Yamamoto, would continue and develop Yamamoto's policies in this regard, since he was known to favour strong action on the mainland. He accordingly came under considerable pressure in 1914 to use the hostilities against Germany as an opportunity for overthrowing Yuan Shih-k'ai. To this idea, however, neither he nor the Foreign Ministry were unduly sympathetic. They regarded negotiations with established authority as more useful than inciting revolution, for which reason they were much more open to a different set of proposals, coming from the army, notably the military attaché in Peking. These, as finally worked out by Kato and a group of government officials, identified a list of concessions to be won from China which were designed, when implemented, to free Japan from dependence on Chinese friendship altogether. They provided, first, for the transfer to Japan of former German rights in the province of Shantung. This meant, in effect, Chinese recognition of a *fait accompli*, since Japanese troops were in occupation of most of the area concerned. Next, they outlined additional railway and mining rights to be obtained in Manchuria and Mongolia, as well as other economic and political privileges in that region to support them. Finally, China was to be forced to give an undertaking not to cede or lease coastal territory to any other power—a promise which was made more specific with respect to Fukien, where Japan had economic interests—and arrangements were to be made for the appointment of Japanese political, financial and military advisers to the Chinese government, joint Sino-Japanese police administration in key areas, the purchase by China of Japanese munitions and joint operation of certain Chinese arsenals.

Such in substance were the Twenty-one Demands, a draft of which was handed to Japan's minister in Peking at the beginning of December 1914, with instructions to use it when a chance arose. He did not have long to wait. In January 1915 Yuan Shih-k'ai announced his intention of revoking the war zone declared during operations in Shantung and asked that foreign troops in China be withdrawn, since China was a neutral in the European struggle. To his dismay, this was described as an unfriendly act by the Japanese, whose prepared demands were at once presented. What is more, they went not through normal diplomatic channels, but secretly to Yuan, with a hint that if he rejected them help might be given to those groups in China which sought his fall.

Yuan could do little in face of Japan's obvious determination when those most likely to help him were already involved in war. Inspired leaks of information from Peking brought protests to Japan from various quarters, especially the United States, but none were strong enough to prevent Foreign Minister Kato from pressing his advantage home. In May, after several weeks of fruitless talks, he modified the proposals, leaving out the most objectionable of those in the final section, but making the rest an ultimatum. This brought quick compliance. Treaties signed on May 25, 1915, together with an accompanying exchange of notes, gave Japan most of what she wanted. It included Chinese approval of any agreement about German rights in Shantung that might be concluded between Japan and Germany, with the proviso that Japan would restore the Kiaochow lease to China in return for the port being opened to foreign trade; an extension of existing leases in Manchuria and a promise of Japanese priority in all development there; and a number of useful, if less sweeping, gains elsewhere.

The agreement, notwithstanding the fact that it gave Japan a preponderance she could not have dared to hope for ten years earlier, was not received without criticism in Tokyo. Some thought it had fallen short of what might have been achieved, some that the effort had been geographically too diffuse, others again that it was a betrayal of the Chinese radicals and reformers. These were the objections of minorities, however, coming chiefly from outside the ruling circle. More important were the objections raised by Yamagata Aritomo and the new leader of the Seiyukai, Hara Kei (Takashi), who, although far apart in politics, were united in condemning the methods by which the new privileges had been obtained. By his bullying, they said, Kato had aroused the hostility of both China and the powers. Consequently, when the latter tried to resume their pre-war position in the Far East at the end of hostilities, as inevitably they would, Japan would be handicapped in resisting them by Chinese enmity. The solution, as Yamagata saw it, was to limit the government's immediate objectives to securing Yuan's acceptance of two basic propositions: first, that Japan's expansion in Manchuria was inevitable, both as an outlet for her growing population and as a means of defending China from Russian attack; second, that the two countries must co-operate against the West.

Yamagata failed to force this plan on Okuma, though his strictures had the effect of getting Kato excluded from the cabinet when it was reorganized in the following August. Moreover, a year later Yamagata was able to block an attempt by Okuma to bring Kato back as premier, securing the appointment instead for his own protégé, Terauchi Masatake, who as governor-general in Korea had already come to much the same conclusions about the mainland as his mentor. Thus when he formed his government in October 1916 it was with certain intentions clearly in his mind. Policy towards China, which he kept under his own control, was to be directed towards conciliation. This was to be attained, however, not by reducing Japan's requirements, but by working closely with such Chinese leaders as were willing to promote them, especially Tuan Ch'i-jui, most likely successor to Yuan Shih-k'ai, who had died in June. Accordingly, between February 1917, when Nishihara Kamezo visited Peking as Terauchi's personal emissary, and September 1918, when Terauchi himself resigned, Tuan and his immediate colleagues received consistent Japanese support. It helped to keep them most of the time in office, chiefly through a series of so-called 'Nishihara loans', totalling 145 million yen, which were ostensibly for the development of telegraphs, railways, mining and timber concessions, but in fact did more for Tuan's political funds than for China's economic growth.

Notwithstanding the fact that Tuan's government had little authority, since effective power in most parts of China had been seized by local warlords, former henchmen of Yuan Shih-k'ai, Terauchi found it highly convenient to have a measure of co-operation from the country's official rulers.

Nevertheless, this by itself was not sufficient to guarantee Japan's position. As a corollary to the policy, therefore, he set out to gain European recognition of the benefits his predecessors had secured. A first move in this direction had been made by Okuma, who had taken advantage of Russia's desperate need for munitions to negotiate a secret Russo-Japanese alliance in July 1916, designed to protect the Far Eastern interests of its signatories, including those which Japan had just obtained in Manchuria and Mongolia. Terauchi determined to complete the pattern by gaining similar assurances from the other powers, using as his bargaining point the question of Japan's participation in the war. She had several times refused requests to send troops to Europe or to provide naval forces for the Baltic, Mediterranean and Dardanelles, on the grounds that all her strength was needed for her own defence; but in January 1917, when he received another such request, this time from Britain for naval assistance against German submarines, Terauchi did not reject it. Instead, he seized the opportunity to conclude a secret agreement, dated February 16, 1917, by which he promised to provide a naval escort group for service in European waters and to support British claims to the former German islands in the Pacific south of the equator, in return for a British undertaking to back Japan's claims in Shantung, the Carolines, Marianas and Marshalls. Within a few weeks France and Italy had been induced to make similar commitments, in this case as the price for Japanese help in persuading China to declare war on Germany.

There remained the United States, sympathetic towards China and much less susceptible to blackmail over military co-operation. Here Japan tried promises, not threats. In September 1917 she sent a special ambassador to Washington, Ishii Kikujiro, who in November carried out a public exchange of notes with Lansing, the American Secretary of State. They committed Japan to respecting the independence and territorial integrity of China, as well as to promoting equal opportunity for all in China's foreign trade. On the other hand, America recognized that 'territorial propinquity' gave Japan 'special interests', which she was entitled to protect.

This was all that could immediately be done to prepare against the expected recriminations. But when the war was over the peace conference at Versailles provided an occasion for Japan to get her rights and status written into a general treaty. Hara Kei was by this time premier, having succeeded Terauchi in September 1918, and Saionji, youngest of the Genro at seventy-four, was sent as Japan's chief delegate; but the change of men did not involve a change of policy. Saionji, starting with the advantage of having known Clemenceau as a student and of being accepted on equal terms by Wilson and Lloyd George, soon showed that he was determined to hold his country's allies to their promises. He was the better able to do so, moreover, because of Japan's known reserves of military strength. Indeed, considering how little part she had played in wartime operations, it was a great tribute to her general standing that she was one of the five powers to have representatives on the Council of Ten, which began discussion of the peace terms in January 1919.

For the most part the Japanese delegates spoke only on matters which their government regarded as its direct concern: Shantung; the Pacific islands; and racial equality. The first of them, Shantung, proved from the beginning to be a major stumbling block. China had sent a strong delegation, which engaged vigorously in propaganda to convince both the council and the press that the 1915 treaties were invalid because they had been signed under the threat of force; and although the argument was not convincing legally—as well as suffering tactically from the disadvantage that it could be extended to all the other treaties of the powers with China—it had American sympathy, so that considerable efforts were made to find a compromise. Japan, trusting to the promises made in 1917, remained unmoved, rejecting first an American proposal for joint action by the powers, then a British proposal for a Shantung mandate; and she gained her point at last on April 30, when it was decided to include in the treaty a clause admitting her claim to Germany's former rights, subject to such arrangements as she might make with China. This was not the end of the story, however, for the Chinese representatives refused to sign the treaty in that form. Thus when the conference ended late in June, Japan's position, though she was in *de facto* control of Shantung and diplomatically unassailable, still lacked legal sanction.

The Pacific islands question caused little dispute and Japan was given those she claimed as a League of Nations mandate. But in the negotiations concerning the establishment of the League itself she suffered a reverse. Prompted partly by memories of the unequal treaties, partly by more recent restrictions on Japanese emigration to Australia and the American west coast—by this time population pressure at home was causing a good many Japanese to seek opportunities of settlement overseas, chiefly in those parts of the world where standards of living were relatively high—public opinion in Japan had seized on the idea of embodying a racial equality clause in the League of Nations charter. This was proposed in February 1919 by Makino, the Japanese member of the drafting commission, and was supported by China, Czecho-Slovakia, France, Greece, Italy and Poland. However, bitter opposition from Hughes of Australia caused a decision to be postponed and before Makino raised the matter again in April at the commission's last meeting, Australian and Californian pressure had made certain that neither Britain nor the United States would accept the motion. This ensured its defeat, leaving Japan with a feeling of resentment that was never entirely assuaged, even by her permanent seat on the Council and full representation in the League's committees and secretariat.

Another failure, more costly both in money and reputation, had meanwhile arisen from a matter that was not on the Versailles agenda at all. This was the Siberian affair, stemming from the Russian revolution of 1917. For the revolution had not only robbed the allies of Russia's military assistance, it had also brought chaos to Russia's Far Eastern possessions, which threatened to spread to neighbouring Manchuria and aroused fears that in the long run revolutionary doctrines might contaminate the rest of the area too, including China. If they did, they were likely to undermine Japan's position there. This, at least, is how the Japanese army saw it, with the result that by December 1917, only a month after the Bolshevik *coup*, it was discussing plans to put a military shield round the whole of China's northern frontier. It proposed to send troops into Siberia, seize the railways and support whatever anti-Bolsheviks it could find. The Foreign Ministry, under Motono Ichiro, made similar proposals, though it arrived at them independently, largely from fear of possible moves by Germany. Indeed, so independent were the two plans that their sponsors found it impossible to co-operate with each other. This proved embarrassing when Terauchi, who was still premier at this time, called meetings to decide on policy at the end of 1917, particularly since Saionji, Hara and Makino all believed that military action would involve a risk of war, which they were quite unwilling to take. The result was deadlock among the government's advisers, not resolved until March 1918, when Yamagata declared himself opposed to intervention. It would, he thought, almost certainly mean fullscale hostilities against both Germany and the Soviets, which Japan could only contemplate if she had the backing of her allies, especially the United States.

This did nothing to change the views of the army, which was much less under Yamagata's control than in the past and went on working out the details of extensive operations. It did, however, bring Terauchi temporarily into alliance with Hara and force the resignation of Foreign Minister Motono, leaving his successor to set about the task of gaining American agreement to some kind of Japanese move. For some weeks he could make little headway, though it was known that both Britain and France were prepared to approve the idea in general terms. Then in June and July Czech forces, fighting their way out of Russia in an attempt to continue the war against Germany despite Russia's surrender, seized Vladivostock and the eastern sections of the Trans-Siberian railway. At this the United States proposed limited intervention to cover the Czech withdrawal, an offer which precipitated another crisis in Japanese policy formation by resurrecting the arguments of the winter and spring. The army by this time was thinking of a force of seven divisions, operating throughout the area east of Irkutsk. The American plan, by contrast, which Hara and his friends preferred, envisaged a single division at most, based on Vladivostock. In such circumstances Terauchi had to work hard to preserve even a semblance of government unity and the final decision, reached on August 2, 1918, was the best compromise he could effect: one, or perhaps two, Japanese divisions to be sent to Siberia, with another force, rather smaller, supporting them in Manchuria. Nothing beyond this would be undertaken, he promised Hara, without further consultation.

Despite this assurance, it was the army's original plans, or something like them, that were actually carried out. By the end of 1918 four or five Japanese divisions were operating in the Amur basin, controlling the whole of the railway and far outnumbering the American and other allied contingents. Hara, now Prime Minister, found it impossible to exercise control or to effect withdrawal, even though Japan's policy was unpopular both at home and abroad. Nor was anything of substance being achieved. White Russian and Cossack puppet leaders proved more a liability than a help. They were quite unable to govern, equally unable to check the advance of Soviet forces from the Urals which began in the following year, so that by November 1919 the Soviets were in Omsk and moving steadily east. In January 1920, therefore, the American government announced the recall of its troops, an example quickly followed by Britain, France and Canada. Only the Japanese remained, actually extending their occupation to northern Sakhalin soon after, in retaliation for a massacre of Japanese citizens at Nikolaevsk; but even to them it was clear by the middle of 1920 that the venture was doomed to failure within a very short time.

Siberia was one of several problems in the Pacific area that had yet to be settled, all of them concerning Japan in one way or another. China still refused to come to terms over Shantung, though it was obvious that Japan had built up too great a stake there to evacuate entirely. American-Japanese relations, already strained by disagreement over Siberia, were being exacerbated by continued disputes over immigration, while a naval armaments race had developed between the two countries which involved Great Britain as well. In fact, there seemed to many governments a real danger that the hostility between America and Japan might end in war, a prospect which filled British statesmen, in particular, with alarm, in view of their obligations under the Anglo-Japanese alliance. In June 1921, therefore, they decided, largely at the instigation of Canada, that the alliance could more safely be replaced by a multilateral agreement. This opened up the possibility of a general discussion of

Pacific affairs, which the United States now took the initiative in arranging.

Accordingly the representatives of the powers gathered in Washington in November 1921 to consider a whole range of Pacific and Far Eastern questions, decisions on which confirmed the new pattern of international relations that the war had shaped. The first to be announced was a Four Power Pact of December 13, 1921, by which Britain, Japan, France and the United States agreed to respect each other's rights in the area and to consult together in the event of a crisis arising. This took the place of the Anglo-Japanese alliance, which was eventually allowed to lapse in August 1923. On the subject of naval armaments, the United States proposed limiting the size and firepower of capital ships and scrapping many of them altogether, with Britain, America and Japan maintaining their respective tonnage for the future at a ratio of 5 : 5 : 3. Japan argued for a ratio of 10 : 10 : 7, but when the other two were stubborn she substituted a suggestion for a standstill in Pacific fortification, which they accepted. Thus the treaty, as signed, not only fixed a 5 : 5 : 3 ratio for total tonnage of capital ships, but also provided that battleships were not to exceed 35,000 tons or aircraft carriers 27,000 tons, that naval guns were not to be larger than 16-inch in calibre, and that no new fortifications were to be constructed at Guam, Hong Kong, Manila or any other base nearer to Japan than Hawaii and Singapore. This gave Japan naval predominance in the West Pacific and an unbreakable grip on the approaches to the China coast.

As to China itself, a Nine Power Treaty, signed by Belgium, Italy, the Netherlands, and Portugal, as well as China and the parties to the Four Power Pact, was concluded in February 1922. It gave China greater control over her own customs revenue and put into due form the platitudes reiterated for the previous twenty years: that the powers would respect Chinese independence and integrity, would refrain from seeking special rights at each other's expense and would avoid interference with China's attempts 'to develop and maintain for herself an effective and stable government'.[61] That such promises were needed at all was itself significant. That they would be fulfilled was unlikely, especially as the treaty set up no machinery for enforcement. The one real gain was that an atmosphere was created in which Japan and China could settle their differences over Shantung, a bilateral agreement on February 4, 1922, restoring Chinese sovereignty in the province and ratifying Japan's economic privileges.

In fact, an easing of international tensions was the main achievement of the Washington meetings, demonstrated in October 1922 by Japan's decision at last to withdraw her divisions from Siberia. Although it was another three years before she evacuated the north of Sakhalin and resumed diplomatic relations with Russia, the decision, coupled with those on naval armaments and China, seemed to make a fresh start possible. Certainly the next few years were marked by an emphasis on economic, not military, expansion, a phase of policy which is associated with the name of Shidehara Kijuro, Foreign Minister from June 1924 to April 1927 and again from July 1929 to December 1931.

On the other hand, the air of compromise which characterized Shidehara's actions was in some respects misleading. Japan's wartime gains were not renounced, but were on the contrary fully exploited. Nor was the political balance within Japan, which made moderation possible, as firmly established as it seemed. Ominously, there had already been signs of institutional weakness in the conduct of Japanese foreign affairs, stemming from the disappearance or declining influence of the Genro, which made the basis of Shidehara's policy unstable. Outstanding was the fact that the army had not only developed views of its own on what it wished to see done, especially in China and Manchuria, but had also found means of putting these into effect, regardless of cabinet decisions. The problems which this posed, first illustrated in the disputes over Siberia, were not solved by the army's temporary loss of popularity thereafter and were to become acute again in 1931.

Before pursuing this topic further, however, it is necessary that we examine another aspect of Japanese history since 1914: the growth in the economy, occasioned by the war, and its effects on domestic politics. It was developments in this field, after all, that made Shidehara's methods a valid, if not a lasting, reflection of Japanese desires. Equally, they contributed to the activities of those who sought to turn foreign policy once again in the direction chosen by Okuma and Terauchi, coupling their arguments with strictures on the kind of society that evolved during the decade of 'the liberal 'twenties' and finding their support increasingly among those segments of the population that acquired grievances—or ambitions—as a result of economic change.

CHAPTER XII

THE LIBERAL 'TWENTIES

Industrial expansion—party politics—inflation and recession
—radicalism

THE GREAT WAR of 1914–18 was important to Japan not only because it provided an opportunity for raising her international standing and prestige, but also because of the stimulus it gave to her economy. By the war's end she had become in the full sense an industrial state. As such she faced political problems of a kind new in her experience, arising both from the pressures of industrial wealth on political and social privilege and from the unrest that infused a growing urban proletariat. Moreover, extension of the 'modern' element in her society had by this time brought changes in patterns of wage-earning, of consumption and of social custom to much of the country's population, changes that were to be of lasting effect, notwithstanding the vociferous—indeed, hysterical—traditionalist reaction they provoked in the next two decades.

The beginnings of industrialization, fundamental to this process, date back to the Meiji period, but it was the outbreak of war in Europe that gave it greater pace and scale. For Europe's pre-occupation with her own affairs proved to be Japan's economic, as well as diplomatic, opportunity. Diverted to war production, European factories could no longer supply many of the goods they had formerly exported, enabling Japan to increase her sales in markets she had already begun to exploit, like China and America, and to penetrate new ones, like India and South East Asia. With little war effort of her own to support she was also able to accept orders for munitions from her allies, while increased demands for shipping, due to the losses which U-boats inflicted on the maritime powers, made it profitable for her greatly to expand her mercantile marine. Her total of steamships and motor vessels doubled, from 1·5 million tons in 1914 to 3 million tons in 1918. In the same years her annual income from freights multiplied ten times, reaching over 400 million yen. Meanwhile the country's growing foreign trade had turned an annual average import surplus of 65 million yen into an export surplus of 350 million, raising Japan's net wartime earnings on international account to some 3,000 million yen in all. Though much of this was frittered away on political loans to China, much was still held as an overseas balance when the peace treaty was signed.

The end of hostilities brought a temporary recession, occasioned partly by the cancellation of munitions contracts, partly by the renewal of European competition; but this had the effect of eliminating the less efficient firms rather than of cutting back industrial growth in general. Many of the export markets that had been won were still retained. Much of industry continued to expand. In fact, the index of manufacturing production (1910–14 =100) rose from an average of 160 in 1915–19 to 313 in 1925–29, while in foreign trade (1913 =100) the index of imports by volume moved from 126 in 1919 to 199 in 1929, that of exports from 127 to 205.

Textiles accounted for a large percentage of the export trade, raw silk, sold mostly to the United States, comprising about 36 per cent of the whole by value in 1929 and cotton goods, notably piece-goods for India and China, only a little less. These two items together totalled two-thirds of Japan's exports in that year, as compared with just over half in 1913. Among imports, food and raw materials (Korean rice, Formosan sugar, Indian cotton) were an even larger proportion. In other words the country's foreign trade, though highly specialized as to both markets and commodities, now reflected chiefly the needs and achievements of Japanese manufacturers.

Similar growth had taken place in heavy industry. Despite continued dependence on imports for a good deal of engineering equipment, Japan was producing much of her own textile and electrical machinery, railway rolling stock and bicycles, as well as building a substantial quantity of the world's ships. Electric generating capacity increased from 1 million kilowatts in 1919 to 4 million in 1929, two-thirds of the power being used in manufacturing and mining. Coal production, however, after rising from 21 to 31 million tons between 1913 and 1919, had failed to keep up with demand, especially for coking coal, so that in 1929, with an output of 34 million tons, Japan was a net importer. Neither steel nor iron was yet in sufficient supply, though for the former, at least, the gap between need and output was quickly narrowing. A quarter of a million tons of steel had been produced in 1913, twice that amount in 1919 and over 2 million tons in 1929, these figures representing about 30, 45 and 70 per cent of contemporary consumption. Pig iron production had no more than doubled, the output of 1 million tons in 1929 being only 60 per cent of the country's needs. Nevertheless, the great increase in the use of metals that this and the other figures represented was itself significant of economic change.

One feature of this industrial development, as we have mentioned earlier, was the emergence side by side of two very different types of organization: the small workshop, usually a family business, on the one hand, and the large factory on the other. In the light engineering trades, for example, and in many industries catering for the domestic rather than the export market, the spread of technical education and the availability of cheap electric power had made it possible for many individual entrepreneurs, despite a relative lack of capital, to engage in the manufacture of goods which others more widely organized would market, or parts which the large-scale factories could use. By 1930 workshops of this kind, each with less than five employees, numbered over a million. They employed 2·5 million people and were responsible for some 30 per cent of Japan's manufacturing product. In sharp contrast were the huge plants engaged in the production of iron and steel, cement, chemicals, heavy engineering equipment and similar goods, as well as some of those on the export side of the textile trades. In these both the factories and the firms that owned them were growing larger. Thus in cotton spinning, the 2·4 million spindles installed by 1913 were owned by forty-four companies controlling 152 mills, while 6·6 million spindles in 1929 were divided between only fifty-nine companies with 247 mills, an increase from 16,000 to 27,000 in the number of spindles per mill and from 55,000 to 113,000 in the number per company. Much the same trend is apparent in cotton weaving, especially where firms used the wide looms needed for export cloth.

The outstanding examples of large-scale organization were the concerns which were known as *zaibatsu*, with Mitsui, Mitsubishi, Yasuda and Sumitomo chief among them. Their origins were diverse—the Mitsui had been a wealthy merchant house in Tokugawa times, whereas Mitsubishi was founded after the Restoration by an ex-samurai of Tosa, Iwasaki Yataro —but all had been closely linked with the Meiji government, owing much in their early days to its subsidies and contracts. In return they had supported it financially and invested in the new industrial undertakings which it sought to promote. This put them in a position to profit greatly by developments of the early twentieth century. They extended their operations into banking, heavy industry, shipping, commerce (both whole- sale and retail) and all other forms of economic activity that promised large returns, thereby creating a web of interlocking financial, industrial and commercial holdings that could survive, because of their multiple interests, the crises from which the economy intermittently suffered. In doing so they absorbed many older and smaller rivals. They also acquired enormous wealth, controlled as a rule through a family holding company and administered by an extremely able managerial group whose members often married into the founder family. Close con- nections with leaders of government, the Diet, the bureaucracy and the Imperial Court made their position wellnigh im- pregnable.

Yet increasing scale, of which the *zaibatsu* firms were extreme examples, was not everywhere typical of Japanese develop- ment. One could argue that the workshops of the cities were not truly exceptions, in that they formed part of a structure which the major distributors and manufacturers were able to dominate. Even farm households raising silk cocoons—and by 1929 this was secondary employment for 40 per cent of them— were subject in some degree to external control by large-scale undertakings, exercised through financing and purchase of the crop. Nevertheless, agriculture in general, employing half the country's working population, remained a matter of individual family holdings, growing rice as a staple food by labour-intensive methods. In the 1920s almost 50 per cent of Japan's farmers held less than half a *cho* (1 *cho* = 2·45 acres). About 24 per cent held between half a *cho* and a *cho*, 18 per cent between one *cho* and three *cho*. Very few, therefore, could be described as important landowners, despite the fact that two-thirds were wholly or partly tenants.

This fragmentation undoubtedly made radical changes in the technique of cultivation difficult, if not impossible, though it is by no means certain that larger units would have helped to raise production, as distinct from making economies in man-power. In the Meiji period, as we have seen, fairly simple technical improvements, such as a more widespread use of fertilizers, had brought an increase in yield per acre of about 50 per cent. Thus with only a small area of new land coming under cultivation it had still been possible to increase the rice crop from 30 million *koku* in 1880–84 (1 *koku* = 5 bushels approximately) to 51 million in 1910–14. Thereafter, however, the rate of increase slowed, apparently because the scope for technological advance was now more limited. Certainly yield per acre rose by less than 10 per cent in the following twenty years and rice production in 1930–34 averaged only 62 million *koku*. Since population was growing more quickly—from 46 million in 1903 to 64 million in 1930—and consumption per head remained unchanged, imports of rice moved inevitably upward. Over 10 million *koku* were imported in 1930–34, compared with less than 3 million in 1910–14.

Rice imports amounting to nearly 15 per cent of consumption can be taken as symbolic of the shift of emphasis from agriculture to industry in the Japanese economy. So, too, can the increasing degree of urbanization. The fact that the numbers engaged in farming remained constant at about five and a half million families throughout this period means that all those who in any given year comprised the population increase were finding their way to urban areas, where the new forms of economic activity were in greatest concentration and the chance of jobs was best. Townships of less than 10,000 persons accounted for 72 per cent of the population in 1913, only 59 per cent in 1930. Cities of 50,000 persons and more held 14 per cent in the first of these years, 25 per cent in the second. Agriculture, in other words, seemed to have reached something like the limit of its potential in absorbing manpower, as well as producing food.

The cities that were now emerging undoubtedly brought misery and hardship to many people, for these seem everywhere to be concomitants of industrial growth. To this aspect we shall have to return. But not all the change was for the worse. On average the Japanese diet became more varied and more sustaining in the early twentieth century. More fish, fruit and sugar were eaten; and the increase in *per capita* consumption of rice that had been achieved in the Meiji period was maintained, despite a sharply rising population. Moreover, Japanese were better clad as well as better fed, to judge by sales of clothing textiles in the domestic market, while those who lived in towns, at least, could enjoy amenities like electric light, improved facilities for travel, cheaper and more plentiful books and daily newspapers.

Prices, of course, had risen, as was evident on every side. The cost of living, if one takes 1914 as the base, had doubled a decade later. Yet money wages had trebled, so that real wages had risen by a half and were to hold the gain, even increase it slightly, for some time to come. It is true that the figures conceal wide variations between different groups and different occupations, farm workers being worse off than those in industry, the unskilled relatively less favoured than the skilled; but on balance society was more prosperous than it had been before the war. Some of its members were very much so. Successful businessmen had begun to build themselves country villas, the well-to-do to add a Western-style room or wing to their homes for entertaining. Geisha, the most expensive providers of entertainment in Japan, found their patrons more numerous and more lavish in spending. For the less affluent there were the dance-halls, whose taxi-dancers provided a cheaper, if untraditional, alternative. Restaurants flourished. And the Japanese became, as they have remained ever since, inveterate travellers: so much so, wrote a British resident, that 'it came to a pitch where, especially on Sundays and holidays, it was easier to find room in a third-class railway carriage than in the superior classes'.[62]

One result of this expansion of the economy was greatly to increase the size of the industrial and commercial middle class.

This was a matter of political importance, for members of that class, men of substance and education, began to seek ways of getting their interests served. Some, like the *zaibatsu*, already had means of doing so through their connections with government. Others, if they were really wealthy, might hope to achieve their ends by bribes. Almost all found it possible, because of the country's new education system, to put sons or dependants into the bureaucracy, though the effect of this was reduced by that body's conspicuous ability to assimilate its recruits and mould their standards to its own.

Businessmen also began to organize themselves as pressure groups. Among the earliest was the Tokyo Chamber of Commerce, which under the leadership of a banker, Shibusawa Eiichi, had begun to campaign vigorously on several issues of economic policy even before the Meiji period ended. By the 'twenties, chambers of commerce, Rotary Clubs and associations of traders or manufacturers were familiar features of the urban scene. Potentially more effective, however, were the political parties. They alone of the acknowledged components of the constitution opened a way to the control of policy by legal means. What is more, the support of business interests, which were rapidly achieving a position in society that no government could afford to ignore, promised to give the politicians a chance of the power which had so long eluded them.

The timing was apt, for the established order was facing a crisis of leadership that made it less able to resist attack. Of the Meiji statesmen, Ito had died in 1909 and Matsukata had ceased to play an active part in politics long before his death in 1924. Yamagata was a very old man, eighty in the year the war ended. Although he retained immense prestige, his hold on the Choshu faction was beginning to weaken. Itagaki, who had long been in retirement, died in 1919, Okuma, like Yamagata, in 1922. Nor were their successors men of equal calibre. Overshadowed by long-lived elders, the new generation seemed more concerned with power than with its uses, except perhaps in foreign affairs, and had little that was constructive to offer when its authority was challenged. Only Saionji was of any stature; and as a liberal, a protégé of Ito and a former party president, he was least likely to oppose the parties' claims.

The Okuma government of 1914–16 had demonstrated that even under a prime minister of great experience and the highest standing it was easier to manipulate votes in the Diet than to destroy the privileges of bureaucracy and Genro. In fact, only the patriotism of his China policy saved Okuma from early defeat. So when he attempted to name his own successor, choosing Kato Komei (Takaaki), another party man, Yamagata lost little time in bringing him down. Terauchi Masatake was installed in his place, forming an alliance with the Seiyukai and helping it to win an election in April 1917, while Kato organized a new group, the Kenseikai, firmly committed to opposition.

The fact that Kato was irreconcilable gave the Seiyukai a certain negative influence on policy as the only body willing to get government legislation through the Diet. This led it into closer association with Yamagata and the Choshu interests. It had other useful affiliations, too, since several of its principal members were former bureaucrats, including the party leader, Hara Kei (Takashi). Accordingly, when popular criticism of Terauchi reached dangerous levels in 1918, chiefly because of a sharp rise in commodity prices, Yamagata and Saionji were able to agree—the former still with some reluctance—on Hara's appointment to succeed him. Japan thus acquired for the first time a 'commoner' as premier, that is, one who did not claim samurai descent. He was supported by ministers who were all members of his party, except the men holding the portfolios of Foreign Affairs, War and Navy, which went, respectively, to a career diplomat and two senior officers of the services concerned.

To those who hailed this event as a victory for liberalism and democracy the next three years were disappointing. As a good party man Hara tried with some success to get his followers appointed to a number of posts, such as prefectural and colonial governorships, which had previously been reserved for bureaucrats, but he showed little enthusiasm for reform in general. His position depended too much on the Genro and the House of Peers to permit constitutional adventures, for which in any case he had little taste. Hence as long as he remained in office, proposals for an extension of the franchise were steadfastly put aside. Socialist thought, stimulated by news of events in Germany and Russia, was ruthlessly suppressed. Signs of corruption were ignored. Even cabinet attempts to restrain the army's intervention in Siberia failed, though this was evidence of institutional weakness, not lack of will.

Hara's assassination on November 4, 1921, an act carried out by a young fanatic for no very obvious reason, robbed the party movement of an able politician rather than an inspiring statesman. Nevertheless, Hara had held his men together—he could both attract loyalty and impose discipline—and had led them to new positions of responsibility. His immediate successors could not do the same. His place was taken by the Finance Minister, Takahashi Korekiyo, who soon found the task too much for him and resigned the following June. For eighteen months thereafter the Seiyukai majority was used to back non-party governments, rather than give the Kenseikai a chance of power.

However, in the climate of opinion that was now forming in Japan such an arrangement could not last. Kato's demands for responsible party cabinets received increasing popular support and he eventually succeeded in splitting the Seiyukai on this issue, forcing a dissolution early in 1924 and winning the ensuing election. His coalition, which included groups led by Takahashi and Inukai Ki (Tsuyoshi), now made the government's position hopeless in the lower house. It resigned in June. This left the way clear for Kato himself to form an administration, first on the basis of coalition, then, after August 1925, from the Kenseikai alone.

His cabinet contained some notable members. Both the Home Minister, Wakatsuki Reijiro, and the Finance Minister, Hamaguchi Yuko, were to serve as premier in the next few years. The Foreign Minister, Shidehara Kijuro, a non-party man, was to become a symbol of moderation in respect of Sino-Japanese relations and a staunch, though unsuccessful, defender of such policies against army attacks. Yet it was Kato who dominated the scene. Less flexible than Hara, he was better born, wealthy, a former ambassador to London, Foreign Minister to Okuma at the time of the Twenty-one Demands. With this background he could meet oligarchs, bureaucrats and Privy Councillors on equal terms, an advantage which in a Japanese context far outweighed the stiffness and reserve that kept him from being really popular. He was also a man of principle, a sincere advocate of parliamentary rule. In May 1925 he passed the Universal Manhood Suffrage Act, giving the vote to males over 25, which increased the size of the electorate from three million to thirteen. He made economies in the bureaucracy, reducing its membership by 20,000, and cut the service budgets to under 30 per cent of the national total, compared with 40 per cent in 1919–22. The army lost four divisions in the process, though it was partly compensated by a measure of re-equipment. On the other hand, Kato was no more able than Hara had been to reform the House of Peers or reduce the authority of the senior bureaucrats, while only a week after Manhood Suffrage conservative pressure brought the Peace Preservation Law, providing penalties of up to ten years' imprisonment for participation in the more extreme forms of left-wing politics.

Kato died in January 1926. Both the party and the government were taken over by Wakatsuki, who continued along the same lines, despite growing army opposition on foreign affairs, until the Privy Council's refusal to confirm a proposed emergency ordinance in the financial crisis of early 1927. This brought his resignation and—an important step—an invitation to the Seiyukai to provide the next cabinet. Equally important, the Seiyukai, as a minority party, dissolved the lower house and sought to better its position through elections. It began to look as if two principles might become established: first, that the defeat of one party must bring the other to power; second, that the government must have a Diet majority. Such, at least, was the pattern for the next few years.

The Seiyukai, led by a general, Tanaka Giichi, who took office in April 1927, won the 1928 election, but did so only by the narrowest of margins. Notwithstanding police intervention against its opponents—now renamed the Minseito—and extensive use of private strong-arm squads under government patronage, victory was by a mere two seats, a fact which made for turbulent debates in the months that followed. Yet it was the army, not the Diet, that caused the government's fall. Though Tanaka was an advocate of sterner policies in China, the murder of the Chinese war-lord Chang Tso-lin in June 1928, apparently engineered by Japanese officers in Manchuria, brought him into conflict with the high command. His demands for disciplinary action were ignored and he finally resigned, being replaced in July 1929 by Hamaguchi. In 1930 Hamaguchi's Minseito won an election in its turn, doing so by methods that were rather less reprehensible than those of its rivals, but the world slump of that year and the signing of the London Naval Treaty soon brought it trouble. Its attempts to cut civil service salaries as part of an economy drive were fiercely resisted, while its acceptance of limitations on naval armament brought a head-on clash with the military and the Privy Council. At this juncture, in November 1930, Hamaguchi was shot and wounded at Tokyo railway station. He died a few months later and Wakatsuki again stepped in, as he had done at the death of Kato, only to face another dispute with the army in September 1931 over the invasion of Manchuria, which most members of his cabinet opposed, as well as a bitter struggle for power within the party. This led to his resignation in the following December. His successor was Inukai, now the Seiyukai's president, but Inukai had an even shorter tenure. In May 1932 he was assassinated at his official residence by a group of young army and navy officers who hoped to bring about a military *coup d'état*.

By this time it was becoming clear to even the most prejudiced observer that the supremacy of party government had been no more than an illusion, shattered as soon as a few fanatics with army backing put it seriously to the test. Some of the reasons for this were external to the party movement and will be considered in a later chapter. However, there were also sources of weakness in party politics themselves.

One was disunity. The parties had had their origin in sectional protests against Meiji centralization and objections to the Satsuma-Choshu monopoly of power. They had therefore tended to be coalitions of groups, each with its own leader and usually having strong local or regional connections, which found it easier to co-operate in opposition to the government than in putting forward a programme of their own. Since the Meiji Constitution, when put into effect, seemed to condemn them in any case to permanent opposition, there seemed every reason for this situation to continue. Such changes as there were, indeed, were of a kind to perpetuate the worst features of what had gone before. The Diet's ability to obstruct official business undoubtedly gave the parties a weapon, but it was a negative one, which enabled them to blackmail the government for concessions without being able to gain control. The result was that a number of party leaders found it possible to secure office and even to share its fruits with their followers, but only at the cost of bargains with the Genro and Privy Council, with the services and higher bureaucracy, which amounted to a denial of party rule. Since the parties did not differ greatly from each other on matters of policy, the temptation for groups within them to take advantage of this opportunity was overwhelming. Again and again factions shifted from party to party, from the side of opposition to that of government, as ambition or tactics might dictate.

Between 1918 and 1932 there was less change in these habits than might have been expected from the parties' growing strength. Policy differences, after all, remained comparatively unimportant; bargains still had to be struck with powerful interests outside the Diet; and the vote-winning or fund-raising connections of an individual leader were likely to be more useful to his party than the party's organization was to him. This being so, party loyalty was a rare virtue. Nor was principle often put before office. Inukai, for example, who had been a bitter critic of political corruption and intrigue, abandoned Kato's coalition to join the Seiyukai in 1924 because, he said, 'he could not leave his faithful followers as a minor fragment divorced from hope of power'.[63] In 1931 Adachi Kenzo brought down the Wakatsuki cabinet, in which he was Home Minister, in an attempt to substitute for it an administration of his own: when his pretensions were denied, he refused either to carry out his duties or to resign, forcing the government to resign as the only means of getting rid of him.

The rank-and-file showed no more scruple and rather less decorum. Knowing that all major decisions were the result of behind-the-scenes negotiation, not of a Diet vote, they reduced debates to the level of the trivial and turbulent, with speeches directed rather to the press than to the motion. Minority parties, seeing little point in a rational exposition of their views, hooted their opponents down. They even had recourse to violence. 'Flushed gentlemen,' writes Morgan Young, 'clad without in frockcoats but warmed within by too copious draughts of saké, roared and bellowed, and arguments frequently culminated in a rush for the rostrum, whence the speaker of the moment would be dragged in the midst of a free fight.'[64] He goes on to describe how on one occasion pandemonium was caused by a live snake being thrown from the public gallery among the Seiyukai benches. In this, it transpired, there was a certain justice, since it was the Seiyukai who had hired a man to throw it at the other side, only for his aim to be spoiled by 'the awkwardness of the missile'.

Corruption was another element in political life that was always being alleged and sometimes proved. In 1914 the Yamamoto cabinet had had to resign after revelations of bribery connected with naval armaments, which implicated the German firm of Siemens, Britain's Vickers, and several high-ranking Japanese officers. Under Hara in 1921 the South Manchurian Railway company was accused of contributing illegally to Seiyukai funds, and a little later Kato's Kenseikai was certainly financed by Mitsubishi, it being asserted that specific lines of political and economic policy were to be accepted by the parties in return. Tanaka Giichi came under particularly heavy fire in matters of this kind. As a soldier he was said to have appropriated large sums from the secret service vote during the Siberian expedition. As Seiyukai leader after 1925 he was accused of taking bribes to decide the placing of army contracts, of selling peerages, even of being subject to improper influence in the making of a cabinet appointment. Moreover, members of both parties at about this time were involved in some very shady land speculations concerning a projected brothel quarter in Osaka, to say nothing of the smaller-scale but more widespread corruption that accompanied elections.

Many such charges were exaggerated and some invented altogether, for this was the way of Japanese politics; but there is no doubt that bribery existed on a considerable scale. Indeed, the relationship between parties and business made it almost inevitable. The *zaibatsu* concerns had less need of it than most, for they had many channels of influence open to them, links of long standing, reinforced by marriage and adoption. Thus

Saionji and the head of the Sumitomo combine were actually brothers. Iwasaki Hisaya of Mitsubishi, apart from sons and other relatives in banking, industry and commerce, had a sister married to Shidehara, another to Kato, and a nephew married to the daughter of an official in the Imperial Household Ministry. By contrast, firms of later origin, especially those which had sprung up during the 1914–18 war, had to use cruder methods. Bribery was the easiest and most direct—and politicians were among its obvious recipients.

For this reason, business backing, though for a time it strengthened the political parties *vis-à-vis* other interests in the state, was ultimately an element of their weakness. The giving and taking of bribes was not the most stable basis for an alliance; and while it was true that businessmen and politicians had certain aims in common, in pursuit of which they could co-operate, and that as clients of government they had approximately equal standing, the fact remains that their ambitions were different enough to be separately attained. Accordingly, each was willing in the last resort to dispense with the other's help. Big business, in particular, behaved more as the politician's patron than his ally, never convinced that attacks on the parliamentary system were attacks upon itself.

The parties, if they could not rely on business, failed equally to build up any popular support. This was partly because their factionalism, unruliness and corruption were in such striking contrast to the 'samurai' virtues which modern education was trying to implant. Partly it was because their leaders made little attempt to cultivate the appropriate skills, thinking oratory vulgar and mass meetings something to be shunned. Party leaders, in fact, were in outlook and background much more like the men they wished to drive from power, the oligarchs and bureaucrats, than the men they led. One might take as examples some of those who held office as prime minister between 1924 and 1932. Kato, Tanaka, Inukai and Takahashi were all of samurai descent. If one includes Tanaka, a regular soldier, all but one had started their careers in the bureaucracy, Takahashi having risen to be head of the Bank of Japan before he ever joined a political party. The exception, Inukai, had been a newspaperman and a follower of Okuma. Hamaguchi, the non-samurai, was from Tosa, entering government service by what was to become the classic route: from Tokyo University's law faculty to the Ministry of Finance. None, in other words, was a member of the urban middle class they are sometimes said to have represented.

These were not the men to lead a social revolution, for they were liberals of a very conservative kind. They stood for economy, good neighbourliness, the authority of the Diet and civilian control, a programme that was modest to a degree. Yet it was both liberal enough and conservative enough to face a challenge from both sides: from those who objected, in the name of tradition, to parliamentary power and backed their objections by murdering the men who wielded it; and from those who urged the abolition or reform of parliaments in the name of the people's rights. It is to a consideration of the latter that we now turn.

Wartime industrial progress, we have said, contributed on average to a rise in Japanese living standards. Yet it also produced hardship and discontent. Some nine million people were living in towns of over 50,000 population in 1920, three million more than there had been a decade earlier, and the numbers employed in factories with more than five employees had increased from just under a million at the beginning of the war to about 1·6 million at its end. This meant a major dislocation in the lives of many Japanese, forced to earn their living in urban areas whose facilities did not always expand as quickly as their citizens' numbers. It also subjected a growing proportion to the strain of work in factories, where hours were long and conditions were under the minimum of regulation. The 1911 Factory Act, for example, which was not enforced till 1916, had done no more than prescribe an eleven-hour working day for women and children, and a minimum age of twelve. An amendment of 1923, effective in 1926, was to make the hours ten and the age fourteen, with some exceptions.

In 1918 the position was made worse by serious inflation. Overseas demand for Japanese goods and the mushroom growth of firms to meet it had made possible a rise in money incomes and profits, an expansion of note issues and bank credit, a fever of speculation. In the last months of the war this brought a sharp upward trend in prices. Rice that cost 16 yen

Rapid urbanization →

a *koku* in January 1917 was 39 yen in August of the following year. The wholesale price index in Tokyo (1900 = 100) averaged 195 for 1917, 255 for 1918, 312 for 1919. Wages rose more slowly, as one would expect, causing thereby a wave of agitation and industrial unrest. Rice riots, starting with a housewives' protest meeting at Toyama on August 4, 1918, spread rapidly to Kyoto, Osaka, Kobe and other centres, where the mobs attacked and sometimes burned the establishments of rice-dealers, moneylenders and unpopular profiteers. Troops had to be called out to disperse them on several occasions during the next two weeks. Meanwhile, the country was experiencing its first important series of strikes for higher pay and better conditions. Disputes affecting 66,000 workers were recorded during the year, despite the existence of police regulations that made them illegal, and in 1919 the scale of such activity increased still more. There were stoppages by railway workers, teachers, postmen, printers—who deprived Tokyo of its newspapers for over a week—and in September 1919 by 15,000 men at Kobe's Kawasaki dockyard. The latter lacked the funds and organization for a lengthy struggle, but they succeeded in getting the management to agree to an eight-hour day.

Soon after this Japan began to feel the effects of the post-war trade recession, which had its severest impact on those industries, like coal-mining and ship-building, that had expanded most in the previous years. Workers in them were forced on the defensive, fighting hard to maintain their levels of employment. In Kobe the men of the Kawasaki yard were again the leaders, joined on this occasion by those from Mitsubishi, with the result that over 25,000 were involved in the strike, lock-out and demonstrations that lasted from early July 1921 into the second week of August.

Unrest spread also to the countryside, though for different reasons. The earlier inflation had not been nearly so serious for the farmer as for the city worker, because of increases in the price of rice. The trade recession, however, broke and reversed the inflationary trend. The cost of a *koku* of rice fell from 55 yen in 1920 to 25·5 yen in 1921, while the wholesale price index dropped from 343 to 265 in the same two years. This meant real poverty for farmers, now fully involved in producing for the market, especially as their most important subsidiary crop, silk, suffered a similar decline in value. Price support programmes did something to restore the position in the next few years, but competition from colonial rice growers—which governments were bound to encourage for the sake of the urban poor—set a strict upper limit to domestic prices. Villages suffered, too, from the fact that they acted as a shock absorber for urban unemployment. Although population increase forced many to the towns, there to find jobs in shops or factories, each setback to the industrial economy drove them back to seek refuge on the farm. The resulting gain in social stability for the country as a whole was offset in part by the loss to rural standards of living.

It was the poorest farmers, especially the tenant farmers, who experienced the worst conditions. By the 1920s this meant something like half the agricultural population, for 49 per cent held plots of under one-and-a-quarter acres and over two-thirds were tenants for all or part of their land. In area, more than 45 per cent of the total was under tenancy agreements, their terms invariably favourable to the owner, since pressure of population, not all the surplus of which was absorbed by the towns, ensured that competition for the land was keen. Thus rents were payable in kind, which deprived the tenant of most of the benefits of inflation. They were also high, amounting to as much as half the crop on rice-paddy, a third for dry fields. The severity of such conditions had been mitigated before the war by the rapid expansion of agrarian production, but as this slowed down, so the agreements became a focus of rising tension. Tenancy disputes, which had usually been occasioned in the past by floods, typhoons and similar catastrophes, became more frequent, more extensive and more highly organized, especially round the periphery of urban areas. Tenant unions came into existence, claiming 132,000 members by 1922, with more everywhere being formed, all campaigning actively for changes in the law concerning tenure, in addition to acting as their members' representatives in specific local negotiations.

Conditions therefore existed in both the countryside and the towns that encouraged the growth of left-wing political activity: real grievances, made the harder to bear by envy, as those who reaped profits from industrial growth indulged in an extravagance and display that were quite foreign to the Japanese tradition. News of the German and Russian revolutions, distributed by an efficient daily press, suggested the possibility of successful protest. Knowledge of Western literature contributed plans and programmes. From all this a new element in politics emerged, a left-wing movement stimulated partly by the intellectuals, partly by trade unions.

Among the earliest of the radicals was Oi Kentaro, who combined an extreme nationalism with support for Sun Yat-sen in China and demands that the state should exercise economic controls for the protection of the poor. His Oriental Liberal Party (Toyo Jiyuto), founded in 1892, in some ways foreshadowed the kind of link between nationalism and the left that was to characterize the 1930s. More moderate was the Social Democratic Party (Shakai Minshuto) of 1901, with its appeal for free education, an eight-hour day and the abolition of child labour, though its moderation did not stop the police from suppressing it as soon as it was formed. An attempt to create a Socialist Party in 1906 was equally unsuccessful. It was not until 1920, in fact, in the atmosphere of turbulence after the war, that such groups stood any real chance of survival; and even then they often broke up within a matter of weeks or months because of their own disunity. Such, at least, was the fate of the Socialist League, formed in December 1920 as a means of bringing together all shades of left-wing thought. The first Communist Party, too, founded in 1921 after contacts with the Far Eastern Comintern at Shanghai, failed to overcome the combination of police action and doctrinal disputes. It went into voluntary dissolution in March 1924 after a brief but colourful career of argument and propaganda.

The members of these organizations included both those who believed in violence and those who did not. Of the radical leaders, several were Christians: a lawyer, Suzuki Bunji, founder of a national labour organization, the Yuaikai, in 1912; a minister, Kagawa Tomohiko, who was imprisoned briefly for his part in the Kobe strikes of 1921; and the American-trained Abe Isoo, a teacher at Waseda University. A good many other moderates were university professors, like Yoshino Sakuzo, an outstanding political scientist, and Kawai Eijiro.

Kawai, when on trial in 1939, probably best expressed their creed. 'Although I talk about socialism,' he said, '. . . I reject illegal and espouse legal methods, abhor violent revolution, and prefer parliamentary means. Consequently, I do not address myself to the lowly plebs. I have never discussed socialism at a meeting of workers.'[65] Making due allowance for the circumstances in which this statement was made, there is still a quality of the intellectual about it that was characteristic. It was to be found also among the advocates of force. For example, Kawakami Hajime—journalist, poet, professor and Communist—was in many ways typical of the radical idealist, deeply influenced by Christianity and Zen Buddhism in his youth, later a Communist from emotion rather than experience. His outlook was religious in its passion for humility and charity, his belief in Marxism that of a pacifist, who saw in the destruction of capitalism the only way of removing the social and economic evils that bred war.

The trade unions were a very different proposition, despite the fact that their leaders were not necessarily drawn from the ranks of labour. The earliest unions—like those formed among ironworkers in 1897 and railwaymen in 1898—had found their activities severely handicapped by police regulations after 1900, so that numbers remained small until the end of the war. From 1918, however, the movement began to increase in both militancy and size. By 1920 there were over 200 unions, most of them newly formed, and they had begun to organize in larger groups. Suzuki's Yuaikai, which had been hitherto a kind of friendly society, became the Federation of Labour (Sodomei) in 1919 and soon comprised seventy constituent organizations claiming 30,000 members in all. It continued to grow steadily in the next few years.

Nevertheless, it was handicapped from the beginning by bitter struggles between competing factions. The first phase of these ended in September 1922 with the defeat of anarchist and of syndicalist supporters, leaving Communists and social democrats still to resolve their disagreements. Then a year later, on September 1, 1923, a terrible earthquake shook the Tokyo-Yokohama region, bringing in its train an outbreak of panic-stricken attacks on radicals and others, especially Koreans, for alleged looting, plotting and similar crimes. The offences existed largely in the imaginations of police and public, but the arrests and interrogations to which they gave rise had the effect of revealing that Communist penetration of the Sodomei had gone farther than anyone suspected. This led to fresh recriminations at its general meeting in 1924. Thereafter the moderates gradually gained the upper hand, until in May 1925 the Communist unions, in membership a little more than a third, broke away to form an organization of their own.

These events took place against a background of strikes and pamphleteering, for the hostility of the police, together with the restriction of the electorate by a property qualification, seemed to make any attempt to win seats in the Diet a waste of time. This remained so until 1925, but in that year the introduction of universal manhood suffrage rendered the objection largely void. A proletarian party to fight elections now became in theory possible, providing it could skirt the laws about subversion which the Peace Preservation Act had simultaneously reinforced. There was still, however, some difficulty in getting the politicians to reach agreement among themselves. Indeed, the first attempt at action foundered on this problem, since the Sodomei leaders withdrew from the discussions and the proposed party's extremist rump became an inevitable target for official intervention. Called the Farmer-Labour Party (Nomin Rodoto), it was banned thirty minutes after it came formally into existence on December 1, 1925. The moderates were next to try, forming a Labour-Farmer Party (Rodo Nominto) which was pledged to follow constitutional means, but within a few months of its foundation (March 1926) it had split on the question of establishing a popular front. By the end of the year its centre and right had broken off to form no less than three separate parties. Adding to the confusion, the Communist Party was reconstituted in December, but it became so deeply involved in ideological controversy and so violently at loggerheads with every other left-wing group that one can only feel surprise at the reluctance of the police to leave it alone.

On this sort of record the left was no more likely to win popular support than were the Seiyukai and Minseito. Moreover, the latter were very much better organized for rallying votes. This became evident in the 1928 elections, when the four leftwing parties—excluding the Communists, who did not compete—polled less than half a million votes between them, about one-eighth of the number that went to each of their rivals. From eighty-eight candidates they elected only eight, of whom four were social democrats. The failure underlined the need for more co-operation and led to new proposals for alliance, but these were again rejected by both the extreme left and the moderate right. Thus the Japan Mass Party (Nihon Taishuto), founded in December 1928, proved to be no more than a variation on familiar themes. It certainly did nothing to bring greater unity and results in the 1930 elections were therefore no better than those of 1928. Once again the parties savagely attacked each other and split the vote by putting up too many candidates, half a million votes giving them on this occasion only five representatives in the Diet. It was a performance that better planning enabled them to repeat in 1932, despite a 40 per cent drop in their share of the poll.

Throughout this phase of their history the left-wing parties were being hampered by the activities of the police, who used censorship, arrest and even violence against them. Police regulations dating from 1900 already conferred extensive powers, but these had been increased in 1925 by the addition of penalties of up to ten years' hard labour for certain offences, notably that of joining any society which was designed to overthrow the Japanese form of government or abolish private ownership. Directed ostensibly against communists and anarchists, the law was passed enthusiastically by the lower house. Yet it soon transpired that the lack of precision in its wording opened the way for many kinds of interference with personal liberties and did not by any means confine their application to extremists. In March 1928, soon after the elections, police raids on a large scale rounded up about a thousand communists and communist sympathizers. A year later the technique was tried again, this time bringing in many non-communist radicals as well. Thereafter men and women of known left-wing proclivities were always liable to arrest, imprisonment and often torture without apparent cause or warning.

One result of this, both because the extreme left suffered more than any other group and because there was a tendency for factions to unite when under attack, was that most remaining members of the labour movement, chiefly those of the right and centre, were at last brought together to form the Social Mass Party (Shakai Taishuto) in July 1932. This managed to maintain a semblance of unity right down to 1940, when all political parties were dissolved, and even to build up a substantial representation in the Diet, adopting for this purpose the nationalist slogans of the age and exploiting the popular resentment caused by army intervention in national politics.

Nevertheless, before 1945 the parties of the left failed to make any great mark on Japanese society. Their own disunity was partly to blame for this, as was government persecution. In addition, their disputes with the 'liberal' parties had reduced the effectiveness of both in seeking power, in that the struggle for control of the Diet played its part in hampering the Diet's bid for control of national policy. Disunity, in other words, operated not only within parties, but also between them, and this when unity was their greatest need. The Seiyukai and Minseito, while they tried to make cabinets responsible to the lower house, encouraged the police to suppress the left. The left, in turn, was at least as hostile to the bourgeois politicians as it was to oligarchs and Genro.

Fundamentally, however, it was the failure to secure popular support that condemned both kinds of parties to defeat. The reasons for it are not to be found in any single factor, not even wholly in the politicians' defects. They lie rather in those ideas and institutions which had turned the Japanese people away from the pursuit of individual freedoms and towards the attainment of collective goals: the formative pressures of the education system; an emperor-centred state religion; conscription, with its accompanying indoctrination; and the persistence of traditional authoritarian attitudes in important areas of bureaucratic and family behaviour. In sum, these enabled the discontents arising from economic change to be marshalled in the service of ambitions quite distinct from those of either the liberal or the labour movements, ambitions which brought Japan close to another 'Restoration' and plunged her into a major war.

CHAPTER XIII

PATRIOTS AND SOLDIERS
1930-1941

*Ultranationalism—army plots—Manchuria—military factions—
insurrection of February 1936—preparations for war*

THE MODEST advance towards a system of parliamentary
democracy and the emergence of various brands of left-wing
politics were not the only—nor, in the long run, the decisive—
characteristics of the 'twenties in Japan. The decade also saw
the beginnings of a conservative and nationalist reaction that
was soon to overwhelm them. It stemmed in part from an
older tradition of opposition to the course of the country's
modern growth, one which had been reflected in the anti-
Western, often violently chauvinistic, activities of men like
Saigo Takamori in the early Meiji period and of organizations
like the Genyosha and Kokuryukai thereafter. These had been
associated, as we have seen, with ideas of Japanese expansion
on the Asian mainland; but in so far as their aim was to build
up the country's strength, making it possible to resist, or repel,
renewed encroachment by the powers, it involved a consideration of events at home as well. A strong Japan had to have not
only arms and bases, but also unity, loyalty, a sense of purpose.
The patriot, therefore, was concerned with questions of politics, education and morale, in addition to economic and foreign
affairs. As the Kokuryukai's programme put it:

'We shall renovate the present system, foster a foreign policy
aiming at expansion overseas, revolutionize domestic politics to
increase the happiness of the people, and establish a social policy
that will settle problems between labor and capital. . . .'[66]

To many it seemed that the domestic aspects of this programme needed more emphasis than the foreign in the years after the 1914-18 war. The growth of industry, in particular, was helping to undermine the attitudes proper to a disciplined and dedicated people, for its profits tempted those who shared them into new forms of extravagance, nearly all imported from the West, while their unequal distribution led to 'dangerous thoughts', also of Western origin, like socialism, pacifism and democracy. Similarly, modernization of the economy could be blamed for rural distress and hence for weakening the position of the farmer, society's staunchest upholder of traditional behaviour. In fact, dancehalls, luxury, political corruption, big business, trade unions, strikes, agrarian unrest and debased standards of every kind, all could be lumped together as results of an over-indulgence in foreign ways. They thus became a focus for the resentments of men of many different kinds: those who felt that the new order of things gave them less than their proper station; those who genuinely respected the past and the values it represented; and those whose sense of inferiority in the face of the West's achievements brought a hatred of factories, as well as an ambition for empire. The resulting movement embraced conservatives, professional patriots, agrarian idealists, advocates of state ownership and social revolutionaries, all contributing in some measure to the aggressive 'ultranationalism' of the nineteen-thirties.

Much of its leadership was to be found in the so-called 'patriotic societies'. A few of the older ones, such as the Kokuryukai itself, had achieved a degree of respectability with the years, as had their more distinguished patrons. Toyama Mitsuru, for example, now wealthy and influential, was often an official guest on state occasions or at ministerial lunches. Equally respectable were the senior members of some newer bodies, especially those whose avowed purpose was to protect Japan from the threat of socialism, like the Dai Nihon Kokusuikai (Japan National Essence Society), founded in 1919 by Tokonami Takejiro, Home Minister in the Hara government. The Kokuhonsha (National Foundation Society) of 1924 was outstanding in this respect. Its membership included three future prime ministers (Saito Makoto, Hiranuma Kiichiro and Koiso Kuniaki), several generals (Ugaki Kazushige, Araki Sadao, Mazaki Jinzaburo) and a number of party politicians, together with representatives of the *zaibatsu* firms and the higher bureaucracy. Some of these, no doubt, joined as a form of political insurance, for the group was diverse in ideas as well as in affiliations. Nevertheless, the Kokuhonsha remained a most powerful champion of the nationalist cause in Japan's centres of authority.

In sharp contrast were the smaller, extremist organizations which existed on the fringes of politics, dependent for funds on the contributions of non-members—obtained by methods ranging from cajolery to threats or even fraud—and for cohesion on the influence of individual 'bosses'. Often they were little more than strong-arm squads, capitalizing on the fashion for patriotism instead of crime. Sometimes, however, they were the personal following of much more dangerous men, fanatics whose views were as violent as the means by which they tried to spread them. Such was Kita Ikki, author and revolutionary, who was eventually executed in 1937 for his part in an attempted *coup d'état*. With Okawa Shumei he founded the Yuzonsha (Society for Preservation of the National Essence) in 1921 and became the inspiration of many others like it, this despite an egocentric and domineering manner that cost him many allies.

Kita's chief contribution was to the ideology of the movement. In 1919 at the age of thirty-five he wrote a book entitled *An Outline Plan for the Reconstruction of Japan*, which set out his ideas at length and soon won him fame despite a police ban on its circulation. It advocated a radical revision of society in order to fit Japan for leadership in the revolutionary Asia which Kita thought bound to come: the confiscation of personal fortunes greater than one million yen, the nationalization of major industries, the establishment of an eight-hour day, the seizure and redistribution of surplus private landholdings above 100,000 yen in value, and renunciation by the emperor of his family estates. All this was to be achieved through a military *coup d'état*, which would make possible a clean sweep of the country's existing leadership—political, economic and bureaucratic—and the substitution for it of a regime based on direct relationships between the emperor and his people. When completed, it would enable Japan to act more vigorously in foreign affairs. As a member of the proletariat of nations, Kita argued, it was her task to secure justice from the wealthy, like Britain (the millionaire) and Russia (the great landowner). This could be done by launching an expansionist policy on the Asian mainland and supporting the interests of Asians everywhere against the West.

Very different were the views of Gondo Seikyo, apostle of an agrarian-centred nationalism that looked to the village as the nucleus of both political and economic life. Like Kita, he emphasized the role of the emperor in the national polity and accepted the doctrine of Japan's racial mission overseas. Unlike him, however, he wished not to socialize industry, but to destroy it, because it was a symbol of capitalism's exploitation of the countryside for the benefit of the town. His concern was for the simple ways of the farmer, who would look to the emperor as a kind of family head, and for village autonomy. Centralization, bureaucracy and things Western were to him anathema.

Gondo's ideas, too, were first published in 1919 and were propagated through an institute which he established in 1920. Another man of similar outlook, Tachibana Kosaburo, founded a communal village near Mito at this time, later conducting a school there at which he taught farming and patriotism to a handful of students. Eventually he formed links with another group in the same area, Inoue Nissho's Ketsumeidan, a blood brotherhood dedicated to a rather directer method of bringing about the agrarian millenium, namely, the assassination of leading financiers and industrialists.

The attitudes and interests represented in such societies were too varied to make it likely that they could co-operate in putting forward a political programme. Moreover, small numbers and lack of regular finances made them ineffective by themselves. On the other hand, the anti-capitalist, anti-Western prejudices which were common to the thinking of most of their members were shared by men whose ability to influence policy proved in the end to be much greater: the younger officers of the forces, especially the army. Many of these, after reforms carried out in 1924-5, were drawn from new social strata—the families of shopkeepers, small landowners and minor officials—which had not the same loyalty to the established order as had characterized the narrower oligarchy of the past, but were nevertheless unwilling to espouse the cause of communism or the urban poor. Officers with this background were more likely than their predecessors to join the radical right and to be influenced by complaints arising from the stress of economic change. Equally, they had grievances of their own. Civilian control, as advocated by the political parties, had contributed to a decline in the services' prestige. Good neighbourliness and retrenchment threatened their careers. Finally, the wealth and luxury of the privileged, notably in the cities, compared strangely in their eyes with the low pay and spartan ways which society apparently expected its soldiers to accept.

As a result, a number of officers began to form connections with the nationalist movement at a level quite distinct from the recognized channels between the high command, senior bureaucrats and politicians. Some got into touch with Kita Ikki, Okawa Shumei and their like, founding joint military-civilian organizations to discuss the possibilities of reform by force. Some established societies with a membership drawn entirely from the army and navy. Most famous—or notorious —was Lt-Col Hashimoto Kingoro's Sakurakai (Cherry Society), originating in September 1930, which at its peak comprised a hundred members, all army men of the rank of lieutenant-colonel or below. About two-fifths were from the War Ministry and General Staff, as many again from the military training schools, and the rest from units stationed in the Tokyo area.

These officers were no clearer than their civilian allies about what it was they intended to achieve. Two phrases occurred frequently in their statements, 'the imperial way' (Kodo) and 'the Showa Restoration'.[67] Both implied that the emperor would play a special part in any plans, but they were not in other respects at all precise, varying in meaning according to individual taste from a vague assertion of the need for moral regeneration to an insistence on 'a military dictatorship, in which the Emperor in fact, if not in name, would be no more than a sacred puppet'.[68] Yet if there was no agreed policy in the positive sense, there could be no question about who were the targets of attack: the political parties, on the one hand, and big business, especially the zaibatsu, on the other. It was this,

coupled with a determination to organize the country economically and ideologically for war, which suggests a comparison with what in Europe was labelled 'fascism'.

The participation of serving officers, even though they were
junior in rank, was important as giving the fanatics access to
weapons. They used them not in revolution proper, for this
was evidently impossible without far wider support than they
could hope to obtain, but to create a degree of confusion which
might enable their seniors to declare a state of emergency and
martial law. For this reason their chosen methods were terrorism and assassination. Sometimes these were employed on a
large enough scale to give the appearance, at least, of attempted
revolt. Sometimes they were directed at individuals, with the
object of removing those who stood in the way of extremist
ambitions or 'persuading' such persons to a change of heart.
Nor can one deny the technique's success. Accompanied as it
was by pamphlets, newspaper articles, protest meetings and
demonstrations, all harping on the theme of patriotic duty—
and this was invariably equated with the political aspirations
of the nationalists at home, as well as with expansionist policies
abroad—the effect was to make it difficult, indeed dangerous,
for any public figure to oppose the trend. 'The mildest accusa-
tion of disloyalty to the *kokutai*,' it has been said, 'seems to
have been enough to disturb the self-confidence of a Japanese
official or politician at any date between, let us say, the close
of 1931 and the beginning of the Pacific War. Moral courage
was displayed, it is true, by a few men in public life. . . . But
devotion to principle, to a rationally thought-out and accepted
personal point of view, was a very rare phenomenon.'[69]

Nationalism and assassination were by no means new in Japanese politics, as we have seen in earlier chapters. Public opinion,
inflamed by nationalism, had several times encouraged riotous
outbursts since 1890. Both Ito and Okubo, like a number of
late-Tokugawa and Meiji leaders, had been killed by men who
objected to their policies, while more recently there had been
the murders of Prime Minister Hara and the head of the *zaibatsu*
firm of Yasuda in 1921. Moreover, one has only to read Morgan
Young's *Japan under Taisho Tenno* (1928) to find numerous
examples of nationalist violence on a smaller scale, as well as

its lenient treatment by the courts, a pattern that was to become familiar in later years.

Nevertheless, the revolutionary aspects of ultranationalism after 1930 were not a mere continuation of what had gone before. They sprang also from contemporary pressures, especially from rural distress. The adjustment of agriculture to the needs of an industrial economy had already brought a good deal of hardship to the farmer, reflected in the growing proportion of tenancy and frequent bankruptcies. This was increased after 1927 by a steady decline in the price of rice, occasioned by bumper crops, and, more serious still, by a failure of silk prices due to the collapse of American prosperity in 1929–30. By 1931 the index of raw silk prices (1914 = 100) was down to 67, compared with 151 in 1929 and 222 in 1925. Over the same period the index for rice fell from 257 to 114. A world slump in international trade simultaneously reduced Japan's cotton exports, driving a large proportion of unemployed girl factory workers to seek refuge in their native villages. The result was widespread poverty in rural areas:

'In Yamanashi prefecture, it was stated, 22,000 silk reeling girls had not been paid for months, finding it better to work for food and shelter than to get nothing. In Miyagi the electric light was abandoned; from various prefectures came reports of unpaid teachers and of local officials on reduced pay. Children were not sent to school so that the small fee, hitherto cheerfully paid by the poorest, might be saved.'[70]

Conditions were worst in the north and north-east, which, with Kyushu, were the army's favourite recruiting grounds; and since many junior officers also came from hard-hit families, the unrest was quickly communicated to servicemen of every rank.

Military opinion was further offended by the Minseito government's readiness to negotiate a limitation on naval armaments. The London Naval Treaty of 1930, which confirmed, and in some respects extended, the arrangements made at Washington in 1922 (see Chapter XI), was supported by the Navy Minister but opposed by the naval Chief of Staff. Signed on April 21, despite the latter's protests, it again faced opposition when it came before the Privy Council for ratification in

July, though the cabinet stood firm behind its premier, Hamaguchi Yuko, and won the day. However, it did so only by
violating two principles which officers of the services had very
much at heart. The first was that Japan should not accept any
international agreement which limited her freedom of action
in the Far East and the Pacific, even one which similarly
restrained her potential rivals. Acceptance of the 5 : 5 : 3
ratio for capital ships, which it was now proposed should be
applied to other major war vessels as well, was held to have this
disadvantage, to say nothing of the fact that it was a blow to
national pride. Secondly, the way in which the decision had
been made raised an important constitutional issue. The service
ministers and chiefs of staff, both in theory and in practice, had
separate functions. These might be broadly distinguished as
administration, on the one hand, and planning, on the other,
while it was also the duty of the minister, as a member of the
cabinet, to secure government approval for the recommendations they both made and to obtain the funds by which these
could be carried out. It was *not* within his powers—nor, in the
view of most military men, those of the cabinet—to overrule
the chief of staff on essentially operational matters, which included questions concerning the level of armament needed for
defence. On this occasion, the navy's chief of staff had not only
been overruled, he had even been forced to resign. Taken in
conjunction with Kato's reduction of the army by four divisions a few years earlier, the incident made it clear that party
cabinets were a real threat to the treasured independence of
the General Staff.

One result of the turbulence which these events produced
was the shooting of Hamaguchi in November. He died of his
wounds in the following year. The attack, which was made by
a youth connected with one of the lesser-known patriotic
societies, does not seem to have been part of any wider plot.
Nor did it have any great effect on the political situation, since
Hamaguchi was succeeded as Prime Minister and leader of his
party in April 1931 by Wakatsuki Reijiro, a man of similar
background and ideas. All the same, it was symptomatic of a
state of affairs which a number of army officers hoped to use
to their own, or their service's, advantage.

The first move came at the beginning of 1931. It was made

by members of Lt-Col Hashimoto's Sakurakai, in conjunction with civilian extremists led by Okawa Shumei, whose plans envisaged, first, a series of riots and bomb attacks, organized by the civilians and carried out with weapons provided by the army, and, second, a declaration of martial law and the installation of a military government under General Ugaki. It is not at all certain how far Ugaki and other senior officers had advance knowledge of these proposals, though their co-operation would undoubtedly have been necessary for success. The fact that they gave orders calling off the plot in March 1931, just before the date for action, suggests that they only learnt the details at the last moment and promptly withdrew their support. Yet their complicity, no matter how slight, made it difficult to take action against the rest. Moreover, their lack of resolution convinced the conspirators that next time they would have to force the hand of the army leadership, in addition to bringing down the government, a decision that became the basis of a further plot later in the year. Again Hashimoto and Okawa were its architects, though this time they looked to General Araki Sadao as their nominee for office. This time, too, soldiers were to be more directly engaged in the preliminary stages. The cabinet, for example, was to be eliminated by air attack during one of its meetings; a Guards division was to be called out in the resulting confusion; and the War Ministry was to be isolated until martial law had been declared. This plan was betrayed and its authors arrested in October. However, the mild character of the punishments meted out showed that the high command was still reluctant to act strongly in maintaining discipline.

One reason for this was that some of its senior members had themselves been planning to bring about operations on the mainland by methods just as 'rebellious' in their way as those of Hashimoto. There had long been a feeling in military circles, especially in the Kwantung Army, which controlled Japanese troops guarding the railway zone in South Manchuria, that Shidehara's conciliatory policy towards China was causing Japan to miss chances of expansion. Since Chinese disunity was unlikely to last for ever, the argument ran, Japan should exploit it while she could. Indeed, some members of the Kwantung army staff had tried to create an occasion for doing so in 1928, by organizing the murder of the Manchurian war-lord, Chang Tso-lin; and although Tokyo had on that occasion refused to act, they still cherished the same ambitions. In 1931 the time seemed ripe to try again. China was distracted by floods in the Yangtse valley. Britain and the United States were preoccupied with economic difficulties at home. And in Japan itself, some issue was needed which would rally public opinion behind the army in its struggle with the party politicians. Action in Manchuria seemed just the thing, the more so as it was a policy on which most army officers could agree—after the event, if not before—whatever their rank and whatever their differences in domestic politics.

During 1931 members of the staff in both Tokyo and Manchuria were making their preparations, these including much exhortation of the public in speeches and pamphlets, as well as military arrangements for troop movements and reinforcements should an incident take place. On September 15 the Kwantung Army was ordered to assume a state of readiness. On September 18 its plans were at last put into effect. Late that night a Japanese patrol near Mukden heard explosions. Investigating, it found slight damage to the railway line just outside the city and promptly fired on a number of Chinese soldiers who were seen in the vicinity. On this flimsy pretext the occupation of the area began, troops taking over the Mukden arsenal, airfield and radio station before dawn, the city itself, together with Changchun, in the course of the following day, and Kirin two days later. On September 21 reinforcements began to arrive from Korea, making it possible to extend operations in the next three months to the whole of the Manchurian provinces.

In Tokyo the army's Vice Chief of Staff, apparently with the sympathy, if not the active co-operation, of the War Minister, General Minami, took the necessary steps to support the forces in the field. The government, accordingly, faced a *fait accompli*. It had heard rumours of the proposed moves a few days earlier and had tried to stop them by sending a messenger to the Kwantung commander-in-chief; but the officer chosen for this duty, being a party to the conspiracy, took care not to deliver his message until it was too late. Thereafter, with its troops already committed, the cabinet tried vainly to halt the advance. Its instructions were ignored by the field commanders, on the grounds of operational necessity, and they in turn were backed by the War Minister and General Staff. In fact, the end of January 1932 saw hostilities spread to China proper, when a clash between Chinese and Japanese troops at Shanghai led to heavy fighting and at one point to a naval bombardment of Nanking. For some weeks this was the only fighting that was going on, for the occupation of Manchuria had by this time been completed and the army had given evidence of its determination not to withdraw by sponsoring a puppet government there, which declared its 'independence'—of China—on February 18, 1932. Pu Yi, the last of China's former Manchu emperors, was made head of the new state of Manchukuo in March.

The international repercussions of these events, which we shall consider in the next chapter, were serious, but no less so was the effect on developments within Japan. The Wakatsuki government, helpless in the face of the army's action, was brought down by its own disunity in December 1931. Its successor, under Inukai, leader of the Seiyukai, was handicapped in its conduct of foreign affairs by its own past record. Ministers found that the enthusiasm with which they had advocated 'positive' policies while in opposition made it difficult for them to criticize the army for carrying such policies out, however unconstitutional the manner in which it did so. What is more, members of the cabinet now had every reason to fear for their personal safety, especially if they were unwise enough to give any hint of seeking a settlement with China. The patriotic societies were delighted with what had been done. They were anxious, too, that the army be given the fullest support, preferably by establishing a new regime. Thus Inoue Nissho's blood brotherhood, dedicated to the removal of the ruling clique, made out of a list of intended victims and drew lots for the privilege of executing sentence. On February 9, 1932, one of them murdered Inoue Junnosuke, a former Finance Minister, known to oppose the Manchurian venture. Less than a month later another killed Baron Dan, head of Mitsui, though at this point the remainder were arrested and the series came to an end.

Their task was taken over, albeit with some differences of

technique, by a group which had been influenced by Gondo Seikyo's agrarian doctrines. Tachibana Kosaburo was involved, as was Okawa Shumei and a son of Toyama Mitsuru, but the active leaders were some young officers from a naval air base not far from Mito and a handful of army cadets. They were supported by Tachibana's Aikyojuku, youths from the countryside, having little organization and less experience, whom a contemporary journalist described as 'adolescents straying in a pink mist'.[71] With such executants it is not surprising that much went wrong, when on May 15, 1932, they made attacks on Tokyo power stations, a bank, the headquarters of the Seiyukai party and other buildings, in an attempt to create a crisis which would lead to martial law. For the most part their efforts failed. In one thing, however, they were successful: in assassinating Prime Minister Inukai at his official residence. This, if it did not provoke an army *coup d'état*, at least proved to be a death blow to party government.

The atmosphere in which politics were to be carried on hereafter was made very plain by the trials which began in the summer of 1933: separate civil trials for Inoue Nissho and Tachibana Kosaburo, each with his followers, and two court martials, one army and one navy, for the servicemen. All were public, long drawn out and wordy, the defendants being allowed to engage in fierce diatribes, sometimes lasting two or three days, against everything and everybody they thought they had reason to hate. This was their defence, an argument of patriotic motive. What is more, they were encouraged in it by judge and prosecuting counsel. Tachibana at one stage was permitted to announce each day the subject of his next day's discourse. Inoue actually complained of the judge's manners, accusing him of not paying proper attention to the speeches, and forced the appointment of a new one by refusing to go on with the trial.

The sentences, when one considers the nature of the crimes, were light, ranging from four years' imprisonment for the army cadets to life for Tachibana; and this fact did not escape the notice of other patriots or their potential victims. One result was to demoralize the political parties, the Minseito and Seiyukai presenting a spectacle of growing impotence and division in the next few years. Some factions broke away to seek power through an alliance with the ultranationalists. Others remained within the parties, but gave increasing support to army policies. The only important exception was a new left-wing organization, the Shakai Taishuto (Social Mass Party), formed in July 1932, which, despite some internal dissension caused by the attractions of different brands of Japanese national socialism, managed to pursue an anti-capitalist, anti-communist and anti-fascist line until the war with China began in 1937. It was helped, undoubtedly, by the police purge of the extreme left-wing—another 2,000 arrests were made in October 1932—since this, by leaving only the moderates, gave it greater cohesion than earlier parties of its kind. It also profited to some extent from popular dissatisfaction with much that the army was trying to do. Thus in the election of 1936 it polled half a million votes and won eighteen Diet seats, a record for the left. Nevertheless, this was nothing like enough to influence the direction of events.

The defence of the constitution was therefore left more and more to the statesmen surrounding the emperor: Saionji, last of the Genro; the ex-premiers; and those who held such offices as Lord Privy Seal or President of the Privy Council. Many were liberals, who wished to see discipline restored in the services and would have preferred party cabinets to continue. On the other hand, they recognized that this was not acceptable to the army extremists and feared that any attempt to impose their ideas might lead to revolt, by which all established institutions, including the Throne itself, would be put in jeopardy. They were thus left no alternative, as they saw it, but to compromise.

For the time being this meant going back to an earlier device, in proposing governments which included members of both the principal parties, but were led by non-party men. On this basis Admiral Saito Makoto succeeded Inukai as Prime Minister in May 1932 and was followed by another admiral, Okada Keisuke, in July 1934, the choice of navy men being dictated by the belief that they were acceptable to, but more manageable than, Japan's generals. A more lasting solution, however, proved hard to find. The problem was to restore discipline over the radical elements in the army. The logical people to do this, it seemed, were that service's senior officers, for which

Navy more symp. to Govt than Army?

reason it was necessary to secure the help of the high command. This, in turn, meant making concessions: in foreign affairs, by accepting expansion in Manchuria; and at home, by postponing disciplinary action until the senior officers felt able to enforce it. The upshot was a policy of 'control by concession' which ended by sacrificing all it had been devised to save.

One difficulty was that the generals themselves were by no means united in their outlook. A minority, known as the *Kodo* (Imperial Way) faction and centring on Generals Araki and Mazaki, sympathized with the revolutionary ideas of Kita Ikki. Another, the *Tosei* (Control) faction, led at first by Nagata Tetsuzan, then by Ishihara Kanji and Muto Akira, was more conservative, more rational, more willing to work with bureaucrats and capitalists within the existing structure. Both were proud of the army's prestige and constitutional independence, ready to defend them against all rivals. Both pressed for a 'positive' foreign policy. There was a difference here, however, in that the radical *Kodo* group saw Russia as the enemy and were anxious not to get Japan's forces too deeply committed in any other struggle, while *Tosei*, which implied a measure of moderation in domestic politics, usually stood for expansion in Manchuria and China. The two also tended to differ as types: the *Kodo* man a field commander, direct, single-minded, intolerant of compromise and politicians; the *Tosei* man suaver, more experienced in affairs, perhaps a bureau or section chief on the General Staff.

The struggle between the two groups was not fully joined until 1935. From the end of 1931, with Araki as War Minister and Mazaki as Vice Chief of Staff, the *Kodo* faction was in a strong position, though their opponents were more powerful in Manchuria. Then in January 1934 Araki resigned, because of strain and ill health, and his successor, Hayashi Senjuro, began to fall under the influence of Nagata Tetsuzan. Mazaki was by this time Director General of Military Education, one of the army's three top posts, which carried with it control of officer training; but in July 1935 Nagata at last succeeded in securing his dismissal, thereby causing serious trouble. On August 12 Nagata himself was murdered by Lt-Col Aizawa Saburo, one of Mazaki's supporters. In response, the *Tosei* leaders brought Aizawa to trial and took steps to move other troublemakers to Manchuria, a plan which persuaded the *Kodo* adherents to resort once again to force.

Their attempt to seize power was made on February 26, 1936. Early that morning, over a thousand men of the First Division, led by junior *Kodo* officers, took over the centre of the capital. Some attacked the Prime Minister's residence and only failed to kill Okada because they did not recognize him. Others murdered the Finance Minister, the new Inspector General of Military Education and the Lord Privy Seal, in addition to making more or less unsuccessful attacks on several other public figures. Pamphlets were distributed calling for the establishment of a new order, which it was hoped would be led by Mazaki. Yet neither Mazaki nor Araki made any move. Nor did society crumble at their blow, as a reading of ultra-nationalist literature might well have led them to expect. Instead, the high command, at the emperor's prompting, called out the navy and the Imperial Guards, surrounded the rebels and invited them to surrender. They did so, after a period of uneasy waiting, on the afternoon of the 29th.

This time surrender did not bring publicity or nominal sentences. Thirteen of the rebels were tried and executed in secrecy and haste, as was Aizawa, and four of their civilian allies, including Kita Ikki, met a similar fate in the following year. Araki and Mazaki were placed on the reserve; and an old rule was revived, providing that the War Minister must be an officer on the active list, by which it was hoped to keep them out of politics. The earlier arrangements to scatter the radical young officers in posts in the provinces or abroad were completed. Discipline, it was claimed, had been restored.

True enough, indiscipline within the army after this date was of a less obvious kind. It took the form of what is known in Japanese as *gekokujo*, a phrase which implies the manipulation of superiors by subordinates and meant in this context that those nominally responsible for army decisions were expressing the views of men on their staff, the latter having the right to propose a course of action, as the probable executants thereof, in the expectation that it would be adopted. Traditionally the relationship stemmed from that between feudal lord and samurai, reinforced by Confucian ideas of leadership. In practice it gave the senior staff officer a degree of power not unlike that of the senior bureaucrat. The most important examples in the 1930s were to be found in the activities of the Military Affairs Bureau at the War Ministry, which had the task of negotiating on defence matters with the civil authorities, and the Operations Division of the General Staff, which formulated strategy, both offices assuming functions in fact much more far-reaching than those they possessed in theory. A similar situation existed in the navy and also on the staffs of overseas commanders.

It was largely by controlling these intermediate stages of the decision-making process that the *Tosei* faction was able after 1936 to exercise a dominant influence on army affairs. By doing so, moreover, it could determine national policies as a whole. If the service chiefs were, as it was sometimes said, 'robots' controlled by their subordinates, the government was rapidly becoming a robot of the service chiefs. This, too, was a kind of indiscipline, one that increased, rather than diminished, after the events of February 1936. The army, having regained its unity and saved the country from its own extremists, could operate a form of *gekokujo* at a higher level, partly by insisting on its independence in military matters—which came to include, ultimately, even the choice between peace and war—and partly by exploiting constitutional advantages to decide the composition of successive cabinets. No government could be formed without War and Navy Ministers. Since the latter had to be serving officers, no government could be formed without the co-operation of the high command. Thus when Hirota Koki became premier in March 1936, his first choice as Foreign Minister was vetoed by the army as unreliable. Hirota himself was brought down in January 1937 by army opposition, which also stopped General Ugaki from succeeding him—Ugaki was invited to form a government, but could find no one to serve as War Minister—and then foisted General Hayashi on a reluctant Court. When Hayashi resigned in May, the palace advisers turned in despair to a descendant of the old nobility, Konoe Fumimaro, in the hope that he would be able to satisfy service demands without giving way to them altogether, only to find that he became little more than a figurehead doing the army's bidding. By the time he left in January 1939, to be followed by the nationalist Hiranuma, the high command was in a position to choose, as well as to veto, nominees for cabinet appointment.

Japan's civilian statesmen, therefore, found that they had exchanged one kind of danger for another. Establishing control over *Kodo* extremists had perhaps saved the constitution and averted a threat to the basis of society. But the price they had had to pay was high. It involved an increase in the army's power to intervene in politics and the acceptance of a course which proved in the end no less destructive than revolution: expansion abroad and the building of a country organized for war.

War—though the word itself was carefully avoided—was not long in coming. In July 1937 one more in the long series of clashes between Chinese and Japanese troops in China took place near Peking. Hostilities spread and became general, so that by the end of the year, by decision of her field commanders and the military staff in Tokyo, Japan was fully committed. The resulting struggle will be discussed in the next chapter, but it can be said here that it was to be long and difficult beyond all expectations. It also had considerable impact on affairs at home. On the one hand it diverted the attention of many army hotheads from political to military matters. On the other it created an atmosphere in which their seniors could press for measures to prepare the country for a sterner test to come: re-armament, the further development of heavy industry, close government control of the economy, the destruction of liberalism, a reform of education.

An outline of these policies had been blocked out by army planners and adopted by the Hirota cabinet in August 1936, but it was not until Konoe became premier in June 1937 that their implementation really began. Within a few days of Konoe taking office, steps had been taken to bring civil aviation and the distribution of fuel under stricter government supervision. In October and November of the same year a Cabinet Planning Board was established, chiefly to co-ordinate economic policy, and an Imperial Headquarters was set up to provide for co-operation between army and navy, though neither organization ever fully achieved its ends. Other regulations had the effect of giving the services formally much of the power they already possessed in fact. All key decisions, it was agreed, were to be made at liaison conferences between the Prime Minister, Foreign Minister, War and Navy Ministers, and service Chiefs of Staff. They would then be confirmed at a meeting in the emperor's presence. This excluded other ministers, except by invitation, so that when the plan was put regularly into operation—which was in 1940—cabinet responsibility became no more than a pretence. Meanwhile the Asia Development Board, created at the end of 1938, had taken over the conduct of Japan's relations with China, a Greater East Asia Ministry being formed in November 1942 to absorb this and to handle matters pertaining to the other countries of the region. In the secretariat of all these bodies service officers held vital posts.

The extension of army influence on policy formation, which these innovations revealed, was accompanied by an increase in the government's powers of economic control. The National Mobilization Law, especially, which was passed by the Diet in March 1938, gave it a vast reserve of emergency authority, providing among other things for the direction of labour and materials, the regulation of wages and prices, government operation of certain industries, even a compulsory savings scheme and a system of national registration. Not all these measures were brought immediately into effect by any means. But their existence made it possible to establish clear priorities in economic growth.

There had already been some recovery from the trade slump of 1929–31, partly as a result of devaluation of the yen, so that both exports and imports by 1936 were about 25 per cent above the pre-slump value. Raw silk sales had fallen, but a rise in exports of textile fabrics compensated for this and stimulated a modest improvement, as well as some diversification, in the textile industry. Markets were also more varied. Less went to the United States, more to the countries of Asia and the south, where cheap manufactured goods were appropriate to local needs. The outstanding feature, however, was the growth in heavy industry. Between 1930 and 1936 the output of producer goods rose much more quickly than that of consumer goods, while the figures for both pig-iron and raw steel doubled. Coal production increased from about 30 million to 40 million metric tons, providing over half the country's fuel and power. In fact, Japan at this time accounted for a third of Asia's total coal consumption, about 90 per cent of what she needed being home produced. Shipbuilding had also recovered, the annual launch reaching nearly 300,000 tons in 1936 and the merchant marine over 4 million tons by 1937.

Government policy played an important part in these developments. At first this was because of attempts to overcome the economic crisis, but it came later to depend very largely on military needs. Military spending, for example, rose sharply, from under 500 million yen and 30 per cent of the budget in 1931 to 4,000 million yen and 70 per cent of the budget in 1937–8. After 1938, moreover, the use of controls authorized by the Mobilization Law, particularly those on raw materials, gave a more selective stimulus to chosen industries and firms. This brought significant gains in the production of motor vehicles, aircraft and warships, and helped to raise heavy industry's share of total industrial output to 73 per cent by 1942.

Manchukuo, too, conformed to the general trend. Indeed, it served in some ways as a pilot scheme for Japan itself, since military influence was paramount there from the very beginning. Its early investment pattern, directed by the South Manchuria Railway, proved too limited to meet the Kwantung Army's wishes; and in March 1938, the Manchuria Industrial Development Corporation was formed, with capital from the Manchukuo government and a new generation of Japanese industrialists (the 'new *zaibatsu*'), with whom the army had close relations. Money was channelled into the coal, iron and steel industries and into automobile and aircraft plants. Similar steps were taken in north China, through the North China Development Corporation, and by 1940 the two areas were producing on an important scale. Together they furnished most of the country's high quality coal, about 30 per cent of its pig-iron needs, and substantial quantities of cement, chemicals and machinery.

Changes of this kind bore a family likeness to those which the Meiji government had brought about under the slogan *fukoku-kyohei* ('rich country, strong army') in the nineteenth century, though it is true that their economics had become more complex. A comparison might also be made of the methods used in fostering unity and morale. In both periods these were conspicuously successful, but in the 1930s they were technologically more advanced. Censorship, as the Mobilization Law recognized, now embraced radio as well as press, while improvements in communications, transport and bureaucratic method made it easier to influence opinion and to bring dissentients under police control.

The main targets were still the liberals, both in and out of politics. They faced the danger of arrest whenever they criticized the government's policies and were subject to a number of public pressures which officialdom did nothing to abate. Professor Minobe, for example, a leading authority on constitutional law and a member of the House of Peers, was attacked strongly in 1934-5 on the grounds that some of his writings described the emperor as an 'organ' of the State. This, it was said, was *lèse majesté*; and in face of such a charge few had the courage to defend him. Eventually he was forced to resign from the Peers and relinquish all his honours, his books were banned, and early in 1936 he narrowly escaped assassination.

In incidents like this Japanese nationalism became hysterical. In others it was little short of nonsense. Thus the wording of the Kellogg Pact, stating that the signatories accepted it 'in the name of their respective peoples', brought quite serious—and successful—objections that this was disrespectful to the emperor. Foreign visitors were accused of spying on the flimsiest pretexts. There were arguments about the use of foreign words and whether nameboards at railway stations should read from right to left (Japanese style) or left to right (Western style). And in 1935 the Foreign Ministry tried to substitute 'Nippon' and 'East Asia' for the older, Europo-centric terms 'Japan' and 'Far East'. This proved difficult to enforce, since habits, once established, died hard: as a British journalist put it, 'throughout many years of military aggression Japan got so thoroughly into the habit of "keeping the peace of the Far East" . . . that nothing was heard of Nippon keeping the peace of Eastern Asia'.[72]

Much of this chauvinistic atmosphere was injected into the schools and universities. Many foreign books used in them were proscribed by the police—often without a very clear idea of their contents—and textbooks were rewritten in nationalist terms. Even works of serious scholarship might well begin with a precautionary reference to Japan's mission overseas. Military training was made a compulsory part of education in 1938 and the time devoted to it, including that spent on indoctrination, increased steadily thereafter, always at the expense of 'unnecessary' subjects, that is, those which contributed little to patriotism or practical knowledge. Army officers were attached to the schools to supervise this process, their work made more important by an ordinance of March 1941, which emphasized the need to induce qualities appropriate to a wartime State.

Indeed, by then a good deal had already been achieved in this direction. In 1937 the Ministry of Education had issued a book called *Kokutai no Hongi* (Principles of the National Polity), which at once became the main text for the course in 'ethics'. Over two million copies were sold and special commentaries on it were issued to teachers, with the result that its doctrines became the basis of an intensive propaganda directed at the young. For the most part these doctrines were conservative, in the sense that they rejected the revolutionary, anticapitalist elements in the thinking of the radical right. But they were anti-liberal in the extreme. Individualism was anathema, service to the State was service in its highest form. Moreover, patriotism taught that what was bad was foreign:

'The various ideological and social evils of present-day Japan are the fruits of ignoring the fundamentals and of running into the trivial, of lack in sound judgment, and of failure to digest things thoroughly; and this is due to the fact that since the days of Meiji so many aspects of European and American culture, systems, and learning have been imported, and that, too rapidly.'[73]

It did not take long for the combined resources of press and radio, of schools and universities, of patriotic societies and army publicists, to drive such a lesson home.

This brings us back to the kind of criticisms which had for years been levelled at the Diet parties: in sum, that they were the representatives of a corrupting West. In the atmosphere that obtained after 1937, it is clear, they found the hostile chorus overwhelming. The elections of April 1937 had revealed signs of popular support for a campaign against the military's control of politics, not least in the million votes and thirty-six seats that went to the moderate left, the Shakai Taishuto; but

once hostilities broke out on the mainland in July, most politicians raised the cry of national unity and showed themselves
ready to pass every government bill. Even the Shakai Taishuto
found arguments to rationalize its coming into line, while its
opponents, if divided among themselves, solemnly denounced
any move to divide the country. Before long there was talk of
a united front—united, not *against* the army, but *behind* it—and
in 1940 plans to form one reached fruition. The Imperial Rule
Assistance Association (Taisei Yokusan Kai) was organized on
October 12 of that year. It replaced the parties, absorbed their
members and pledged itself to rally opinion behind 'the nation's'
policies, thereby making itself a symbol of the army's victory.
From this time on, the only restraints that remained on
Japan's actions overseas were those which might be exercised
within the inner circles of her leadership.

CHAPTER XIV

AN EMPIRE WON AND LOST
1937-1945

*Invasion of Manchuria—war with China—Anti-Comintern Pact
—Pearl Harbour—victory and defeat*

JAPANESE ADVOCATES of expansion after 1931 had behind
them a people easily persuaded that aggressive policies were
just. History, as taught in their schools, showed their country
starting its international career in the nineteenth century under
a number of handicaps imposed by a greedy West, then suffering under racial discrimination a generation later, when
Australia and the United States introduced controls on immigration—a grievance made all the harder to bear by the fact
that in Asia Japanese often had the status of Europeans—and
more recently facing new tariffs, quota regulations and other
'defensive' arrangements by the powers, designed to protect
their economies from Japanese competition during a time of
world recession. It is not surprising that the Japanese, acutely
conscious of their large and growing population, felt resentment, nor that the apostles of empire had little difficulty in
turning it to account. As Hashimoto Kingoro of the Sakurakai
wrote in his *Addresses to Young Men*:

'We have already said that there are only three ways left to Japan
to escape from the pressure of surplus population . . . namely
emigration, advance into world markets, and expansion of territory.
The first door, emigration, has been barred to us by the anti-
Japanese immigration policies of other countries. The second door,
advance into world markets, is being pushed shut by tariff barriers
and the abrogation of commercial treaties. What should Japan do
when two of the three doors have been closed against her?'[74]

To Hashimoto, like most of his compatriots, this reasoning

fully justified the pursuit of territorial ambitions, notably in
Korea, China and Manchuria. On the other hand, it was always
with mixed feelings that Japan's neighbours were made subject
to attack. For there still lingered the idea that they ought
properly to be allies in the struggle against the West, were it
not for the obstinacy which made them reject Japan's offers of
co-operation; and this line of thinking led in the end to the
concept of a 'New Order' in East Asia, announced by Prime
Minister Konoe in a broadcast in November 1938. It envisaged
the co-ordination under Japanese leadership of the military,
political, economic and cultural activities of Japan, China and
Manchukuo, so as to rescue all of them from subservience to
American and European pressure, the process involving—in a
manner reminiscent of the Twenty-one Demands—the establishment of Japanese bases on the mainland, Japanese control
of communications, and Japanese participation in running
China's police and army. A few years later came the more
ambitious proposal for a Greater East Asia Co-prosperity
Sphere, extending the same principles to South East Asia. This,
it was believed, would strengthen the alliance, politically by
marshalling anti colonialism in its favour and economically by
providing access to supplies of oil and other raw materials. Nor
was it to be confused with the building of an empire in the old
manner. Rather, Japan insisted, it was a response to the past
encroachment of the West. Hashimoto even tried to dis-
tinguish between colonization, as the West knew it, and his
own plans for 'some place overseas where Japanese capital,
Japanese skills and Japanese labour can have free play'.[75]

However unconvincing the argument of all this, the emotions
behind it are understandable enough and had a powerful effect
on Japanese opinion. There nevertheless remained a good deal
of room for disagreement about the methods by which the
programme might be carried out. Some groups had a vested
interest in one part of it more than another, like the Kwantung
Army staff and its industrialist friends, who were concerned
with the development of Manchukuo. Other army men had a
similar preoccupation with north China, whereas the navy,
because of its need for oil, tended to dwell on the importance
of moving south. Then there was the division between the
services, on the one hand, with their greater readiness to use

force, and the career diplomats and civilian statesmen, on the other, who, in the tradition of their Meiji predecessors, sought policies which would seem 'respectable' in international terms. If one adds the different attitudes that groups and individuals might adopt towards specific countries—fear of Russia, a desire for alliance with Germany (or Britain), friendship for America, perhaps—it is easy to see why a general acceptance of the necessity for increasing Japanese strength did not automatically lead to the shaping of a consistent course.

The complexities were made greater by the struggle for power within Japan, an account of which was given in the previous chapter. The decline of the political parties undoubtedly meant that less attention was paid to commercial objectives in Japanese activities abroad, but the new leaders, it transpired, were no better able to enforce a positive and coherent policy in their place. The services, after all, like the parties, suffered both from factions and indiscipline. Thus the defeat of the *Kodo* extremists in 1935–6 contributed to a shift of emphasis from defence against Russia to advance against China, in addition to weakening the right-wing radicals at home; while at another level, the fact that army field commanders, members of their staff and officers in Tokyo of varying seniority were able at times to control events quite independently of the supreme command, provoking incidents which would commit their superiors whether they liked it or not, ensured that no group's ideas were ever likely to be followed without question. One result of the army's growing dominance, in fact, was to put it in question whether there was a truly 'national' policy at all. Statesmen close to the emperor, fighting a rearguard action to defend the constitution and the prestige of the Throne— a cause to which they rather too readily sacrificed their principles in foreign affairs—might make concessions in discussion with the War Minister or representatives of the General Staff, only to find that these had already been anticipated and put into effect by officers of lower rank. Such a situation makes it difficult for the historian, as it did for contemporaries, to allocate responsibility for decisions, a circumstance that needs to be borne in mind when reading the narrative which follows.

The invasion of Manchuria in 1931 set an ominous pattern, for the Japanese troops who occupied Mukden on the night of September 18-19 were following the plans of the Kwantung Army staff, not the policies of Tokyo. The cabinet, indeed, was first consulted when it came to sending reinforcements. In the next few months, moreover, the high command as a whole gave full support to the officers in the field, repeatedly accepting orders to limit the advance, then allowing them to be ignored on a plea of operational necessity. It was by this technique that the occupied area was constantly enlarged and the diplomats faced with a series of *faits accomplis*. As a final step came the creation of the puppet state of Manchukuo in February 1932, which gave the Kwantung Army something not far short of a private empire. Its commander-in-chief, as Japanese ambassador, acquired so large a measure of independence, by exercising civil, as well as military, control, that Admiral Okada, Prime Minister in 1934-36, later stated that the government 'had no way of learning what the plans and activities of the Kwantung Army were'.[76]

Diplomacy, meanwhile, had been doing what it could to repair the damage to the country's reputation. On September 21, two days after the outbreak, China had appealed to the League of Nations and Japan had promptly denied that she was pursuing territorial ambitions. She also promised to withdraw her troops, only to find, as time passed, that Tokyo lacked the authority to do so. For several weeks, explanations and recriminations prevented further progress. Then in November, with Japanese consent, the League appointed a commission of inquiry, its members, under the chairmanship of Lord Lytton, being nominated in January 1932 and reaching Yokohama in the following month. By then their investigations had already been made abortive by the announcement of the 'independent' state of Manchukuo. Nor did anything they saw or heard thereafter give much credence to the Japanese army's case. Though it was not until years later that the true story of the military conspiracy became known, the commission's report, submitted in September 1932, firmly condemned Japan's aggression and rejected the arguments on which it stood. This made it inevitable that recognition would be withheld from the regime which the Kwantung Army had established, so Japan, making public her own recognition of it, withdrew altogether from the League as soon as the matter came to debate at Geneva in February 1933.

China gained nothing from these moves and found Western sympathy of little help when the Japanese army resumed operations in her northern provinces at the beginning of 1933. In the first few weeks of that year a pretext was found for adding Jehol to Manchukuo. In May a truce at Tangku, negotiated without reference to the diplomats, created a demilitarized zone which insulated Japan's gains from the areas further south and gave military commanders a basis for fresh demands at a later date. In June 1935, for example, they called for the withdrawal of Chinese troops from Hopei and Chahar, on the grounds that their presence threatened the maintenance of peace. Simultaneously they encouraged such Chinese political movements in the north as might be willing to accept 'autonomy' under the patronage of Japan.

For the most part the advances Japan made in China in these years were local, intermittent and small-scale, rarely causing the sort of scandal that would have brought international intervention. They were also the army's work, though its success was bringing increasing political support at home. The Foreign Ministry contented itself with enunciating in April 1934 the doctrine that the relationships between Japan and China—which it described in terms more appropriate to suzerainty or protectorate than to diplomacy between independent states—were in no sense the concern of the League of Nations or the powers. Eighteen months later it proposed a basis for a general settlement: Chinese recognition of Manchukuo; suppression of anti-Japanese activities in China; and an anti-communist Sino-Japanese alliance.

Even this, however, fell short of an attempt at total domination, such as was to come before very long. Chinese stubbornness and hostility in the resulting negotiations soon began to convince Japanese leaders that their piecemeal methods were of no avail, an attitude that became more widespread when Chiang Kai-shek reached agreement with the communists at the end of 1936 on making common cause against Japan. Similarly, the Japanese high command was finding its hotheads harder to restrain, or rather, had found fresh grounds for not trying to restrain them. The failure of the military revolt in Tokyo in February 1936 had left behind it a sense of frustration and discouragement among younger officers. This might have been explosive had there been any attempt to exercise moderation overseas, whereas an adventurous foreign policy had the advantage, if successful, that it might ease the political tensions building up at home and possibly show a profit economically as well. Since most members of the Tosei ('control') faction now dominant in the army were men dedicated to pursuing Japan's 'mission' on the mainland—and most members of the public had been led to expect some outstanding achievement from them—by 1937 the prospects of a major clash with China had much increased.

It began with an incident at Marco Polo Bridge, near Peking, on the night of July 7, 1937, when firing broke out between Chinese and Japanese troops while the latter were on manoeuvres. The fighting quickly spread, becoming general in the next few weeks. One reason was that Chinese resistance proved unusually stubborn. Another was the absence of any authority on the Japanese side that seemed willing to effect a local settlement. The cabinet wanted one, as did several members of the high command, for many senior officers were reluctant to get the army deeply committed in China at the cost of leaving Manchuria and Mongolia open to Russian attack; but the field commanders and their allies, the section chiefs of the General Staff, were able to prevent any such restrictive proposals from being carried out. In this sense, the 'China Affair', as it was called, was the result of another military conspiracy.

Once the campaign was properly begun, of course, Tokyo could hardly refuse reinforcements, and this made it possible, as had happened in Manchuria six years earlier, for the scale of operations to be continually increased. By early August Tientsin and Peking had both been occupied. By September over 150,000 Japanese troops had been deployed. Hostilities had also spread to the south, beginning, once again, at Shanghai, where there was heavy fighting, and continuing with a thrust up the Yangtse river to Nanking, Chiang's capital. The city was captured in mid-December and became the scene of what were probably the worst atrocities of the war, as Japanese troops were turned loose to murder, rape, loot and burn at will. Their behaviour gained them a reputation for lust and cruelty that endured until final surrender in 1945.

Their victories, moreover, ensured that hostilities would continue. The Chinese government withdrew to the interior, eventually to Chungking, and showed some signs of a willingness to bargain. In Tokyo, on the other hand, where each success tended to confirm the belief that a solution of the China problem was in sight, the price of peace grew higher. Before the end of 1937 all talk of localizing the conflict had been abandoned and most army men were demanding nothing less than Chiang Kai-shek's removal, especially since it was obvious by this time that China's appeals to the League were not going to bring her substantial help. Accordingly, the terms offered previously were withdrawn and the country prepared itself for waging a full-scale war. A naval blockade was extended to the whole of China's coastline. In addition, Chinese cities were heavily bombed and campaigns were launched to consolidate the territorial gains which had been made so far. During 1938, for example, the forces in north China and the Yangtse valley linked up to establish land communications with each other. In October of that year, troops moving up the Yangtse reached Hankow, others in south China reached Canton. By November, in fact, when Konoe announced his plans for a 'New Order', Japan controlled all the wealthiest and most highly populated parts of China, except Szechwan.

Since none of this brought a Kuomintang capitulation—nationalism seemed to thrive on defeats, as well as victories—the year 1939 saw a pause for reconsideration. Japan was still not fully extended by her efforts. She resembled, it has been said, 'a country engaged in a wearisome colonial war, rather than one exerting all its strength . . . against an adversary of equal power'.[77] Nevertheless, she was experiencing an economic strain and a measure of war weariness, while her military leaders were anticipating a clash with Russia in the next few years for which they needed every possible preparation. They therefore changed their strategy, seeking to exploit political rather than military advantages. As a first step they tried cutting China off from the outside world by exerting pressure on the countries that befriended her, a decision leading in February 1939 to the occupation of Hainan, a French sphere of interest, and in June to a blockade of the French and British concessions in Tientsin. The process was completed by the outbreak of the European war soon after, for in their pre-occupation with it the powers could offer little resistance to Japanese demands. Within a year France had granted Japan access to the south through Indo-China and Britain had—temporarily—closed the route from Burma to Yunnan.

Supplementing these successes was an attempt at subversion from within. Japanese army commanders had tried frequently in the past to acquire the help of Chinese local leaders, but it was not until Wang Ching-wei seceded from the Kuomintang regime that they won over a statesman of any consequence. In March 1940 Wang was established as head of a puppet government in Nanking, which it was hoped would attract support for a peace treaty on Japanese terms. In this it failed, notwithstanding the marks of respect which Japan accorded it. Indeed, both Chiang and the communists continued to wage a bitter guerilla warfare in their respective areas, which was a mounting drain on Japanese resources and proved of considerable value to their allies when the Sino-Japanese struggle merged into a wider conflict.

Events in China had important repercussions on Japan's relations with the powers. Since the spread of Japanese authority gave benefits to Japanese trade, it was in some degree an attack on the interests of Britain and America. Similarly, the means by which it was carried out provoked a number of incidents, involving, for example, British and American ships on the Yangtse, which furnished both countries with specific grievances. All this helped to encourage them in showing sympathy for China. On the other hand, neither—the one because of crises in Europe, the other because of isolationism at home —was willing at first to take any positive steps against Japan. Nor did they, until a change in Japanese policies began to threaten them more directly after 1939.

In the interval Japan was much more concerned at the danger of being attacked by Russia. Her acquisition of the Manchurian provinces had put a check on Russia's traditional aspirations in the area, forcing her among other things to sell to Japan in 1935 the Chinese Eastern Railway (the spur from the

Trans-Siberian which ran to Vladivostock via Harbin). It also gave the two a much longer common frontier, on which friction might develop. Thus a clash occurred at the junction of the Manchurian, Korean and Siberian borders in July 1938, which lasted for nearly a fortnight, and another in May 1939 at Nomonhan, between Manchuria and Outer Mongolia, which was not settled till September. Large forces were used in both, including armour; and Japan's relative lack of success on these occasions made her still more wary of Russian strength.

Her fears, plus a consciousness of the diplomatic isolation in which withdrawal from the League of Nations had left her, prompted a search for friends. This had already led to Hitler's Germany some years earlier—since Germany's enemies, anti-communist convictions and need for allies seemed very like her own—and had resulted in the signature of an Anti-Comintern Pact in November 1936, providing publicly for Japanese-German co-operation against international communism, secretly for a defensive alliance against Russia. Knowledge of it helped to convince the army in 1937 that action in China was a legitimate risk. Indeed, an influential group of officers soon began to urge something more positive and open. Closer Japanese-German ties, they thought, might serve as an insurance against Russian moves and increase the pressure on China to surrender, so in June 1938 their representative, General Oshima Hiroshi, first as military attaché, then as ambassador, began negotiations in Berlin. These failed because Germany did not want to commit herself to an exclusively anti-Russian treaty, nor Japan to an alliance of more general scope, but it was not until a Russo-German non-aggression pact was announced in August 1939 that they came formally to an end.

The second Konoe government, on taking office in July 1940, faced renewed demands from the army for a German agreement. They were enthusiastically sponsored by the Foreign Minister, Matsuoka Yosuke, who was completely confident of his ability to exploit such an arrangement to Japan's, rather than Germany's, advantage. He was also sure of German victory in Europe, from which he drew the conclusion that Japan must lose no time in negotiating a division of the spoils, since the defeat of Britain, France and Holland would leave their colonies in Asia without defence. So enticing a prospect overcame the cabinet's doubts and a Tripartite Pact with Germany and Italy was signed on September 27 of that year. It was reinforced in April 1941 by a neutrality agreement with Russia, designed to free Japan from uncertainty about her northern frontiers. Unfortunately for Matsuoka's reputation, however, the whole policy proved to be based on erroneous calculations. Britain did not succumb to German attack. What is more, Hitler, without warning to Japan, launched an invasion of Russia in June 1941. One of its by-products was Matsuoka's fall, brought about by a cabinet re-shuffle in July.

In his year of office Matsuoka had given a new dimension to Japan's ambitions by formulating plans for expansion in South East Asia. These had been discussed by military staffs as early as 1936, with a view to Japan gaining control of the region's oil, tin, rubber, bauxite and other strategic raw materials, but little had been done to take the formal steps which would have put them into effect, until Matsuoka did so at a liaison conference between ministers and service chiefs on July 27, 1940. Its decision, confirmed by the inner cabinet in September, was that Japan must seize the opportunity which the European war had given her to establish herself in Indo-China, Siam (Thailand), Burma, Malaya and the Netherlands Indies. Diplomacy was to be tried in the first place to attain these ends. In particular, every effort was to be made to avoid a conflict with America. But in the last resort force would be used and the risk of war accepted.

Within a few weeks a beginning had been made in Indo-China, the French government, in return for a guarantee of French sovereignty there, being persuaded in September 1940 to authorize the establishment of Japanese air bases in the north and to grant right of passage for Japanese troops. This was in the context of Japan's strategy in China, rather than South East Asia, but in July 1941 substantial Japanese forces entered the rest of the territory, obviously in preparation for moves further south. On the other hand, attempts to get special economic and political privileges in the Netherlands Indies in this period failed. Demands for co-operation, including the allocation to Japan of most of the colony's production of oil, were made by Japanese missions during the autumn and

Moving N. or S. in Asia *28*

winter of 1940–41, only to meet with interminable difficulties and evasions. It seemed reasonable to conclude that nothing short of force would overcome them.

Germany's attack on Russia raised a different problem, since it opened the way for Japan to strike north, instead of south, if she wished to do so. Equally, of course, it made it possible to launch a campaign in South East Asia with greater confidence. Both points were strongly urged when the matter was debated in Tokyo at the beginning of July 1941, even the army being divided between their rival attractions, and the decisions that were finally taken left the issue open for a time. In effect, Japan was to concentrate on her 'New Order', acting independently of her Axis allies, and continue preparations for a major struggle without getting involved in the Russian war.

The key to a southward move, as most Japanese leaders saw it, was likely to be the reaction of the United States. The risks, in other words, would depend a good deal on whether or not America was prepared to fight, a question they found it difficult to answer. Recent omens had not been favourable. American hostility to Japanese policies in China had led Washington in July 1939 to refuse to renew its commercial treaty with Japan, which expired in the following year. 1940 saw an increase in such economic pressure, with licences introduced for exports of various kinds of oil and scrap-iron in July, an embargo on all scrap for Japan in September, its extension to iron and steel exports after the presidential elections in November. The regulations seriously handicapped Japanese stockpiling of vital materials, even though a total ban on oil supplies was not imposed. A still graver blow came in 1941, when in immediate response to the occupation of southern Indo-China in July the American government froze all Japanese assets in the United States, bringing trade almost to a standstill.

By this time the two countries had for some months been engaged in negotiations, though the effect of exchanges in April, May and June 1941 had been only to clarify the nature of their disagreement. The United States sought an undertaking that Japan would respect the independence and territorial integrity of her neighbours, including China and the Philippines; that she would pursue her policies by peaceful means; and that she would guarantee equality of economic opportunity in the areas under her control. In reply, Japan asserted that her intentions were peaceful and in no way a threat to other states. Conflict could more easily be avoided, she said, if Washington would help her to secure the oil and rubber she needed and persuade China to accept her terms. Implicit in this was an American demand that Japan withdraw from China and halt her advance in South East Asia, and a Japanese refusal to do any such thing. This brought deadlock, which the following weeks did nothing to resolve. Prime Minister Konoe tried to break it in August by proposing a personal meeting between himself and President Roosevelt. The latter, however, would not undertake it unless a measure of success were first achieved in preliminary talks, of which there was little sign. Later in the year Japan sent a special envoy, Kurusu Saburo, to assist her ambassador in Washington; but since neither side was willing to give way on matters of substance the gesture was no more effective than those that had gone before.

In Tokyo, meanwhile, staff officers had been considering the plans they would follow in the event of war. Two factors—the state of stockpiles and anticipated weather conditions—convinced them that operations would have to be begun, if at all, not later than December 1941, which meant, in turn, that a final decision on war or peace must be made by the beginning of October. This conclusion was reported to the inner circle of policy-makers in early September and accepted as setting a timetable within which they should work. Yet accepting a timetable, it proved, was easier than carrying it out. When October came, the services announced that they were agreed on giving priority to South East Asia and adamant against retreat from China, thereby ensuring that the American talks must fail. Civilian members of the government, on the other hand, were equally unwilling to admit that hostilities must be the unavoidable result. Unable to bring about a reconciliation, Konoe felt he had no choice but to resign.

He did so on October 16, 1941, and was succeeded two days later by General Tojo Hideki, promoted from the office of War Minister in the belief that he would have the army's confidence. This he undoubtedly had. A former staff officer and the army's spokesman in the cabinet disputes of the previous weeks, he was an authoritarian of rigidly military outlook who made an exemplary representative of the high command. Even his nickname, 'Razor', implied an uncompromising directness which was more appropriate to a war leader than a saviour of the peace. To make him premier, therefore, was not merely the latest step in a series of civilian attempts to control the army by concession; it was also a fatal one, leading to military dictatorship—a dictatorship of the General Staff—and war.

This rapidly became apparent in the reappraisal of policy which followed his appointment. Operational necessity was argued more strongly than ever, until it was agreed at last, much as it had been in September, that time for only one more diplomatic effort remained. There was the difference, however, that on this occasion the alternative was more clearly war, if the diplomats could not secure at least American abandonment of China and extensive economic concessions, in return for the halting of Japan's advance elsewhere. On November 5, 1941, they were given until the end of the month to secure a settlement on these terms. Inevitably they failed, despite the Kurusu mission. On November 26 Washington rejected the proposals and five days later, on December 1, an imperial conference of civilian and service leaders in Tokyo took the decision to attack. A formal statement breaking off relations was then prepared for transmission to the American government, only to be delayed, first by an excess of security consciousness at home, then by secretarial inefficiency in the Washington embassy, so that it was not delivered until hostilities had actually begun. In fact American intelligence agencies, who had already broken Japan's most important code, were able to pass a copy of the statement to the Secretary of State some hours before he received it from the Japanese ambassador.

Once Japanese strategists were convinced that the United States would not stand idly by while the countries of South East Asia were invaded, it became axiomatic that the American Pacific fleet, the only force capable of threatening Japan's communications with the south, must become the first object of attack. Accordingly, a major air strike was directed at its Hawaiian base, Pearl Harbour, on the morning of Sunday,

December 7, 1941, by planes from a naval squadron which had left the Kuriles ten days earlier. Surprise was complete and success phenomenal. Eight battleships were sunk or damaged, as were seven other vessels. Ninety per cent of America's air and surface strength in the area was immobilized or destroyed. Simultaneously, attacks were launched against targets in Wake, Guam, Midway, the Philippines and Hong Kong, all of them successful, while soon after a British battleship and battle-cruiser from Singapore were attacked and sunk at sea.

These operations, carefully planned and brilliantly executed, opened the way for a series of rapid campaigns in South East Asia. Hong Kong was forced to surrender on Christmas Day. Landings on Luzon brought the capture of Manila on January 2, 1942, followed quickly by the occupation of the whole of the Philippines, though an American force in Bataan held out until the beginning of May. Other Japanese troops landed on the east coast of Malaya, crossed the Kra isthmus, and advanced down both sides of the peninsula, taking Kuala Lumpur on January 11 and Singapore—supposedly impregnable—on February 15. This freed men for an assault on the Netherlands Indies, where Dutch troops capitulated on March 9, and on Burma, which was largely overrun by the end of April. At this point, therefore, Japan controlled everything from Rangoon to the mid-Pacific, from Timor to the Mongolian steppe.

Her war plans, drawn up in November 1941, had envisaged turning the whole of this area into a Greater East Asia Co-prosperity Sphere, with Japan, north China and Manchukuo as its industrial base. The other countries were to provide raw materials and form part of a vast consumer market, building a degree of economic strength that would enable Japan, first, to meet and contain any counter-attack from outside, then, if all went well, to incorporate India, Australia and Russia's Siberian provinces by further wars at a later date.

To achieve these ends it was necessary that Japanese domination be substituted for domination by the West, at least initially, a decision that led to a cultural crusade—widespread teaching of the Japanese language, reforms of education to eliminate 'undesirable' influences, the organization of literary and scientific conferences, even attempts to abolish the siesta and jazz—as well as the creation of a network of new political alignments. Some countries were from the beginning left a large measure of independence. Indo-China, for example, was left in the hands of the French, and Siam (Thailand), after signing a treaty of alliance, retained its own monarchy and administration, though both had to grant a number of special favours to Japan. Occupied China, as represented by Wang Ching-wei's regime, had already signed a peace agreement in November 1940 and was eventually persuaded to declare war on America and Britain in January 1943. This heralded an era of greater formal equality with Japan, marked by the abolition of Japanese concessions in the old treaty ports later in the year. Manchukuo, of course, had always been nominally an independent state, despite the authority of the Kwantung Army there. This situation, like the colonial status of Korea, remained unchanged.

Of the territories that had been newly conquered, Burma produced a puppet leader, Ba Maw, who was made head of a Japanese-sponsored administration on August 1, 1942. However, real power was in the hands of his military advisers and they retained it after the country was given independence in the following year, when it declared war and concluded an alliance in its turn. The Philippines, with the help of pro-Japanese collaborators, achieved independence on October 14, 1943, though its government was able to avoid declaring war on the allies until September 1944. In Malaya and the Netherlands Indies, on the other hand, because they were economically vital, Japan was more reluctant to relinquish direct control. Each was put under military administration, centralized and bureaucratic in its methods, which replaced the officialdom of the former colonial powers. Nor were freedom movements of any kind encouraged in the first two years. Even thereafter no very extensive promises were made, though regional councils were established and local residents were allowed to play some part in government. In Malaya, in fact, this was as much as was done for the rest of the war, though in the Indies a nationalist movement developed and was at last recognized by the Japanese when their defeat was obvious in 1945, a fact that enabled its leader, Dr Soekarno, to declare Indonesian independence immediately after Japan's surrender in August of that year.

Apart from the long-term problem of maintaining these

states as dependencies, Japan's colonial policy was also directed to the task of exploiting their anti-Western sentiments and economic resources in support of her own defence. In this she was a great deal less successful. For one thing, the harshness of her rule tended to alienate the very people whose sympathy she was trying to win. All too often executions and torture produced, not co-operation, but hatred and resistance, which her enemies found it easy to put to use. There was a good deal of inefficiency, too, since the Greater East Asia Ministry, established in November 1942, recruited most of its staff from the diplomats and commercial representatives whom the war had brought back from Europe and elsewhere, or from journalists and traders whose jobs had given them a nodding acquaintance with the areas to be governed. The former lacked local knowledge, the latter administrative experience and expertise, while both found it impossible to pursue any policy which conflicted with the views of army commanders. To this handicap was added a lack of trained technicians capable of restoring the trade and industry of South East Asia, especially the production of oil, to their former efficiency, so that the plan for creating a powerful and self sufficient economic bloc experienced difficulties from the very start.

They were increased by the consequences of military failure. Allied submarine attacks interfered seriously with sea communications among the islands as early as 1942. When they were supplemented by an air offensive later in the war, Japan found herself almost completely cut off from her more distant —and more valuable—possessions. Three-quarters of her merchant marine had been lost by the summer of 1945 in an attempt to keep the sea lanes open. One result was to handicap industrial production at home, so that the traditional rivalry between army and navy was accentuated by disputes over the allocation of equipment, to a point at which even the co-ordination of their respective operations was affected. Their quarrels did much to render useless the fanatical courage with which Japanese units fought.

Indeed, it was soon apparent that it was not going to be easy for the services to fulfil the role which had been assigned them, namely, of holding an extended perimeter while Japan replenished her reserves, so that America could be persuaded to accept a compromise peace. Not only was the economic development of the Co-prosperity Sphere much slower, but the American counter-offensive was much faster, than had been expected. The naval battles of the Coral Sea at the beginning of May 1942 and of Midway a month later foiled Japanese thrusts towards Australia and Hawaii respectively, the former being confirmed by the successful Australian defence of southern New Guinea in the rest of the year. Then, as Japan's first major repulse on land, came the American recapture of Guadalcanal in the Solomon islands, ending after six months' bitter fighting in February 1943. These operations, it later appeared, marked a strategic turning-point.

During them, moreover, a new pattern of warfare was evolving: in naval engagements, action at long range, using aircraft from carriers as the main offensive weapons—a development which largely offset Japan's initial advantage in capital ships—and in island campaigns, close co-operation between land, sea and air forces, preferably under unified command. These became the main ingredients in an American 'island-hopping' technique designed, not to regain territory in any general sense, but to win bases from which ships and aircraft could dominate wide areas of the west Pacific.

In January 1943 allied leaders met at Casablanca and agreed to divert more resources to the war against Japan. In August they followed this up at Quebec by naming their commanders and outlining the strategy to be used. Within a few months forces under Admiral Chester Nimitz, acting in accordance with these decisions, had attacked the Marshall islands in the central Pacific, demonstrating for the first of many times the overwhelming weight of metal that could be brought against an island target and the speed with which it could be reduced if enemy reinforcement were made impossible. The key base of Kwajalein was captured in ten days' fighting in February 1944. Saipan in the Marianas took a little longer (mid-June to early July 1944) and involved a full fleet action, the battle of the Philippine Sea, to cover the landings. This broke the back of Japanese naval resistance, however, and made even more rapid progress possible elsewhere. Guam fell in August, the Palau group in September, completing an 'advance' of over two thousand miles in less than a year.

The emphasis now swung to the South West Pacific, where General Douglas MacArthur was in command. In September 1944, simultaneously with the attack on Palau, his forces landed on Morotai off the northern coast of New Guinea. A month later they reached the Philippines, completing the occupation of Leyte by the end of December and invading Luzon in January 1945. Manila was captured on February 5. From this point the two commands were able to act together, their first target being Okinawa in the Ryukyu islands, which was secured by late June, their next an invasion of Japan itself. The Japanese fleet was no longer a serious threat, having been virtually destroyed in a further naval battle in the Leyte Gulf in October 1944. This left the offshore defence of the homeland to the suicide tactics of planes and midget submarines, a kind of fighting which experience at Okinawa had shown to be terrifying, but not fully effective. Since a land campaign had also begun in Burma, which, together with the guerilla activities of Chinese communists and nationalists, was engaging the attention of a substantial proportion of Japan's available troops, success for an invasion seemed highly probable, the more so as Germany's surrender in May 1945 enabled the allies to devote all their efforts to it.

The first stage of preparation was the bombing of Japanese industries and cities. The use of land-based aircraft for this purpose had begun from Saipan the previous autumn and was made easier by the capture of Iwojima in March 1945. Then operations began from Okinawa, growing rapidly in frequency and extending to the whole of Japan, so that by the summer the country was in a state of siege. Shipping to and from the mainland almost ceased. Most industrial centres, despite attempts at dispersal, suffered heavy damage, while incendiary raids on urban areas, made as an attack on Japanese morale, brought casualties which included over 200,000 killed. Rail transport, suffering not only from bombing but from lack of maintenance, began to deteriorate rapidly, contributing to a situation in which production, even of munitions, dropped sharply from its wartime peaks. Consumer goods became wellnigh unobtainable. Food was scarce, prices rising, black markets everywhere. Nor was there much that was encouraging in the visual scene. People in the streets were drab, the men in a kind of khaki suiting that was virtually a civilian uniform, the women in dark working-trousers or the dullest of kimono. Vehicles were ramshackle, buses having been converted to charcoal-burning to save fuel and their windows, like those of trains and trams, boarded up to save replacing glass. With it all, the population was required to work harder, and for less reward, than ever before. Education had been curtailed to get more students into the army and the factories. Restrictions on child and female labour had been abolished. Even the regulations which limited working hours, mild though they were, had been swept away.

Despite the evidence around them, press and radio constantly assured the Japanese that they could win the war, if only they would make a supreme effort—sometimes it was called a supreme sacrifice—in their own defence. The enemy had over-extended his communications; he had underestimated Japanese strength; he would never accept the casualties which a determined people could make him suffer. All these arguments and many more were used to justify—and make possible —a last-ditch stand.

Nevertheless, most of Japan's leaders had by this time few illusions about the fact of military defeat. Some of them, like Yoshida Shigeru, Shigemitsu Mamoru and others with a diplomatic background, had begun to think of a compromise peace as early as 1943; and their influence, together with a secret war study prepared by a member of the Naval General Staff, which clearly indicated that victory was unattainable, won over men close to the emperor, including the former Prime Minister, Konoe Fumimaro. When Saipan was captured in 1944 they moved to bring about Tojo's fall, helping to force the resignation of his cabinet on July 18. His successor, General Koiso Kuniaki, another member of the Kwantung Army group, proved no more amenable, but he, too, could not survive for long in the face of a deteriorating military situation. Air raids on Tokyo and news of the landings on Okinawa brought his resignation on April 5, 1945. This made way for an aged and much respected admiral, Suzuki Kantaro, who was known privately to favour ending the war, if it could be done with honour.

The War Minister, Anami Korechika, backed by Tojo and the high command, was still resolutely opposed to any peace moves. Accordingly, the talks now undertaken with the Russian ambassador in Japan, which superseded earlier approaches made in Konoe's name to the Swedish minister, were officially to seek a basis for improving Russo-Japanese relations, though many senior statesmen were clearly hoping to get Russian mediation in the Pacific war. Towards the end of June they succeeded, albeit with difficulty, in getting this second purpose formally avowed, only to find Russia unresponsive. Despite a proposal that Konoe should go to Moscow as an imperial envoy to negotiate a peace, no progress had been made in the discussions when the allied powers, with Russia's concurrence, issued the Potsdam Declaration on July 26.

The declaration, made in the names of Britain, America and China, called for the unconditional surrender of Japan, to be followed by military occupation, demilitarization and loss of territory. This left little prospect of the kind of settlement which the uncommitted in Japan, especially in the services, might have been persuaded to accept. Indeed, it brought a temporary closing of the ranks behind those who were willing to go down fighting. This, however, lasted only for about a week. On August 6, 1945, the first atom bomb was dropped on Hiroshima and three days later another destroyed most of Nagasaki, the second coming less than twenty-four hours after a Russian declaration of war upon Japan. To the great majority, these events made surrender imperative—and at once.

Even so, the War Minister and the two Chiefs of Staff refused to give way, arguing throughout meetings of the Supreme War Council and the cabinet on August 9 that conditions must be attached to any acceptance of the allied ultimatum. The result was deadlock, broken at last by the emperor at an imperial conference after midnight, when he gave a ruling in favour of those who urged that surrender be subject only to a reservation of his own prerogatives as sovereign ruler. In this form the message was handed to Swiss representatives on August 10 for transmission to the allies. The latter's reply, making no mention of the imperial prerogative, precipitated another series of disputes in the next few days, which were resolved, like the previous ones, by the emperor's intervention. The decision to surrender on the allies' terms was therefore made public on August 15, 1945.

This was not quite the end of the story, for Japan's career of conquest was to end, as it had begun, with attempted mutiny and disorder. Officers of the War Ministry and General Staff, determined to prevent the emperor from broadcasting the announcement of defeat, broke into the palace on the night of August 14 to search for the recording of his speech, though they did not find it. Others set fire to the homes of the Prime Minister and President of the Privy Council. When all this failed to reverse the decision, many, including War Minister Anami himself, committed suicide, several doing so on the plaza opposite the palace gates. It was in this turbulent atmosphere that orders were given for a ceasefire on August 16 and a new government, headed by an imperial prince to give it greater prestige, formed the following day to see that they were carried out. By September 2, when members of it signed the instrument of surrender aboard the American flagship in Tokyo Bay, American troops had already begun to arrive for the occupation of Japan.

CHAPTER XV

REFORM AND REHABILITATION
1945-1962

---

*American occupation—demilitarization—political and constitu-
tional reform—judiciary—reform of labour laws, land tenure
and education—peace treaty—foreign relations—politics after
1952—industrial recovery and growth*

THE LANGUAGE in which the Japanese emperor told his
people of the decision to surrender was elliptical in the extreme.
'Despite the best that has been done by everyone,' he said,
'. . . the war situation has developed not necessarily to Japan's
advantage.'[78] Accordingly, in order to avoid further bloodshed,
perhaps even 'the total extinction of human civilization', Japan
would have to 'endure the unendurable and suffer what is
insufferable'. For these reasons it had been decided to accept
the allied terms.

What this meant in practice was very soon made clear. The
appearance of American airborne forces in Tokyo and of an
allied fleet at anchor off Yokosuka, the orders given to Japanese
troops overseas to lay down their arms and to those in Japan
to disperse quietly to their towns and villages, all this brought
home vividly the reality of defeat. In the Tokyo-Yokohama
area the population stayed as much as possible indoors, fearing
atrocities and reprisals. Everywhere, as they looked to their
leaders for instructions, or at least for news of what was going
on, they found their country's administration, like its economy,
in chaos. To a nation that had for weeks been exhorted to work
harder and prepare itself for a last-ditch stand, the change was
bewildering, notwithstanding the bombing, the shortages and
the other signs of disaster which had been multiplying on every

side for the previous year. The war's ending brought a sense of relief, therefore, but also a shock of disillusion. In its train came a numbness and a dull apathy, evident in the way people walked, in the silence of the crowds, in the conscientious provision of entertainment for the conqueror.

So sharp was the break with what had gone before that one is tempted to regard it as the end, not of a chapter, but of a story, to treat all that followed as something new. Indeed, in many ways it was. For defeat seems to have been a catharsis, exhausting the emotions which Japanese had hitherto brought to their relations with the outside world, as well as opening the way for experiments in social and political institutions. In both respects it has had a profound effect. On the other hand, the change of direction can easily be overstated. Once the shock wore off and Japanese again began to take the initiative in directing their country's affairs, they gave to the new something of the flavour of the old: in society and politics, a little less of America of the 1940s, a little more of Japan of the 1920s; in attitudes and ideas, a resumption of trends and controversies which had been diverted or suppressed by ultra-nationalism; in economic development, the exploitation of wartime experience to establish a fresh industrial pattern and promote an astonishing growth. The result is that seventeen years after surrender one can trace a far greater continuity with the past—the recent past—than would at one time have seemed possible. Hence an account of this period is not a mere postscript to what has gone before, but the continuation, if at a tangent, of the story of Japan's attempts to come to terms with the modern world.

The occupation of Japan was in all vital respects an American undertaking. It is true that a small British Commonwealth force, mostly Australian, shared the military tasks. It is also true that there was an elaborate machinery of international control, headed by a Far Eastern Commission in Washington, on which were represented all the countries that had fought against Japan. In practice, however, the execution of policy was in the hands of General Douglas MacArthur, the Supreme Commander for the Allied Powers (SCAP). As American commander-in-chief in the area he took orders only from the

United States government, through which the decisions of the Far Eastern Commission were also transmitted to him; and a natural tendency for the distinction between his two functions to become blurred meant that before long he and his immediate superiors were exercising a good deal of discretion in carrying policy out, the more so as the international committees were often deadlocked.

To assist him in Tokyo, the Supreme Commander had an enormous staff, both military and civil, forming a bureaucracy very nearly as complex, if not so large, as that of Japan itself. Few of its members had much knowledge or experience of the country they had to govern, a circumstance which led them at times to transplant American institutions to Japan, not because they were necessarily appropriate, but because they were familiar. Moreover, they lacked the means of ensuring that SCAP directives were put fully into effect, since acceptance of the need to work through a Japanese government, together with the difficulty of checking on its operations because of the shortage of trained allied personnel, made possible a considerable divergence between intention and result. If one adds the problems posed by the attempt to instil democracy through military conquest, it is surprising, one might conclude, not that mistakes were made, but that the occupation achieved so much that was of real significance.

The basic lines on which it was to work were first set out by the American government and later approved by the Far Eastern Commission. Most straightforward was the plan to demilitarize Japan, in accordance with which military supplies and installations were destroyed, over two million men demobilized at home, over three million (and as many civilians) repatriated from overseas. There was talk as well of stripping factories of their equipment to provide reparations for the countries which Japan had attacked, though little was actually done. Punishment, indeed, took a different form. Partly it was accomplished by depriving Japan of all the territorial gains she had made since 1868, including, that is, both the Ryukyu and Kurile islands. Partly it involved the trial of 'war criminals': the leaders who had brought about the war, twenty-five of whom were tried in Tokyo by an international tribunal between May 1946 and November 1948 (seven, including Tojo, being condemned to hang, the rest to prison sentences); senior officers of the services, commanding in areas where atrocities had occurred (all but two of whom successfully denied responsibility); and thousands more, accused of individual acts of cruelty and murder. Of the latter, many were brought before courts abroad, but in Yokohama alone 700 were sentenced to death and 3,000 to various terms in prison.

Nevertheless, punishment was not the only, nor, after the first few months, the primary object of the occupation. The Potsdam declaration had announced the allies' intention of removing 'all obstacles to the revival and strengthening of democratic tendencies among the Japanese people'.[79] One measure immediately taken in this direction was a political amnesty, by which all those who had tried unsuccessfully to oppose the wartime and prewar governments in Japan were released from gaol: communists, socialists, and liberals of every kind, many of whom had been in prison for several years. Another step was the logical corollary to this, namely, the removal from public life—from key posts in administration, politics, education, the press and radio, even certain businesses—of all those whose close connection with the old order would lead them, it was thought, to sabotage the new. A few were identified personally, on the basis of their records. Many more were identified simply by the jobs they held, a method which caused much injustice, but made the procedure quick and thorough in its operation. In fact, the 'purge', as it was called, affected over 200,000 persons, so that the inroads made into Japanese leadership were heavy enough not only to weaken the hold of tradition on society, but also to reduce efficiency for a time as well.

Meanwhile, with American encouragement, parties had been formed to replace the Imperial Rule Assistance Association, the most powerful of them, the Liberals and Progressives, being composed of those prewar conservative politicians who survived the purge. In the centre there appeared an uneasy combination of moderates and socialists, the Social Democratic Party, while a fringe of radical organizations came into existence on the left. Of these, the Communists, free to work openly for the first time in many years, received a great stimulus from the return to Japan in January 1946 of Nosaka Sanzo, the most able of their exiled leaders, who had been working for the Comintern in Moscow and then in China with Mao Tse-tung. By 1949 his slogans of 'peaceful revolution' and 'a lovable Communist Party' had won the support of three million voters, nearly 10 per cent of the electorate.

In addition there were all sorts of small, local parties, their numbers estimated at over 300 by the spring of 1946, which represented everything from the lunatic fringe to ambitious individuals. A good many of their members, like most of the independents—at least those who were successful at the polls —turned out to be conservatives, so that the latter, putting all parties together, were able to command nearly two-thirds of the country's votes. In the elections of April 1946, 24 per cent went to the Liberals and 19 per cent to the Progressives, giving them, respectively, 140 and 94 seats. So in May the Liberal leader, Yoshida Shigeru, an ex-diplomat with a record of opposition to the army, formed a government which included members from both parties. During the next year, however, the Progressives disappeared and the moderate right was reorganized as the Democratic Party, led by Ashida Hitoshi. This gained something like parity with the Liberals in the election of 1947, both winning about 25 per cent of the votes, as did the Social Democrats; but it was the latter, holding 143 seats, who emerged as just the largest Diet party. Ashida threw in his lot with them, first in a coalition government under the Socialist, Katayama Tetsu, in May 1947, then under his own leadership from March 1948, but the inability of the cabinet to be either socialist or liberal, partly because of its own disunity, partly because of conservative strength, forced his resignation six months later. This brought back Yoshida and his party, who remained in power for the next six years. In the elections of January 1949 they secured a clear majority—the first since the war—by returning 264 members to the lower house. The Democrats were relegated to second place with sixty-nine seats; the Social Democrats, badly split between a parliamentary right and a Marxist left, got only forty-eight; and the Communists, winning thirty-five, made their first significant gains.

By this time the parties were operating within an entirely new political and social framework. For during its first three years the occupation had brought changes in the constitution, local government, the judiciary, law, labour relations, land tenure and education which seemed likely to revolutionize Japanese life.

A summary of them begins logically with the constitution, which was drafted in MacArthur's headquarters early in 1946, when it began to appear that Japanese officials were responding too slowly to the hints that they should act themselves. Announced on March 6, 1947, its text, both in language and content, betrayed its origin. For this it has been criticized, even mocked, both in Japan and abroad. Yet by putting power firmly into the hands of the Diet it did something that the Japanese might have found it difficult to do on their own. Both houses of the new assembly were to be elective: a House of Councillors of 250 members, half of them standing for election every three years, of whom 60 per cent were to represent prefectures and 40 per cent to be chosen on a single national vote; and a House of Representatives of 467 members, drawn from 118 electoral districts, which would each choose three to five. The lower house, like the British House of Commons, could be dissolved if the government wished to hold a general election; the upper house, like the American Senate, could not. However, the right of decision on almost all matters rested in the last resort with the lower house. In the event of disagreement a finance bill would become law thirty days after the Representatives passed it and any other bill, after rejection by the Councillors, become law if the lower house passed it again by a majority of two-thirds. Similarly, the lower house was to elect the Prime Minister, whose cabinet was responsible, if to the Diet in name, to the Representatives in fact. The only important limitation on the power of the Representatives was that revision of the constitution required a two-thirds vote of *each* house, ratified by a simple majority in a national referendum.

One object achieved by these constitutional arrangements was to create a system in which there was a single centre of authority, controlled by popular vote, instead of one in which the emperor's supposedly supreme prerogatives were exercised piecemeal by different civil and military groups. Inevitably this involved a restatement of the position of the Throne. The emperor became 'the symbol of the State . . . deriving his position from the will of the people with whom resides sovereign power'.[80] His actions were made subject to cabinet approval and their scope was specified, a change which aroused profound misgivings among conservatives, but which the Court's advisers accepted, even welcomed. They began to shape the monarchy in a new image, doing so with such success that within a few years, by carefully planning the emperor's public appearances and speeches, they had made him the focus of a loyalty based rather on affection than on awe. By this means they did much for the Throne's stability and prestige at a time when defeat had left both seriously threatened.

Other changes, outlined in the constitution and worked out in detail during the next few months, were those in local government. The Home Ministry was abolished and most of its functions were dispersed, being entrusted to prefectural and city administrations which were to be headed by elected governors and mayors. Local assemblies were also to be elected, as in the past, but they were now to be given extensive powers. Education became largely a local matter, while each area acquired its own police force and civil service, paid for out of local taxes, the intention being to foster 'grass-roots democracy' by giving communities a chance to run their own affairs. Unfortunately, as it transpired, the units were often made too small, so that many of them found finance an intractable problem. The smaller the unit, moreover, the more parochial its outlook—to the detriment of social services, in particular—and the easier it was for political 'bosses' to control it. For these reasons, notwithstanding the degree of popular participation that was achieved, this aspect of reform was among the least successful.

American example, which inspired decentralization, was also followed in separating the judiciary from the executive. Administrative supervision of the courts was transferred from the Ministry of Justice to a newly-established Supreme Court, to which was deputed also the task of appointing judges (except its own members, which were to be nominated by the cabinet) and of pronouncing on the constitutionality of laws. This meant that it became the guardian of a wide range of provisions concerning human rights which had been written into the constitution, not least those giving women full legal and political equality with men. And votes for women meant the addition of several million voters to the electoral register, all, presumably, with reason to support the new regime.

Equally important was the revision of the labour laws, for this, too, had the effect of creating powerful interests committed to maintaining the reforms. A Trade Union Act in 1945 and a Labour Relations Act in 1946 gave Japanese workers the right to organize and strike, while a Labour Standards Act in 1947 gave them a guarantee of better working conditions, a health insurance scheme and accident compensation. They were quick to seize the opportunities this offered. By the end of 1948 some 34,000 unions had been formed, having a total of nearly seven million members. This represented over 40 per cent of the industrial labour force; and although there was a drop to 5·5 million members in 1949–51, because of government action against the left-wing movement generally, numbers rose again to over 6 million thereafter and have remained at about that level. Something like half are affiliated to the General Council of Trade Unions (Sohyo), formed in 1950 under Socialist leadership, which has been the most influential of several postwar national federations.

The encouragement of trade unions had the result, not entirely premeditated, of increasing the turbulence of Japanese politics, especially in the towns. Land reform, by contrast, which was planned in the belief that agrarian unrest had contributed to Japanese aggression, reduced tensions in the countryside to a point lower than they had ever been in modern times. The first proposals for it were prepared by Japanese officials and submitted to the government in November 1945. They were emasculated by the Diet, which would have thrown them out entirely had it not feared American intervention, and in their revised form were promptly vetoed by MacArthur, who substituted a draft proposed by the Australian representative in Japan, MacMahon Ball. This was sent privately to the Japanese cabinet in June 1946 and forced through a reluctant lower house, becoming law on October 21. It provided for the compulsory purchase of all land held by absentee landlords. Owner-farmers and resident landlords were to be allowed to retain an area ranging from 12 *cho* (just under 30 acres) in

Hokkaido to an average, varying with local conditions, of 3 *cho* elsewhere, not more than a third of which was to be let to tenants. Everything above these limits was to be sold to the government—at rates fixed in relation to the artificially low *controlled* prices for agricultural products ruling in 1945, which had long since been overtaken by inflation—and offered to the existing tenants on easy terms. The terms were made all the easier in the event by a fall in the value of money and the farmer's ability to charge black market prices for food, which wiped out farm debts and left even the poorest families with a modest cash reserve.

Some idea of the scope of what was done can be gained from the overall statistics: more than a million *cho* of rice-paddy and a little less than 800,000 *cho* of upland (1 *cho* = 2·45 acres) bought from 2·3 million landlords by August 1950 and sold to 4·7 million tenants. To put it differently, land under tenancy agreements, over 40 per cent of the whole before 1946, dropped to a mere 10 per cent, while the share of owner-cultivators rose to 90 per cent. There were still inequalities, of course. Since the least affluent landowners, who were the great majority, had had to get rid of only a small proportion of their land, their tenants had less chance of buying it than did those of former absentees. Similarly, there was room for much manoeuvring in the choice of plots to be sold, a topic which greatly exercised the land committees, each consisting of five tenants, three landlords and two owner-farmers, which were set up in every village to settle details and prevent evasion. Nevertheless, the reform made Japan substantially a country of peasant proprietors. Even such tenancy as remained was of a very different kind from that which had existed before the war. In place of high rents, which on rice-paddy had been almost invariably paid in kind and represented approximately half the crop, were substituted moderate rents in cash, with written contracts providing security of tenure. Although one must set against this a measurable decline in paternalism, which in backward areas, at least, had to some extent mitigated the harshness of the previous system, it would be difficult to deny that the changes brought 'a considerable increase in the sum of human happiness in Japanese villages'.[81]

One is tempted to say that education reforms performed a

similar service for Japanese children, since they affected the manner, as well as the matter, of teaching and introduced a far freer atmosphere into schools. Wartime chauvinism had caused a re-writing of textbooks in nationalist terms, together with an increase in military training and indoctrination. The first correctives, therefore, were negative: the abolition of suspect courses, the withdrawal of offending books. Early in 1946, however, an educational mission arrived from the United States, and its recommendations, quickly carried out, led to a complete reorganization on American lines. Administration, as we have already said, was decentralized, being put under elected boards at the prefectural and municipal level. Compulsory education was extended to a full nine years. The first six of these were to be in elementary school, the rest in a new kind of co-educational middle school, which would offer pupils a wide choice in the courses they wished to take. Beyond this came an optional three-year high school course, leading to university entrance.

At first there were many problems. A desperate shortage of buildings for a school population so suddenly enlarged was only partly solved by a recourse to shift-work. Teachers, struggling with huge classes, had to do so without books—it was several years before new ones were written and available—and under a barrage of advice about educational method. 'Subjects' were to disappear, in favour of a 'core' curriculum and 'integrated projects'; 'ethics' was to give way to 'civics'; and the day's work was no longer to begin with an obeisance to the emperor's portrait. It is not surprising that there was confusion and many mistakes, provoking the criticism that postwar children knew less and behaved worse than their fathers had ever done. Yet as the teachers gained experience and were joined by a generation that had itself been trained in the newer ways, something appeared on the credit side as well: a liveliness of outlook, more flexibility, less formality and restraint. It remains to be seen whether this will be, as it was intended that it should, a guarantee of continuing democracy.

University education fared little differently, in the sense that an attempt was made to impose on it an alien pattern. A decision, taken by the occupation authorities in 1946, that there should be at least one university in every prefecture, precipitated a scramble among special high schools, technical colleges and similar bodies, either singly or in combination, to win university status. As a result Japan's universities, already seventy in number before the war, increased to over 200, the majority being of little consequence or reputation. On the other hand, the fact that academic staffs were both conservative and entrenched has prevented much change in the curriculum. A certain reduction in specialization for undergraduates and the introduction of new graduate courses of the American type are the most obvious changes, at least in the older and more respected institutions; though many observers would add, perhaps, that the students have changed much more, notably in their political allegiance to the radical left. In this, indeed, as in the activities of trade unions, the occupation reforms had effects which their authors might not have described as democratic.

On the other hand, democracy and reform were no longer the chief preoccupations of MacArthur's headquarters after the enthusiasm of the first two years died down. For by 1948 considerations of international politics were beginning to shape matters in a different way: first, because of a sharp deterioration in Russo-American relations; secondly, because of the growing strength of the communists in China, which threatened to leave America without a Far East ally. Together these developments shifted the emphasis to the strategic aspects of America's position in Japan, giving greater importance to the country's role as a base, less to its interest as a subject of political experiment. The trend became stronger after the communist victory in the Chinese civil war in 1949 and the outbreak of hostilities in Korea in June 1950, when Japan became vital to the United Nations forces, mostly American, which were defending Syngman Rhee's republic against Korean and Chinese incursions from the north.

One early sign of the change in atmosphere was the pressure put on left-wing movements in Japan. The right of Japanese trade unions to strike had always been subject to the veto of occupation officials, as had been demonstrated in February 1947, when a proposed general stoppage of work was banned on economic grounds. But strike action was now to be limited for other than strictly economic reasons. In July 1948 at SCAP insistence civil servants were prohibited from resorting to it, the rule being extended to local government employees shortly after. Then came revision of the Trade Union Act in 1949, putting restrictions on the political activity of many workers, and revival of the 'purge' regulations, in order that they might be applied to communists. Over 20,000 were said to have been dismissed from jobs in government, education and industry during 1949 and 1950, some even from the unions themselves.

Tightening up It was also in 1949 that MacArthur authorized the Japanese government to review the application of the purges of 1946 and 1947. Progress in this was slow at first, but the pace quickened after June 1950, so that almost all those originally affected had regained their political rights by the end of 1951. Not many of them were restored to positions of influence, for their successors were by this time well established and showed little desire to make room for an older generation at the top; but a number won election to the Diet or even places in the cabinet, their presence there helping to intensify the growing conservatism of Japanese public life.

Further evidence that American policy-makers were reconsidering the past came from their handling of the question of rearmament. The 1946 constitution, supposedly at the insistence of the Supreme Commander, had included a clause to the effect that 'the Japanese people forever renounce war as a sovereign right of the nation'. It also bound them never again to maintain an army, navy or air force. In the situation immediately after the war, in which Japan appeared as a defeated enemy, whose military revival was to be prevented, this provision had seemed good sense; but there was much less to be said for it in 1950, when she was a potential ally. Accordingly, in July of that year permission was given for the creation of a National Police Reserve, a para-military force 75,000 strong, which was to take over from American troops the responsibility for security within the country. Thereafter, American urging plus Japanese right-wing support got the force's size and functions gradually extended—despite fierce opposition from those Japanese who objected to the cost or the flagrant evasion of the constitution which this entailed—until by 1960, renamed the National Defence Force, it had emerged as a fully military organization, having land, sea and air arms of substantial size, all equipped with the most modern weapons.

Revival of the "Military"

Long before this had happened, Japan had also regained her formal independence. Logic suggested that a free Japan under a friendly and conservative government would make America a better ally than one condemned to continuing foreign rule. Equally, most of what could be done by an occupying power to promote democracy had been completed in the first few years, the rest depending on Japanese acceptance of the changes and a willingness to make them work. General MacArthur—whose reports consistently overstated the success of 'democratizing' policies in any case—had been considering the possibility of concluding a peace treaty on these grounds as early as 1947; and although he was not at that time able to carry Washington with him, the international developments of the next three years, especially the Korean war, gave his arguments much greater weight. They also ruled out any possibility of joint action by the Far Eastern Commission, leaving America to conduct the negotiations very largely on her own.

The resulting treaty was signed at San Francisco in September 1951 by most of the countries which had fought in the Pacific War. Russia refused to accept it, as did India and mainland China. But since these three played no direct part in governing Japan the military occupation came to an end when the treaty was ratified in April 1952. This did not mean a withdrawal of the occupation forces, however, since Japan, having little choice in the matter, had also signed a defence agreement by which she undertook to continue providing bases for American troops, ships and aircraft, thereby committing herself to an American alliance which was to cause considerable difficulties in her relations with Russia and the Asian neutrals.

Russia was in a position to drive a hard bargain. In the first place, having occupied the Kurile islands and southern Sakhalin at the end of the war, she controlled all routes of access to Japan's former fishing grounds in the Sea of Okhotsk. These she could threaten to close or limit, at the same time holding out the hope that Japan might, if amenable, recover one or two of the islands nearest Hokkaido. Moreover, possession of a veto in the United Nations Organization enabled her to block all Japanese attempts to seek election to that body. Yet while Russia was willing to use these weapons to strengthen her diplomacy, Japan's economic, as well as military, dependence on the United States ensured for her part a resistance to both threats and temptation, so that there was little improvement in the relations between the two for several years. It was not until June 1955, in fact, that an easing of international tension made it possible for them to open peace talks through their ambassadors in London. These ended in deadlock in March 1956 because of disagreement on the territorial issue—Japan demanded, and Russia refused, a return to the 1855 division of the Kurile islands, that is, with Japan holding Kunashiri and Etorofu—and the Japanese Foreign Minister, Shigemitsu Mamoru, was unable to make any progress on this point when he visited Moscow in August. But in October 1956 a settlement was reached on other matters: normal diplomatic relations were to be restored and a trade pact signed, the territorial question being temporarily shelved. As a result Japan became a member of the United Nations in December, as soon as ratifications of this agreement had been exchanged, and was elected to the Security Council in October of the following year. Nevertheless, fisheries and the dispute over the Kuriles continued to bedevil Russo-Japanese relations, with Russia still seeking to use them to weaken Japanese ties with the United States. In 1961–62 she added a further inducement, namely, proposals for an expansion of trade, though still not on a scale which could match what America had to offer.

it is still important

Trade, in fact, was a weapon which Communist China could use to better advantage, for as a market and a source of raw materials the mainland had always been of immense importance to Japan. This was reflected in the readiness with which Japanese businessmen overcame their conservative scruples about dealing with the communists after 1949. On the other hand, America's policy imposed severe limitations on 'trading with the enemy', applying to her friends as well as to herself, and Japanese governments held firmly to the American alliance in refusing recognition to Peking. This was much resented in Japan, even though it was easy to see that the new China— powerful, nationalist, and committed to a programme of rapid industrialization—was not going to offer opportunities for profit in any sense comparable with those of the recent past. Businessmen, to say nothing of left-wing politicians, did their best to get the restrictions eased. In July 1957 they were partly successful, for Japan agreed to put the China trade on the same footing as that with Russia, removing embargoes on the export of rubber, various metals and a wide range of industrial equipment in which China was showing interest. Within a year a number of valuable contracts had been signed, notwithstanding the fact that political relations between the two countries showed little change.

Japan's relations with the non-communist world, too, came to be determined for the most part by the needs of trade. Her attempts to revive it were for some time hampered by resentments arising from the war or her former colonial policies, especially on the part of countries like Australia and South Korea, while in South East Asia there were difficulties about reparations to be solved. Again, many people retained suspicions, dating from the 1930s, about Japanese commercial practices, such as led Britain among others to refuse to extend to Japan the full benefits of the General Agreement on Tariffs and Trade, to which she became a party in 1955. Nor did the Japanese themselves always act in a manner best calculated to overcome foreign prejudice. On one occasion, for example, when on a goodwill tour to India and her neighbours, the Prime Minister, Kishi Nobusuke, let slip the word 'Co-prosperity'. On another a Japanese politician, visiting Manila, took with him two ex-members of the gendarmerie who had helped to terrorize that city during the war. Fortunately such incidents were rare and had only a temporary effect, so that progress was steady, if slow, and the reputation for quality which Japanese goods increasingly enjoyed did a great deal to maintain it. This, however, is a subject to which we must return when we discuss economic development in general.

The peace treaty and its repercussions in foreign affairs were not the only results of the events of 1949-51, for in domestic politics they confirmed the domination of the conservatives and gave them an opportunity to effect a change of policy which they had long desired. The anti-left-wing proclivities of occupation headquarters in its last two years greatly helped them in this, of course. More important, however, was a change that occurred in Japanese opinion. Time, perhaps inevitably, brought a revulsion against the spate of 'Western' innovations in Japan, such as had occurred at the end of the nineteenth century and again in the 1930s; and it led to a turning back a little towards tradition, albeit a tradition expressed in terms of a very Westernized modern growth. The upshot was the 'reverse course', a re-examination, sometimes a revision, of a number of the occupation reforms.

The constitution was one target, for to many it seemed that the country's military establishment, now that independence had been regained, ought to be made more obviously legal than it had been so far. Decentralization was another, partly because it was said to be inefficient, partly because it had been applied most vigorously to conservative institutions like the bureaucracy and the police. Education also came under fire, chiefly for its failure to provide a training in ethics. Advocates of such training were careful to deny that they wished to restore prewar nationalism under another guise, but they were loud in their condemnation of a system which failed to substitute for it standards of any kind at all. Politics apart, they even found a certain sympathy for this view among the teachers, some of whom were finding it difficult to discover what kind of citizen the course in civics—at anything more than a very elementary level—was intended to produce.

Since the 'reverse course' was a policy of the right-wing parties, usually coupled with strictures on the 'excessive' liberties which had been granted to trade unions and the individual citizen in the postwar years, it is not surprising that the socialists and the labour movement opposed it bitterly. On the other hand, they had less power to do so in the Diet than they would have liked. Yoshida's Liberals, profiting from the peace treaty's popularity, won an absolute majority in the elections of October 1952. The Reform Party, formerly the Democrats, also held a substantial number of seats, thus ensuring the conservatives a firm hold on the lower house. They maintained it in the elections of April 1953 and February 1955, despite factional struggles which led to shifts in party labels and allegiances. Yoshida, for example, was challenged within his own party in 1953 by its former leader, Hatoyama Ichiro, who had been purged in 1947 and apparently expected to take over the reins again when he returned to politics in 1951; and the split, together with a steady decline in the government's popular appeal, forced the Prime Minister's resignation in December 1954. Only two weeks earlier Hatoyama had formed a new Democratic Party, composed of forty-two Liberal renegades and eight-two members of the other rightwing Diet groups, whose votes helped to make him premier in Yoshida's stead. He then won a general election at the beginning of 1955, relegating the Liberals to second place. Since he commanded no more than a plurality, however, he was unable to remain in office without their help, a fact which led to a merger in November, creating the Liberal-Democrats. Hatoyama, though not without difficulty, became their leader. Indeed, it was soon apparent that the reorganization had not so much achieved unity as turned separate parties into factions of a larger whole. When Hatoyama resigned because of ill health in December 1956, he was succeeded, again after much debate, by Ishibashi Tanzan, but within two months Ishibashi's health had given way in turn and Kishi Nobusuke had taken over. This was at the end of February 1957, the Kishi cabinet surviving until July 1960, when it was replaced by that of Ikeda Hayato.

All the cabinets after Yoshida's—Kishi's was reshuffled in the summer of every year—had the look of conservative coalitions. Despite this, the Liberal-Democrats were able to secure about 58 per cent of the votes and 290 seats in the elections of May 1958 and November 1960. Against this the Socialists had little more than half as many, the disparity revealing how slowly they had recovered from the setbacks of 1949. The peace treaty had in fact brought into the open the basic ideological divisions with the Socialist Party, so that it went to the polls in 1952 as two independent units, the right supporting the treaty, the left rejecting it. Each secured something over fifty seats, a little more than they had won between them in 1949. In the 1953 elections the right increased its total to sixty-six seats, the left to seventy-two, and in 1955 the figures were sixty-seven and eighty-nine respectively. But this was not enough to give either a chance of power. In October 1955, therefore, they re-united, setting an example, as we have seen, which their opponents were quick to follow. Nevertheless, the Social Democrats, as they were now to be called, continued to make only modest progress: 166 seats in 1958, 172 in 1960, the latter including seventeen held by a splinter group of moderates, the Democratic Socialists, who had broken away at the end of 1959.

Nor could the opposition expect much help from Communists, whose parliamentary representation had been wiped out by the Korean war. Russian, or rather Cominform, criticism of Nosaka's peaceful line in 1950, together with suspicions that the party had had foreknowledge of the North Korean attack, had cost it most of its public support. Government action, the so-called 'Red Purge', had then completed its discomfiture. As a result, Communist leaders and much of the party machinery went underground, preparing to pursue 'militant' policies instead of wooing votes. They lost every single seat in the elections of 1952, regained one in April 1953, two in February 1955; and although there were signs of a return to the Nosaka policies soon after, confirmed by his emergence from hiding and assumption of leadership later in the year, the long interval of militancy had done damage which it proved impossible to repair. The left-wing Socialists, chief beneficiaries of Communist failure at the polls, held what they gained, so that no more than three Communist members were elected to the lower house in 1960.

One might summarize what has been said above as follows: the conservative membership of the House of Representatives had fallen slightly, from over 70 per cent in 1952 to just under 65 per cent in 1960; that of the socialists had risen from 25 per cent to 35 per cent in the same period; and the Communists had ceased to be a major factor in Diet proceedings. It follows that governments and their policies in these years, whatever their labels, were consistently conservative. Surprisingly, however, the 'reverse course' met with less success than these facts would have led one to expect.

One of its elements, constitutional reform, without which rearmament could not be made official, was blocked by the left continuing to hold more than a third of the seats in the upper house, even when it was at its weakest in the lower. Other proposals, like those for education, suffered a similar fate for different reasons, being defeated not by votes but by extra-parliamentary pressures. Thus a draft for an ethics course in schools, prepared by the Education Minister in 1951, was so widely criticized by press and public for its reactionary content that it was withdrawn. A bill to give the ministry power to license textbooks met the same response and was defeated in the Diet in 1956. Local education boards, in fact, were the only part of the educational structure to be effectively attacked, being revised in April of that year. The pattern held good for efforts to revise the police administration, too: in 1954 the Diet abolished all the smaller forces, consolidating them into prefectural units, with a national police to carry out co-ordination; but a bill to give the police more powers, including rights of arbitrary arrest, aroused such an outcry in October and November 1958 that the Kishi government found it best to drop it.

The methods adopted by the Socialist Party in these disputes were in some respects as retrogressive as the measures they were designed to oppose. Attempts to obstruct Diet business, sometimes by a refusal to conduct debates, sometimes even by the use of force, were reminiscent of the 1920s. So, indeed, was the situation in which they were applied, since the Socialists were an opposition with little immediate hope of coming to power and an extremist wing, never fully committed to parliamentary means, which was willing to sacrifice long-term interests to short-term gains. Certainly the extremists, becoming steadily stronger as the prospects of office grew more remote, took the lead in exploiting the party's links with trade unions, student organizations and similar bodies. At their instigation, strikes, demonstrations and petitions were constantly used to influence the Diet vote, so that in 1958, for example, during the struggle over the Police Duties Bill, the General Council of Trade Unions (Sohyo) brought out over four million workers in protest rallies against the government's proposals.

This kind of politics was effective because there was a measure of public sympathy for the aims it tried to achieve—itself a tribute to the success of what America had set out to do—and because the nature of Japanese society made it easier to organize such sympathy behind specific protests than to rally it against the government in elections. Many Japanese, who for one reason or another were committed to supporting a conservative candidate, were not entirely at one with the policies his party pursued. Accordingly, they welcomed the opportunity to criticize some of its actions without taking the more drastic, and perhaps more embarrassing, step of recording their sentiment at the polls.

The tendency was greater still in discussions of foreign affairs. The American alliance was accepted as necessary, even beneficial, by a majority, their arguments reinforced by gratitude for the humanitarian and constructive purposes of the occupation. On the other hand, there was a certain uneasiness at Japan becoming involved in the 'cold war'. There was also a lingering Pan-Asianism, which led to the feeling that Japan 'ought' to belong to a neutralist Afro-Asian bloc; a revulsion against the atomic bomb, more often evident in hostility to American nuclear tests, which got more publicity, than to Russian; and a stirring of nationalism, bringing resentment of Japan's apparently 'dependent' status *vis-à-vis* the United States. All these were emotions which the Socialists, backed by Communists and the surviving ultranationalists, could use. And incidents inevitably arose on which they could be focused. In October 1956 hundreds were injured when residents of the village of Sunakawa, helped by students and trade unionists, demonstrated against a plan to extend a neighbouring American airbase at the expense of agricultural land. Legal wrangles over the arrests that were made dragged on for nearly three years, including at one point a surprise ruling from the Tokyo District Court—quickly overruled on appeal—that the presence of American bases in Japan was contrary to the constitution. In 1957 came another *cause célèbre*, concerning an American sentry who shot a Japanese woman collecting metal for scrap on a firing range. The issue this time was whether the trial was to be in a civil (Japanese) court or a military (American) one, raising questions of legality which involved the constitutions of both countries; and it was not until after much publicity that the Japanese court was adjudged to have priority. It promptly released the man on a suspended sentence.

The most famous of all these affairs, which arose in 1960, brought down a government. Recognizing that no administration could afford to ignore entirely the objections to the American connection—many of which were traditionalist and hence conservative—Prime Minister Kishi sought new arrangements which would provide sops to Japanese pride. For example, he said, Japan ought to have some kind of say in deciding the use to which American bases on her soil were put. Unfortunately, however, an agreement embodying this and other changes, signed in Washington in January 1960, instead of soothing nationalist feelings by its provisions, exacerbated them by drawing attention to the two countries' inevitable inequalities of strength. When it came before the Diet in April there were violent student demonstrations against it outside the building. By May the Socialists had boycotted the proceedings and picketed the House, having to be physically removed by the police. Then in their absence the government party voted to ratify the treaty. This made the dispute one of constitutional rights and raised the protests to the level of hysteria: mass demonstrations throughout Japan on May 26; student riots in Tokyo causing several hundred casualties; enormous public petitions; a railway strike at the beginning of June.

Within two weeks of these events President Eisenhower was expected on a visit to Japan, it having been assumed that he would arrive in time to celebrate the exchange of ratifications. The turbulence, increasingly anti-American in its tone, for all that it was directed chiefly at the Kishi government, made this impossible. On June 16 an emergency cabinet meeting decided to ask Eisenhower not to come. Two days later the Diet vote for ratification of the agreement took effect and on June 23 America ratified in turn. Kishi at once resigned.

Yet the tumult had not really changed the nature of Japanese politics. Kishi's successor, Ikeda Hayato, was a member of the Liberal-Democrats, chosen by the usual manoeuvrings, as his distribution of office to competing factions showed. In November, moreover, he won an election, demonstrating that Japanese voting patterns remained the same, despite the passions of the early summer. Japan, it seemed, had not suddenly achieved a system in which politics fully represented opinions. All the same, in announcing his intention to concentrate on promoting economic growth the new Prime Minister was showing a proper discretion, as well as a personal bent. He was also underlining the importance of an aspect of Japan's postwar history which was just beginning to impress the outside world.

Japan's economy had faced very considerable difficulties after the surrender, quite apart from the damage and dislocation which bombing had left behind. Shortages of fuel, power and raw materials, inadequate transport, the apathy of defeat, and fears that equipment might be seized for reparations, these combined with the loss of colonies and foreign markets to hamper development for several years. Even when the future became a little less uncertain there were still factors which worked against recovery. A multilateral trade, on which Japan had depended prewar, proved harder, if not impossible, to maintain in a world divided into sterling and dollar blocs. Division between hostile camps had the same effect, as was exemplified in the political problems of trade with China, to which we have already referred. At home there were handicaps stemming from reform: a loss of trained leadership because of the purge; the disorganization arising from an American decision to break up the giant *zaibatsu* firms, which led to the abolition of their central holding companies and the dissolution of the combines into their component parts. If more democratic, the result was less efficient than what had existed before, as American policy-makers themselves were forced to admit at a later stage.

To balance these drawbacks were a number of advantages, though it was a little time before they could be realized. Creation of a war economy had appreciably raised the level of Japanese technical skill in several industries. Again, the destruction of plant which bombing had entailed at least ensured that rebuilding, if achieved at all, would be undertaken with the most up-to-date methods and machinery. Nor was American intervention in economic matters entirely to the bad by any means. In the early days it brought vital shipments of food and raw materials. Later, when intensification of the cold war caused a fresh approach, there was a relaxation of the anti-*zaibatsu* policy and help towards the ending of inflation. In many respects, in fact, American aid provided a substitute for a stagnant foreign commerce. The outbreak of the Korean war greatly increased it, since it brought large orders for equipment for the United Nations forces, which gave Japanese production its first considerable stimulus of the postwar years; and even after 1952 aid was maintained in the form of procurement orders for American troops and bases in Japan. It has been estimated that from 1952 to 1956 these paid for about a quarter of Japan's commodity imports every year.

Once started, the growth of Japanese industry was rapid and almost continuous. In 1948 production stood at only 40 per cent of the 1937 figure, but this was the end of the really hard times. In 1950 the industrial production index was 84 (1934–6 = 100), in 1953 it was 155. Prices rose, handicapping exports, and government corrective measures caused a mild recession in 1954; but expansion was resumed thereafter, the index standing at 262 by 1957, where it levelled out for a year because of balance of payments problems, then jumped to 325 and 410 in 1959 and 1960. In the second of these years the economy achieved a real growth rate of 13·2 per cent, accompanied by an almost 12 per cent rise in individual consumption.

Much the largest share in this advance was due to manufacturing industry, especially in fields like chemicals and engineering, which had been relatively undeveloped before the war. Finished steel products, only 4·5 million metric tons in 1936, were 9·4 million in 1955 and 22·1 million in 1960, with iron ore totalling approximately half as much throughout. Commercial motor vehicles in use, 700,000 in 1955, were six times as many then as in 1936 and nearly doubled again in the next five years, during which period Japan also became the world's biggest—and in many ways most enterprising—shipbuilder, having an annual average launch of 1·75 million tons. In electric generating capacity she ranked sixth in 1960, her 23 million kilowatts being about two-thirds that of Britain and three times her own capacity in 1937. A start had also been made with atomic power, there being five reactors in operation by the end of 1961.

Evidence of the growth was to be seen in the sprawling, industrial cities, like Tokyo and Osaka, where, instead of the debris and dilapidation of 1945, modern factories were producing a range of goods which could compete with the very best. Japanese motor-cycles were winning European races; Japanese cameras and optical goods were threatening to drive those of Germany from international markets; Japanese sewing-machines and transistor radios were to be bought everywhere in the world. Nor was this merely a question of price. Many technical improvements now originated in Japan, so that for the first time she was in a position to sell patents—and accuse others of copying her designs.

Significantly, metal, chemicals and engineering represented over 60 per cent by value of the country's gross factory production in 1959, compared with only 30 per cent in 1930, demonstrating how greatly the war, and preparation for it, had influenced the direction of development. Textiles, which had long held pride of place in both domestic production and foreign trade, were perhaps half as important in 1960 as in 1936. What is more, the balance within the industry had changed. Raw silk, facing severe competition from man-made fibres, totalled less than a third of the prewar figure in 1950–54 and increased only a little thereafter. Cotton yarn output was smaller in 1960 than in 1935–7, as was the number of spindles in use. Exports of cotton piecegoods, unable to match the price of those from areas like South East Asia, had dropped by over 40 per cent. By contrast, rayons and other artificial fabrics, relying on an expanding chemical industry for materials, were more important, as was wool.

Foreign trade naturally reflected the pattern of industrial growth, as well as the different opportunities and limitations of the postwar world. Textiles, especially the new varieties, remained a major export, but were much less dominant than before, being joined by the mechanical, electrical and optical equipment we have already mentioned. Ships were the most valuable item among heavy manufactured goods, though they represented a slowly declining proportion by 1961. Railway equipment, motor vehicles and chemicals, including fertilizers, were also substantial export items. Among imports, textile materials declined, except for Australian wool, because of the shift to man-made fibres, while the country's much greater needs for power brought oil up to 16 per cent of the whole by 1959. Imports of metals and food also remained considerable. In terms of the trade's geographical spread, the United States was Japan's biggest customer, taking about 27 per cent of exports in 1958–9, mostly labour-intensive manufactured products, and providing about a third of imports. China played a much smaller part than before, the areas to the south of it a larger one; but perhaps the outstanding feature was that Japan's foreign trade was more widely distributed than it had

Diversification in goods offered & countries traded with

been in the past, as well as being less concentrated on a narrow range of goods.

The fact that food imports have remained stable in the post-war period, despite the loss of food-producing colonies like Korea and Formosa and an increase in population from 73 million in 1940 to 93 million in 1960, is a tribute to the efficiency of Japanese agriculture. Land reform helped to make it possible, of course, partly by giving greater incentives to the owner-farmer, partly by limiting the opportunities for investing in land to rent, thus making capital more readily available for improvements. So did the refugees from the towns, who swelled the numbers working on the farms just after the war and so contributed extra labour. When they returned to urban employment, as most of them eventually did, their place was often taken by machines, a tendency reflected in the spread of motor ploughing in recent years, whether by the hire of ploughs from local contractors, or by the purchase of small hand-guided rotors. Most important of all, however, have been technical changes: better drainage and irrigation; more use of chemical fertilizers; the development of insecticides, making possible effective pest control. These factors, taken together, have raised the production of rice, the staple crop, to an average of 30 per cent more in 1955–60 than in the middle 'thirties. Simultaneously, farm produce has been diversified, with conspicuous growth in the figures for vegetables, fruit, dairy products and livestock, especially pigs.

As a result the Japanese diet has continued to become more varied, with wheat products, for example, actually making inroads on what used to be a universal preference for rice. Indeed, since there is no longer a large percentage of the national income being spent on arms, the increases in productivity have raised the standards of living in every way. Real wages in manufacturing industry, the most favoured sector, reached the 1934–6 level in 1952, were almost 50 per cent above it in 1960. It is true that there were inequalities, which such averages tend to conceal. Workers in large modern enterprises were appreciably better off than those in small ones, both in pay and conditions, while farmers, after long being at a disadvantage, were only just beginning to catch up. Nevertheless, prosperity was now being spread much more evenly through Japanese society than ever in the past; and although *per capita* income was closer to that of southern Europe than the more heavily industrialized countries of the West, it was well above anything else in Asia (and gained over 16 per cent in 1960 alone). Consumption expenditure in the same year rose nearly as sharply: by over 12 per cent in the villages, by just under 10 per cent in the towns. Much of this went on luxury foods, travel, superior clothing. Much went on new electrical equipment, like television sets—owned by four out of five urban households in 1962 and half the rural ones—refrigerators, vacuum cleaners, washing machines and heaters. A good deal went on savings and insurance. In fact, by comparison with conditions of a hundred years ago, or even with the rest of contemporary Asia, one is tempted to conclude that Japan today is well on the way to becoming an affluent society.

CHAPTER XVI

POSTWAR JAPAN

THIS BOOK began with a description of Japanese society in the early nineteenth century. To end it with one of Japan today, therefore, will serve to summarize the enormous changes that have taken place in the intervening century and a half. Nevertheless, the task of describing the contemporary is by no means easy, partly because generalization, without the perspective given by time, can become misleading, partly because Japan seems now more complex, perhaps more disordered, than it was before. In one of its aspects, for instance, modern history has seen a Western challenge to the established Sino-Japanese tradition, contributing to the breakdown of what was formerly a coherent hierarchical society and the substitution for it of one in which the locus of power, the composition of the ruling class and the standards of behaviour to which it subscribes have all become difficult to determine. Similarly, while change has in most things been rapid, it has not maintained an equal pace in every segment of Japanese life. It is largely for these reasons that every author writing about modern Japan finds it necessary to emphasize the admixture of East and West, of old and new, that is to be found there.

In 1800 Japan had an emperor in seclusion, whose authority, in so far as feudal particularism allowed, was wielded by an hereditary, *de facto* monarch, the Shogun. A hundred years later the Shogun had vanished, the emperor had become quasi-divine and there was a Westernized bureaucracy ruling in his name. Now, after sixty years more, power rests in the hands of an elected Diet. It is exercised on the Diet's behalf by a Prime Minister and a cabinet responsible primarily to the lower house, with the emperor a mere 'symbol of the State'. Moreover, the mechanisms of politics have also changed. Influence is no longer a matter of hereditary status and regional affiliation, backed by force. Nor does it depend primarily on possessing land, or friends in office, though both remain important. Instead, it is attained—publicly, at least—by the manipulation of votes in the lower house, with the result that it involves parties and pressure groups; local 'machines' and professional representatives of the people; businessmen and trade unions; newspapers, radio and television; elections and electioneering.

At the higher levels, as we have seen, faction is still a significant element in Japanese politics, since neither conservatives nor socialists have fully outgrown the days when the activities of the Diet were concerned with spoils, not policies. Thus a Prime Minister has more need for the skills appropriate to maintaining a balance of power within his cabinet than for the qualities of forceful leadership. On the other hand, the sharp reduction in the privileges of bodies like the Privy Council, the bureaucracy and the services since the war has removed one obstacle to the growth of a sense of responsibility among party politicians, by eliminating rivals who made their efforts ineffective. The end of the occupation has removed another, in that it terminated the veto exercised by the Supreme Commander for the Allied Powers, which was hardly compatible with parliamentary sovereignty. What is more, there has been a measure of progress towards a two-party system in the last few years, with alliances shaped by outlook rather than tactical convenience. On the right the Liberal-Democrats, on the left the Socialists, have maintained their coalitions, despite occasional secessions; and the Communists, though influential outside the Diet in many ways, no longer have the representation within it to play an important part in the struggle between the two.

It has to be granted that there is a great disparity between conservative and socialist strength. As a recent comment put it:

'One party remains dominant and always in power. It knows only how to govern. The other is a perennial minority, unable to command more than a third of the electorate. It knows only how to oppose. . . .'[82]

This state of affairs might easily endanger the stability of the constitution, in that the frustrations it provokes—and the government's determination to press its advantage to the full—have on several occasions led the Socialists to adopt extra-parliamentary methods. Equally disturbing, it might be thought, is the fact that there are still groups outside the Diet which are capable of exerting a disproportionate influence on decisions. The bureaucracy, an able and self-conscious élite, is one of them, providing a core of members to the lower house and a number of ministers in each conservative cabinet. Business associations and organized labour are others, linked with the right-wing and left-wing movements, respectively, as much by the funds they provide as by the interests they legitimately represent. All the same, there is a significant difference between this situation and that which obtained before the war. Pressure, to be successful, must now be exerted *on* the parties, not independently of them, a sure sign that a transfer of authority has really taken place.

Membership of the parties is small, consisting mostly of bureaucrats, full-time politicians, businessmen and trade unionists who can expect to be election candidates. Little has been achieved by attempts to gain popular participation and support. Accordingly, since the party as such has little to offer its recruits, other than its label and financial backing, organization in the constituencies tends not to be very closely bound to that within the Diet. Success at the polls, in fact, depends on the extent to which a man can cultivate local leaders, acquire a local reputation and raise money for posters, broadcasts, loudspeaker vans and other kinds of publicity while electioneering. It helps if the candidate is of some repute, still more if he is of local origin; but the policies for which he stands matter a good deal less, except, perhaps, in the sense of whether he belongs to the right or left of the political spectrum.

This is especially true of rural constituencies, which are more numerous than the distribution of population fully justifies. In the countryside, local issues are of greater interest than national ones and a recommendation from village dignitaries has far more effect than a noisy campaign. Village cohesion, which makes voting a community obligation, ensures a voting rate higher than the towns; and the farmer's respect for tradition— combined with the fact that the party in power has important means of wooing rural councils, by promises about subsidies from central government funds or the allocation of money to provide schools, roads and irrigation—ensures that between

50 and 60 per cent of the vote goes to the conservatives. The latter, therefore, although no longer a party of landlords, as they were at the beginning of the century, dare not appear to be too openly the champions of commercial and industrial enterprise.

The Socialists are more sectional in the support they receive, a fact which is reflected in their electoral record. The solid footing which business and the farm give to the conservatives is for them provided by trade unions, whose resources furnish candidates, funds and organization on a substantial scale. This strengthens the socialist position, especially in the industrial towns, but it is not without its disadvantages. For one thing, too close an association with organized labour tends to alienate voters of the centre and middle class, without whose help the party is unlikely to obtain the majority it needs if it is to come to power. For another, since the trade union movement is no less divided ideologically than the left-wing politicians, the relationship between the two makes unity harder to achieve. Thus there are two national federations: the General Council of Trade Unions (Sohyo), a radical organization with about three million members, and the much more moderate Trades Union Congress (Zenro), about a quarter its size. For some years the division corresponded to that between the two separate socialist parties of the left and right. In addition there are a large number of company unions, each comprising the workers in a single factory or firm, many of them not affiliated to the national bodies at all.

In an economy in which wages and conditions of work vary widely from one type of employment to another, particularly as between large concerns and small, there is much to be said for such an arrangement, in so far as the unions exist primarily to negotiate with employers; but the multiplication of units, plus the fact that they differ greatly from each other in political outlook, serves to increase the fragmentation which an emphasis on local connections gives to Japanese politics as a whole. The socialist who owes his election to the patronage of a local union, like the conservative who relies on personal influence in a rural area, does not feel much beholden to the party whose badge he wears. He can even afford to treat its discipline with a certain disrespect. This does much to explain the kaleidoscopic qualities of Japanese party history—its shifts in factional or party allegiances and its numerous independants, who often do not join a party until after they have won a parliamentary seat—as well as the way in which parties reach decisions by reconciling differences behind closed doors before proceeding to a Diet vote.

The men who are elected to the local assemblies and the House of Representatives, of course, are not the only element in Japan's ruling class. Senior bureaucrats and the managerial staff of the larger businesses are at least equally influential, while the owners of small firms, trade union leaders, labour 'bosses', mayors and prefectural governors, local officials and landowners (despite the reduction in their holdings which the land reform effected) all wield a good deal of power. Unlike the samurai of the Tokugawa period, however, these groups do not have a status that can readily be defined. Their position does not depend on hereditary rank, which has been abolished. Nor does it rest on birth in the wider sense, which is important for the kind of upbringing it affords and the connections it provides, but not as something which confers absolute privilege. Certainly birth without ability, though it might lead to a pleasant enough existence as one of the pensioners of the great—and gives social kudos at any level—would not now guarantee the possession of authority. The doctrines of Japanese family life have long approved the use of marriage and adoption as a means of recruiting the able to take over a family's affairs, superseding in the process those whose only claim to do so is that of blood; and society, which accords to the person so recruited the standing proper to the position he attains, not that from which he came, also accepts the technique as a way of advancing a man's career outside the family as well. Of two young men of equal ability, therefore, the better born will make rapid progress, because of his father's friends; but the other, if he is reasonably lucky, might do so by acquiring a patron or a wife. What is more, he will end no worse regarded for having risen in this way, provided his achievements are real.

Yet this is not to say that Japan is the land of the fairytale, where the poor commoner marries the princess amid general rejoicing. Marriage and adoption take place within fairly narrow social limits as a rule. Moreover, enough of the old 'status society' still remains to ensure that an individual's wealth or power can rise—or fall—faster than his standing. To put it differently, there is a 'right' and a 'wrong' manner of speaking in Japan, a 'good' and a 'bad' part of town in which to be born, a 'polite' and a 'vulgar' way of eating and behaving, all having undertones of the traditional distinctions between samurai, merchant and commoner. Such things can play a major part in determining a man's success, for to get a good job, or to win promotion in it, he must be socially presentable, even if he does not possess the appropriate connections. Education is the one means by which the majority can hope to overcome the initial disadvantages of humble origin, a fact which makes entry to the best schools and universities vital to those who are ambitious. It is not merely that the quality of their academic training is superior, making it easier for their students to pass examinations. It is also that the years spent acquiring that training will give the student an acceptable manner and well-placed friends, the latter being by no means the least useful acquisition in a country where it may be highly desirable in later life to have a former classmate in a particular government office, company, or political party. As a consequence, university education in Japan suffers from more competition, more preoccupation with marks, and more suicides, than anywhere else in the world, an atmosphere which pervades the high schools, too. This is one price that is paid for a society in which there is a fair degree of mobility from class to class. Another, paradoxically, is a widespread self-consciousness, which seems to make all Japanese acutely aware of just what their status is in relation to those with whom they come into regular contact. Or ought this, perhaps, to be described as a survival from the past?

Government and social structure have changed no more radically in Japan than the factors which determine where people live and how they earn their living. Population is some 95 million in 1962, approximately three times as great as it was a hundred years ago; and this inevitably makes the country both industrial and urban. Over 45 per cent live in cities of 50,000 inhabitants or more, their numbers increasing every year. Another 10 per cent live in towns of smaller size, leaving rather less than 45 per cent in areas designated 'rural'. In terms of occupation, the 1955 census showed only 38 per cent of the labour force as engaged in agriculture, compared with 47 per cent in 1930, this being the continuation of a trend which has been consistent throughout modern times. By contrast, there has been a steady increase in the numbers in manufacturing industry (from 16 to 18 per cent during the same period) and in distribution, transport and similar services (from 30 to 35 per cent), while the total labour force itself has grown from 29 million to 39 million people. There have also been great changes in the size and nature of the firms in which the urban population works. Numbers in the textile trades have halved, those in the machinery and engineering industries doubled, since 1936. More significant still, the very smallest firms, those with less than ten employees, provide only a fifth of the jobs, compared with nearly three-fifths in 1930, and those employing fifty or more account for about a half, instead of a third. About one industrial worker in seven earns his living in a factory with at least a thousand employees.

There is nevertheless a great disparity still between the two segments of Japanese industry. On the one hand are a comparatively few, very large concerns—some of the former *zaibatsu* empires have been rebuilt since 1952, though no longer under family ownership—with huge, modern factories, a highly-trained managerial bureaucracy, a world-wide network of offices and representatives. On the other are the much more numerous small and medium businesses, highly competitive with each other and usually under the owner's management. They are often sub-contractors, especially those which are engaged in making components for Japan's newer electrical and mechanical products; and although they tend to be much better equipped than in the past, they offer lower wages and poorer conditions than their bigger rivals. The man with a permanent job at one of the larger factories will almost certainly have a powerful union to defend his interests, giving him a measure of security which his counterpart in a smaller enterprise does not share. Moreover, his wages, including allowances for age, length of service, size of family, cost of living and so on, to say nothing of annual bonuses based on profits, which are sometimes of considerable size, might be fully half as much again as those of the temporary workers whom most of the smaller firms employ. It is the latter whose wages suffer most, or whose hours are cut, when times are hard, a circumstance which helps to explain the country's competitiveness in foreign trade, but leaves it with a social problem of significant proportions.

Real wages in manufacturing industry, which regained the 1934-6 level in 1952, have risen another 40 per cent in the last ten years. This is an average, concealing, as is clear from what we have said above, some important variations between workers of different types; but it represents a major advance in living standards even for those who profit least. This has been achieved by other sections of the working population, too: the army of white-collar workers, whose growth in numbers is perhaps the surest index to modernization; the employees of construction firms, which have been enjoying an unprecedented boom; the men in transport, the girls in shops, the labourers (often women) on the roads. All have more money to spend now than most of them, certainly the younger ones, have ever had. There are also more things for them to buy. Before the war it was usual for urban households to have a radio, but it was a sign of some affluence to have a sewing-machine or electric fire. Now both are common, as are television sets, while refrigerators and vacuum cleaners have a ready sale. And although motor-cars are still a luxury—if one which the middle class can increasingly afford—a greater ability to pay for holidays by train or coach has filled the beaches everywhere and brought a hundred million visitors a year to the mountainous national parks.

It would be wrong to suggest, however, that ways of living in urban Japan cannot be distinguished from those of Europe, even though at first glance a Japanese city—with its heavy traffic, its crowds in Western dress, its office buildings, modern shops and neon lighting—contains little that is obviously oriental. In fact, one reason for the high levels of consumption is precisely that some of the population's basic needs are simpler, and hence less expensive, than their Western equivalents. Few Japanese have a Western-style house, for example, though a good many have a Western-style room. Apartment blocks, while becoming more popular than they were, as land gets dearer, are still exceptional. Most people live in houses of the traditional kind, which are flimsier and cheaper to build, as well as being safer in earthquakes. They require less furniture and make a more economical use of interior space. Moreover, not many of them have modern sanitation; and this, when applied to an entire suburban area, means an enormous saving in the capital expenditure which would otherwise have to be made on sewage. In the same way, the practice of making residential roads narrow, poorly lit and only roughly surfaced further reduces the cost of running towns.

The farmer, at least in the more accessible parts of the country, has facilities which are not so very much worse. He will have electricity and will not be far from the nearest telephone. There will be village shops, which are less imposing than those of the city, but stocking similar goods, and an efficient bus or train service to whatever is the local centre, from which he can reach Tokyo or Osaka, if he wishes, in a matter of hours. His daughter will have no difficulty in getting a permanent wave; his wife might well have a television set to watch—49 per cent of rural households were said to own one in 1962—possibly a washing-machine to use; and there is about one chance in four that he or his son will have a motor-cycle. Furthermore, in 1960 the average surplus of his family income over expenditure was 10 per cent, most of which was saved.

Some of this prosperity is due to land reform, which has served to equalize the distribution of village wealth and so create a wider market for goods and services. Some of it is due to a conservative government's policies of price support, a return for rural votes. Some springs from greater investment, in the form of mechanization, chemical fertilizers, insecticides and so on, which have raised the crop to record heights, while giving the farmer more leisure, which he and his family can devote to side-employment. All the same, agriculture still has its problems, several of them becoming more acute. The average holding remains very small, so that to divide it on inheritance—as the law actually enjoins—would soon reduce it to unmanageable parcels. Usually, therefore, younger sons renounce their rights; and since machines make their labour less and less needed on the land, they emigrate to the city or find jobs in local firms and factories. It is essentially the same process that has been going on throughout the century, keeping the farm population at a more or less steady figure and providing a source of cheap labour for industrial towns. Its speed, however, is now increasing as industry booms, with the result that the cost of seasonal agricultural labour is getting higher— wages rose by 16 per cent in the year 1960 alone—and farmers are finding it difficult, so they complain, to secure husbands for those of their daughters who stay at home.

From a different standpoint, this situation raises the question of whether the towns can continue to absorb the surplus population of the countryside, in addition to that which they produce themselves. The 'population problem', in other words, is still very much an issue, even though the rate of increase has been slowed down by better living standards and legalized abortion. Most people today realize that there is no solution to it to be found in emigration or attempts at creating an empire overseas. This only leaves industrial development, which in the last resort depends on foreign trade. Accordingly, the public shows much concern with subjects like balance of payments, relations with Communist China, or the restrictions imposed on Japanese exports by foreign powers, recognizing that Japan is committed by necessity to encouraging commercial growth. Compared with the views on the subject expressed by Tokugawa scholars and reflected in the cry to 'expel the barbarians' at the time of the first opening of the ports, this, too, is a measure of how things have changed.

It is not only with respect to trade that attitudes towards the outside world differ from those of the past. Resentment and a sense of inferiority, engendered in the nineteenth century, which in the twentieth fed the chauvinism that brought war, seem to have been purged by defeat. Consequently, although traces of the former passions remain—in the prickliness about American bases, for example, and the exaggerated humility with which individual Japanese occasionally praise all things foreign—postwar nationalism has taken a different line. At home, as we said in the previous chapter, it has manifested itself as nostalgia for a social order which events since 1945 have nearly destroyed. Thus the call to revive filial piety and for the country's youth to show a proper attitude towards authority is partly an appeal to nationalist sentiment. Abroad, nationalism has taken the form of a search for the world's respect: generally, through membership of the United Nations and co-operation in international development plans; specifically, through opposition to atomic tests and overtures towards Asian neutralism. In both, with only rare exceptions, there has been a scrupulous, even over-scrupulous, care to avoid claims to leadership of any kind.

In a wider sense, Japan's relationship with the West involves every aspect of her modern life. Many of its physical and institutional components, like buses, electricity, factories, joint-stock companies and water taps, to name but a random few, have become far too familiar to be thought of now as 'foreign'. Indeed it is doubtful whether the millions who watch baseball on television every day think of it as being 'American', for it has become a national game. Similarly, tastes in music are overwhelmingly for that of Europe and America, whether Beethoven or jazz, there being an awareness that it is imported, of course, but not, apparently, any feeling that it is part of an alien culture. An exception would seem to be Western food, which, although everywhere available, is rarely understood. 'They have done to our food,' a British resident observed, 'what they have done to our language: assimilated odds and ends and adapted them to their own needs.'[83] No doubt this is because Japan's own food follows such totally different gastronomic rules.

It is significant, however, that the Japanese show much less skill in performing, than they have taste in appreciating, some of the elements of Western civilization, notably those which are most difficult to communicate or teach. Japan has yet to produce either a composer or a poet of note who uses the Western idiom, while her art, which has contributed so much to that of Europe, seems to have exhausted itself by giving its own, or choked itself by ingesting others', techniques. The result is a great deal of uninspired imitation of either contemporary Europe or traditional Japan, with only occasional flashes of an ability to reconcile the two.

The novel, by contrast, continues to be the most successful of the country's literary imports. Between 1918 and 1945 it suffered from too great a pre-occupation with the social and political movements of the time, as authors became either proletarian or ultranationalist in outlook, and so made their books more rewarding than good. There was a similar danger after 1945, when democracy threatened to become the only theme and 'the people' the universal hero. It extended even to interpretation of the classics:

'The attempt had formerly been made to proclaim how the Japanese race under the wise and benevolent rule of the unbroken line of emperors had risen to greatness. The new attempt was to show . . . how every advance had been the result not of guidance from above, but of the efforts of the common people.'[84]

By these standards the eleventh-century novel, *The tale of Genji*, which in the 1930s had been dismissed as frivolous, was made to appear as an exposé of Court corruption, while an eighth-century chronicle, the *Kojiki*, ranked by prewar militarists as almost a religious revelation, became a critique of military rule.

Fortunately the best of the novelists, although they are far from ignoring the world in which they live, have managed to resist the temptation to write books that are no more than thinly-disguised political pamphlets. Of the older generation, Tanizaki Junichiro and Nagai Kafu survive from the great days after the Russo-Japanese War. Of the younger men, Mishima Yukio and Dazai Osamu more fully represent the middle of the century, the former being under forty now, the latter under forty when he committed suicide in 1948. All are as much the heirs of European as of Japanese literature, for their manner of writing and concepts of what they wish to do owe more to French and Russian novelists than to anything in Japan before the Meiji Restoration. It may be for this reason that their work has been accorded great acclaim when translated into European languages. At the same time, they are Japanese in the subjects they choose and the society they so vividly describe, demonstrating, as most Japanese artists have failed to do, that Western technique and Japanese material can in fact be brought together.

The intellectuals of modern Japan—and their numbers are great enough to maintain the circulation of an astonishing range of serious periodicals—have all received an education in Western literature and thought which enables them to compare these eminent writers with those of the rest of the world. Gide, Sartre and Malraux are names frequently heard in Tokyo's cafés, where the youth of the *avant-garde* meet and talk, while a walk through the Kanda will reveal in almost every second-hand bookshop window Japanese editions of de Maupassant, Tolstoy (who ranks among the country's ten most popular authors), Chekhov, T. S. Eliot and others like them. What is more, many of the young men and women who buy these books are better able to understand them than, say, *The tale of Genji*, which they will read, if at all, in a modernized version. From this point of view, at least, education is producing a generation which can face the West on equal terms, albeit at the cost of abandoning tradition.

Indeed, for most of its members Japan's own past is something romantic or entertaining, rather than real. It is *sumo* wrestling, for example, which rivals baseball as a television programme, or a feudal castle, carefully restored, where one may picnic. Alternatively, if one wishes to be cynical on the subject, it is the *kabuki* theatre, where businessmen take their guests on expense accounts, or simply the theme of one of the country's more exportable films. It is certainly not an inherited complex of ideas from which one's art draws its inspiration and one's life its standards.

This is partly because change has been so rapid in the last hundred years that 1850 and 1950 seem to belong to different worlds. Partly it is because the present is divided from the immediate past by the gulf of defeat, by which Japan's carefully fostered image of herself was shattered. In its light, it has been said, 'the entire set of expansionist slogans that had been drummed into people's ears for so many years . . . stood starkly revealed as false and, what was perhaps rather more damaging, as risible'.[85] The very inclusiveness of the doctrines that were thus destroyed made all the greater the sense of vacuum their disappearance left behind; and although this made it easier for America to win support for the introduction of democracy, for instance, it also made it necessary for democracy to compete for the nation's loyalty with other creeds. Many, especially the young, soon demonstrated that they found the American ideal disappointing, because materialistic—or possibly too difficult, since self-reliance was a quality they had never been encouraged to acquire—and in any case tainted with military occupation. Disillusion turned some to hedonism and irresponsibility, manifesting themselves among intellectuals as a vogue for existentialism and an excessively bohemian way of life. It turned others to the more radical forms of left-wing thought. Marxism, having all the charm of a fruit that had long been forbidden, became for a time so common in some circles as to be an emblem of intellectual respectability. Even after the novelty wore off, its satisfying dogmatism, by accepting which its adherents may derive a 'positive' approach to every kind of problem, has continued to ensure it a wide appeal, the more so because of its prevalence among teachers and in the serious journals.

On the other hand, if nationalism, generating ultranationalism, was Japan's response to the nineteenth century preponderance of the West, one cannot say that Marxism has established itself as a mid-twentieth century successor. It is still confined to a relatively small segment of the population, which has more stridency than power. It is being weakened, moreover, by prosperity, as well as by the conservatism which comes to students with increasing age. This makes it an important, but not a dominant, strand in Japanese thought.

It is not easy, in fact, to identify a dominant strand at all. Confucianism, which provided the ethical content of the pre-war structure, has not only lost its foothold in the schools, but is also under attack within the family, where equality between man and wife, which is fast becoming a reality, plus the ability of children to earn their living independently and even to choose their marriage partners for themselves, makes nonsense of the hierarchy of relationships Confucianism once enjoined. Hence precepts based upon such relationships, though still taught in the majority of households, have ceased to form an organized and generally accepted body of belief.

Nor have the religions of Japan fared any better, though defeat, one would have thought, should have produced an atmosphere which might have favoured their revival. State Shinto was abolished in 1945, together with the emperor's divinity, and the great shrines—except as tourist attractions—have never fully regained their following. Local shrines receive support, since this is considered a community duty; and Shinto ceremonies, most of which concern the crop, are punctiliously observed in rural areas. Festivals everywhere draw crowds, though this, perhaps, depends less on piety than prosperity, since one needs money to spend at sideshows and stalls. Yet there is little evidence of Shinto practices in the home; and such signs of growth as there have been among the Shinto sects have been largely in those whose appeal is to emotion, most of them small in size and obscure in doctrine.

Buddhism was less affected by defeat than Shinto, because it was less involved in the nationalist myth. As a result, its rites still seem to be observed in a majority of families and it continues to profit by conducting funerals and rituals for the dead. It has not, however, made any great progress since the war. Christianity has been more successful, though its adherents, having become fewer in the 1930s, are little more numerous now than they were at the beginning of the century. Their present total, a figure of something under half a million, may well be all that can be achieved. For it remains true that Christianity is put at a disadvantage by its refusal to recognize local, especially family, customs of a quasi-religious kind, a fact which outweighs—in the matter of gaining converts, if not in exercising influence—its association with Western civilization in the popular mind.

One might sum this up by saying that there is no immediate indication of Japan ceasing to be a secular society. This is what Tokugawa Confucianism made it and what the pursuit of national strength thereafter, for all its Shinto trappings, has confirmed. Where it essentially differs now is not that the country is becoming less religious than it used to be, but that it no longer has a single pattern of belief to which the majority of its citizens will subscribe. Marxism, for all its influence, is a minority view. Democracy, though more firmly established than many of its critics would have one believe, is not apparently a thing to fire men's imaginations or to give them drive. Nor is the pursuit of wealth, despite the fact that it is the objective on which people can most readily agree. Japan, in other words, has not fully come to terms with the spiritual problems to which her modern development has given rise. But then, what country has? Perhaps the present malaise, like the present affluence, is no more than evidence that Japan has at last achieved the distinction of being 'modern'.

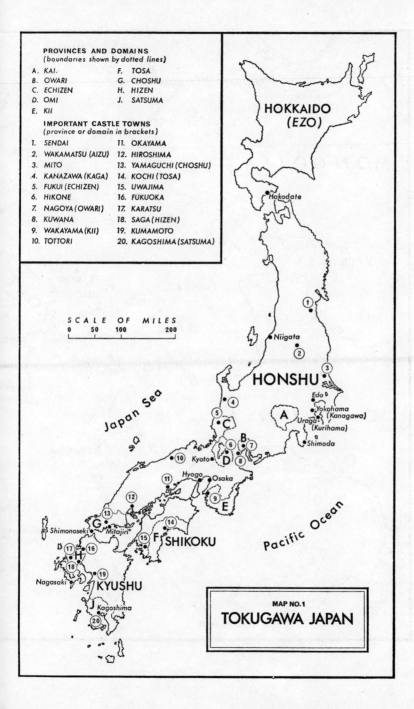

PROVINCES AND DOMAINS
(boundaries shown by dotted lines)

A. KAI.
B. OWARI
C. ECHIZEN
D. OMI
E. KII

F. TOSA
G. CHOSHU
H. HIZEN
J. SATSUMA

IMPORTANT CASTLE TOWNS
(province or domain in brackets)

1. SENDAI
2. WAKAMATSU (AIZU)
3. MITO
4. KANAZAWA (KAGA)
5. FUKUI (ECHIZEN)
6. HIKONE
7. NAGOYA (OWARI)
8. KUWANA
9. WAKAYAMA (KII)
10. TOTTORI

11. OKAYAMA
12. HIROSHIMA
13. YAMAGUCHI (CHOSHU)
14. KOCHI (TOSA)
15. UWAJIMA
16. FUKUOKA
17. KARATSU
18. SAGA (HIZEN)
19. KUMAMOTO
20. KAGOSHIMA (SATSUMA)

HOKKAIDO
(EZO)

Hakodate

SCALE OF MILES
0   50   100   200

Japan Sea

HONSHU

Niigata

Edo
Yokohama
(Kanagawa)
Uraga
(Kurihama)
Shimoda

A

Kyoto
Hyogo   Osaka

B
C
D
E

Shimonoseki   Mitajiri
G
Nagasaki
H
KYUSHU
J   Kagoshima

F   SHIKOKU

Pacific Ocean

MAP NO. 1
TOKUGAWA JAPAN

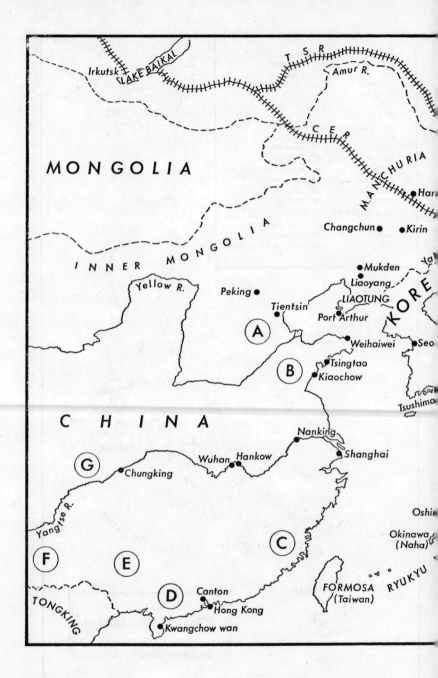

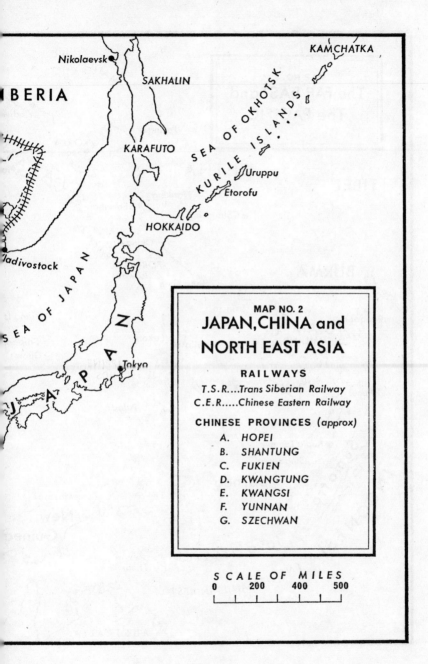

KAMCHATKA

Nikolaevsk

SIBERIA

SAKHALIN

SEA OF OKHOTSK

KARAFUTO

KURILE ISLANDS

Uruppu

Etorofu

Vladivostock

HOKKAIDO

SEA OF JAPAN

JAPAN

Tokyo

MAP NO. 2

JAPAN, CHINA and
NORTH EAST ASIA

RAILWAYS

T.S.R....Trans Siberian Railway
C.E.R.....Chinese Eastern Railway

CHINESE PROVINCES (approx)

A. HOPEI
B. SHANTUNG
C. FUKIEN
D. KWANGTUNG
E. KWANGSI
F. YUNNAN
G. SZECHWAN

SCALE OF MILES
0   200   400   500

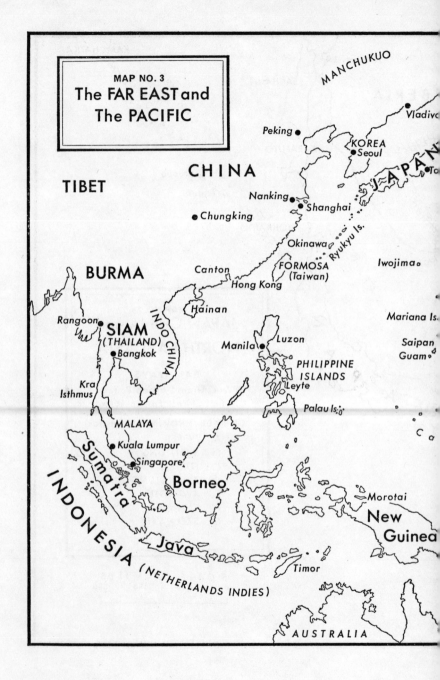

MAP NO. 3
The FAR EAST and
The PACIFIC

MANCHUKUO

Vladiv[o]

Peking

KOREA
Seoul

JAPAN

To

CHINA

TIBET

Nanking

Shanghai

Chungking

Okinawa

Ryukyu Is.

Iwojima

BURMA

Canton

FORMOSA
(Taiwan)

Hong Kong

Hainan

Mariana Is.

Rangoon

SIAM
(THAILAND)

Manila

Luzon

Saipan
Guam

Bangkok

PHILIPPINE
ISLANDS

Leyte

Kra
Isthmus

Palau Is.

Ca

MALAYA

Kuala Lumpur

Singapore

Borneo

Morotai

Sumatra

New
Guinea

INDONESIA

Java

Timor

(NETHERLANDS INDIES)

AUSTRALIA

INDO CHINA

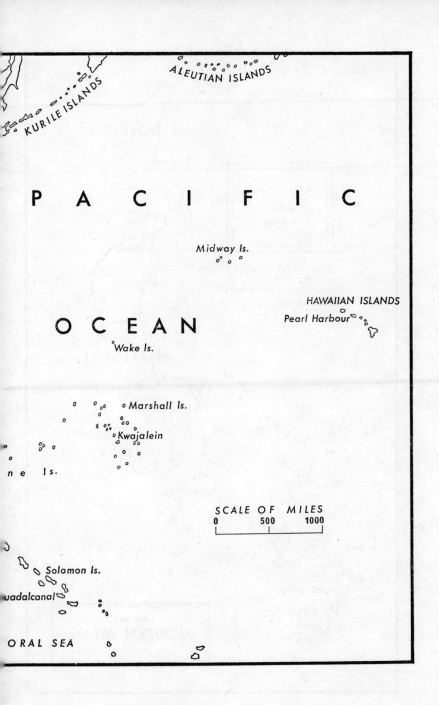

KURILE ISLANDS

ALEUTIAN ISLANDS

P A C I F I C

Midway Is.

HAWAIIAN ISLANDS
Pearl Harbour

O C E A N

Wake Is.

Marshall Is.

Kwajalein

ne Is.

SCALE OF MILES
0   500   1000

Solomon Is.

uadalcanal

ORAL SEA

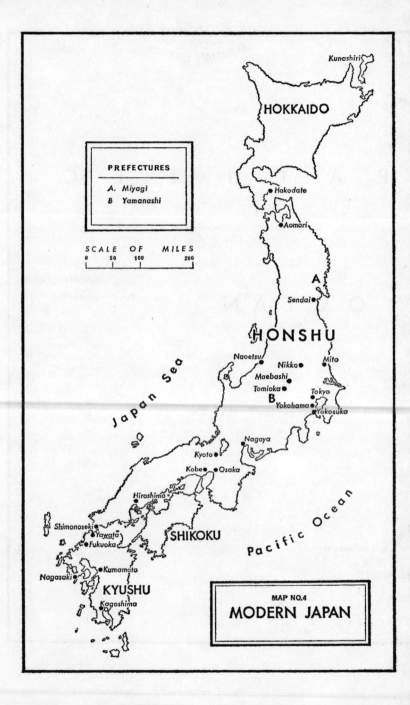

PREFECTURES

A. Miyagi
B Yamanashi

SCALE OF MILES
0   50   100   200

HOKKAIDO

Kunashiri

Hakodate

Aomori

A

Sendai

HONSHU

Naoetsu

Nikko

Mito

Maebashi

Tomioka

Tokyo

B

Yokohama

Yokosuka

Nagoya

Kyoto

Kobe

Osaka

Hiroshima

Shimonoseki

SHIKOKU

Yawata

Fukuoka

Nagasaki

Kumamoto

KYUSHU

Kagoshima

Japan Sea

Pacific Ocean

MAP NO.4
MODERN JAPAN

SOME JAPANESE TERMS

BAKUFU: The central administration of Japan under a Shogun.

DAIMYO: A feudal lord of the Tokugawa period whose domain was estimated to yield an annual crop equivalent to 10,000 *koku* of rice or more. FUDAI DAIMYO were hereditary vassals of the Tokugawa. TOZAMA DAIMYO were those who were subject to the Shogun's control only by virtue of the authority which the Shogun derived from the Emperor.

KAMPAKU: The senior minister at the Imperial Court before 1868.

KAN (KWAN): Measure of weight. 1 *kan* = 8·27 lbs.

KOKU: Measure of capacity. 1 *koku* = 4.96 bushels.

ROJU: A feudal lord (specifically, a *fudai daimyo*) who was a member of the Shogun's Council of State in the Tokugawa period.

RYO: Gold coin of the Tokugawa period. Before 1850, approximately equivalent in value to 1 *koku* of rice.

SAMURAI: A member of Japan's feudal ruling class before 1871. Technically the term included the Shogun and the *daimyo*, but it was more often used of those below this rank.

SHOGUN: The Emperor's military deputy. Before 1868 the office was in effect that of an hereditary *de facto* monarch.

YEN (Y): Monetary unit of modern Japan. Until 1934 it exchanged at about 10 to the pound sterling; from 1934 to 1939 at about 17; since 1950 at about 1,000.

ZAIBATSU: 'Financial clique', or plutocracy. Term used to describe a handful of great family holding companies in modern Japan, distinguished by their enormous size and the wide spread of their economic interests.

A SELECT BIBLIOGRAPHY OF WORKS
IN ENGLISH

Many Western visitors to Japan have written books about their experiences, sometimes good ones. Moreover, Western scholars, especially in the last fifteen years or so, have devoted a good deal of attention to the country's modern development. There is therefore a considerable literature which one might cite in a bibliography of Japan's modern history; and although I have tried to mention all works of outstanding importance in the lists which follow, it must be emphasized at the outset that the selection as a whole reflects a degree of personal taste and prejudice.

General works
Those readers who would like to acquire a knowledge of Japanese history before the nineteenth century will find the best accounts in G. B. Sansom, *Japan. A short cultural history* (rev. ed., London, 1952) and the chapters on Japan in E. O. Reischauer and J. K. Fairbank, *East Asia: the great tradition* (Boston, Mass., 1960).

The standard account of Japan's modern history is H. Borton, *Japan's modern century* (New York, 1955). C. Yanaga, *Japan since Perry* (New York, 1949) is more detailed, but more appropriate for reference than for general reading, while G. B. Sansom, *The Western World and Japan* (New York, 1950) is a brilliant and readable study of cultural relations between Japan and the West from the sixteenth to the nineteenth centuries. Also important for the nineteenth century is E. H. Norman, *Japan's emergence as a modern state* (New York, 1940). Two good political histories, one emphasizing parties and institutions, the other nationalism, are R. A. Scalapino, *Democracy and the party movement in prewar Japan* (Berkeley, 1953) and D. M. Brown, *Nationalism in Japan: an introductory historical analysis* (Berkeley, 1955). Economic history is treated more or less chronologically in G. C. Allen, *A short economic history of modern Japan 1867–1937* (2nd rev. ed., with a supplementary chapter on the period 1945–1960; London, 1962) and by topics in W. W. Lockwood, *The economic development of Japan. Growth and structural change 1868–1938* (Princeton, 1955).

W. T. de Bary, ed., *Sources of the Japanese tradition* (New York, 1958) consists of translated extracts from Japanese writings of all periods, including the nineteenth and twentieth centuries, together with lengthy introductory notes. It provides an excellent survey of the history of ideas. On Shinto there is also D. C. Holtom, *The national faith of Japan. A study in modern Shinto* (London, 1938). A number of works of Japanese literature, especially novels, have been translated into English; and some representative translations are to be found in D. Keene, ed., *Anthology of Japanese literature from the earliest era to the nineteenth century* (London, 1956), the same author's *Modern Japanese literature from 1868 to the present day* (London, 1956), and I. Morris, ed., *Modern Japanese stories* (London, 1961), all three of which have informative introductions on literature generally.

The Tokugawa period (Japan before 1868)

Apart from the general works cited above there are two important studies of economic history for this period: C. D. Sheldon, *The rise of the merchant class in Tokugawa Japan 1600–1868* (Locust Valley, N.Y., 1958) and T. C. Smith, *The agrarian origins of modern Japan* (Stanford, 1959). M. B. Jansen, *Sakamoto Ryoma and the Meiji Restoration* (Princeton, 1961) is a first-rate account of the years after 1853. It is usefully supplemented by A. Craig, *Choshu in the Meiji Restoration* (Cambridge, Mass., 1961).

Monographs on various aspects of Japan's foreign relations before 1868 include D. Keene, *The Japanese discovery of Europe: Honda Toshiaki and other discoverers 1720–1798* (London, 1952); C. R. Boxer, *Jan Compagnie in Japan 1600–1850. An essay on the cultural, artistic and scientific influence exercised by the Hollanders in Japan from the seventeenth to the nineteenth centuries* (rev. ed., The Hague, 1950); G. A. Lensen, *The Russian push toward Japan: Russo-Japanese relations 1697–1875* (Princeton, 1959); and W. G. Beasley, *Great Britain and the opening of Japan 1834–1858* (London, 1951). In addition, W. G. Beasley, *Select documents on Japanese foreign policy 1853–1868* (London, 1955) contains translations which illustrate Japanese attitudes and policy, while among accounts by contemporary Western visitors to the country the following might be found of interest: M. E. Cosenza, ed., *The complete journal of Townsend Harris, first American Consul General and Minister to Japan* (New York, 1930); Sir R. Alcock, *The capital of the Tycoon. A narrative of a three years' residence in Japan* (2 vols., London, 1863); Sir E. M. Satow, *A diplomat in Japan. The inner history of the critical years in the evolution of Japan when the ports were opened and the monarchy restored* (London, 1921).

The Meiji period (1868–1912)

The most recent general history of this period is J. Fujii, *Outline of Japanese history in the Meiji era* (Tokyo, 1958), a rather loosely organized work with an emphasis on cultural change, though it is not too well translated. N. Ike, *The beginnings of political democracy in Japan* (Baltimore, 1950) treats the early development of political parties; G. M. Beckmann, *The making of the Meiji Constitution. The oligarchs and the constitutional development of Japan 1868–1891* (Lawrence, 1957), which includes some translations of Japanese documents, views much the same subject-matter from the standpoint of the Meiji government. T. C. Smith. *Political change and industrial development in Japan: government enterprise 1868–1880* (Stanford, 1955) is important for the study of economic policy. On diplomatic history, W. L. Langer, *The diplomacy of imperialism* (2nd ed., New York, 1951) remains the standard work for the years 1894–1902. Two later books, making fuller use of Japanese materials on more limited topics, are M. B. Jansen, *The Japanese and Sun Yat-sen* (Cambridge, Mass., 1954) and H. Conroy, *The Japanese seizure of Korea: 1868–1910* (Philadelphia, 1960).

Works which enable one to see the period to some extent through Japanese eyes include: S. Okuma, ed., *Fifty years of new Japan* (2 vols., London, 1910), a collection of essays on a wide range of topics, mostly by leaders of Meiji Japan; W. W. McLaren, ed., *Japanese government documents* (being vol. XLII, Part 1, of the *Transactions of the Asiatic Society of Japan*; Tokyo, 1914), which selects chiefly constitutional and administrative papers of the years before 1890; and *The autobiography of Fukuzawa Yukichi*, trans. E. Kiyooka (Tokyo, 1934). Of the very large number of contemporary accounts by Western writers, the following are of interest and have been cited in the text: J. R. Black, *Young Japan. Yokohama and Yedo. A narrative of the settlement and the city from the signing of the treaties in 1858 to the close of the year 1879* (2 vols., London, 1880–81); G. W. Browne, *Japan. The place and the people* (Boston, Mass., 1901); and B. H. Chamberlain and W. B. Mason, ed., *Murray's Handbook for Travellers in Japan* (8th ed., London, 1907; or any other edition of about this period).

The period 1912–1945
Except for J. W. Morley, *The Japanese thrust into Siberia, 1918* (New York, 1957), most of the monographs dealing with this period have concentrated on developments after 1930. R. Storry, *The double patriots: a study of Japanese nationalism* (London, 1957) deals chiefly with the patriotic societies, while Y. C. Maxon, *Control of Japanese foreign policy. A study of civil-military rivalry 1930–1945* (Berkeley, 1957) approaches the same problems through an analysis of institutions. Something of the atmosphere of the 1930s is conveyed in the translation of the principal 'ethics' text for schools: *Kokutai no hongi. Cardinal Principles of the National Entity of Japan*, ed. R. K. Hall, trans. J. O. Gauntlett (Cambridge, Mass., 1949). There are also several lively accounts by foreign journalists in Japan, including H. Byas, *Government by assassination* (London, 1943); A. M. Young, *Japan under Taisho Tenno 1912–1926* (London, 1928); and the same author's *Imperial Japan 1926–1938* (London, 1938).

F. C. Jones, *Japan's New Order in East Asia: its rise and fall 1937–45* (London, 1954) is a valuable study of the years after the outbreak of the China war, written from Western sources. It can best be supplemented, especially on questions of Japanese policy-making, by the two books of R. J. C. Butow, *Tojo and the coming of the war* (Princeton, 1961) and *Japan's decision to surrender* (Stanford, 1954), which both make extensive use of Japanese documentary materials. There are also two good foreign eye-witness accounts of Japan at the beginning of the war and during it: J. Morris, *Traveller from Tokyo* (London, 1943) and R. Guillain, *Le peuple japonais et la guerre: choses vues, 1939–1946* (Paris, 1947).

Postwar Japan

Source materials are not readily available for the postwar years, a fact which is reflected in the nature of the historical studies on the subject so far published. There are, however, a number of works of high quality on several aspects of recent Japanese society. K. Kawai, *Japan's American interlude* (Chicago, 1960) discusses the period of military occupation, as does W. Macmahon Ball, *Japan—Enemy or Ally* (London, 1948), written by the British Commonwealth Representative on the Allied Council. H. Borton and others, *Japan between East and West* (New York, 1957) is a group of papers on Japan after 1952. On politics there are three useful books: N. Ike, *Japanese politics. An introductory survey* (London, 1958); R. A. Scalapino and J. Masumi, *Parties and politics in contemporary Japan* (Berkeley, 1962); and I. Morris, *Nationalism and the right wing in Japan. A study of postwar trends* (London, 1960). G. C. Allen, *Japan's economic recovery* (London, 1958) is the best summary of postwar economic history, while R. P. Dore, *Land reform in Japan* (London, 1959) deals at some length with village life, as well as the land reform itself, thus becoming in some respects a companion volume to the same author's earlier sociological study, *City life in Japan. A study of a Tokyo ward* (London, 1958).

NOTES

CHAPTER I: JAPAN IN THE EARLY NINETEENTH CENTURY

1. In Tokugawa Japan it was usual to indicate the extent of landholding not by area, but by the estimated annual crop which the land would yield. This was expressed in *koku* of rice: 1 *koku* equals approximately 5 bushels.

2. Wherever possible I refer to a domain by the name of its castle-town, which is relatively easy to identify on a map. However, the greatest of them were often known by the names of the provinces which they comprised, and these names have been used extensively in books written in western languages. Where this is so, I give the name of the province in brackets and often use it alone. The most important examples are those of domains which played a major part in nineteenth-century politics: Kagoshima (Satsuma); Yamaguchi (Choshu); Kochi (Tosa); and Saga (Hizen).

3. Translated in W. T. de Bary (ed.), *Sources of the Japanese tradition* (New York, 1958), pp. 409–10.

   It might be relevant here to comment briefly on the subject of samurai literacy. All samurai were encouraged to study the Confucian classics; and although many achieved only the sketchiest knowledge of them, most had an education of sorts and some became scholars of great repute. Certainly the society in which they lived set a great value on books and learning, so that their opportunities for reading were considerable. The technique of printing, which had been brought to Japan from China in very early times, was much improved by the use of movable type, learnt from both Europe and Korea at the end of the sixteenth century; and this helped to bring about a great increase in the number of books available. They were soon being printed not only by the Tokugawa and domain governments, but also by commercial booksellers, now emerging for the first time in the great cities. The libraries of feudal lords, usually open to samurai of their domains, were numerous and often large, while the poorer samurai and merchants were in a position as a rule to borrow books from their more affluent friends and neighbours. Even residents of the countryside were able to read the more popular works, by borrowing them from itinerant pedlars for a fee.

4. Donald Keene, *Anthology of Japanese literature* (London, 1956), p. 358.

5. Population figures for the period are unreliable in detail, but are a reasonable enough guide to relative size. They were drawn up for tax purposes and therefore exclude figures for samurai families; and this makes the real size of towns a matter of some conjecture, since most samurai were town-dwellers and they accounted in all for about 2,000,000 persons of a national total of some 30,000,000 in the nineteenth century.

6. G. B. Sansom, *Japan. A short cultural history* (rev. ed., London, 1952), p. 477.

CHAPTER II: ECONOMIC PROBLEMS AND REFORMS

7. The *ryo* was a gold coin which in the money markets of Edo and Osaka exchanged on average for about 60 *momme* (225 gm.) of silver in the period 1750–1800, about 64 *momme* (240 gm.) in 1800–50. Since this, despite fluctuations, was also approximately the price of 1 *koku* of rice, one can roughly

equate the *ryo* and *koku* in considering financial statements of these years. The same does not hold good after 1850, however, because of rapid inflation.
8. E. H. Norman, *Japan's emergence as a modern state* (New York, 1940), pp. 61–2.

CHAPTER III: JAPAN AND THE WEST

9. *Edinburgh Review*, xcvi, 196 (October, 1852), p. 383.
10. Quoted in W. G. Beasley, *Great Britain and the opening of Japan 1834–1858* (London, 1951), p. 93.
11. The old Chinese tag, 'to know one's enemy and know oneself brings constant victory', was often used in the mid-nineteenth century to avert conservative criticism of the study of things Western.
12. Quoted in G. B. Sansom, *The Western World and Japan* (New York and London, 1950), p. 258.
13. de Bary, *Sources of the Japanese tradition*, p. 544.
14. Quoted in S. Toyama, *Meiji ishin* [The Meiji Restoration] (Tokyo, 1951), p. 78. [The translation is mine. W.G.B.]

CHAPTER IV: TREATIES AND POLITICS, 1853–1860

15. The texts of the President's letter and that of Perry are to be found in F. L. Hawks, *Narrative of the Expedition of an American Squadron to the China Seas and Japan* (3 vols., Washington, 1856), I, 256–9.
16. W. G. Beasley, *Select documents on Japanese foreign policy 1853–1868* (London, 1955), p. 117.
17. Beasley, *Select documents*, pp. 130–1.
18. Memorandum translated in Beasley, *Select documents*, p. 138.
19. Townsend Harris, *The complete journal of Townsend Harris*, ed. M. E. Cosenza (New York, 1930), p. 507.
20. Memorandum translated in Beasley, *Select documents*, p. 180.
21. Harris, *Complete Journal*, p. 505.
22. Text of imperial decree, translated in Beasley, *Select documents*, p. 194.

CHAPTER V: THE FALL OF THE TOKUGAWA, 1860–1868

23. I here follow the figures given in H. Borton, *Japan's modern century* (New York, 1955), p. 57.
24. R. Alcock, *The Capital of the Tycoon* (2 vols., London, 1863), I, 126.
25. Memorial by Bakufu Council, translated in Beasley, *Select documents*, p. 203.
26. Russell to Neale, December 24, 1862, *Parliamentary Papers 1864*, vol. LXVI, pp. 179–80.
27. Letter of Okubo Toshimichi, September 23, 1865; translated from *Okubo Toshimichi Monjo* (10 vols., Tokyo, 1927–9), I, 298.
28. E. Satow, *A diplomat in Japan* (London, 1921), p. 129. Most Western visitors at this time knew the Shogun as 'the Tycoon'.

CHAPTER VI: NEW MEN AND NEW METHODS, 1868–1873

29. Variant translations of the Oath are given and their significance discussed in Sansom, *The Western World and Japan*, pp. 318–20.
30. W. W. McLaren, *Japanese government documents* (Trans. Asiatic Soc. Japan, vol. xlii, part 1; Tokyo, 1914), pp. 26–7.
31. Ito Hirobumi, writing in S. Okuma, ed., *Fifty Years of New Japan* (2 vols., London, 1910), I, 122.
32. The text is given in McLaren, *Japanese government documents*, pp. 29–32, where it is wrongly dated March 5, 1869, instead of March 2.

CHAPTER VII: GOVERNMENT AND POLITICS, 1873–1894

33. Satow, *A diplomat in Japan*, p. 340.
34. Memorial of February 20, 1874, in McLaren, *Japanese government documents*, p. 445.
35. R. A. Scalapino, *Democracy and the party movement in prewar Japan* (Berkeley & Los Angeles, 1953), p. 63.
36. Translated in G. M. Beckmann, *The making of the Meiji Constitution* (Univ. of Kansas, 1957), p. 149. The memorials by Ito, Yamagata and Okuma are also translated, *ibid.*, pp. 126–42.
37. This, like other standard translations of Japanese party names, is open to serious objections. However, the usage is hallowed by time and it would only cause confusion to propose alternatives here.
38. Press Law of June 28, 1875, in McLaren, *Japanese government documents*, p. 542.
39. McLaren, *Japanese government documents*, p. 503.
40. Ito Hirobumi, 'Some reminiscences of the grant of the new constitution', in Okuma (ed.), *Fifty Years of New Japan*, I, 125.
41. Decree of April 28, 1888, in McLaren, *Japanese government documents*, p. 128.
42. Ito, 'Some reminiscences', in Okuma, *Fifty Years of New Japan*, I, 127.

CHAPTER VIII: MODERNIZATION, 1873–1894

43. Satow, *A diplomat in Japan*, p. 391.
44. *Murray's Handbook for Travellers in Japan*, ed. B. H. Chamberlain and W. B. Mason (8th ed., London, 1907), p. 11.
45. The *yen* (Y) was a new coin, introduced with the opening of the Osaka Mint in April 1871 to replace the *ryo* and *ichibu* of the Tokugawa period. Its normal value before the 1930s was about 2 to the dollar, 10 to the pound sterling.
46. J. R. Black, *Young Japan* (2 vols., London, 1880–1), II, 455.
47. W. W. Lockwood, *The economic development of Japan* (Princeton, 1955), p. 584.
48. *The autobiography of Fukuzawa Yukichi* (Tokyo, 1934), p. 264.
49. Fujii Jintaro, *Outline of Japanese history in the Meiji era* (Tokyo, 1958), p. 166. The novel is summarized at some length in G. B. Sansom, *The Western World and Japan* (New York, 1950), pp. 412–5.

CHAPTER IX: NATIONALISM AND FOREIGN AFFAIRS, 1890–1904

50. In Okuma, *Fifty Years of New Japan*, I, 211.
51. The relevant article is quoted in Langer, *The diplomacy of imperialism* (rev. ed., New York, 1951), p. 777.

CHAPTER X: THE END OF AN ERA

52. In Okuma, *Fifty Years of New Japan*, I, 128–9.
53. G. W. Browne, *Japan* (Boston, 1901), p. 408.
54. Murray's *Handbook for Travellers in Japan* (1907), ed. B. H. Chamberlain and W. B. Mason. The quotations used here are taken from p. 10, but the whole book is invaluable as a source of information on Japan in the early 20th century.
55. Lockwood, *The Economic Development of Japan*, p. 556.
56. Black, *Young Japan*, II, 407.
57. Murray's *Handbook* (1907), p. 8.
58. Scientific education was firmly enough established by the end of the Meiji period for Japan already to be producing research of some distinction, even

though the country's first-class scientists remained very few. Thus Nagaoka Hantaro's work on atomic structure resulted in his name being linked with those of Rutherford and Bohr (and established a tradition of work in nuclear physics which was maintained later by Yukawa Hideki, whose meson theory gained him a Nobel Prize in 1949); Suzuki Umetaro independently discovered vitamins in 1910; and others made important contributions in the fields of astronomy, seismology and botany, in particular.

CHAPTER XI: JAPAN BECOMES A WORLD POWER, 1914–1922

59. A. M. Young, *Japan under Taisho Tenno* (London, 1928), p. 88.
60. Yamagata to Okuma, August 1914; in de Bary, *Sources of the Japanese tradition*, p. 714.
61. From Article I. The texts of Articles I and III, containing the core of the agreement, are quoted in Borton, *Japan's modern century*, p. 317n.

CHAPTER XII: THE LIBERAL 'TWENTIES

62. Young, *Japan under Taisho Tenno*, pp. 112–3. It might be added that the rich also travelled a good deal abroad and often sent their sons to foreign universities—though the high standards maintained by the best Japanese universities ensured that a foreign education was usually regarded as a desirable addition to, rather than a necessary substitute for, that which could be obtained at home.
63. Scalapino, *Democracy and the party movement*, p. 232.
64. Young, *Japan under Taisho Tenno*, p. 280.
65. de Bary, *Sources of the Japanese tradition*, p. 834.

CHAPTER XIII: PATRIOTS AND SOLDIERS, 1930–1941

66. Translated in D. M. Brown, *Nationalism in Japan: an introductory historical analysis* (Berkeley and Los Angeles, 1955), p. 139.
67. Showa is the era-name for the reign of the present emperor, beginning in 1926, just as Meiji was for that of his grandfather.
68. Richard Storry, *The Double Patriots* (London, 1957), p. 52.
69. Storry, *Double Patriots*, p. 300. The word *kokutai*, meaning something like 'national polity', was a favourite with the ultranationalists and came to have strong connotations of emperor-worship, loyalism and right wing ideas generally.
70. A. M. Young, *Imperial Japan 1926–1938* (London, 1938), pp. 179–80.
71. Hugh Byas, *Government by assassination* (London, 1943), p. 47.
72. Young, *Imperial Japan*, p. 250. The word 'Japan' is a European corruption of the Chinese pronunciation of the ideographs by which the Japanese describe their country (literally they mean 'sun-origin'; hence 'land of the Rising Sun'). The Japanese themselves pronounce these ideographs 'Nihon' or 'Nippon', the latter having slightly more nationalistic connotations.
73. *Kokutai no Hongi*, trans. J. O. Gauntlett (Cambridge, Mass., 1949), p. 52.

CHAPTER XIV: AN EMPIRE WON AND LOST, 1937–1945

74. Translated in de Bary, *Sources of the Japanese tradition*, pp. 796–7.
75. *Ibid.*
76. Quoted in Y. C. Maxon, *Control of Japanese foreign policy . . . 1930–1945* (Berkeley, 1957). p. 94.
77. F. C. Jones, *Japan's New Order in East Asia* (London, 1954), p. 83.

CHAPTER XV: REFORM AND REHABILITATION, 1945–1962

78. The translated text can be found in R. J. C. Butow, *Japan's decision to surrender* (Stanford, 1954), p. 248.
79. The text is given in Borton, *Japan's modern century*, p. 486.
80. Article 1. The text of the 1946 Constitution is given in Borton, *Japan's modern century*, pp. 490–507, where the provisions of the Constitution of 1889 are also tabulated for comparison.
81. R. P. Dore, *Land reform in Japan* (London, 1959), p. xvii.

CHAPTER XVI: POSTWAR JAPAN

82. R. A. Scalapino and J. Masumi, *Parties and politics in contemporary Japan* (Berkeley and Los Angeles, 1962), p. 53.
83. John Morris, *Traveller from Tokyo* (London, 1943), p. 29.
84. D. Keene, in H. Borton and others, *Japan between East and West* (New York, 1957), p. 188.
85. Ivan Morris, *Nationalism and the right wing in Japan* (London, 1960), pp. 30–31.

INDEX